The Canadian Rockies
TRAIL GUIDE

The Canadian Rockies
TRAIL GUIDE

A hiker's guide to Banff, Jasper,
Yoho, Kootenay, Waterton Lakes,
Mount Assiniboine & Mount Robson

Brian Patton & Bart Robinson

SUMMERTHOUGHT
Banff, Alberta

ISBN 0-919934-14-5

Third edition, revised

Summerthought Ltd.
P.O. Box 1420
Banff, Alberta T0L 0C0
Canada

Printed and bound in Canada

Preface to the Third Edition

The publication of the third edition of *The Canadian Rockies Trail Guide* marks the fifteenth year that this book has been in print. Much water has tumbled down the creek since the authors first ventured forth, pushing their trail measuring wheels before them, to write a book on the trails of the mountain parks. Had we grasped the immensity of the task, we may have spent the summer of 1970 pursuing more mundane pleasures. But the first edition of this guide was published the following summer, and projects like this have a way of grabbing hold of one's life.

Lucky are those authors who write books that will never be revised. Most novelists, poets, and historians finish their tomes and move on to other things. Guidebooks, on the other hand, are supposed to be revised and updated. No sooner is one edition off the press than information starts to trickle in for the next: the parks department moves a trail head 300 metres down the highway; a footbridge is built over a previously impassable river; or new regulations are introduced to protect a heavily visited area. Knowing that changes will have to be made, the authors can never be satisfied with what has gone before: there is always one more obscure trail that they'd like to hike; one more popular area needs to be revisited; or some old, seldom-seen piece of horse trail out on some distant park boundary line must be accurately measured.

The third edition of our book reflects all the above considerations. Expanded by more than 100 pages, it now contains complete descriptions for every reasonably defined trail in the Rocky Mountain national parks, as well as the provincial parks of Mount Assiniboine and Mount Robson. By utilizing trail measurements made by the authors since 1978 and inventories carried out by Parks Canada during the late 1970s, distance outlines are now available for nearly every trail. The shorter trails (one to three kilometres in length), eliminated from the second edition, have been reinstated in special sections at the end of each chapter.

Most importantly, every trail in this book has been reconsidered and rewritten. Most of the trail descriptions in the second edition of *The Canadian Rockies Trail Guide* were compiled from one-visit experiences. The descriptions for the majority of trails in this edition are drawn from three, four or more visits. Simply stated, we have learned a lot more about matters like the flora, the fauna, trail conditions, hiking seasons, visitor use, and the text incorporates this knowledge. After nearly twenty years in the Canadian Rockies, we have a much different feel for the country and the trails than we did when the first edition appeared in 1971.

The only thing that hasn't changed in this edition is our dedication to preserving the mountain environment. As we noted in the preface to the second edition, if every person who uses this book makes the small effort necessary to leave the wilderness exactly as he or she found it, we will feel that providing this key to the backcountry has not been a detriment to our mountain parks.

Brian Patton, Bart Robinson
Banff, 1986

Acknowledgments

No guidebook containing the amount of detail and information found in the third edition of *The Canadian Rockies Trail Guide* could have been compiled by just two individuals. This edition owes a great deal to a great many people.

This revision could not have been completed without the assistance of the park administrators, visitor services personnel, wardens and naturalists of the mountain parks. While it is impossible in this limited space to mention all of those who provided information, advice and encouragement, some of the more important contributors were as follows: in Banff National Park, Tim Auger, Doug Harvey, Rick Kunelius, Ian Pengelly, Alan Westhaver and Cliff White; in Jasper National Park, Dave Biederman, John Kellas, Shirley Klettl, and Mary Porter; in Yoho National Park, Frances Klatzel, Rick Langshaw, Randy Robertson, and Gord Rutherford; in Kootenay National Park, Cal Bjorgan; in Waterton Lakes National Park, Simon Lunn; and in Mount Assiniboine Provincial Park, Raymond Gaudart.

A very special thanks to Perry Davis of Visitor Services, Banff, and Ruth Remple of Visitor Services, Jasper, who spent many hours advising the authors and reading the manuscript to insure accuracy.

Until one has pushed a bicycle wheel over hundreds of kilometres of mountain trail, one cannot fully appreciate the dedication of the trail measurer. A number of trail inventories were instituted by Parks Canada during the 1970s, and we must express our deep appreciation to Halle Flygare, Leslie Scrimshaw and Linda Webb for selflessly passing along the results of their arduous fieldwork to supplement our own measurements.

Many recreational hikers write the authors, pointing out errors and suggesting corrections. Edmonton backpacker Phil Lister has been a faithful correspondent over the past decade, and many of his notes are incorporated into our text.

And finally, special recognition to San Francisco backpacker Mike McReynolds, who has visited the Canadian Rockies every summer since 1976 and hiked more than 3,000 kilometres in the mountain parks. Mike has contributed information from all of his trips, and the text for most of the trails in Banff's Front Ranges and Jasper's North Boundary country is condensed from detailed descriptions which he wrote for us.

The proofreading and paste-up of this edition was completed with the generous assistance of Jon Whyte and Susan Hammond. Their support during the final stages of production was invaluable.

The photograph on page 113 is provided courtesy of the Whyte Museum of the Canadian Rockies, Banff. All other photographs published in this edition were taken by the authors.

Cover photos by Brian Patton
Front cover: Wolverine Plateau, Kootenay National Park
Back cover: Carthew Summit, Waterton Lakes National Park

Contents

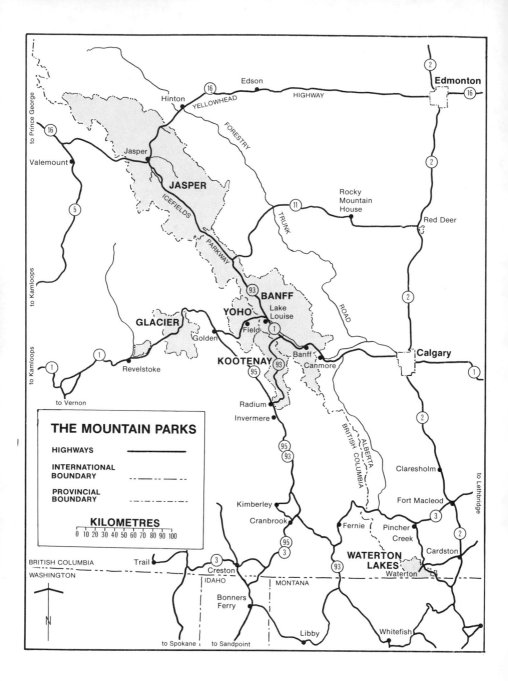

Introduction

In 1885, the Dominion of Canada created a special ten square mile reserve near Banff, Northwest Territories, to protect the Sulphur Mountain Cave and Basin hot springs from commercial despoilation. The reserve, after name and boundary changes, became Banff National Park—the first national park in Canada. Today, five mountain national parks occupy over 20,000 square kilometres of prime mountain wilderness in the Canadian Rockies.

Several million people visit the parks each year, but a great many of them experience the mountains at only the most superficial level—the Canadian Rockies as seen from a rapidly moving automobile. Although the scenery is magnificent, it represents but a small portion of what the Rockies offer. Just as it is necessary to leave the front seat of an automobile to fully appreciate a great museum or cathedral, so is it necessary to walk a bit (and preferably a great deal) to gain a true sense of these living museums of nature. Hiking is an appropriate and effective way to appreciate the national heritage of the parks, and those who have walked the mountain trails are best prepared to understand the importance of preserving the park lands, leaving them "unimpaired for the enjoyment of future generations."

This book is an invitation to the byways of the Canadian Rockies: to the more than 3,000 kilometres of trail that thread through the valleys and passes, by the lakes and glaciers of Banff, Jasper, Kootenay, Yoho and Waterton Lakes National Parks, as well as the adjacent British Columbia provincial parks of Mount Assiniboine and Mount Robson. It is an invitation to experienced hikers to examine a whole new realm — an area so large it would take a lifetime of summers to thoroughly explore. And it is an invitation to the novice to discover the three-dimensional living museum that lies beyond the automobile windows.

Weather, Climate and the Hiking Season

Despite their northerly latitudes, the Canadian Rockies have climate and weather patterns that compare closely with mountain areas hundreds of kilometres to the south. Because the elevation of the range increases progressively from north to south, mean temperature and annual precipitation in Banff and Jasper relate very closely with those of West Yellowstone, Montana and Leadville, Colorado.

The following chart shows average daily maximum and minimum temperatures, precipitation averages, and the average number of days per month with significant precipitation for Banff townsite during the hiking season, May through October. It should be remembered, though, that precipitation increases and temperatures decrease as one gains elevation or approaches the continental divide.

1

BANFF TOWNSITE CLIMATE:*	May	June	July	Aug.	Sept.	Oct.
Average max. temp./C.	14	18	22	21	16	9
Average min. temp./C.	1	4	7	6	2	-1
Mean rainfall/mm.	51	65	48	48	38	36
Average no. days rain	9	11	9	9	9	8

*Because of its location and lower elevation, Jasper townsite averages one degree warmer on all temperatures and is slightly drier.

The mountain snowpack begins to disappear with the spring temperature moderation, usually in April. By mid-May hiking is possible on a handful of low elevation trails in the major valleys as well as on south-facing slopes in the Front Ranges. By the first of July most trails below timberline are open, but many are still wet and muddy. Alpine zone trails open gradually from early July to early August, depending on slope exposure and snowpack.

The hiking season often lingers into late October. High country temperatures start to drop in mid-August, and early September usually sees the first snow drifting over the peaks. A fall of fifteen centimetres or more is not unusual at higher elevations in early September. These initial storms are usually short-lived, though, and the latter weeks of September and early October often are blessed by a beautiful Indian Summer. However, the weather changes quickly at this time of year, so autumn backpackers should be prepared for surprise storms and the possibility of some cold, snowy hiking.

A final cautionary note: don't rush the season in the spring. Not only does hiking too high too early mean muddy boots and slippery trails, but it can be damaging to both the trails and the adjacent terrain. Check with park information bureaus for current trail conditions before starting any hike in the high country.

Equipment

While the authors assume that the reader possesses common sense and a reasonable level of experience, we recognize that hiking conditions vary from one part of the continent to the other and thus suggest a few prerequisites for any day trip in the Rockies.

Your clothing is the most important consideration on any trip which will take you into the backcountry for more than an hour or two; no matter how warm and promising the day appears, always be prepared for weather that might include high wind, rain or snow, and freezing temperatures. Absolute essentials include a waterproof parka, poncho or rainsuit and a wool sweater or pile jacket.

While many day trips can be hiked in running shoes, sturdy leather or leather/Gore-Tex hiking boots will keep your feet drier and provide more protection and warmth on muddy or snowy trails. Boots increase your mobility, particularly for off-trail excursions, and decrease your chances of a debilitating injury. A wool outer sock worn in combination with an inner sock of lightweight wool, cotton or polypropelene is the best combination with boots and for keeping your feet dry and warm.

Other options which every day hiker should seriously consider include a toque, a water repellent hat, wool or polypropelene gloves, insect repellent, sunglasses, sun tan lotion, and a first aid kit. While unnecessary for most day trips, a map and compass can be useful and informative. And a small flashlight is a nice piece of insurance should your trip extend into darkness.

For backpackers there are dozens of publications dealing with the techniques of backcountry travel and camping (our favourite is Colin Fletcher's *The Complete*

Walker, currently in its third edition). Such manuals will help with the theoretical end of hiking, but, as with most things, experience is the true teacher. Novice backpackers in the Rockies should start with short trips before trying the longer treks outlined in this guide: avoid a week-long epic as your first ever backpack if you want to keep hiking as a hobby. Meanwhile, you can get some ideas about minimum impact hiking and camping by turning to the final section of this introduction.

Hiking and climbing specialty shops in Banff, Jasper and Waterton townsites carry a wide variety of quality outdoor equipment. Freeze-dried food is also available.

Topographic maps

Most of the hikes in this book do not require a map. For extended trips into more remote regions, however, a topographic map is a prerequisite. Whatever the case, many hikers like to carry topo maps wherever they go, finding them invaluable for identifying natural landforms.

All areas in the mountain parks have been mapped on a 1:50,000 scale (approximately two centimetres equal one kilometre). These sheets provide a high degree of detail and are extremely useful for both navigation and landform identification. Unfortunately, it takes over 40 of these maps to cover the mountain parks. Furthermore, many of the cultural features (i.e., roads and trails) are often out-of-date or not accurately marked.

For casual hikers who don't read maps or desire only a general overview of the parks and their trail systems, the national park topographic sheets are helpful. The Banff-Yoho-Kootenay sheet and Jasper sheet are both scaled at 1:200,000, while the Waterton Lakes sheet is on a 1:50,000 scale. All three sheets are very accurate as to trail placement and provide good detail on adjacent provincial park and forest areas.

Produced by the Department of Energy, Mines and Resources, the park maps and the 1:50,000 sheets are available at park information bureaus and official map dealers in the major townsites. Maps may also be mail ordered from the Canada Map Office, Department of Energy, Mines and Resources, Ottawa, Ontario (write for a price list and ordering information).

Bears, ticks and other hazards

The Canadian Rockies, by and large, are free of pestiferous fauna. Nonetheless, there are several animals of which hikers should be forewarned.

The mountain parks are home to a modest population of black bears and a smaller number of grizzlies, and the greatest single paranoia of hikers concerns an unpleasant confrontation with members of either species. Statistically, hikers are much safer in the backcountry than they are driving the highways, but such information is cold comfort to the person awakened by a hoarse snuffling outside his tent in the middle of the night. There are several courses of action that will minimize the chances (as well as the effects) of an ursine encounter.

First, keep a clean camp. In the hiking manuals, all cooking and washing should take place 50 metres from the tent, and all food should be stashed in a pack and hung another 50 metres from the tent on a tree branch five metres off the ground; clothes sporting spilled soup, fish guts and melted chocolate bars are thoughtfully included with the food. In the real world, however, such distances and elevations usually are adjusted according to the time of day one pitches camp, one's fatigue, the weather, the temperature, and the availability of trees with clear branches at the correct height. (Many campsites have specially constructed bear bars or cables for hoisting food out of reach.) Nonetheless, at all times and under all conditions, it is prudent to consider the potential cost of a sloppy, smelly campsite.

3

Dogs have no place in the backcountry of the national parks, but if you must take your pet along, make sure that he is always on a leash; dogs have been known to engage bears and then come yipping back to their masters for protection once they realize the nature of the foe.

Second, stay alert on the trail. Bears have as little desire to confront humans as humans do bears, and by serving nearby bruins notice of your presence, you can do much to forestall sudden meetings. Since your vision is sharper than a bear's, you should always be scanning the surrounding countryside, and before you descend from a pass, you should peruse the valley ahead (binoculars come in handy for this type of reconnaissance).

Some hikers wear bells, but those that are loud enough to do any good will be maddening to others in the party in a matter of minutes. The preferred practice is to whistle occasionally, or, approaching an open slope of willow or alder laced with berries, whistle frequently, shout greetings to the forest, sing old rock-and-roll favourites, rattle stones in a can, or beat on the bottom of a cooking pan.

Third, in case of a confrontation, keep a cool head. Those best experienced suggest facing the bear and talking to it in a quiet, reassuring manner. Indicate a willingness to give it the room it wants, and let it pass. The worst action is to turn and run since running often triggers a pursuit reflex in bears. Climbing a tree has saved many a hiker from an attack, but finding a climbable tree and getting far enough off the ground to be out of reach is often a problem. You should be reasonably confident of your ability to get up a tree safely; remember, the simple act of scrambling for a tree might inspire pursuit.

There is also evidence that many people fall down and play dead too readily; a curious bear with no inclination to attack may become more aggressive when confronted by a prone hiker in a defensive posture. If a bear is charging at close range and you believe it is about to complete the attack, you can drop to the ground, roll onto your stomach, lock your hands over your neck and leave your elbows spread wide, making it difficult for the bear to roll you.

And finally, it is always good practice to check at park information centres to get a current report on bear activity for your backcountry destination (these reports are compiled from sightings made by wardens and other hikers). If there is a particularly troublesome bear operating in a certain area, you may want to change your itinerary.

Anyone who is really concerned about how to act in bear country, or who has an abiding interest in bear behaviour, should go beyond the very general guidelines provided above and read one of several current books devoted specifically to the subject. Our favourite is *Bear Attacks: Their Causes and Avoidance* by Dr. Stephen Herrero (published by Winchester Press in the U.S. and distributed by Hurtig Publishers in Canada).

There are no other mammals that pose a significant threat to backcountry travellers. While such animals as cougar and wolverine have fierce reputations, they are very shy around humans and are seldom even seen. Of course, no animal should ever be harassed or fed (the most common injury is probably the bitten fingers of those who persist in feeding red squirrels). Some animals can be a nuisance, however: Porcupines have been known to dine sumptuously on hiking boots left out overnight, and ground squirrels have accomplished Houdini-like feats in gaining access to food left in unattended tents.

Second to bears, visitors worry about wood ticks—small, flat-bodied insects that require a meal of mammal blood as part of their reproductive cycle. Ticks are abundant in the Rockies in the early spring on dry, grassy slopes at elevations up to 2130 metres (7,000 feet), where they creep through low-lying shrubs and grasses, waiting for a potential meal to brush by. Once on a mammal, they spend up to three hours exploring before burying their heads in its flesh, so hikers have a fair chance to find and remove the beasts before the feast begins.

Although ticks of the Canadian Rockies are free of Rocky Mountain Spotted Fever, they can cause a potentially fatal tick paralysis if they burrow at the base of the skull. The best precaution is to wear long pants with gaiters, keep moving and examine yourself frequently. Ticks are partial to heads, armpits and crotches, and a thorough search of same before bedtime is recommended.

When a tick is discovered, a simple touch or gentle tug often dislodges it. If that fails, an application of insect repellent or sun lotion may do the trick. Still failing, give it a ride to the nearest physician and put a scalpel to it. The time-honoured methods of spotting it with kerosene or touching it with a warm match are rarely effective.

Mosquitoes are much less a problem in the parks of the southern Canadian Rockies than they are in the mountains and tundra farther north, but they can still be irritating from time to time. Hikers do not need headnets or anklets, but a supply of repellent should be carried throughout the hiking season until early September.

A fourth addition to the list of hiker's miseries is the protozoan *Giardia lamblia,* a waterborne parasite that can cause severe gastrointestinal distress. *Giardia* is carried by many species of animals, but the human infective strain is most frequently found in beaver, domestic dogs and, of course, humans. The parasite finds its way into mountain streams and rivers through the feces of these animals, but beaver are the animals best equipped to perpetuate the parasite in wilderness water systems. Most local hikers are willing to take their chances in the upper portions of the watersheds, particularly above timberline, or where they feel secure that there is no beaver activity or human sources of infestation. But the only way to be totally safe is to boil your drinking water for five to ten minutes.

The only other hazard worth noting here is unbridged stream crossings which occur on some remote backcountry trails. While the creeks and rivers of the Canadian Rockies are relatively tame compared to the thundering torrents of the Interior and Coast Ranges, they can still be quite dangerous at certain times of the year (a few large rivers like the Bow and the Athabasca are always hazardous). As a general rule of thumb, rivers run highest in June and July, tapering away toward their lowest runoff in September and October. In the Front Ranges (east of the Trans-Canada Highway and Icefields Parkway) streams are usually highest during cool, rainy periods when runoff sluices down into drainages from the bare, limestone peaks; stream levels in the Front Ranges often drop dramatically once the rain stops. In the Main Ranges (along the Great Divide) the highest runoff usually occurs during hot spells in July and August when the glaciers are in full melt; these rivers are usually easier to cross in the morning, after the flow has subsided with the cool of the night.

Any trail listed in this book which includes a major ford, should only be attempted by river-wise backpackers. It is best to leave your boots on when walking across rocky river bottoms. Leave the waistbelt of your pack unbuckled so that you can get it off quickly if you lose your balance. When waters are above your knees, improvise a staff from a sturdy piece of downed timber to brace yourself against the current (place the staff on the downstream side). If the current is strong and the water threatens to rise above your crotch, you should consider abandoning the ford altogether. Either wait for water levels to subside or, if that is unlikely, retreat the way you came and live to ford another day.

Backcountry information and regulations

In the four contiguous national parks of Banff, Jasper, Yoho and Kootenay, backpackers must obtain a park use permit. These are issued at all park information centres and warden offices (locations are listed in the introduction to each park) and are mandatory for any trip involving an overnight stay in the backcountry. Permits for any of the four parks can be obtained in advance by writing to Parks Canada, Western

5

Regional Office, 520 - 220 4th Avenue S.E., Calgary, Alberta T2P 3H8. All requests must contain the name of the party leader, the number of hikers, destination, route, and the dates you expect to be on the trail.

The four parks also offer a voluntary registration option for hikers who feel at risk in their backcountry activities. A registration form lists the hikers' route, destination and estimated time of return. If the party fails to register back on schedule, the warden service begins search operations. Obviously, registered hikers must be back on time and register in (by phone or by returning the registration form) immediately upon their return.

It is possible to register or obtain park use permits in any one of the four parks for any of the other three, but it is recommended that hikers do all they can to deal directly with the park in which the hike is planned.

Hikers interested in Waterton Lakes National Park will encounter a slightly different system. Because Waterton limits the number of users at all backcountry campsites, it is necessary to obtain a backcountry camping permit. These can be picked up at either the information centre or the administration building in the townsite. There is no reservation system or advanced booking; permits must be picked up in person immediately prior to the hike, and they are issued only to groups of six or less. Furthermore, unlike the four contiguous parks, registration is mandatory for any off-trail mountaineering activity.

While it doesn't affect the procedure that backpackers must follow, Jasper, Kootenay and Yoho Parks also have quotas on certain backcountry trails and campsites. Such quotas could upset hiking plans, particularly if the objective is a popular backcountry area, so hikers should arrive at all parks with several hiking alternatives in mind.

Campfires are permitted in many designated backcountry campsites, but should be built only in existing fire circles or fireplaces. If precut firewood is not provided at the site, you can only use dead branches or downed timber for your fire; it is illegal to cut a living tree for firewood in any of the parks. Open fires are prohibited in several high country campsites, usually because of a scarcity of wood, so campers must cook with camp stoves in these areas.

Hikers wishing to fish park lakes and rivers must purchase a national park fishing license, available from any park information centre or warden office and selected commercial outlets.

It is recommended that all hikers stop by one of the information centres before beginning any serious hiking. The centres serve as clearing houses for all hiking activity in the parks. In addition to issuing permits and registration forms, they dispense maps and up-to-date information on trail conditions, as well as free publications covering everything from grizzly bears to hypothermia. They also can inform hikers of any policy changes that may have occurred since the last printing of this guide.

Mountain cycling and ski touring

While this book is primarily written for pedestrians, it has an obvious value for all-terrain bicycle enthusiasts. We have provided few notes specific to mountain cycling, but the descriptions herein should be detailed enough to be useful for this activity. Most of the park fire roads are ideal bike routes, and the authors have provided more detailed descriptions of these roads in this edition primarily for the use of cyclists.

As of this writing, Parks Canada is moving in the direction of limiting bicycles to the fire roads and a few major horse trails. Even though the authors are avid mountain cyclists (many of the fire roads in this book were measured by mountain bike), we can sympathize with these limitations. Bicycles are an unpleasant intrusion on narrow trails, and it is impossible not to startle hikers when you come upon them at speed. It is also virtually impossible to enjoy one's environment when your attention is riveted on the next rock in front of your wheel. You can pick up a brochure listing trails that are open to bicycles at any park information centre. And remember, off-trail use of bicycles is absolutely forbidden.

Finally, this book is not intended as a ski guide. While many of the summer trails make excellent winter ski trips, many others are not only difficult to ski but traverse avalanche slopes as well. There are both private and park publications detailing ski tours in the Canadian Rockies.

Using this book

It is the intention of this guide to provide descriptions for all trails of any significance within the mountain parks of the Canadian Rockies. Readers will find these trails loosely divided into three general catagories:

Primary trails are those commonly recognized as the most exceptional and scenically rewarding. These trails are presented with full and detailed descriptions spread over two or more pages and are illustrated with a photograph. All have been hiked at least once by the authors.

Wilderness access routes and secondary trails are usually less scenic and more utilitarian. These tracks usually follow along forested valley bottoms and often they take the form of rather flat, tedious fire roads. Trails in this category are given a more limited description over one page and are not illustrated. (A few trails with outstanding scenery are presented in this abbreviated fashion because of their remoteness and unbridged river crossings.)

Short hikes and nature trails have been included for persons with limited time or energy. Though these are often wonderful hikes, their length (always less than three kilometres) begs a shorter description. These trips are described at the back of each park chapter. Some very short nature trails, those less than a kilometre long, are not included in this guide.

While the authors have hiked most of the trails catalogued in The Canadian Rockies Trail Guide (including all of the primary trails), there remain several they have yet to survey. In such cases, as much detail as possible has been collected from reliable sources (the warden service and experienced backpackers), and, in a few instances where necessary, approximate distances have been calculated from 1:50,000 maps.

The primary trail displays are divided into four distinct elements: trail summary, outline, descriptive text and photo. A few notes may clarify their intended use.

Beneath the name of each trail is its distance in both kilometres and miles. Most of the distances are one way calculations since the hiker goes out and comes back over the same trail. But for loop trips and long distance trails which end at a different trail head than the point of origin, total distances are provided. The authors have pushed a bicycle wheel with an odometer over most of these trails to obtain accurate distances. Where we have been forced to estimate distances, this is indicated by a footnote.

In recent years Parks Canada has devoted considerable energy to measuring and correctly signing all park trails. While these sign distances often disagree with the distances in this book, the discrepancies are usually small. As of this writing, however, the park signing and measuring program is not complete and, in some areas, the accuracy of measuring has not been well controlled. So when major discrepancies appear, you would do well to rely on the figures in this guide.

The general round trip duration of hikes is categorized as 'half-day,' 'day,' and 'backpack,' to assist hikers in finding outings tailored to their desires.

Hiking time is the number of hours, usually one way, the hiker can expect to spend on the trail. The times are usually calculated for the trip to the hiking objective, which in most cases runs uphill. These times are provided for those unaccustomed to estimating their own hiking speed. Strong hikers may often beat the listed times, while the less fit and experienced, or those who take extended breaks for nature study or photography, might find it takes longer to reach their destination.

The elevation gain is the total ascent, listed in both metres and feet, over the one way course of the trail. In cases where the trail rises and falls significantly (e.g., a trail that carries the hiker over two high passes and through a deep connecting valley), maximum and minimum elevations are provided instead of elevation gain.

The maximum elevation is the highest point above sea level reached on the hike, usually at the trail's destination. This elevation is also expressed in both metres and feet.

The topographic map references given are for the 1:50:000 sheets covering the hiking area. A note is made if the trail is not shown or has been badly misplaced.

The trail outlines are included to provide the reader with a brief, graphic profile of the route. All basic directions are given in the outline, thereby freeing the text for more interpretive material. The exact kilometre breakdown can be used either as an odometer for judging distance or to help locate natural features. The outlines also contain important highway directions for reaching the trail heads.

The text is written to describe the scenic rewards of the trail and to interpret some of the human and natural history of the area. Because most park trails are well-defined, a minimum number of words is devoted to long, tedious directions. Where applicable, optional routes are described at the end of the text.

All contemporary photographs were taken by the authors and selected to illustrate the objective of the hike or an outstanding point of interest along the way.

The maps included in the book were drawn by the authors using information from the Department of Energy, Mines and Resources maps in conjunction with corrections noted in the field. They are abbreviated and meant to give a general impression of a given area rather than specific directions. The shading of areas above 2300 metres is to provide a general impression of the relief, particularly the relative location of major mountains and passes; this elevation also happens to be fairly close to the average level of timberline for this latitude in the Rocky Mountains, though the shading should not be considered an accurate representation of same.

Some final words

- Plan ahead. Choose trips you are in shape to handle. Allow time for unexpected events and changes to your route and itinerary. Plan ahead to avoid busy trail heads, crowded campsites and holiday weekends.

- Stay on the trail even if it occasionally means muddy boots. Going around obstacles creates parallel trails and widens existing trails. Utilize switchbacks to minimize erosion and conserve your energy; shortcuts quickly become erosion gullies.

- Pack out all garbage. Carry plastic bags (you can pick some up from Parks Canada when you receive your park use permit) and, whenever possible, pack out litter that previous, less considerate visitors have left behind. Do not, under any circumstances, throw garbage into privies.

- Never leave smelly garbage or food around your camp—it attracts bears and other animals. Seal all food and garbage, and hang it from a bear bar or cable (where provided) or in a tree, 50 metres from the tent and as high off the ground as possible.

- Always leave rocks, flowers, antlers and all other natural objects where you find them; minimize disturbance of stones, soil and plant life. Never pick wildflowers or edible plants. Avoid disturbing living trees or plants when setting camp.

- Firewood is scarce in many areas and campfires are prohibited; use lightweight gas

8

stoves for cooking. Such stoves are recommended even where campfires are permitted, but if you insist, use only dead wood gathered from the ground for fuel. Keep all fires small and make certain they are cold before you depart. Flood the fire circle and stir the ashes.

- Keep food, soap, toothpaste, and detergent out of lakes and streams. Dispose of wash water on well-drained soil at least 50 metres from the nearest surface water. Even biodegradable soaps are pollutants.

- Where facilities are not provided, one's toilet should be tended to well away from trails, campsites, lakes and streams. Dig a small pit (no more than 15 cms deep), bury toilet paper, and restore the ground as closely as possible to its original state. Improper disposal of human waste is a major factor contributing to the spread of *Giardia* in North America.

- While they are permitted on a leash, dogs are a threat to wildlife, have been known to incite grizzly attacks, and are an aesthetic intrusion for other visitors. They are often carriers of *Giardia*. Please leave your dog at home.

- Never feed, disturb or harass wildlife. It is illegal, harmful to the animal's health, and alters their natural behaviour. Observe all wildlife from a distance—do not disturb or entice.

- Be considerate of fellow hikers when sharing a campsite or backcountry shelter. Be considerate as well of horseback riders: move well off the trail (preferably down-slope), remain still and be prepared to comply with the guide's requests.

- All-terrain bicyclists should avoid surprising hikers, horses and wildlife. Be considerately wary at all corners and rises.

In other words, treat the wilderness areas of the national parks as an experienced mountain traveller would, displaying at all times a keen awareness of the diverse and delicate mountain world.

Banff National Park

Banff National Park, with an area of 6,641 square kilometres, lies due west of Calgary, Alberta, on the eastern slope of the Rockies. It is second in size only to Jasper among the mountain parks. Banff's western boundary, a 240-kilometre run of the Great Divide, is also the eastern margin of Yoho and Kootenay National Parks and Mount Assiniboine Provincial Park; to the north, Banff shares a common boundary with Jasper National Park.

Banff contains more than 1,500 kilometres of trail, more than any other mountain park; since much of this trail development is in the form of short hikes near well-known beauty spots, the park is also the most heavily hiked in the Canadian Rockies. The two most popular centres for day hiking are Lake Louise and Banff townsite. Lake Louise is by far the most famous hiking area, and the three important valleys of the region — Louise, Paradise, and the Valley of the Ten Peaks — offer spectacular scenery. Banff townsite is the hub of an extensive trail network that branches out in all directions to all elevations, but mainly up into the jagged limestone mountains of the Front Ranges. The Sunshine Meadows area, some 20 kilometres southwest of Banff, is rapidly emerging as another focal point for day trips now that the Sunshine Village gondola lift is operating in the summer. Most of the other popular day trips originate in the Bow Valley between Banff and Lake Louise or from the Icefields Parkway in the northern section of the park.

The two most popular backcountry hiking centres are the Skoki Valley area east of Lake Louise and the Egypt Lake region west of Banff townsite; most visitors backpack into these areas and then spend several days exploring the excellent day hikes which radiate from the core campsites. More serious backpackers tend to concentrate their efforts on the longer trails running between Banff and Lake Louise — the Sawback Trail and the Bow Valley Highline route — or on the trails traversing the Upper Spray and Bryant Creek Valleys at the southern end of the park. For even more adventurous souls, the trails in Banff's remote Front Ranges offer the ultimate in challenge and solitude.

All persons planning an overnight trip into the backcountry must obtain a park use permit. Such permits, along with information on trails and other regulations, are available in Banff from the Park Information Centre at 224 Banff Avenue and the warden office (open 24 hours) in the industrial compound on the north edge of town. Use permits for Banff are also available from the Park Information Centre and warden office in Lake Louise. (Information centres and warden offices in Yoho, Kootenay and Jasper Parks can also issue permits for Banff.) Persons wishing to obtain permits in advance may write to the Superintendent, Banff National Park, Box 900, Banff, Alberta T0L 0C0; the requests should include the name of the leader, the number of hikers, the route, destination, and the dates of the days in the field. Hikers wishing to use the shelters at Bryant Creek or Egypt Lake must make reservations through the Banff Information Centre.

Park visitors can find gas, food and accommodation in Banff townsite, Lake Louise and, in a more limited fashion, Saskatchewan River Crossing. In addition to the basics, Banff provides all the amenities normally found in much larger centres, including a number of hiking and climbing specialty shops.

Access: The town of Banff is located just 130 kilometres west of Calgary and 920 kilometres east of Vancouver on the Trans-Canada Highway, the main east-west route through Banff National Park. Access to the park from the north is gained via the Icefields Parkway, running south from Jasper to an intersection with the Trans-Canada Highway near Lake Louise. Highway #93 runs north and east from Radium, B.C., through Kootenay National Park, to intersect the Trans-Canada Highway at

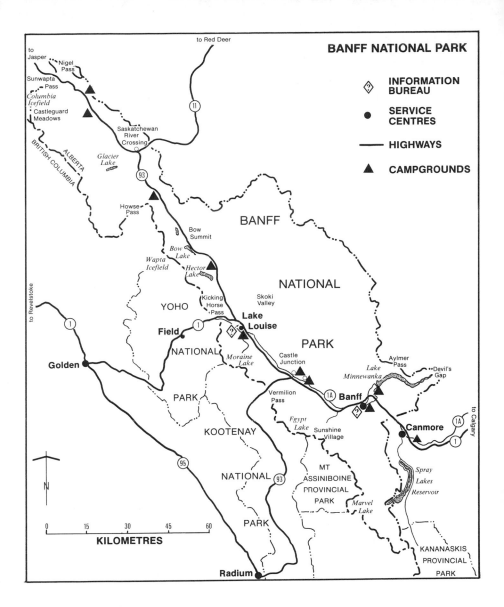

BANFF NATIONAL PARK

◈ INFORMATION BUREAU

● SERVICE CENTRES

—— HIGHWAYS

▲ CAMPGROUNDS

to Red Deer

to Jasper

Nigel Pass

Sunwapta Pass

Columbia Icefield

Castleguard Meadows

Saskatchewan River Crossing

Glacier Lake

BRITISH COLUMBIA

ALBERTA

Howse Pass

Bow Summit

Wapta Icefield

Bow Lake

Hector Lake

BANFF

NATIONAL

Kicking Horse Pass

Skoki Valley

YOHO

to Revelstoke

Field

Lake Louise

NATIONAL

Moraine Lake

PARK

Castle Junction

Golden

Aylmer Pass

Lake Minnewanka

Devil's Gap

PARK

Vermilion Pass

Banff

Canmore

to Calgary

Egypt Lake

Sunshine Village

KOOTENAY

MT ASSINIBOINE PROVINCIAL PARK

Marvel Lake

NATIONAL

Spray Lakes Reservoir

PARK

0 15 30 45 60

KILOMETRES

N

Radium

KANANASKIS PROVINCIAL PARK

Castle Junction. And Highway #11 (the David Thompson Highway) connects the city of Red Deer, Alberta, with the Icefields Parkway at Saskatchewan River Crossing.

No other major hiking area in North America is as well served by public transportation as Banff National Park. East and westbound transcontinental VIA Rail trains make daily stops at Banff and Lake Louise; numerous Greyhound buses run east and west on the Trans-Canada Highway, with regular stops at Banff and Lake Louise and flag stops at Castle Junction; Brewster Transportation operates a daily bus service between the Calgary International Airport and Jasper, travelling via Banff, Lake Louise and the Icefields Parkway (backpackers have the option of buying tickets to trail head drop-off points anywhere along the way).

11

Bourgeau Lake

Trans-Canada Highway to Bourgeau Lake—7.5 kilometres (4.6 miles)
Trans-Canada Highway to Harvey Pass—9.7 kilometres (6.0 miles)

Day trip

Allow 2½ - 3 hours one way

Elevation gain: 725 metres (2,380 feet)

Maximum elevation: 2160 metres (7,100 feet)

Topo maps: Banff 82 O/4†
　　　　　　†trail incorrectly marked

Point of Departure: Follow the Trans-Canada Highway to the Bourgeau Lake parking area, 2.8 kilometres (1.7 miles) west of the Sunshine Village junction and 700 metres east of the Wolverine Creek Picnic Area. The parking area is set back in the forest on the southwest side of the highway.

0.0—Trail sign (1435 m).

　　—Moderate but steady uphill.

1.6—Trail stops switchbacking, heading straight up southeast side of the valley.

3.7—Trail crosses tributary stream.

5.5—Wolverine Creek crossing. Cascades.

　　—Steep switchbacks.

6.8—Trail levels out into meadows.

7.5—Bourgeau Lake (2160 m).

　　—Trail veers away from northwest side of lake, climbs steeply to obvious notch due west.

8.8—Small, unnamed lake in alpine bowl.

　　—Veer left and climb to pass.

9.7—Harvey Pass and Lake (2470 m).

Set within an amphitheatre carved from the limestone walls of the Massive Range, Bourgeau Lake exhibits a wide variety of alpine and subalpine life forms. Bordering its waters are fir-laced meadows and barren talus slopes where ptarmigan, marmots and pikas are often seen pursuing their daily chores. In spring, avalanches thunder down through the couloirs above, and mountain goats stroll placidly on the slopes of Mount Brett to the north. These attractions coupled with the lake's easy access from Banff townsite make it a popular spot with local hikers.

Rising from the Trans-Canada Highway, the trail quickly buries itself in a forest of lodgepole pine and spruce, then slowly gains altitude up the Wolverine Creek drainage. After 2.4 kilometres views open back to the Bow Valley and the sharp, serrated peaks of the Sawback Range beyond. The broad summit of Mount Brett (2984 m), the highest mountain in the Massive Range, dominates the scenery ahead.

At the 5.5 kilometre mark the trail crosses Wolverine Creek, passing beneath a long cascade of tumbling white water. The log bridge offers an excellent spot for rest and refreshment before tackling the steep switchbacks that climb into the cirque above.

The amphitheatre containing the lake is carved into the northwest side of Mount Bourgeau (2930 m). Like other peaks in the range, it is composed of Devonian and Mississippian aged limestones and shales—formations which bear fossils of brachiopods, corals, and other species of early ocean life. Dr. James Hector named the mountain for the French botanist Eugene Bourgeau, his comrade-in-exploration with the Palliser Expedition during the summer of 1858.

Snowbanks often linger in the meadows bordering the lake until mid-July, their meltwaters feeding a wide variety of

Bourgeau Lake

subalpine wildflowers. White-tailed ptarmigan nest in the talus above the lake, their mottled summer plumage making them all but invisible among the piles of broken rock. Pika, golden-mantled ground squirrels and chipmunks scurry back and forth through the boulders, watching any passing hikers closely for a possible handout.

Strong hikers may wish to explore beyond Bourgeau Lake into the alpine basin which lies above and to the west. A path follows above the forested north shore of Bourgeau Lake then climbs steeply toward a notch dividing the ramparts of Mounts Bourgeau and Brett. After some strenuous climbing, the track emerges into an open, alpine bowl complete with small tundra ponds.

While this lofty cirque is quite pleasant, hikers will want to continue upwards and to the south to yet another pass at the foot of the long ridge which descends from the main peak of Mount Bourgeau. In less than fifteen minutes of hiking the traveler will crest this col and be greeted with unparalleled views to the south—the matterhorn peak of Mount Assiniboine framed perfectly within the narrow pass. A small tarn set within this gap is known locally as Harvey Lake.

Edith Pass

Fireside Picnic Area to Edith Pass—4.5 kilometres (2.8 miles)

Mount Edith Circuit—13.0 kilometres (8.1 miles)

Day trip

Allow 1½ - 2 hours one way

Elevation gain: 640 metres (2,100 feet)

Maximum elevation: 2075 metres (6,800 feet)

Topo maps: Banff 82 O/4†

    †trail incorrectly marked

Point of Departure: Follow the Trans-Canada to the junction with the Bow Valley Parkway, 5½ kilometres (3½ miles) west of Banff townsite's west interchange. Continue on the Bow Valley Parkway for 500 metres and turn right onto the access road to the Fireside Picnic Area. Continue one kilometre to the picnic area at the road's end. The trial sign is located at the bridge which crosses a creek into the picnic area proper.

0.0—Trail sign (1435 m).

    —Cross bridge. Trail angles away beyond lower edge of picnic area on old road bed.

0.2—Trail cuts left into forest from old road bed.

    —Contours east on valley side.

1.1—Junction. Cory Pass uphill to left. Straight ahead for Edith Pass.

    —Trail enters forest and angles uphill at gradual to moderate grade.

4.0—Junction. Edith Pass Low Route stays right, reaching pass in 0.6 km and the Forty Mile Valley trail in 2.9 km. Keep left for Edith Pass High Route.

4.5—Trail levels out in pass.

4.8—Open avalanche slope.

    —Trail switchbacks steeply up avalanche slope then contours north at high level.

5.9—Descent to mouth of Gargoyle Valley on steep scree.

6.2—Entrance to lower Gargoyle Valley. Intersection with *Cory Pass* trail at Km 6.8.

The trail to Edith Pass offers three interesting options for day hikers: a six kilometre-long climb to an outstanding viewpoint for the limestone monolith of Mount Louis; a strenuous but spectacular 13 kilometre loop trip around Mount Edith via Edith and Cory Passes; or a pleasant forested walk through the pass to the Forty Mile Valley, eventually emerging at the Mount Norquay Ski Area. All three options can be started from the trail head at the Fireside Picnic Area.

From the picnic area the trail to Edith Pass contours through a typical Bow Valley montane forest of aspen, white spruce, and Douglas fir, reaching the junction with the Cory Pass trail at Kilometre 1.1 where the route to Edith Pass stays right, enters heavy forest, and begins its climb toward the pass summit. Though the trail is forest-enclosed from the Cory Pass junction to the pass, for much of the way it follows near a sparkling stream bordered by a mossy forest floor—a cool, green woods with its own magical, fairy tale charm.

At Kilometre 4.0 the trail splits again at a rather poorly marked junction. Most hikers will want to keep left and take the high route that climbs above Edith Pass proper and onto the open avalanche slopes of Mount Edith. Not only does this option provide the best overview of the pass environs, it is also the route for those planning to loop around Mount Edith to Gargoyle Valley and Cory Pass.

The high route option reaches the forested summit of Edith Pass just 500 metres beyond the junction, but it continues to climb from that point, switchbacking up an open avalanche slope and then contouring due north along the slopes of Mount Edith toward the looming "hand" of Mount Louis. From this lofty viewpoint it is possible to look back down onto the summit of Edith Pass and across the valley to Mount Norquay. Views of Mount Louis improve as you continue

Mount Louis from Edith Pass

the traverse, as do those up the Forty Mile Valley to its headwaters, some 15 kilometres distant to the north.

At Kilometre 5.9 the trail emerges through stands of stunted spruce and fir onto a steep scree slope leading down to the mouth of the Gargoyle Valley—an obvious gap between the northern cliffs of Mount Edith and Mount Louis. Most day trippers will turn back at this viewpoint, but strong hikers who have lots of energy to spare can continue down to the Gargoyle Valley and then climb to the 2350 metre summit of Cory Pass, eventually looping back to connect in with the Edith Pass trail at Kilometre 1.1 (see *Cory Pass* trail description).

Edith Pass-Forty Mile Creek Option. Hikers planning a one-way arrangement hike over Edith Pass to Mount Norquay

Ski Area will want to stay right at the 4.0 kilometre junction and cross the pass via the low route. This trail crests Edith Pass at its lowest point (1950 m) and never really emerges from the forest, though there are some openings and meadows which provide glimpses of Mount Louis to the northwest. From the pass the trail continues north, losing elevation rapidly, to reach Forty Mile Creek and the junction with the Forty Mile Creek trail in another 2.3 kilometres. From this junction it is a pleasant six kilometre walk to Mount Norquay, making a total distance of 12.8 kilometres for this option. Many hikers prefer to start the trip from Mount Norquay, however, thereby saving approximately 240 vertical metres of climbing (see *Mystic Lake* trail description).

15

Cory Pass

Fireside Picnic Area to Cory Pass—5.8 kilometres (3.6 miles)
Mount Edith Circuit—13.0 kilometres (8.1 miles)

Day trip

Allow 3 hours to pass

Elevation gain: 915 metres (3,000 feet)

Maximum elevation: 2350 metres (7,700 feet)

Topo maps: Banff 82 O/4†
　　　　　　†trail not shown

Point of Departure: Follow the Trans-Canada Highway to the junction with the Bow Valley Parkway, 5½ kilometres (3½ miles) west of Banff townsite's west interchange. Continue on the Bow Valley Parkway for 500 metres and turn right onto the access road to the Fireside Picnic Area. Continue one kilometre to the picnic area at the road's end. The trail sign is located at the bridge which crosses a creek, the entrance to the picnic area.

0.0—Trail sign (1435 m).

　—Cross bridge. Trail angles away beyond lower edge of picnic area on old road bed.

0.2—Trail cuts left into forest from old road bed.

1.1—Junction. Trail to Edith Pass straight ahead. Keep left and uphill for Cory Pass.

　—Extreme uphill climb.

2.4—Crest of narrow forested ridge.

　—Trail rolls along ridge then climbs steeply across valley headwall to pass.

5.8—Cory Pass (2350 m).

　—Steep descent over scree slopes into Gargoyle Valley.

6.8—Entrance to lower Gargoyle Valley. Intersection with *Edith Pass—High Route* at Km 6.2.

A rugged defile that stands at over 2300 metres above sea level and looks out upon the monolithic south face of Mount Louis, Cory Pass is the objective of the most spectacular hike in the immediate Banff vicinity. But after gaining a vertical kilometre of elevation in just over five kilometres of hiking, the traveler will have paid dearly for the view.

The hike to Cory Pass starts at the same trail head as the trip to Edith Pass, and indeed both of these passes can be combined to make an interesting loop trip. From the Fireside Picnic Area the trail runs east along the north slope of the Bow Valley to where the trails divide at Kilometre 1.1. While the right hand branch to Edith Pass immediately dives into the forest to begin a rather leisurely ascent to its destination, the Cory Pass option cuts uphill to the left and begins a heart-pounding climb on an open south-facing slope. After what may seem like an eternity, a forested ridge is crested and the grade relents somewhat. From this viewpoint, the sharp summit of Mount Edith is visible ahead with the notch of Cory Pass just below and to the left. The trail follows along the uneven ridge for the next kilometre or so before ascending across a broad open slope to the pass (take care if snow is lingering in the steep gullies traversed by the trail).

In contrast to the usual warm, dry climb on the southerly exposed trail, Cory Pass is often a very cold and windy place. Sandwiched between the rocky summits of Mount Edith (2555 m) on the east and Mount Cory (2800 m) on the west, this high, rockbound gap might more appropriately be called a *col*—a French mountaineering term for a high, steep-sided gap between two peaks.

However, the views are worth any discomforts of trail or pass, the highlight being the towering slabs of grey limestone which form the 500 metre face of Mount

Mount Louis from Cory Pass

Louis. Termed a 'dogtooth' mountain, Mount Louis' extraordinary shape was created by the erosion of layers of sedimentary rock which were tilted almost vertical during the uplift of the Rockies some 60 million years ago. Because of its spectacular and unapproachable aspect, the peak has been a popular ascent for experienced mountaineers ever since it was first climbed by the Austrian guide Conrad Kain and his companion A. H. MacCarthy in 1916.

Instead of returning via the approach trail, the hiker may wish to continue on into the Gargoyle Valley and make a loop trip around Mount Edith, returning to the trail head by way of Edith Pass. Barring late season snow, a vague trail can be followed down the steep talus slope north of the pass. After a quick initial loss of elevation, the track traverses right just beneath the cliffs of Mount Edith to a narrow opening between that mountain and Mount Louis. The valley has an appropriate name as rugged cliffs and rock pinnacles loom on all sides, the stark landscape relieved only by a small, green meadow nestled at the foot of Mount Louis' south face.

Stay high and to the right once out of the Gargoyle Valley (the trail is faint here) and climb directly up an open scree slope. Approximately 300 metres up this scree slope, near its top, watch for a well-defined trail leading off into the stunted trees on the left. From here there is a high, open traverse across the slopes of Mount Edith before descending through Edith Pass and back to the junction at Kilometre 1.1 (see *Edith Pass—High Route* trail description). Total distance for the loop trip is 13 kilometres, and taking into account the steep climbs and descents, it makes for a most energetic day.

17

Cascade Amphitheatre

Mount Norquay to Cascade Amphitheatre—6.6 kilometres (4.1 miles)

Day trip

Allow 2 - 3 hours one way

Elevation gain: 610 metres (2,000 feet)

Maximum elevation: 2195 metres (7,200 feet)

Topo maps: Banff 82 O/4†

†last 3.5 kms not shown

Point of Departure: Follow the Mount Norquay Road north from the Trans-Canada Highway at Banff townsite's west interchange, climbing 6 kilometres (3½ miles) of twisting switchbacks to the Mount Norquay Ski Area. Turn into the first parking lot on the right (Lot #3) and drive to the far end.

0.0—Trail sign (1705 m).

—Follow ski area service road down past lower lift terminals.

0.8—Old fire road descends into forest below ski area.

1.1—Junction. Trail to Edith Pass and Mystic Lake cuts to left. Keep straight ahead for Cascade Amphitheatre.

3.1—Forty Mile Creek bridge (1555 m).

—Steady uphill.

4.3—Junction. Elk Lake straight ahead. Cut uphill to right for Cascade Amphitheatre.

—Steady, switchbacking climb.

6.6—Trail levels out into Amphitheatre.

7.7—Head of Amphitheatre (2195 m).

One of the more popular day hikes in the Banff environs is the trek up the western flank of Cascade Mountain to a large natural amphitheatre lying some 2200 metres above sea level. Featuring the beauties of subalpine meadows, glacial-carved rock and an excellent survey of Elk Valley, the trip is certainly worth a long day's outing.

From the trail sign at the Mount Norquay Ski Area, the route follows a service road down through the ski development, passing beneath a number of ski lifts and runs. Once you are through the ski area, a distance of less than a kilometre, the trail takes the form of a broad cat track which continues the gradual descent of this small tributary valley of Forty Mile Creek. (Beware of the well defined trail which intersects from the right side of the creek just below the ski area; this is merely a horse trail which climbs from the Buffalo Paddock corrals on the Trans-Canada Highway.)

At the 3.1 kilometre mark the trail reaches the floor of the Forty Mile Valley, crosses the creek on a substantial bridge, and begins angling up the western slope of Cascade Mountain. The bridge is a good place to fill a canteen as the trail beyond is dry and quite steep.

Shortly beyond the crossing the trail offers a good view of the sheer 390 metre face of Mount Louis (2682 m) which lies directly west across the valley. The precipitous Palliser limestone "pope's hat" of Louis is one of the better known rock climbs in the Banff region. The summit of Mount Edith (2554 m), another popular climb, can be seen to the south of Mount Louis, behind Mount Norquay.

The last trail fork of the hike is at the Elk Lake junction, 1.2 kilometres beyond the Forty Mile Creek bridge. The right hand fork climbs steeply through a forest of spruce and lodgepole pine for 2.3 kilometres before levelling out into the Cascade Amphitheatre.

Cascade Amphitheatre

The Amphitheatre is a delicate subalpine meadow sheltered on three sides by the rugged limestone of Cascade Mountain's summit ridges. The open meadowland along the valley bottom is carpeted with wildflowers throughout the summer, starting with the showy white western anemone and nodding yellow glacier lilies which appear along the edges of the receding snow banks in late June. Two small sink lakes also appear in the meadows with the spring melt-off, but these usually dry up and disappear entirely by mid-July. The rockslides which fringe the upper end of the vale are home to large numbers of hoary marmots, pikas, and white-tailed ptarmigan.

For the hardier hiker the ridge forming the southern wall of the Amphitheatre represents the popular route to the summit of Cascade Mountain (2998 m). Although this is really a climb, the route is little more than a long, gruelling scree scramble and the view is quite spectacular. A crude but discernible trail climbs out of the Amphitheatre to the south and runs up the ridge as far as a false summit. This is the only confusing and possibly dangerous point on the ascent, and climbers should descend the right side of the ridge (south) about 10 metres on easy rock to regain the scree slopes leading to the final summit slopes.

19

Elk Lake

Mount Norquay to Elk Lake—13.5 kilometres (8.4 miles)
Mount Norquay to Stony Creek—21.0 kilometres (13.0 miles)*

Day trip or backpack

Allow 4 - 5 hours to Elk Lake

Elevation gain: 610 metres (2,000 feet)

Maximum elevation: 2165 metres (7,100 feet)

Topo maps: Banff 82 O/4

Castle Mountain 82 O/5

Point of Departure: Follow the Mount Norquay Road north from the Trans-Canada Highway at Banff townsite's west interchange, climbing 6 kilometres (3½ miles) of twisting switchbacks to the Mount Norquay Ski Area. Turn into the first parking lot on the right (Lot #3) and drive to the far end.

0.0—Trail sign (1705 m).

—Follow ski area service road down past the lower lift terminals.

0.8—Old fire road descends into forest below ski area.

1.1—Junction. Edith Pass and Mystic Lake to left. Keep right for Elk Lake.

3.1—Forty Mile Creek bridge (1555 m).

4.3—Junction. Cascade Amphitheatre to right. Elk Lake straight ahead.

6.8—Trail enters subalpine meadows.

11.5—Elk Pass (2055 m), campground and junction. Elk Lake trail branches uphill to left just past campsite, reaching lake in 2.0 kms.

14.4—Junction. Branch trail right to unnamed lake (4.5 kms). Keep straight ahead down valley.

18.0—Bridge to left side of creek.

20.2—Cascade River footbridge. Crossing to east bank.

20.4—Stony Creek footbridge. Crossing to south bank.

—Horse trail leads across flats to fire road.

21.0—Junction (1645). Intersection with *Cascade Fire Road* at Km 13.8.

*Distances beyond Elk Pass approximate.

Mount Brewster, visible from Banff between Mount Norquay and Cascade Mountain, is the southern end of a 20 kilometre-long massif which runs due north, deep into the eastern wilderness of Banff Park. All along the eastern face of this unbroken chain of peaks (misnamed the Vermilion Range on recent maps) are numerous glacially carved amphitheatres, some containing small lakes. Almost a third of the way down the range is Elk Lake, the largest and most scenic of these tarns. The lake is often visited as a long day trip or an easy overnight, and the trail which continues north to the Cascade River is a key route for trips into Banff's Front Ranges.

The first 4.3 kilometres of trail are the same as for the Cascade Amphitheatre hike, cutting down through the Mount Norquay Ski Area, across Forty Mile Creek, and up the western flank of Cascade Mountain. At the Cascade Amphitheatre junction the traveller should stay to the left, continuing northward through a typical coniferous forest of lodgepole pine, spruce and alpine fir on a path that is wide and well-defined.

A little over two hours of walking will bring the hiker to an extensive subalpine meadow, characterized by few trees, low willows, shrubby birch and cinquefoil, and a profusion of showy wildflowers. The scenery is dominated by the summit of Mount Brewster (2859 m) and its subsidiary peaks to the west, a mountain which is named for John Brewster, one of the early settlers and businessmen of Banff. The trail wanders through such terrain for some five kilometres—a beautiful piece of hiking where an occasional over-the-shoulder glance reveals a long and clear view downvalley to Mount Norquay, Sulphur Mountain and, beyond Sulphur, portions of the Sundance Range.

The trail eventually reaches Elk Summit and a campground at Kilometre 11.5.

Elk Lake and Mount Brewster

Just beyond the campground the trail to Elk Lake branches left from the main trail and gradually ascends a forested ridge for a short distance before dropping into the amphitheatre that contains Elk Lake. The high point on this ridge offers an excellent unobstructed view back down the length of the approach valley to Mount Norquay and points south.

Not far from timberline, backed by a sheer limestone face of some 500 metres, Elk Lake's aspect differs markedly from the gentle meadows leading up from Forty Mile Creek. The forest cover at the lake, predominantly alpine larch, offers a distinct contrast to the earlier forest canopy— a good indication of a transitional life zone. The boggy meadows around the lake contain a number of wildflower species typical of saturated tundra regions, such as globeflower, marsh marigold, elephant head, and mountain laurel. The rock slides above the lake are home to marmots and pikas.

Since there is no camping allowed at the lake, backpackers should set camp at the campground near the 11.5 kilometre junction and day hike to the lake. In addi-

tion to Elk Lake, the ridges and slopes of Cascade Mountain to the east are gentle and open, offering an infinite number of day trip possibilities in that direction from the campground. An unnamed lake, almost identical in size to Elk, is hidden behind one of these long ridges descending from Cascade, and it can be reached by continuing north on the main trail beyond Elk Summit for nearly three kilometres, then hiking southeast up the lake's outlet stream for another 4.5 kilometres to the 2345 metre level.

For backpackers who are bound for the more remote regions of eastern Banff Park, the trail north from Elk Summit to the Cascade Valley is a good optional route. It is particularly useful for those headed to Dormer Pass since it intersects with the Cascade Fire Road just a few metres from the Dormer Pass trail head, thereby providing a somewhat longer but more aesthetic approach than that broad, well-graded road. The trail descends to the Cascade Valley in a well-defined, straightforward fashion, and all major stream crossings including the Cascade River and Stony Creek have been bridged.

21

Spray River Circuit

Spray River Circuit—13.1 kilometres (8.1 miles)

Day trip

Allow 4 hours round trip

Elevation gain: 65 metres (200 feet)

Maximum elevation: 1435 metres (4,700 feet)

Topo maps: Banff 82 O/4

Point of Departure: From downtown Banff, cross the Bow River bridge and turn left onto Spray Avenue. Follow Spray Avenue for 0.8 kilometre (0.5 mile) to Rundle Avenue. Turn left on Rundle and follow it downhill and to the right for 0.6 kilometre (0.4 mile) to the parking area for Bow Falls. From the parking area walk south to the Spray River bridge—the entrance to the Banff Springs Hotel Golf Course.

0.0—Spray River bridge (1370 m).

—Cross bridge and follow golf course access road.

0.6—Junction. Hiking-horse trail branches right from golf course road.

—Follow around end of 1st Hole and into forest margin beyond.

0.9—Junction. Keep left and uphill on broad track.

1.2—Game control fence.

1.6—Junction. Mount Rundle trail branches left. Keep straight ahead.

2.1—Banff Springs Hotel viewpoint.

5.8—Campground.

6.6—Spray River footbridge.

6.7—Junction and picnic area (1435 m). Intersection with Spray River West Road. Turn right to return downvalley.

8.8—Youth Hostel.

12.6—Spray River West Road access gate.

—Follow first right-hand road downhill past log house then bear left to emerge on golf course south of clubhouse.

13.1—Spray River bridge (1370 m).

Most short fire road walks at lower elevations are not worthy of mention, but the thirteen kilometre circuit of the lower Spray River is an exception. Despite the wide track which hikers are forced to follow, the proximity of the Spray River gorge throughout the trip and the option of returning down the opposite side of the river make for a varied and pleasant forest outing.

The easiest spot to start the loop is from the Bow Falls parking lot at the entrance to the Banff Springs Hotel Golf Course. Follow the golf course road across the Spray River bridge and watch for a "hiker" symbol sign on the right hand side just beyond the first hole. From this junction a broad track skirts behind the first hole, then branches up to the left to exit the golf course via a gate in the animal control fence.

The Spray River East Road climbs above the river's gorge at a gradual rate and soon emerges on open bluffs that provide a fine view for both the river below and the Banff Springs Hotel, rising like a medieval castle from the forest back to the north. From this viewpoint the trail rolls southward into more closed forest, passes a large campground, and eventually crosses a footbridge to the west side of the river to reach the head of the loop.

The Spray River West Road is very straightforward as it descends the valley. The road is still occasionally driven by park wardens, so it is usually a bit more muddy than that on the east side. The road passes the Canadian Youth Hostel 2.1 kilometres below the junction and continues to provide occasional views to the river gorge and to the mountains north of Banff, mainly Mounts Norquay and Brewster.

Once you've arrived at the Spray Fire Road access gate just above the hotel, you can make your way back down to the Bow Falls by any one of several routes.

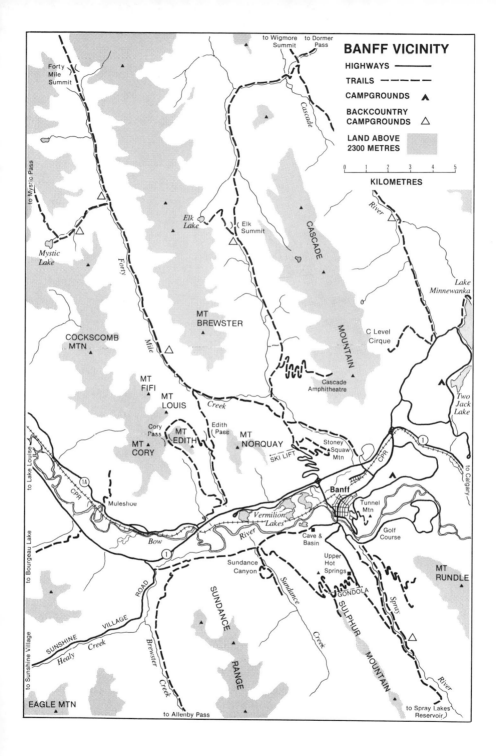

BANFF VICINITY

HIGHWAYS ———
TRAILS – – – –
CAMPGROUNDS ▲
BACKCOUNTRY
CAMPGROUNDS △

LAND ABOVE
2300 METRES

0   1   2   3   4   5
KILOMETRES

to Wigmore   to Dormer
Summit   Pass

Forty
Mile
Summit

to Mystic Pass

Mystic
Lake

Elk
Lake

Elk
Summit

CASCADE

River

Lake
Minnewanka

Forty

Mile

COCKSCOMB
MTN

MT
BREWSTER

MOUNTAIN

C Level
Cirque

Cascade
Amphitheatre

Two
Jack
Lake

MT
FIFI

MT
LOUIS

Creek

Cory
Pass

MT
EDITH

Edith
Pass

MT
NORQUAY

Stoney
Squaw
Mtn

MT
CORY

to Lake Louise

CPR

SKI LIFT

CPR

Banff

1

to Calgary

Muleshoe

Vermilion
Lakes

Tunnel
Mtn

Bow

River

Cave &
Basin

Golf
Course

1

to Bourgeau Lake

Sundance
Canyon

Upper
Hot
Springs

MT
RUNDLE

Sundance

GONDOLA

Spray

ROAD

SUNDANCE

SULPHUR

to Sunshine Village

SUNSHINE

VILLAGE

Healy

Creek

Brewster

Creek

RANGE

MOUNTAIN

River

EAGLE MTN

to Allenby Pass

to Spray Lakes
Reservoir

23

Mount Rundle

Banff Springs Golf Course to Trail's End—5.3 kilometres (3.3 miles)

Day trip
Allow 2 hours one way
Elevation gain: 460 metres (1,500 feet)
Maximum elevation: 1830 metres (6,000 feet)
Topo map: Banff 82 O/4

Point of Departure: From downtown Banff, cross the Bow River bridge and turn left onto Spray Avenue. Follow Spray Avenue for 0.8 kilometre (0.5 mile) to Rundle Avenue. Turn left on Rundle and follow it downhill and to the right for 0.6 kilometre (0.4 mile) to the parking area for Bow Falls. From the parking area walk south to the Spray River bridge — the entrance to the Banff Springs Hotel Golf Course.

0.0—Spray River bridge (1370 m).

—Cross bridge and follow golf course access road.

0.6—Junction. Hiking-horse trail branches right from golf course road.

—Follow around end of 1st Hole and into forest margin beyond.

0.9—Junction. Keep left and uphill on broad track.

1.2—Game control fence.

1.6—Junction. Mount Rundle trail branches left from Spray River east side fire road.

—Trail climbs and switchbacks through pine forest.

4.5—Junction. Trail to 1st peak of Mount Rundle branches up to left. Main trail contours on along slope.

5.3—Trail's end (1830 m). Route to main peak of Mount Rundle continues on across gully and up along ridge on opposite side.

The hike up the southwest slope of Mount Rundle is one of the most arduous in the Banff townsite vicinity. While the trail offers some limited views of the Spray Valley and the town of Banff, its primary function is as an approach route for summit-bound climbers.

The first 1.6 kilometres of the trail is the same as that for the Spray River Loop. The trail strikes off from the golf course access road just beyond the first hole and eventually leaves the golf course area as a fire road running south along the east side of the Spray River. Just 400 metres after passing through the golf course game control fence, the Mount Rundle trail branches left from the fire road and begins its steady climb of the mountain's southwest slope. Beyond the fire road, the hiker is enclosed in forest for the next 2.4 kilometres. Finally the trail switchbacks onto open slopes where there are good views of the Spray Valley and the Banff townsite vicinity.

At the 4.5 kilometre mark, the route to the first peak of Mount Rundle cuts uphill to the left. Just 800 metres farther along the main trail ends at a large gully. Looking up this gully, the main summit of Mount Rundle can be seen above in the form of grey limestone slabs and steep talus slopes. The climb to the summit can be made by experienced rock scramblers, but the peak lies a gruelling 1120 vertical metres above. The correct climbing route to the main peak follows across this gully and up the ridge on the opposite side (ascending the gully leads to serious problems). But remember, any ascent of the mountain beyond the established trail requires previous climbing experience and good route-finding skills; a number of inexperienced hikers have lost the route and their lives on this "easy" climb.

Be sure to carry water on the hike or the climb, as this slope of Mount Rundle is usually bone dry.

Sulphur Mountain

Upper Hot Springs to Upper Gondola Terminal—5.5 kilometres (3.4 miles)

Day trip
Allow 2 hours one way
Elevation gain: 655 metres (2,150 feet)

Maximum elevation: 2255 metres (7,400 feet)

Topo map: Banff 82 O/4

Point of Departure: From downtown Banff, cross the Bow River bridge and turn left onto Spray Avenue. Follow Spray Avenue for 100 metres and bear right on Sulphur Mountain Drive at the signed intersection. Follow Sulphur Mountain Drive to its termination at the Upper Hot Springs parking lot. The trail starts on an access road (with locked gate) just above the entrance to the parking lot.

0.0—Upper Hot Springs parking lot (1600 m).

—Follow access road and then trail upwards through forest. Steady ascent on long switchbacks.

2.4—Trail passes within 200 metres of waterfall.

2.7—Old trail shelter.

—Steady uphill on switchbacks, passing beneath lift line.

5.5—Upper gondola terminal (2255 m).

For those who distain using a gondola lift as a means of reaching a mountaintop, the 5.5 kilometre trail leading off from the Upper Hot Springs will be the preferable route to the top of Banff's popular Sulphur Mountain. While the trail gains 655 metres of elevation along the way, well graded switchbacks ease the strain of ascent. Though the trail is frequently near or immediately below the gondola line, the hike is usually quite peaceful and provides a number of fine viewpoints for the Banff townsite environs.

The track is wide and the uphill grades are moderate as the trail climbs into the forest and begins its somewhat tedious switchbacking ascent of the mountain. Views open up near the halfway point of the trip as the trail passes just north of a waterfall on the mountain's east face. A small trail shelter lies just beyond the end of a switchback at Kilometre 2.7. (Prior to the completion of the gondola lift in 1959, a tractor and wagon were used to pull visitors up the trail to this point.) The slope of the mountain steepens near the summit and the trail enters into a cool, north-facing subalpine forest. A few scattered alpine larch in the dense forest herald the summit ridge and the upper gondola terminal.

From the gondola terminal, it is possible to hike north along the summit ridge for 0.4 kilometre to the old stone meteorological observatory which was built on rocky Sanson Peak in 1903 (also used as a station for the study of cosmic rays during the 1950s and 60s). Another trail runs south along the ridge for 0.8 kilometre through a scattered forest of alpine fir, Engelmann spruce, alpine larch, and whitebark pine.

Many Sulphur Mountain hikers ride the gondola to the top of the mountain and then walk back down the trail. However, at the time of this writing, hikers who walk up the trail can ride the gondola back down for free.

C Level Cirque

Half-day trip

Allow 1½ hours one way

Elevation gain: 1920 metres (6,300 feet)

Topo maps: Banff 82 O/4†
　　　　　　†trail not shown

Point of Departure: Follow Banff's main street, Banff Avenue, north out of the village to the junction with the Trans-Canada Highway. Continue straight through this interchange onto the Lake Minnewanka Road and follow it to the Upper Bankhead Picnic Area, situated on the left side of the road 3½ kilometres (2 miles) beyond the Trans-Canada underpass. A 100 metre-long gravel entrance road leads to the picnic area parking lot. The trail strikes off from the west corner of this parking lot.

0.0—Trail sign (1465 m).

　—Steady uphill through closed forest.

1.1—Old mine buildings.

1.3—Lake Minnewanka viewpoint.

1.8—Old mine vent shafts.

　—Steady climb through forest.

3.9—C-Level Cirque (1920 m).

Despite its short length, the C Level Cirque trail is one of the more attractive hikes in the Banff townsite vicinity. In less than four kilometres it climbs past the remains of a long defunct coal mine, a panoramic viewpoint for the broad Minnewanka Valley, and finally emerges in a high, rockbound pocket beneath the looming east face of Cascade Mountain.

The hike begins its ascent through a pleasantly varied forest of lodgepole pine, aspen and spruce where calypso orchids, blue clematis and many colourful violets bloom in early summer.

Within a half-hour two skeletal buildings are reached, the remnants of an anthracite coal operation which flourished in the area from 1904 to 1923. A substantial town of some 1,000 inhabitants called Bankhead was spread across the valley near where the trail begins, and these old buildings along the trail were a part of the "C Level" operation—the highest level at which shafts were driven into the mountain. From a tailings pile 100 metres beyond the buildings there is an excellent view out to Lake Minnewanka, and above the viewpoint several fenced holes in the ground indicate the location of old mine vent shafts.

For the remainder of the hike travel is through closed forest. The forest finally opens up over the last 200 metres or so before reaching the cirque with views down the Bow Valley, past Mount Rundle, to the Three Sisters and other mountains beyond the town of Canmore.

The cirque is carved into the eastern flank of Cascade Mountain where a small alpine glacier was obviously at work during a previous ice advance. Snow often lingers in this basin into midsummer, and as it retreats, a carpet of yellow glacier lilies spreads across the damp, subalpine soil near the mouth of the cirque. A tiny pond at this entrance provides water throughout the summer, fed by the extensive snowfield on the talus slopes above.

Lake Minnewanka from C Level Cirque trail

From the rockslide near the mouth of the cirque, a faint trail continues up to the right along a sparsely forested ridge to an even higher vantage point on a knoll above the basin. But most visitors prefer to "boot ski" the snowfield beneath Cascade's cliffs or simply relax on a convenient rock to watch the antics of the cirque inhabitants—the hoary marmots, pikas and golden-mantled ground squirrels.

Aylmer Pass

Minnewanka Parking Area to Aylmer Lookout—11.8 kilometres (7.3 miles)
Minnewanka Parking Area to Aylmer Pass—13.5 kilometres (8.4 miles)

Day trip or backpack

Allow 4 - 5 hours one way

Elevation gain: 810 metres (2,650 feet)

Maximum elevation: 2285 metres (7,500 feet)

Topo maps: Canmore 82 O/3
Lake Minnewanka 82 O/6†
†trail to lookout not shown

Point of Departure: Follow Banff's main street, Banff Avenue, north out of the village to the junction with the Trans-Canada Highway. Continue straight through this interchange onto the Lake Minnewanka Road, following it to the west end of the lake 5½ kilometres (3½ miles) beyond the Trans-Canada Highway junction. Park in the large parking lot just above the tour boat concession entrance.

0.0—Boat concession gate (1480 m).

—Follow paved limited access road past boat concession and picnic area.

0.6—Pavement ends, official trail begins (trail sign).

1.4—Stewart Canyon bridge.

—Trail cuts back to right after crossing canyon and eventually emerges above lakeshore. Trail rolls along above lakeshore next 6 kms.

7.8—Junction. Take left fork to Aylmer Pass and Lookout. Short branch trail to lakeshore and campground cuts down to right. Minnewanka ,Lakeshore trail continues straight ahead.

—Steep climb.

10.1—Junction. Trail to Aylmer Fire Lookout site cuts up to right (1.7 kms to lookout viewpoint). Keep straight ahead for pass.

—Steady climb gradually emerging above tree-line.

13.5—Aylmer Pass (2285 m).

When Sir George Simpson, Governor of the Hudson's Bay Company, made the first recorded visit to Lake Minnewanka in August, 1841, he marvelled at the beauty of the lake and exclaimed that "the surrounding mountains were very grand, of every varied form ... their craggy summits resembling battlements among which dizzy heights the goat and sheep delight to bound." Hikers who journey to Aylmer Pass and the old Aylmer fire lookout can retrace part of Sir George's route and visit those "dizzy heights" where "sheep delight to bound."

Though the first 7.8 kilometres of the journey follow Minnewanka's north shore over gentle, undemanding trail, hikers should beware of the ordeal which rises beyond. Forking uphill, away from the tranquility of the lake, the trail to the pass and lookout is strenuous indeed. Water bottles should be filled at the stream near the junction in preparation for gaining 600 vertical metres in the next two kilometres. The next water is at least an hour beyond this stream, and the south-facing slope which permits hikers to climb to over 2000 metres above sea level in early June is also one of the hot spots in the Rockies on sunny summer days.

Most day hikers opt for the shorter trip to the fire lookout which is situated on the crest of an open ridge below the summit of Mount Aylmer. From this 2040 metre viewpoint nearly all of Lake Minnewanka can be seen. The water, over 500 metres below, is of the deepest blue, and the boats look much like tiny water insects skimming to and fro. Across the lake stand the twin peaks of Mount Inglismaldie (2965 m) and Mount Girouard (2995 m), displaying massive cliffs of Mississippian and Devonian age limestone. Directly behind the lookout site, a short distance to the north, is Mount Aylmer (3162 m), the highest mountain in this section of the park. To the southwest lie the Mount

Aylmer Pass

Rundle massif and the Bow Valley near Banff townsite, with range upon range beyond, disappearing into the distance.

Though the lookout hasn't been manned for many years, the open ridge is often visited by herds of mountain sheep who, perhaps, remember the days when fire lookouts used to put out salt blocks. Another form of wildlife which proliferates on the ridge in early summer, partially due to the presence of the sheep, is the wood tick (check your body carefully upon returning from this trip).

From the fire lookout trail junction at Kilometre 10.1, the left fork continues on to the park boundary and the tundra of, Aylmer Pass. The pass is a prime alpine area above the last forest cover and it is free of snow considerably later than the lookout ridge. From its summit views open onto the highly folded and faulted mountains of the Palliser Range. Directly above the pass to the east is the summit of Mount Aylmer, a gruelling but straightforward scramble for strong hikers with good boots. Like the Aylmer Lookout vicinity, the slopes above the pass are prime mountain sheep habitat.

Though strong hikers can visit the lookout or the pass and return in one long day, the hike lends itself well to overnight camping. There is an excellent campground on the shore of Lake Minnewanka near the 7.8 kilometre junction, and both the lookout and pass can be reached from this base camp in an easy day. And if backpackers have a few days to spare they may want to continue over the pass to explore the Ghost River Wilderness Area.

29

Lake Minnewanka

Minnewanka Parking Area to Ghost Lakes—25.6 kilometres (15.9 miles)

Minnewanka-Carrot Creek Circuit—48.6 kilometres (30.2 miles)

Backpack

Allow 8 - 10 hours to Ghost Lakes

Elevation gain: nil

Maximum elevation: 1525 metres (5,000 feet)

Topo maps: Lake Minnewanka 82 O/6

Point of Departure: Follow Banff's main street, Banff Avenue, north out of the village to the junction with the Trans-Canada Highway. Continue straight through this interchange onto the Lake Minnewanka Road, following it to the west end of the lake, 5½ kilometres (3½ miles) beyond the Trans-Canada Highway junction. Park in the large parking lot just above the tour boat concession entrance.

0.0—Boat concession gate (1480 m).

—Follow paved limited access road past boat concession and picnic area.

0.6—Pavement ends, official trail begins (trail sign).

1.4—Stewart Canyon bridge.

—Trail cuts back to right after crossing canyon, eventually emerges above lakeshore.

—Trail rolls along gently not far above lakeshore.

7.8—Junction. Aylmer Pass and Lookout to left. Lakeshore campground to right. Main trail straight ahead.

9.3—Campground.

11.1—Campground.

18.8—Campground.

20.4—Trail cuts away from shoreline.

22.8—East end of Lake Minnewanka.

23.8—First Ghost Lake.

25.6—Ford and junction (1495 m). Cross stream between 1st and 2nd Ghost Lakes to south side. Intersection with *Carrot Creek* trail at Km 22.9. Devil's Gap and park boundary to left.

29.5—Devil's Gap and park boundary.

The hike down the north shoreline of Banff's largest lake is definately a departure from the usual alpine meadow-cirque lake routine, and it is especially attractive to early and late season backpackers since the lake's low elevation and easterly location in the range often result in dry, snowless hiking from May until mid-autumn.

Departing from the boat dock complex and picnic area at Minnewanka's western end, the trail rolls along the north shore for the next 20 kilometres with little gain or loss of elevation the entire way. There are many fine campsites along this shore, and pleasant gravel beaches scattered with driftwood provide numerous places to stop and relax (though not as pleasant on weekends when motor boat traffic is heavy on the lake).

Approaching the eastern end of the lake, the countryside becomes noticeably drier and the vegetation more typically montane. Limber pines are scattered among the ubiquitous lodgepole stands and western wood lilies cover the open hillsides and meadows.

After passing beyond the eastern end of the lake, the trail skirts the first of the three Ghost Lakes, crosses through an arm of forest, and emerges on the short channel connecting the first and second lakes. An easy ford can be made here, and from the junction on the opposite side you can either wander eastward into the Devil's Gap or turn right and return to civilization by way of the Carrot Creek trail (see *Carrot Creek* trail description).

The rather haunting names found in this part of the park relate to local Indian legends concerning a cannibal ghost which was observed picking over the bones of Stoney warriors killed in battle on the nearby Ghost River (just a bit of local colour to ponder as you slip into your sleeping bag for the night).

Lake Minnewanka

Carrot Creek

Trans-Canada Highway to Carrot Creek Summit—10.5 kilometres (6.5 miles)
Minnewanka-Carrot Creek Circuit—48.6 kilometres (30.2 miles)

Day trip or backpack

Allow 4 - 5 hours to summit

Elevation gain: 550 metres (1,800 feet)

Maximum elevation: 1920 metres (6,300 feet)

Topo maps: Canmore 82 O/3†
†trail not shown

Point of Departure: Follow the Trans-Canada Highway west from the Banff Park East Gate 2 kilometres (1.2 miles) to the Carrot Creek landfill side road (landfill road is also accessible via a crossover from the eastbound lane of the highway). Follow the landfill access road for 100 metres to a small parking area on the left. The trail starts at the hiker's walk-through gate in the animal control fence.

0.0—Fence walk-through (1370 m).

—Faint path along animal control fence.

0.3—Junction. Keep right onto old abandoned access road.

—Flat walking through aspen parkland.

1.6—Junction. Trail from hamlet of Harvie Heights intersects from right. Keep straight ahead.

1.8—Old road narrows to a single trail.

2.6—Mouth of Carrot Creek canyon. First crossing of creek (via log).

—Trail zigzags up the canyon crossing creek 24 times, usually on makeshift log bridges.

7.6—Last crossing of Carrot Creek.

8.0—Campsite.

8.4—Grade steepens toward pass.

10.5—Carrot Creek Summit (1920 m).

—Moderate downhill.

12.1—Downhill grade steepens, crossing back and forth over creek.

14.0—Lake Minnewanka (1495 m). Trail follows shoreline to right.

20.6—East end of Lake Minnewanka.

22.9—Junction. Intersection with *Lake Minnewanka* trail at Km 25.6.

The Carrot Creek trail is a masochist's delight. In all its 14 kilometres to the south shore of Lake Minnewanka, it never once emerges from the forest, and it comes close to setting a Rocky Mountain record by crisscrossing the creek 24 times in the space of five kilometres, all of these traverses either fords or narrow log-walks. But the Carrot Creek canyon is a cool, unique environment of overhanging walls and sparkling water, and the exquisite Peechee Meadows above Carrot Creek Summit provide a view that is well worth the bushwhack and steep climb.

After crossing an open alluvial plain dotted with stands of aspen and cottonwood, the mouth of the canyon and the first of the 24 crossings are encountered. Nearly all of the crossings are necessary since the walls of the narrow canyon force the trail back and forth across the stream but most have some sort of rough log bridge, so it is possible for acrobatic log walkers to negotiate the entire canyon with dry feet.

Beyond the last crossing, the trail begins its steep ascent to Carrot Creek Summit. Just south of this forested pass, a narrow avalanche path allows a glimpse up to the open Peechee Meadows. These meadows can be attained up this steep opening or by continuing on to the summit and then climbing due west until you emerge from the trees. The summit of the Peechee Meadows is an open 2200 metre-high ridge which commands a breathtaking view of Lake Minnewanka.

From Carrot Creek Summit the trail plunges straight down a major tributary stream to reach the south shore of Lake Minnewanka, then runs east along the shore to eventually intersect with the Lake Minnewanka trail between the first and second Ghost Lakes. These two trails can be linked together to create a fine early season backpack covering some 48.6 kilometres (see *Lake Minnewanka-Ghost Lakes* trail description).

Spray River Fire Road

Banff Springs Hotel to Spray Lakes Reservoir—38.8 kilometres (24.1 miles)

Backpack

Allow 2 -3 days one way

Elevation gain: 335 metres (1,100 feet)

Maximum elevation: 1735 metres (5,700 feet)

Topo maps: Banff 82 O/4
Canmore 82 O/3
Spray Lakes Reservoir 82 J/14

Point of Departure: From downtown Banff, cross the Bow River bridge and turn left onto Spray Avenue. Follow Spray Avenue for 1.0 kilometre (0.6 mile) to the Banff Springs Hotel. Park along the street below the hotel and walk uphill, past the hotel and the upper parking lot, to a locked access gate at the end of the street.

0.0—Access gate (1400 m).

3.7—Youth Hostel.

5.7—Junction. Spray River East Road intersects from left (see *Spray River Circuit* trail description).

9.8—Junction. Goat Creek trail branches left. Keep right.

10.2—Junction. Warden cabin to left 100 metres. Keep right.

15.1—Campground.

22.7—Spray River Warden Cabin and campground.

23.2—Spray River bridge.

33.7—Campground.

34.9—Spray River bridge.

35.6—Junction. Fortune Warden Cabin to right 50 metres. Keep left.

37.2—Park boundary.

38.8—Spray Lakes Reservoir and junction (1705 m). Intersection with Spray Lakes West Road. Canyon Dam to left 1.8 kilometres. Keep right for Trail Centre.

43.6—Access gate and parking area.

44.3—Trail Centre Junction (1705 m).

Starting near the Banff Springs Hotel in Banff townsite, the Spray River Fire Road follows the course of the Lower Spray River south to its source near the west end of the Spray Lakes Reservoir. It is a closed access road that is popular with mountain bicyclists and is still utilized on occasion by warden service vehicles, and though it is a long and rather dull way for backpackers to reach the southern part of Banff Park, it does traverse a peaceful, forested valley appointed with some very fine campgrounds.

While the main fire road starts at an access gate on the west side of the valley just beyond the Banff Springs Hotel, another road starting from the hotel's golf course and following along the east side of the river for the first 6.7 kilometres is a more pleasant way to initiate the journey (see *Spray River Loop* trail description). After the east side road crosses the river to join the main road to the west, the ascent of the Spray becomes quite straightforward and mainly forest-enclosed.

At Kilometre 10.9 the Goat Creek trail junction is passed and the road immediately bends to the southwest to cut through a gap in the chain of peaks which comprises the Sulphur Mountain—Goat Range. After traversing the gap, the road takes a southeasterly tack once again until it reaches the Spray Lakes Reservoir. At this junction with the reservoir's old west side access road, most travellers will want to turn right and hike 5.5 kilometres to Trail Centre—the trail head for trips up Bryant Creek and the Upper Spray River.

Goat Creek. This is another old fire road which connects the Spray River Fire Road to the Spray Lakes Road eight kilometres south of the town of Canmore. For all of its 9.3 kilometre distance it runs along a wooded valley bottom between the Mount Rundle massif and the Goat Range.

Brewster Creek

Sunshine Road to Allenby Pass—29.5 kilometres (18.3 miles)

Sunshine Road to Lake Magog Campground—46.6 kilometres (29.0 miles)

Backpack

Allow 2 - 3 days one way

Elevation gain: 1020 metres (3,350 feet)

Maximum elevation: 2440 metres (8,000 feet)

Topo maps: Banff 82 O/4

Mount Assiniboine 82 J/13

Point of Departure: Follow the Trans-Canada Highway 9 kilometres (5½ miles) west from the Banff townsite west exit to the junction with the Sunshine Village access road. Follow the Sunshine Village Road for 0.8 kilometre to a well-defined turnout and parking area on the left hand side of the road.

0.0—Healy Creek bridge (1420 m).

2.1—Junction. Left hand branch leads to the Sundance Canyon bicycle path (2.9 kms) and Banff (7.7 kms). Keep right and uphill.

11.1—Ten Mile Cabin (outfitter's camp).

12.7—Junction. Fatigue Pass to right (10.8 kms). Keep straight ahead for Allenby Pass.

25.4—Half-way Cabin (outfitter's camp).

—Trail crosses creek just south of cabin.

26.2—Trail swings southeast and begins steep switchback ascent toward Allenby Pass.

29.5—Allenby Pass (2440 m).

—Moderate to steep grades descending from pass.

34.1—Junction. Trail straight ahead descends to Bryant Creek trail in 0.5 km (reaches trail 5.4 kms above Bryant Creek Warden Cabin). Keep right for Og Pass and Mt. Assiniboine.

36.6—Trail turns northwest and begins ascent to Og Pass.

39.7—Og Pass (2300 m). Intersection with *Og Pass* trail (see Assiniboine Park chapter).

—Descent to Lake Magog via Og Pass trail.

46.6—Lake Magog Campground (2165 m).

The trail up Brewster Creek to Allenby and Og Passes is a long established horse route from Banff to Mount Assiniboine. While the passes at the southern end of the trail are very fine indeed, heavy horse travel and a comparatively long approach to Mount Assiniboine have discouraged most backpackers from using this route.

While it is possible to reach Brewster Creek from Banff townsite by following the Sundance Canyon bicycle path west from the Cave and Basin and then connecting in with the old Healy Creek access road, the bridging of Healy Creek has made the trail head on the Sunshine Village Road the shortest and most direct point of access. From the bridge an old road track leads due east for 2.1 kilometres to meet the main access road from Sundance Canyon. From this junction the Brewster Creek trail branches uphill to the south to begin its long ascent of the valley.

From the junction at Kilometre 2.1 to the Ten Mile Cabin, you follow a broad, well-beaten path utilized by horses and the commercial outfitter's supply vehicles. Beyond the cabin the horse trail continues upvalley through a forest of spruce and lodgepole pine which allows occasional views of the Sundance Range to the east. The outfitter's Halfway Cabin is passed at Kilometre 25.4 and the steep ascent to Allenby Pass begins immediately thereafter.

From the summit of Allenby Pass — a spectacular defile composed of rockslides and beautiful alpine meadows — it is possible to continue south and descend to the Bryant Creek trail in another five kilometres (see *Bryant Creek* trail description). Most Assiniboine-bound travellers will prefer to contour off to the right above the valley, however, and traverse Og Pass—a summit which is just as scenically rewarding as Allenby.

Fatigue Creek

Backpack

Allow 2 or more days

Elevation gain: 780 metres (2,560 feet)

Maximum elevation: 2395 m (7,850 feet)

Topo maps: Banff 82 O/4†

†trail not shown

Point of Departure: To reach the north end of the trail hike the *Brewster Creek—Allenby Pass* trail to the junction at Km 12.7. To reach the south end of the trail hike the *Citadel Pass* trail to the junction at Km 9.3.

0.0—Brewster Creek Junction (1615 m).

0.2—Brewster Creek crossing (knee-deep ford).

1.0—1st Fatigue Creek crossing.

—Trail swings back and forth across creek, six fords in 4 kms.

5.1—6th Fatigue Creek crossing.

7.9—Primitive campsite.

—Steep ascent to pass.

10.9—Fatigue Pass (2395 m).

—Contour right and descend toward Citadel Pass.

13.4—Citadel Pass and junction (2360 m). Intersection with *Citadel Pass* trail at Km 9.3.

The Fatigue Creek trail is a backcountry link that connects the Brewster Creek trail to the Citadel Pass-Mt. Assiniboine trail. It is an old outfitter's route that is steep, rough, and seldom traversed by hikers. While Fatigue Pass is one of Banff Park's highest trailed passes and very scenic, it is usually visited as an extended day trip from Sunshine Village via Citadel Pass. But the valley that runs away from the pass to the north is remote and peaceful, and the trail may prove to be a useful connection for some wilderness travellers.

From its junction with the Brewster Creek trail, follow the Fatigue Creek trail 200 metres to a ford of Brewster Creek, the first of many foot-soaking encounters. From this crossing, the slog up the Fatigue Valley begins. The valley is narrow and the horse trail swings back and forth across the creek six times in the first five kilometres— all unbridged fords. Above the last ford the grade steepens as the trail begins its ascent to Fatigue Pass. Nearing the head of the valley, the forest opens out into subalpine meadowland.

From the upper meadows, the trail climbs up and over 2395 metre-high Fatigue Pass. The way is steep and rocky, but above timberline and glorious all the way to the junction in Citadel Pass on the other side. From there you can head south toward Mount Assiniboine or north to Sunshine Village.

While the trail is described here as an option from the Brewster Creek valley, the few hikers who do travel its length usually start from the Citadel Pass end. The elevation advantages are obvious and the fords not nearly so unpleasant when one is heading downhill. If you do start from Citadel Pass, be aware that the trail is indistinct for the first kilometre or so across the alpine tundra. Take a topo map along so you can locate the obvious gap of Fatigue Pass to the southeast, then look for the trace of the trail on the slopes above.

Banff Park South

The southern end of Banff National Park is quite removed from the park's highway system, and trails extending into the region from the north are long and somewhat tedious. As a result, most hikers utilize the road system in the Spray Lakes Reservoir area as their approach to such southern areas as the Upper Spray Valley and Bryant Creek. The two main trail heads are Trail Centre at the south end of the Spray Lakes Reservoir and Mud Lake at the headwaters of Smith Dorrien Creek, and both are reached from the town of Canmore via the Spray Lakes Road.

To reach Canmore, follow the Trans-Canada Highway to the interchange four kilometres east of Banff Park's east gate. Exit onto the 1-A Highway and cross the CPR tracks into downtown Canmore by either of two main entrance streets. Near the west end of the town's main street, at the intersection of 8th Avenue and 8th Street, watch for a prominent "Spray Lakes" sign. Follow the street as indicated and cross the Bow River bridge to the west edge of town. Turn left on Three Sisters Drive and follow the "Spray Lakes" signs as they lead you out of town on the Spray Lakes Road.

The Spray Lakes Road reverts from pavement to a well-graded gravel road as it climbs to Whiteman's Pass—a narrow gap in the cliffs above Canmore. From the gap the road levels out and runs due south to the Spray Lakes Reservoir. Seventeen kilometres from downtown Canmore the Spray Lakes Road splits: the Spray Lakes West Road branches right, crosses an earth-fill dam, and follows the west shoreline to Canyon Dam (16 kilometres) and the reservoir's south end (22.4 kilometres); the Smith Dorrien—Spray Road continues due south along the east side of the valley to the Watridge Creek logging road (21 kilometres), Mud Lake (27.2 kilometres), and the Kananaskis Lakes.

Spray Lakes West Road. There are two approaches to the Trail Centre trail head at the southern tip of the Spray Lakes Reservoir: one utilizes the Spray Lakes West Road, the other the Smith Dorrien — Spray Road and the Watridge Creek logging road. Of the two, the Spray Lakes West Road has been the most popular route over the years, partially because many people are willing to drive the last 6.4 kilometres of road beyond Canyon Dam to the parking area near Trail Centre. If you are travelling by mountain bicycle, motorcycle, or four-wheel drive vehicle, this stretch of road is no problem, but the first 1.5 kilometres after the dam are steep, muddy and severely eroded, and vehicles with low clearance find the going very slow and rough. If you decide against sacrificing the family car to the vagaries of this section, drive to Canyon Dam and walk the rest of the way—an option that adds 7.1 kilometres to all hikes starting from Trail Centre.

Watridge Creek. If you don't want to drive beyond Canyon Dam, you might consider the Watridge Creek approach to Trail Centre—an option which entails a mandatory 6.0 kilometre hike, approximately one kilometre less than the walk from the dam. To reach the Watridge trail head, take the road which branches right from the Smith Dorrien—Spray Road 38 kilometres from downtown Canmore (watch for the "Karst Trail" sign at the junction) and follow it due west into the old Watridge Creek logging area, keeping right at all road intersections. The trail begins where the road has been washed out at Kilometre 7.0, and it is well marked as it makes its way through a kilometre or so of logging debris on old cat-tracks. From the edge of the clearcut the route follows pleasant if sometimes boggy trail through heavy forest to the north shore of Watridge Lake and then through more forest to a bridge across the Spray River just upstream from the end of the reservoir. Across the bridge the Palliser Pass trail is joined 700 metres south of the Trail Centre junction (if you are heading south up the Spray River, this option will actually save you nearly two kilometres over the Canyon Dam approach).

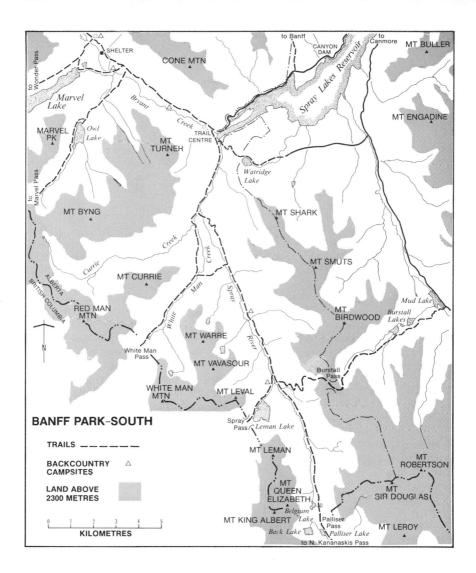

BANFF PARK-SOUTH

TRAILS — — — — —

BACKCOUNTRY △
CAMPSITES

LAND ABOVE
2300 METRES

0 1 2 3 4 5
KILOMETRES

Of the two approaches to Trail Centre, the authors have a slight bias in favour of Canyon Dam when heading for Bryant Creek or Mount Assiniboine: the road is pleasant, as roads go, with open views along the shore of the reservoir, and even though it is a kilometre or so longer than the Watridge Creek option, the broad, solid surface allows for a much brisker walking pace. For trips to Palliser Pass or White Man Pass, the saving of two kilometres probably favours Watridge Creek.

Mud Lake. Another point of access into the southern park region utilizes Burstall Pass as an approach to the Leman Lake—Palliser Pass area of the Upper Spray Valley, an option which saves at least four kilometres over the hike from Trail Centre. The trail head is located at the south end of Mud Lake, 45 kilometres from downtown Canmore on the Smith Dorrien—Spray Road. (See *Burstall Pass* trail description.)

37

Palliser Pass

Trail Centre Junction to Palliser Pass—21.4 kilometres (13.3 miles)

Backpack

Allow 1 - 1½ days to pass

Elevation gain: 400 metres (1,300 feet)

Maximum elevation: 2105 metres (6,900 feet)

Topo maps: Spray Lakes Reservoir 82 J/14
Kananaskis Lakes 82 J/11

Point of Departure: Follow directions to the Trail Centre area at the head of the Spray Reservoir as described in the *Banff Park South* introduction (see page 36). Starting from Canyon Dam or the Watridge Creek logging area, add 7.1 kms or 4.6 kms respectively to this trip.

0.0—Trail Centre junction (1705 m). Bryant Creek trail to Mt. Assiniboine, Marvel Lake straight ahead. Take left hand trail for Upper Spray—Palliser Pass.

0.2—Bryant Creek bridge.

0.7—Junction. Trail from Watridge Creek logging area intersects from left. Keep straight ahead for Palliser Pass.

3.9—Junction and Spray River. White Man Pass trail cuts off to right. Cross Spray River on bridge (upstream from old ford) and continue upvalley for Palliser Pass.

7.5—Junction. South cutoff to White Man Pass branches right. Palliser Pass straight ahead.

10.2—Palliser Warden Cabin.

—Open, willow-dwarf birch meadows.

14.0—Keep left on higher and drier bench trail above creek.

14.6—Junction. Burstall Pass trail intersects from left. Keep straight ahead for Palliser Pass.

14.7—Junction. Trail to Leman Lake (1.3 kms) branches down to right. Keep straight ahead for Palliser Pass.

19.3—Steep ascent to Palliser Pass begins.

20.6—Belgium Lake.

21.4—Palliser Pass and park boundary (2105 m).

The valley containing the headwaters of the Spray River forms the extreme southern tip of Banff Park. It is a narrow valley just over twenty kilometres in length running from the southern end of the Spray Lakes Reservoir to Palliser Pass. Flanked by the craggy peaks of the Spray Mountains, the valley offers a variety of hiking options in an area receiving only moderate use during the hiking season. Using Palliser Pass as a basic objective, a backpacker can spend several days in the valley, taking side trips to White Man Pass and Leman Lake, and, having reached Palliser Pass, either continue beyond the pass for a longer trek into Kananaskis Provincial Park or turn back down the Spray to exit via Burstall Pass.

From the Trail Centre junction at the south end of the Spray Lakes Reservoir, the trail works south through heavy forest then emerges into open willow meadow to cross the Spray River at Kilometre 3.9. The trail to White Man Pass cuts west from the Palliser Pass trail at the north end of the crossing footbridge (see *White Man Pass* trail description).

At Kilometre 7.5 you pass the poorly marked southern cutoff to White Man Pass and less than three kilometres further along the Palliser Warden Cabin. Approximately two kilometres beyond the cabin, now travelling through the open willow and dwarf birch meadows that characterize the upper portion of the valley, you will encounter an area where there is some confusing multi-trailing. Theoretically, there are two main trails, one that runs along the river's edge and another that stays high along the slight benchland above the river. Both trails make their way upvalley successfully, but the higher (and drier) trail is the preferred route.

At Kilometre 14.6, at the base of a large avalanche slope, the Burstall Pass trail intersects from the left, and, 100 metres farther on, the short spur trail to Leman Lake branches right and crosses the river

Spray Valley

via a footbridge. Those bound for Palliser Pass should tread the middle ground, continuing upvalley.

After crossing the second of two small streams near the 18.5 kilometre mark, the trail begins a steep ascent toward the pass, eventually leaving the forest for the open subalpine meadows surrounding Belgium Lake (there is a primitive campsite at the lake). The boundary marker signifying Palliser Pass and the southernmost tip of Banff Park is passed at Kilometre 21.4, and Palliser and Back Lakes lie just beyond.

Leman Lake. Lying at 1935 metres above sea level between Mounts Leval and Leman, Leman Lake is often a primary objective for backpackers visiting the Upper Spray Valley. Certainly it is no great hardship to drop your pack at the 14.7 kilometre junction and walk the 1.3 kilometre trail to this pleasant lake. After crossing the Spray River and Leman Creek footbridges, a primitive campsite is passed, then the trail climbs a short but steep ridge and descends to the lakeshore. The trail continues high along the western margin of the lake for just over another kilometre to reach the park boundary at Spray Pass—a gap which is well forested and provides no views.

Burstall Pass. This 10.9 kilometre-long trail originating at Mud Lake in Kananaskis Provincial Park is the shortcut route to the Leman Lake area and Palliser Pass. Anyone desiring to save time on their trip to the Upper Spray environs should definately examine this option. (See *Burstall Pass* trail description.)

Burstall Pass

Smith Dorrien-Spray Road to Spray River Junction—10.9 kilometres (6.8 miles)

Day trip or backpack

Allow 2 - 3 hours to Burstall Pass

Elevation gain: 455 metres (1,500 feet)
loss: 490 metres (1,600 feet)

Maximum elevation: 2375 metres (7,800 feet)

Topo maps: Spray Lakes Reservoir 82 J/14†
†trail not shown

Point of Departure: Follow directions to the Spray Lakes Road as described in the *Banff Park South* introduction (see page 36). From downtown Canmore follow the Spray Lakes Road 17½ kilometers (11 miles) to the junction with the Spray Lakes West Road. At this junction stay left on the main road designated Smith Dorrien–Spray Trail, continuing another 27 kilometres (17 miles) to Mud Lake—a one-kilometre-long lake on the right hand side of the road. A parking area, locked access gate, and trail sign at the south end of the lake indicate the start of the trail.

0.0—Trail sign and access gate (1920 m).

—Follow old logging road up along lower slopes of Mt. Burstall.

2.9—Road passes above Burstall Lakes.

—Road reverts to single path.

3.7—Trail skirts Burstall Creek flats, begins ascent to pass.

7.4—Burstall Pass (2375 m).

—Steep switchbacks.

10.9—Junction (1905 m). Intersection with *Upper Spray River—Palliser Pass* trail at Km 14.6.

The Burstall Pass trail, though lightly travelled, offers diversion and scenery to equal any in the Rockies. To the day hiker, the route means easy access to high, rolling alpine meadows and rich mountain vistas; to the backpacker, it is a fast, spectacular entrance to the Upper Spray Valley and the far southern tip of Banff National Park.

The trail actually begins in Kananaskis Provincial Park, striking off from a well-marked trail head at the south end of Mud Lake on the Smith Dorrien—Spray Road. The trip begins inauspiciously as hikers find themselves trudging up an old access road through a logged-over pine and spruce forest. At the three kilometre mark, however, the road passes above the Burstall Lakes and reverts to a well-defined trail. Another 800 metres finds it skirting a large dryas meadow and crossing the braided channels of Burstall Creek.

At the western edge of the flats, the trail climbs away from Burstall Creek, rising first beside a small tributary creek through mature forest and then out onto a large avalanche slope on the southeastern flank of Mount Birdwood. From the avalanche path it again enters the forest for a steep 150 metre ascent before levelling off in a large meadowy cirque. The hiker's relief is temporary, however, for the climb resumes within a kilometre, this time pushing 215 vertical metres to the pass.

The descent into the Upper Spray can be problematic, particularly when snow blankets the pass. The trail skirts to the left of the obvious sinkhole just west of the pass and begins to descend a large gully (watch for cairns or markers). As the path emerges from the gully onto the slope of the Spray Valley it swings south to catch the next creek gully down the mountainside. A long series of steep switchbacks descends to the valley below. At Kilometre 10.9 the trail meets the Palliser Pass trail at a marked junction. (See *Palliser Pass* trail description.)

White Man Pass

Trail Centre Junction to White Man Pass—11.6 kilometres (7.2 miles)

Backpack

Allow 4 - 7 hours one way

Elevation gain: 430 metres (1,400 feet)

Maximum elevation: 2135 metres (7,000 feet)

Topo maps: Spray Lakes Reservoir 82 J/14

Point of Departure: Follow directions to the Trail Centre area at the head of the Spray Lakes Reservoir as described in the *Banff Park South* introduction (see page 36). Starting from Canyon Dam or the Watridge Creek logging area, add 7.1 or 4.6 kms respectively to this trip.

0.0—Trail Centre junction (1705 m). Take left hand fork for Upper Spray River and White Man Pass.

0.2—Bryant Creek bridge.

0.7—Junction. Trail from Watridge Creek intersects from left. Keep straight ahead.

3.9—Junction and Spray River. Palliser Pass trail crosses river via bridge. Keep right on west side of river for White Man Pass.

5.2—Currie Creek ford.

5.5—White Man Creek ford.

—Gradual climb.

7.8—Junction and primitive campsite. South cutoff from Palliser Pass trail intersects from left. Keep right for White Man Pass.

9.5—Steep ascent to pass begins.

11.1—Small lake.

11.6—White Man Pass (2135 m).

Whatever White Man Pass may lack in scenic splendour, it more than compensates with its rich, colourful past. This is the pass James Sinclair led the Red River emigrants and their livestock through on the way to the Oregon Territory in 1841. Here, beside the small lake just east of the pass, the halfbreed guides of the Jesuit missionary Father Pierre DeSmet erected a wooden cross in his honour in 1845. The cantankerous fur trader Peter Skene Ogden, the British spies Henry Warre and Nigel Vavasour, and the tireless explorer-geologist George M. Dawson all passed this way.

While the trip to White Man Pass and back can be made in a long day from the end of the Spray Lakes Reservoir, most visitors prefer packing-in to spend a night on the pass, particularly if their hike begins further back at Canyon Dam or Watridge Creek (see Banff Park South introduction).

This hike begins on the Upper Spray River-Palliser Pass trail, but at the Spray River crossing at Kilometre 3.9 it stays on the west side of the river and bends right toward the White Man Creek valley. Unfortunately, access to the valley is not without its toll—a knee-deep ford of Currie Creek at Kilometre 5.2 followed by a ford of White Man Creek less than 300 metres further along.

The remainder of the ascent to White Man Pass is straightforward and uneventful as the trail travels through a mix of meadow and subalpine forest before it starts a strenuous climb over the last two kilometres to the divide. The pass itself is comprised of a forested ridge, but a tiny lake just east of the summit makes a fine camping spot with open views to White Man and Red Man Mountains.

Latter-day explorers can continue this historical journey by bushwhacking down the Cross River drainage to reach a B.C. forest logging road 6 kilometres below the pass.

Bryant Creek

Trail Centre Junction to Assiniboine Pass—16.3 kilometres (10.1 miles)

Trail Centre Junction to Lake Magog Campground—20.1 kilometres (12.5 miles)

Backpack

Allow 5 - 6 hours to pass

Elevation gain: 455 metres (1,500 feet)

Maximum elevation: 2165 metres (7,100 feet)

Topo maps: Spray Lakes Reservoir 82 J/14

Mount Assiniboine 82 J/13

Point of Departure: Follow directions to the Trail Centre junction at the head of the Spray Lakes Reservoir as described in the *Banff Park South* introduction (see page 36). Starting from Canyon Dam or the Watridge Creek logging area, add 7.1 or 6.0 kms respectively to this trip.

0.0—Trail Centre junction (1705 m).

0.3—Junction. Warden cabin to left. Keep straight ahead.

2.9—Campground.

5.3—Junction. Owl Lake to left 3.5 kms. Keep straight ahead.

6.3—Junction. Campground to left (0.6 km) and shortcut to Marvel Lake (1.6 km). Assiniboine Pass straight ahead.

6.9—Junction. Bryant Creek Shelter 0.2 km to left. Keep straight ahead.

7.6—Bryant Creek Warden Cabin and junction. Campground 0.2 km to right. *Marvel Lake* and *Wonder Pass* to left. Assiniboine Pass straight ahead.

10.8—Junction and campground. Horse trail crosses stream to left (1.5 kms shorter than hiker's route). Hiker's highline route branches right.

11.3—Junction. Allenby Pass to right. Keep left.

15.7—Junction. Horse trail rejoins hiker's trail from left.

—Steady uphill switchbacks.

16.3—Assiniboine Pass (2165 m). Intersection with *Assiniboine Pass* trail (see Assiniboine Park chapter).

—Descent to Lake Magog via Assiniboine Pass trail.

20.0—Lake Magog Campground (2165 m).

Few people think of Bryant Creek as a backcountry destination but rather as the most direct access route to Mount Assiniboine. Yet, the valley's shelter cabin and campgrounds serve as centres for as great a variety of hiking as can be found anywhere in the Rockies, with such scenic highlights as Assiniboine Pass, Marvel Lake, Wonder Pass, Owl Lake, and Allenby Pass all being within easy reach of your camp.

While the trail up Bryant Creek officially starts from the Trail Centre junction at the west end of the Spray Lakes Reservoir, chances are good that you will have to walk an extra 7.1 kilometres from Canyon Dam or 6.0 kilometres from Watridge Creek to reach this point (see *Banff Park South* introduction). From the junction the trail cuts through dense lodgepole pine forest, working up the Bryant Creek valley between Cone Mountain and Mount Turner—a straightforward if uninspiring trek. The Owl Lake trail junction is passed at Kilometre 5.3 and a shortcut trail to Marvel Lake branches left a kilometre beyond. At Kilometre 6.9 the Bryant Creek Shelter is reached, lying just off the main trail to the left. The shelter is open to the public but is usually well-populated from late June through Labour Day.

A little less than a kilometre beyond the shelter is the Bryant Creek Warden Cabin and the junction with the Wonder Pass trail. A campground just behind the warden cabin provides a good, centrally-located alternative for back-packers who don't want to stay at the shelter cabin.

Assiniboine Pass. The Bryant Creek trail continues upvalley from the warden cabin and immediately enters an extensive meadow covered with shrub willow and dwarf birch. At Kilometre 11.3 a hiker's trail branches right from the old horse trail. While this trail stays on higher and drier ground on the north side of the val-

Bryant Creek Warden Cabin

ley, it adds approximately 1.5 kilometres onto the total distance to the pass. Since the horse trail is no longer used by commercial outfitters, we recommend you stay left at this junction, hop across the creek, and stick to the more direct route up the south side of the valley.

While the subalpine meadows of Assiniboine Pass would be a pleasant enough destination on many other trails, hikers who take the trouble of climbing to its summit are inevitably bound for Lake Magog at the foot of Mount Assiniboine just 2.4 kilometres beyond (see *Mount Assiniboine* chapter). For day hikers working out from a base camp in the upper Bryant Creek valley, Assiniboine Pass can also be coupled with Og Pass to the north to make a scenic loop trip around Cave Mountain.

Marvel Lake. Ringed by heavy subalpine forest, Marvel is one of Banff Park's largest backcountry lakes and the closest point of interest to the Bryant Creek Shelter and campgrounds. The main attraction of the lake is not the scenery but the fishing, and its deep waters have been known to produce some large trout on occasion. The east end of the lake can be reached via the 1.6 kilometre shortcut trail that branches from the Bryant Creek trail at Kilometre 6.3 or by hiking the

Wonder Pass trail from the Bryant Creek Warden Cabin junction. (See *Wonder Pass* trail description.)

Allenby Pass. This lofty, rockbound pass is usually associated with the long, tedious backpack up the Brewster Creek valley. However, it can be reached as a day trip from any of the campgrounds in the upper Bryant Creek valley.

At Kilometre 11.3, where the Assiniboine Pass horse and hiker routes diverge, keep right on the hiker's trail. A short distance beyond this junction, watch for the Allenby Pass trail branching right. From this junction the trail climbs steadily up Allenby Creek for the next 5.1 kilometres to the 2440 metre summit of the pass. The trail traverses some delightful wildflower meadows and alpine larch stands along the way. Total distance to the pass from the Bryant Creek Warden Cabin is 10.5 kilometres. (See also *Brewster Creek* trail description.)

Other worthwhile trips from the Bryant Creek area include a loop around Marvel Peak via Owl Lake, Marvel Pass, and Marvel Lake and a loop to Mount Assiniboine and back utilizing Wonder and Assiniboine Passes. (See *Owl Lake* and *Wonder Pass* trail descriptions.)

Marvel Lake—Wonder Pass

Bryant Creek Junction to Wonder Pass—8.9 kilometres (5.5 miles)

Bryant Creek Junction to Lake Magog Campground—13.5 kilometres (8.4 miles)

Backpack

Allow 3-4 hours to Wonder Pass

Elevation gain: 550 metres (1,800 feet)

Maximum elevation: 2395 metres (7,850 feet)

Topo maps: Spray Lakes Reservoir 82 N/14

Mount Assiniboine 82 J/13

Point of Departure: Hike the *Bryant Creek-Assiniboine Pass* trail to the 7.6 kilometre junction, opposite the Bryant Creek Warden Cabin. The Marvel Lake trail branches southwest from this junction.

0.0—Bryant Creek Warden Cabin Junction (1845 m).

—Trail crosses large meadow.

0.3—Bryant Creek bridge.

—Trail runs southwest from meadow into subalpine forest.

1.1—Junction. Marvel Lake (east end) to left 0.5 km. Keep right for Wonder Pass.

2.0—Avalanche path.

—Trail contours above Marvel Lake across avalanche paths.

5.6—Junction. Marvel Lake (west end) to left 0.5 km. Keep right for Wonder Pass.

—Steady ascent with switchbacks along steep, forested slope.

7.3—Trail enters scattered subalpine forest.

—Moderate climb north through meadows toward pass.

8.9—Wonder Pass (2395 m). Intersection with *Wonder Pass* trail (see Assiniboine Park chapter).

10.5—Gog Lake.

11.5—Naiset Cabins.

13.5—Lake Magog Campground (2165 m).

The trail running above the north shore of Marvel Lake and over the 2395 metre-high summit of Wonder Pass is one of several routes leading to Mount Assiniboine, and even though it is only a kilometre longer than the shortest approach over nearby Assiniboine Pass, a very steep climb of more than 400 vertical metres to the pass discourages many from ascending it from the east. As a result, it is often coupled with the Assiniboine Pass trail to make a loop trip, utilizing Assiniboine Pass on the way in and Wonder Pass on the way out. For many hikers, however, the attraction of this trail is not Wonder Pass or Mount Assiniboine, but rather the fishing at Marvel Lake.

The Wonder Pass trail begins at the junction with the Bryant Creek trail 7.6 kilometres beyond Trail Centre (see *Bryant Creek* trail description). Just 1.4 kilometres from the junction the first side trail to Marvel Lake branches left, reaching the lake's east end in just 500 metres. The lake is surrounded by a dense forest of Engelmann spruce and alpine fir, but its popularity with fishermen has produced a number of rough but passable trails along the shoreline.

The main trail continues upvalley, contouring well above the lake along the lower slopes of Wonder Peak. The trail passes across numerous avalanche slopes from Kilometre 2.0 to Kilometre 5.3 where views are open to the ice-covered summits of Aye and Eon Mountain at the head of the valley and the deep waters of Marvel Lake below. At the 6.1 kilometre mark the trail bypasses another cutoff to Marvel Lake, a branch which not only provides access to the lake's west end, but also continues across Marvel Creek to Marvel Pass (see *Owl Lake* trail description).

Lakes Gloria and Terrapin can now be seen at the head of the valley. Since these two lakes filter out much of the silt which

Marvel Lake

pours down from the nearby glaciers on
the Great Divide, their milky, turquoise
waters are a stark contrast to the dark
blue of Marvel Lake below.

Beyond the branch trail to the west end
of Marvel Lake, the trail begins its steep
ascent to the pass, a tough climb on a hot
day. However, the scenery encountered
near the summit more than compensates
for the work involved in getting there.
The view back to Marvel Peak, Mount
Gloria and Eon Mountain is truly spectacular, and to the north of the pass there
is a fine prospect up the Og Valley which
stretches all the way to the peaks surrounding the Sunshine Meadows. From
the pass the trail gradually desends
through subalpine meadows, skirts Gog
Lake, and arrives at Lake Magog three
kilometres below. (See *Wonder Pass,*
Mount Assiniboine chapter.)

Owl Lake

Day hike or backpack

Allow 3 -5 hours one way

Elevation gain: 185 metres (600 feet)

Maximum elevation: 1890 metres (6,200 feet)

Topo maps: Spray Lakes Reservoir 82 J/14
Mount Assiniboine 82 J/13

Point of Departure: Follow directions to the Trail Centre area at the head of the Spray Lakes Reservoir as described in the *Banff Park South* introduction (see page 36). Starting from Canyon Dam or the Watridge Creek logging area, add 7.1 or 6.0 kms respectively to this trip.

0.0—Trail Centre junction (1705 m). Keep right for Owl Lake.

0.3—Junction. Trail Centre Warden Cabin to left. Keep right.

2.9—Campground.

5.3—Junction. Turn left for Owl Lake.

5.6—Bryant Creek crossing (footbridge 200 m upstream).

7.2—Trail crests rise, enters Owl Lake basin.

8.7—Junction. Left fork to Owl Lake north shore (100 m). Right fork follows west shoreline to south end (1.5 kms).

8.8—Owl Lake (1890 m).

Owl Lake is a charming blue-green body of water which occupies the central portion of a valley formed by Marvel Peak to the west and Mounts Morrison and Byng to the east. Its pleasant subalpine setting makes the lake a worthy objective in itself or a scenic highlight on the way to the Marvel Pass environs.

From the south end of Spray Lakes Reservoir, the trip to Owl Lake and back can be made in an easy day, but starting from Watridge Creek or Canyon Dam makes for a very strenuous outing. The lake is probably most often visited from one of the campgrounds on Bryant Creek, either as a short day trip or as a part of a Marvel Pass loop.

From the Trail Centre junction at the south end of the Spray Lakes Reservoir, the route follows the major Bryant Creek trail for just over five kilometres, working northwest along the foot of the Sundance Range. The trip is essentially level and scenically uneventful.

At the 5.3 kilometre mark the Owl Lake trail branches off to the left, gradually descending to the valley bottom and the swift-flowing Bryant Creek (crossed on a footbridge located some 200 metres above the horse ford). Beyond the creek the trail climbs moderately for a little over 1.5 kilometres to enter the Owl Lake basin. Once the valley bottom has been reached the hiker begins to traverse some intriguing meadows, characterized by low ridges of peculiarly jumbled rock, probably the remnants of a terminal moraine. This section of twisted and broken terrain also provides a good opportunity for the hiker to take his bearings on the surrounding country.

At the 8.7 kilometre mark the hiker encounters a trail split and must decide either to descend to the left to the north end of the lake or continue around to the right to its western shore—a trail which contours above the shoreline to the lake's south end.

Mount Alcantara from Marvel Pass

Marvel Pass. Lying 4.3 kilometres beyond and 300 vertical metres above the southern end of Owl Lake, Marvel Pass offers an interesting option for experienced hikers in the Owl Lake—Marvel Lake vicinity. Located at the apex of three high alpine valleys, the pass is a truly spectacular spot in an area celebrated for its scenic wonders.

From the end of Owl Lake a clear-cut trail exists as far as an old campsite in a broad meadow 400 metres distant. There you are confronted with a variety of trails leading back into the woods and should look for the distinctive combination of a double-topped fir and a dead snag in the forest at the edge of the meadow. The main trail lies about 20 metres on the uphill side. At all following junctions you should take the fork that leads to the right (uphill) to avoid some stints of discouraging bushwhacking.

For adventuresome hikers, the trek can be extended beyond Marvel Pass by descending into the Marvel Creek drainage, following it down to Marvel Lake and then steeply up the northern shore to the Wonder Pass trail. However, some rather sketchy pieces of trail across boggy meadows and a double ford of Marvel Creek just above Marvel Lake make a good nose for trail and some solid wilderness experience a definite asset for this option. The total distance of the Owl Lake-Marvel Pass-Marvel Lake combination, starting and ending at the Trail Centre junction, is 34.4 kilometres. (See also *Marvel Lake-Wonder Pass* trail description.)

Sunshine Meadows

The Sunshine Meadows region is unique in all the Canadian Rockies. Unlike most of the Great Divide which is composed of heavily glaciated peaks and limestone walls, this fifteen kilometre run along the crest of the continent between Citadel Pass and the Monarch Ramparts is a mixture of rolling subalpine meadowland and alpine tundra. The moist Pacific weather systems which flow up from the west deposit copious amounts of rain and snow here, and the result is a lush alpine rock garden containing an incredible variety of wildflowers, some of which appear nowhere else in the range.

In the centre of this exceptional area is the Sunshine Village Ski Area. For fifty years the area operated only in winter, but in 1984 the resort opened for its first summer season. With the improved access provided by a five kilometre-long gondola and the subsequent promotion of the lodge and its facilities, visitation to the area increased from a few hundred hikers per season to many thousands. This heavy impact was anticipated, and the resort management together with Parks Canada initiated a comprehensive program designed to protect the surrounding terrain. Much of this activity centred on trail improvement and restoration of areas where multi-trailing and severe erosion had occurred. An interpretive centre was also opened just above the upper gondola terminal, and hikers can receive directions and current information on trail conditions at the information desk inside.

As of this writing, there are three main trails which radiate from Sunshine Village: Rock Isle Lake, Citadel Pass, and Simpson Pass (Meadow Park). All the trails provide outstanding scenery — open views to the mountain ranges of British Columbia and glimpses of the lofty spire of nearby Mount Assiniboine — and excellent wildflowers from late July to mid-August. Rock Isle Lake is by far the most popular of the three trails, and by eleven a.m. on any sunny summer day many dozens of hikers will be climbing over the divide on this broad gravel pathway. Since it travels through open country and gives an excellent survey of the best the meadows have to offer, the 9.3 kilometre-long trail to Citadel Pass is also heavily used, though most hikers go only as far as Howard Douglas Lake.

The Meadow Park trail to the top of Wawa Ridge provides the best overview of the entire region, and from near the summit of Wawa a connecting trail can be followed south behind Standish Ridge to link up with the Rock Isle Lake trail — an excellent half-day loop trip. By continuing over Wawa Ridge to Simpson Pass, hikers can visit the Healy Meadows at the foot of Healy Pass and then return directly to the gondola parking area via the Healy Creek trail.

Access: Follow the Trans-Canada Highway to the Sunshine Village interchange, 9 kilometres (5.5 miles) west of Banff townsite and 21 kilometres (13 miles) east of Castle Junction. Continue on the Sunshine Village Road for another nine kilometres to the parking area at the foot of the gondola lift. From here you can either buy a one way or round trip ticket on the gondola or hike the 6.5 kilometre access road which leads up to the ski area. The Sunshine Village gondola normally operates from the Canada Day weekend (July 1st) through Labour Day (9:30 a.m. - 8:00 p.m. Monday through Thursday, 9:30 a.m. - 10:30 p.m. Friday through Sunday), and any hiking in the area prior to the seasonal opening of the lift is discouraged. After Labour Day, hikers can only reach the meadows by walking the access road. For up-to-date information on gondola schedules and lodge accommodation, please contact Sunshine Village, P.O. Box 1510, Banff, Alberta T0L 0C0 or phone (403) 762-4000.

Howard Douglas Lake and the meadows leading to Citadel Pass

Rock Isle Lake

Sunshine Village to Rock Isle Lake—1.6 kilometres (1.0 mile)
Sunshine Village to Larix Lake—3.2 kilometres (2.0 miles)

Half-day trip

Allow 1½ - 2 hours one way

Elevation gain: 105 metres (350 feet)
loss: 75 metres (250 feet)

Maximum elevation: 2300 metres (7,550 feet)

Topo maps: Banff 82 O/4

Point of Departure: Travel to the Sunshine Village Ski Area as described in the *Sunshine Meadows* area introduction (see page 48). The trail begins in front of the Sunshine Village Interpretive Centre.

0.0—Interpretive Centre (2195 m). Follow gravel road leading left and uphill.

0.2—Avalanche Control Warden Cabin. Trail branches left from road immediately above cabin.

1.3—Summit of Great Divide (2300 m).

1.6—Rock Isle Lake viewpoint.

—Trail continues around lake to right.

2.4—Rock Isle Lake outlet.

—Moderate to steep downhill.

3.2—Larix Lake (2225 m).

—Trail skirts around east and south shores of lake.

4.5—Grizzly Lake.

In the early morning, the waters of Rock Isle Lake are often a mirror reflecting its rocky island and shoreline, and there is a peacefulness and natural symmetry in the scene that has attracted artists and photographers for many decades. The lake's setting, on the edge of the rolling Sunshine Meadows near the crest of the Great Divide, also allows it to serve as a window to the jagged peaks of Kootenay Park to the south and west. And beyond its west shore, where its outlet stream slides down steep slabs of limestone, there is the option of descending a less travelled path to a pair of pretty lakes set among the larches—Larix and Grizzly.

With the opening of Sunshine Village as a summer resort in 1984, the short hike to Rock Isle Lake became one of the most popular in the Canadian Rockies. This increase in use was not unexpected, and the resort, working with Parks Canada, prepared for it by upgrading the trail to a wide gravel path and developing interpretive displays. Though use is unpleasantly heavy after eleven o'clock on the average summer day, the broad trail absorbs it a lot better than would the surrounding tundra, and it does so without detracting from the experience, the way that many paved alpine trails do.

The climb from Sunshine Village to the Great Divide is steady but brief, passing from the open stands of fir and lush meadows indicative of a north-facing, upper subalpine forest to the treeless tundra of the alpine zone. On the summit, at an elevation of 2300 metres above sea level, hikers have an excellent perspective of the Sunshine Meadows—a vast expanse of open terrain which is only occasionally broken by clusters of stunted trees and the spidery cables of ski lifts. To the south the pyramid-shaped summit of Mount Assiniboine is just barely visible, while beside the trail grow a myriad of wild-

Rock Isle Lake

flowers — alpine forget-me-nots, Indian paintbrush (of all shades and hues), contorted lousewort, western anemone, buttercups, fleabane (purple, wooly and golden), red stemmed saxifrage, pearly everlasting, and many, many more.

From the crest of the divide, the gravel path continues on into Mount Assiniboine Provincial Park to the Rock Isle Lake overlook. Beyond this classic viewpoint for the lake, the trail skirts around and above the shoreline to the right and eventually drops down to the lake's outlet on the opposite side. Here views open out to the valleys and peaks of British Columbia and to the waters of Larix and Grizzly Lakes immediately below.

Though Larix Lake is only 0.8 kilometre beyond Rock Isle, a steep descent discourages the many inexperienced hikers who walk this trail from visiting its shores. The lake lies within a very pleasant setting of meadow and larch forest (*Larix lyallii* is the botanical name for alpine larch). The trail skirts around the lake's south shore, then reverts to a rather vague path which eventually descends to the marshy meadow at the south end of Grizzly Lake. (Another sketchy trail descends to Grizzly more directly from the meadow just north of Larix Lake.)

Citadel Pass

Sunshine Village to Citadel Pass—9.3 kilometres (5.8 miles)

Sunshine Village to Lake Magog Campground—29.0 kilometres (18.0 miles)

Day trip

Allow 3 - 4 hours one way

Elevation gain: 165 metres (550 feet)

Maximum elevation: 2360 metres (7,750 feet)

Topo maps: Banff 82 O/4†
               †trail not shown

Point of Departure: Travel to the Sunshine Village Ski Area as described in the *Sunshine Meadows* area introduction (see page 48). The trail begins in front of the Sunshine Village Interpretive Centre.

0.0—Interpretive Centre (2195 m). Follow gravel road leading left and uphill.

0.2—Avalanche Control Warden Cabin. Trail branches left from road immediately above cabin.

—Steady uphill on well-tended gravel trail.

1.3—Summit of Great Divide (2300 m) and junction. Rock Isle Lake to right (500 metres). Keep left for Citadel Pass.

—Gentle, rolling across meadows.

5.2—Trail climbs over crest of ridge below Quartz Hill.

5.8—Howard Douglas Lake. Campground.

9.3—Citadel Pass and junction (2360 m). Trail to Fatigue Pass branches uphill to left. *Og Lake* trail to Mt. Assiniboine continues straight ahead and descends to Golden Valley (see Assiniboine Park chapter).

16.5—Junction and campground. Trail from Golden Valley and Policeman's Meadows intersects from right.

22.2—Og Lake and campground (2060 m).

29.0—Lake Magog Campground (2165 m).

The hike to Citadel Pass is one of the most scenic and popular day trips in the Sunshine Village region. Throughout most of its distance it is never more than a few hundred metres from the crest of the Great Divide, rolling through wildflower meadows which are justifiably renowned as some of the finest in the Rockies and providing continual vistas of the rugged peaks of British Columbia to the west. Beyond the pass, the trail continues into British Columbia as a favourite approach route to Mount Assiniboine.

The trail climbs from the Sunshine Village Interpretive Centre to the open alpine meadows which straddle the Alberta-B.C. border then rolls southeastward toward Citadel Pass through timberline stands of larch, spruce and fir. It remains fairly level throughout most of its course except for a short climb at Kilometre 5.2 when it traverses a short spur ridge beneath Quartz Hill. On the opposite side of this ridge, the trail drops to the shore of Howard Douglas Lake (misnamed Sundown Lake on the current topo sheet) and a trailside campground.

Another small lake lies off to the right of the trail less than two kilometres beyond Howard Douglas, its basin set beneath a gap in the Great Divide which serves as a window to the great 3618 metre peak of Mount Assiniboine. This is one of the best views of this famous 'horn' mountain from the Sunshine Meadows trail system, and though its summit seems to loom near, it is over 15 aerial kilometres from this lookout point.

Citadel Pass offers several options to the day hiker with a little time to spare and a yen for exploration. One of the most interesting is the climb to Fatigue Pass—a 2395 metre crest to the southeast which can be reached in an hour or less. A trail runs to this high summit, but the junction in Citadel Pass is vague, so scan the slopes above for the obvious track lead-

Mount Assiniboine from Quartz Hill

ing across the scree to the pass. (See also *Fatigue Pass* trail description.)

Mount Assiniboine via Golden Valley. South of Citadel Pass, backpackers bound for Mount Assiniboine make a steep descent toward the Golden Valley and the headwaters of the Simpson River. Campers who wish to spend the night at Porcupine Campground or Policeman's Meadows can continue to the bottom of the valley, but the most direct route to Assiniboine branches left from the main trail on a steep, open slope well above the valley floor then contours to the south-west into the Valley of the Rocks.

The Valley of the Rocks is a long, dry valley enclosed in a forest of pine and spruce and featuring a wild array of peculiarly shaped boulders—the aftermath of an ancient rockslide. Og Lake marks the end of the valley, and the trail

veers south through subalpine forest and meadows to finally reach Lake Magog and the foot of Mount Assiniboine 29.0 kilometres from Sunshine Village. (Be sure to carry water on the long slog through the Valley of the Rocks.)

The Citadel Pass route to Mount Assiniboine was used by pioneer outfitter Bill Peyto when he led the alpinist James Outram and his Swiss guides to the peak in 1901; because it was so much shorter than the traditional approach route, Outram and his guides were able to complete the first ascent of Mount Assiniboine just hours before the first snows of autumn descended on the mountain. The trail was improved over the ensuing years by a variety of outfitters, most notably Pat Brewster in the 1920s. (See also *Og Lake* trail description in Mt. Assiniboine chapter.)

Simpson Pass

Day trip

Allow 2-3 hours to Healy Meadows

Elevation gain: 165 metres (550 feet)

Maximum elevation: 2360 metres (7,750 feet)

Topo maps: Banff 82 O/4

Point of Departure: Travel to the Sunshine Village Ski Area as described in the *Sunshine Meadows* area introduction (see page 48). From the Sunshine Village Interpretive Centre, walk downhill between the upper gondola terminal and the day lodge to the bottom of the Wawa Ridge ski lift. Follow the Meadow Park trail leading uphill beyond the ski lift.

0.0—Trail sign (2195 m).

—Steady uphill along open meadow.

1.9—Wawa Ridge summit (2360 m).

—Gradual descent.

5.6—Simpson Pass (2135 m) and junction. Right hand branch leads down draw to Healy Creek. Keep straight ahead for Healy Meadows and Pass.

—Short climb.

6.0—Junction. Eohippus Lake to left (3.2 km). Keep right for Healy Meadows and Pass.

7.6—Junction. Intersection with *Healy Pass* trail at Km 7.7. Healy Pass to left 1.5 kms.

While Simpson Pass can be reached by ascending Healy Creek from the Sunshine gondola parking lot and then cutting up to the summit on a short branch trail (the historic route used by George Simpson), the most scenic approach is from Sunshine Village via Wawa Ridge. It is a trail which can be used by daytrippers looking for a scenically varied hike from Sunshine Village or by backpackers seeking a fine highline option into Healy Pass and Egypt Lake. One word of warning, however: more than any other trip in the area, the Wawa Ridge trail to Simpson Pass can be very sloppy early in the season or during wet weather.

Ascending the most northerly ski run on Wawa Ridge, the trail soon climbs through the upper fringes of the subalpine forest and onto the treeless summit of the ridge at Kilometre 1.9. From this high crest, hikers can see most of the Sunshine Meadows country. Views include the Citadel Pass region and the sharp summit of Mount Assiniboine to the southeast and the massive pyramid of The Monarch to the southwest. This is definitely the best viewpoint on the trail.

Beyond Wawa Ridge the trail begins to drop back into the forest. Small ponds fringed with cotton grass dot the meadows and, like many open areas in the Sunshine vicinity, this ridge is a wildflower-lover's dream.

After following along a low but sheer rock escarpment for nearly two kilometres, the trail drops down to a small meadow on the summit of Simpson Pass. Here a shortcut trail from Healy Creek crests the pass from the right, providing a quick route of descent to the Sunshine gondola parking lot for those who are so inclined; on the B.C. side of the pass, a vague trail quickly disappears into overgrown meadow and forest.

The pass was crossed by Sir George Simpson, governor of the Hudson's Bay

Healy Meadows

Company, in the summer of 1841. It was a disappointment as an improved route for the company's fur brigades bound for the Oregon Territory, but Sir George did linger long enough to allow his guide to carve their initials and the date in a nearby tree. The monument was salvaged by a local outfitter in the early part of this century and now resides at the Park Museum in Banff.

On the west side of the Simpson Pass meadow, the trail rises quickly onto the open, lake-studded meadows which lie beneath the long ridge of the Monarch Ramparts. Just before the meadows are reached, 0.4 kilometre beyond the pass, the 3.2 kilometre-long side trail to Eohippus Lake branches left—a good option for strong hikers who have time and energy to spare.

At Kilometre 7.6 the Healy Pass trail is joined. From here you can either continue to Healy Pass or Egypt Lake by veering left (see *Healy Pass—Egypt Lake* trail description), turn right to descend Healy Creek to the gondola lift parking lot, or simply retrace your steps to Sunshine Village.

Healy Pass

Sunshine Parking Lot to Healy Pass—9.2 kilometres (5.7 miles)

Sunshine Parking Lot to Egypt Lake Campground—12.4 kilometres (7.7 miles)

Day trip or backpack

Allow 3 - 4 hours to Healy Pass
4 - 5 hours to Egypt Lake Shelter

Elevation gain: 655 metres (2,150 feet)
loss: 335 metres (1,100 feet)

Maximum elevation: 2330 metres (7,650 feet)

Topo maps: Banff 82 O/4

Point of Departure: Follow the Trans-Canada Highway west from Banff townsite 9 kilometres (5½ miles) and turn left onto the Sunshine Ski Area access road. Follow this road for 9 kilometres to its end at the lower terminal for the gondola lift. Continue on past the lift terminal to the right to the trail head parking lot. A few metres beyond the rear of the terminal building, the trail begins on a broad cat-track.

0.0—Sunshine Village Parking Lot (1675 m).

—Follow broad cat-track uphill from lower terminal.

0.8—Junction. Turn right as trail leaves cat-track.

3.1—Bridge over Healy Creek.

5.2—Old cabin foundation.

5.5—Campground.

5.9—Junction. Simpson Pass to left (1.3 km). Keep straight ahead.

—Trail begins to climb.

7.7—Junction. Simpson Pass to left (2.0 kms). Keep straight ahead.

—Steady climb through open meadows with alpine larch.

9.2—Healy Pass (2330 m).

—Steady downhill grade.

12.2—Junction. Egypt Lake Warden Cabin to right 50 m. Natalko Lake to left 4.2 km. Keep straight across meadow and bridge to campground and shelter.

12.4—Egypt Lake Campground (1995 m). Shelter cabin.

While Healy Pass and its adjoining meadows make a worthy objective for any day hiker, it is the area beyond the pass, centred on Egypt Lake, that is the focal point for the backpackers who are the most frequent travellers on this trail. A number of factors contribute to the popularity of the Egypt Lake area: its proximity to Banff townsite and the Bow Valley; the presence of a shelter cabin at the area's central campground; and a large concentration of subalpine lakes that create a plethora of day hiking options amid some of the finest scenery to be found anywhere in the Rockies.

Most people hike to Egypt Lake by way of Healy Pass since that route is shortest and also quite scenic. Climbing from the Sunshine gondola parking lot, the trail follows along a wide, bulldozed track for nearly a kilometre before cutting off onto a more pleasant forest path. Gradually, but steadily, the trail ascends the Healy Creek valley, rising from a dense canopy of Engelmann spruce and alpine fir to subalpine meadows where wildflowers bloom in lush profusion from mid-July to late August.

Trails from Simpson Pass intersect the main trail at Kilometre 5.9 and 7.7, providing some interesting day trip loop options between Sunshine Village, the Simpson-Healy Pass environs, and the gondola parking lot. From the latter junction it is 7.6 kilometres to Sunshine Village, making this higher and more scenic route an excellent choice for hikers who are willing to pay the price of a gondola ticket (see *Simpson Pass* trail description).

The climb finally culminates among the last scattered alpine larch on Healy Pass. At an elevation of 2330 metres above sea level, the pass offers an excellent perspective on the surrounding landscape. The block of peaks beyond the ridge to the northeast is the Massive

The Monarch and Ramparts from Healy Pass

Range, dominated by Mount Brett on the left and Mount Bourgeau to the right. Standing as a landmark to the southeast —nearly 30 kilometres distant—is the 'horn' spike of Mount Assiniboine (3618 m), the highest mountain in Banff National Park. Less than six kilometres away to the south is the massive pyramid of The Monarch (2904 m), while the long, wall-like ridge which extends from its flanks to Healy Pass is known as the Monarch Ramparts. And due west of the pass, stacked beneath the Pharaoh Peaks, lie Egypt and Scarab Lakes.

The trail drops downhill rapidly from the pass, reaching the junction near the Egypt Lake Campground in just over three kilometres. Situated in the middle of the campground is a shelter cabin, constructed in 1969 to sleep approximately 16 backpackers. (Don't mistake the warden's cabin near the trail junction for the shelter; the shelter is directly across the creek from the junction on a raised benchland.) Since all major trails for the area radiate out from the campground, it is ideally situated as a centre for day tripping.

57

Egypt Lake

Egypt Lake, a popular backpacking area, lies near the continental divide just 25 aerial kilometres west of Banff townsite. Though Egypt Lake itself is often the focal point of trips into the area there are many other beautiful lakes, bearing exotic names such as Scarab, Mummy, Haiduk and Sphinx, scattered about in the open subalpine environment. The options for the hiker are many, limited only by time.

Pharaoh Creek. The 8.7 kilometre trail running up Pharaoh Creek from the Shadow Lake trail is primarily used as an optional route of access to or exit from Egypt Lake. It is a longer trip than the Healy Pass hike (19.6 kilometres from the Trans-Canada Highway at Redearth Creek), but because it runs at lower elevations, it is a good option early in the season when snow is lingering in the high country. It can also be used as a low level connector to Shadow Lake in place of the more demanding Whistling Valley trail.

From the 10.8 kilometre junction on the Shadow Lake trail, branch left and follow the trail which leads up along Pharaoh Creek from the Redearth Warden Cabin. The valley bottom trail and the bridges which take it back and forth across the creek are usually in good condition, the grade is gentle, and strong hikers can make better time here than on Healy Pass — a consideration during periods of foul weather. A campground is located beside the creek halfway up the valley, and above this point there are open meadows with views ahead to the Pharaoh Peaks. (The high trail which branches uphill to the left just beyond the Redearth Warden Cabin and rejoins near the campground was a failed attempt to create a hiker's route and should be ignored.)

Egypt Lake. The shortest hike from the campground is the 800 metre stroll to the region's namesake. From the south edge of the campground, just beyond the shelter cabin, follow the Whistling Valley trail through the forest for 500 metres and turn left at the Egypt Lake junction. From there it is only 300 metres to the lakeshore. Egypt is a peaceful, unassuming lake whose only backdrop is a small, cone-shaped peak known locally as Sugarloaf Mountain.

Natalko Lake. Situated 4.2 kilometres away, just across the Great Divide in Kootenay National Park, Natalko Lake is a popular day trip from the Egypt Lake area (with a campground on its shores, it can even be an alternate base camp for those who want to escape the Egypt crowds). From the junction near the Egypt Lake Warden Cabin, follow the trail which runs due south into Redearth Pass. At Kilometre 2.3, just 500 metres short of the park boundary on this brushy and rather unremarkable pass, watch for the Natalko trail branching to the right. It is a stiff 1.9 kilometre climb to the lake from this junction.

In the 1920s, Natalko Lake was the site of a talc mine operated by the National Talc Company. The talc was trucked by wagon from the lake all the way down Pharaoh Creek to the CPR line in the Bow Valley — a distance of over 23 kilometres! Some relics of this unlikely operation can still be found near the lakeshore.

Experienced rock scramblers armed with a topo map can make a very scenic trip across the high col northwest of the lake and descend to Mummy Lake on the other side. In fact, this option is often included as part of a loop trip from the Egypt Lake Campground, but it can only be completed by strong, well-shod hikers who are good route-finders. Total distance for this loop is approximately 9.0 kilometres.

Scarab Lake—Mummy Lake. These two lakes, situated in cirques immediately above Egypt Lake, make an outstanding day trip from the main campground. Often they are visited in conjunction with a hike to Whistling Pass or as a side-trip for backpackers who are bound for Haiduk Lake and points north. The total dis-

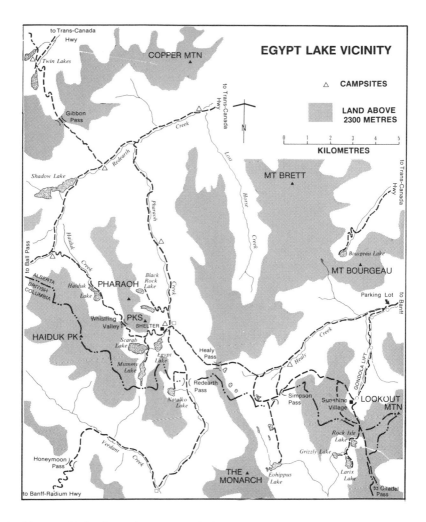

EGYPT LAKE VICINITY

△ CAMPSITES

◾ LAND ABOVE 2300 METRES

0 1 2 3 4 5
KILOMETRES

tance to Mummy Lake from the campground is 3.3 kilometres. (See *Whistling Valley* trail description.)

Pharaoh Lake. The 2.4 kilometre hike to Pharaoh and Black Rock Lakes is a pleasant half-day outing from the Egypt Lake Campground. Follow the Pharaoh Creek trail to the junction 500 metres north of the campground and take the left hand branch to make the short but steep climb to Pharaoh Lake. Black Rock Lake lies 1.1 kilometres beyond Pharaoh via a rocky and rooty trail, and tiny Sphinx Lake can be reached via yet another 1.6 kilometres of trail-less bushwhacking.

One final word concerning the Egypt

Lake area: this is one of the most heavily used backcountry destinations in the mountain parks, so don't go there seeking solitude. The shelter cabin is inevitably crammed to the rafters during the summer months, and because the area seems to attract an inordinate number of inexperienced backpackers there are many horror stories concerning inconsiderate individuals clattering about the premises at all hours of the night. Because of this high impact and the delicate nature of the subalpine environment, it behooves all hikers to take special care when visiting the area.

Whistling Valley

Egypt Lake Campground to Whistling Pass—3.3 kilometres (2.1 miles)

Backpack

Allow 3 - 4 hours one way

Elevation gain: 305 metres (1,000 feet)
   loss: 380 metres (1,250 feet)

Maximum elevation: 2300 metres (7,550 feet)

Topo maps: Banff 82 O/4

Point of Departure: Hike to the Egypt Lake Shelter/Campsite as described in the *Healy Pass—Egypt Lake* or *Egypt Lake via Pharoah Creek* trail descriptions. The Whistling Pass trail passes in front of the shelter cabin and runs southwest from the campground area. Southbound travellers can reach the north end of the trail by hiking the *Shadow Lake—Ball Pass* trail to the junction at Km 18.6.

0.0—Egypt Lake Campground (1995 m).

0.5—Junction. Egypt Lake to left (0.3 km). Keep right for Whistling Pass.

—Steep uphill, switchbacks.

1.9—Junction. Trail branches left to Scarab Lake (0.6 km) and Mummy Lake (1.4 km). Keep right for Whistling Pass.

—Steady ascent.

3.3—Whistling Pass (2300 m).

—Moderate to steep downhill, rocky sections.

5.5—Haiduk Lake (2055 m). Trail follows east shore, crosses outlet stream just below lake.

—Gradual descent down valley; steep downhill last km to junction/campsite.

8.7—Junction and campground (1920 m). Cross bridge to intersect *Shadow Lake-Ball Pass* trail at Km 18.6.

No trip to the Egypt Lake area is complete without visiting Whistling Valley— a spectacular gap nestled between the Pharaoh Peaks and the sheer escarpment of the Great Divide. The valley, along with Scarab and Mummy Lakes, can be hiked as a day trip from the Egypt Lake campground, or it can be experienced as part of a backpack to Haiduk Lake and points north.

From the shelter cabin at the main campground, follow the trail that runs southwest toward Egypt Lake. Stay right at the junction to the lake and climb a steep series of switchbacks leading up through forest and rockslides along the south slope of the Pharaoh Peaks. With an occasional rewarding glance back to Egypt Lake, the trail grinds relentlessly upward for more than a kilometre, finally emerging in a meadow above Scarab Lake. Beyond the Scarab Lake junction the trail continues upward into the meadows and talus slopes of the Whistling Valley.

The term 'valley' is actually a misnomer for one of the more spectacular and rugged passes in Banff Park. Its larch-laced meadows and rockslides are the home of the hoary marmot, whose shrill whistle of warning gives the area its name. Another inhabitant is the pika, an elusive bundle of fur that may be seen darting among the rocks. From the summit of the pass, views open northward to Haiduk Lake and the long east-facing escarpment of the Ball Range. Scarab Lake is visible back to the south.

Strong hikers can easily descend to the shores of Haiduk Lake and return back through the Whistling Valley to the Egypt Lake campground in a day, but most traffic over the pass is comprised of backpackers bound to or from the Ball Pass— Shadow Lake environs. On the north side of Whistling Pass the trail drops abruptly through a large rockslide and then levels out into the marshy meadows along Hai-

Haiduk Lake from Whistling Pass

duk Lake. Beyond the lake, the trail crosses to the true left bank of Haiduk Creek and descends through subalpine forest to the campground at the junction with the Shadow Lake—Ball Pass trail. (See *Shadow Lake—Ball Pass* trail description.)

Scarab and Mummy Lakes. The side trip to Scarab Lake is a must for anyone hiking to the Whistling Valley, and stronger hikers who aren't bothered by a little steep rock scrambling will want to visit Mummy Lake as well. The spur trail to these two tarns branches from the main trail at Kilometre 1.9 and descends through a lush wildflower meadow to the shore of Scarab Lake in 0.6 kilometre. The north and east sides of the lake are contained by a typical timberline forest of Engelmann spruce and alpine fir with a liberal sprinkling of alpine larch, while the west and south sides are backed by steep scree slopes and vertical cliffs. Just a few metres from Scarab's east shore, the lake's outlet stream tumbles off a 100 metre-high cliff to Egypt Lake below.

Mummy Lake lies totally within the alpine zone, its shores rimmed by tundra and talus. To reach the lake, you must cross the Scarab outlet stream and scramble up a short but steep track. At the base of a cliff the trail splits, the right hand branch ascending a 10 metre-high cliff to the meadow at the lake's north end, while the left branch takes a longer but less demanding route around to the east shore. Experienced rock scramblers can continue down Mummy's rugged east shoreline to a narrow gap that serves as a window into Kootenay Park's Verdant Creek valley or climb due east of the lake to a high col on the crest of the Great Divide which provides access to the Natalko Lake cirque and an alternate way back to the Egypt Lake campground. (See *Natalko Lake* trail description).

Concerning the exotic names which are scattered about the Whistling Pass area, the early topographical surveyor A. O. Wheeler wrote: "How Pharaoh Peaks received the name is not recorded. Egypt, Scarab and Mummy Lakes were named by me as a sequence when mapping that area. Haiduk Lake was named from a Polish word meaning 'lively, vigorous,' and when first seen with the sun, like diamonds, sparkling on its wind-blown ripples the name seemed to apply."

Shadow Lake

Trans-Canada Highway to Shadow Lake—14.3 kilometres (8.9 miles)

Trans-Canada Highway to Ball Pass—21.3 kilometres (13.2 miles)

Day trip or backpack

Allow 4 - 5 hours to Shadow Lake

Elevation gain: 440 metres (1,450 feet)

Maximum elevation: 1840 metres (6,050 feet)

Topo maps: Banff 82 O/4

Point of Departure: Follow the Trans-Canada Highway to the Redearth Creek parking area, situated on the south side of the highway 20 kilometres (12½ miles) west of Banff or 10½ kilometres (6½ miles) east of Castle Junction. Trail leaves from the east end of the parking lot.

0.0—Redearth Creek parking area (1400 m).

—Foot trail merges with Redearth Fire Road in 300 metres.

7.2—Redearth Creek bridge and campground.

10.8—Junction. Shadow Lake trail cuts away from road to right.

—Moderate uphill grades.

13.2—Shadow Lake Cabin (outfitter cabin).

13.4—Junction and campground. Gibbon Pass uphill to right 3.1 kms. Shadow Lake straight ahead.

14.3—Shadow Lake (1840 m). Outlet and bridge.

18.6—Junction and campground (1920 m). Trail to Haiduk Lake (3.2 km) and Whistling Pass across bridge to left. Ball Pass straight ahead.

—Moderate uphill climb; last 600 metres to summit steep and rocky.

21.3—Ball Pass (2210 m). Connects with Kootenay Park's *Hawk Creek—Ball Pass* trail.

Situated beneath the massive cliffs of Mount Ball, Shadow Lake is one of the more impressive subalpine lakes along the Great Divide. In addition to its own charms, the lake has gained popularity as a centre for a number of excellent side trips: Haiduk Lake, Ball Pass and Gibbon Pass are all worthwhile day hikes which can be made from the Shadow Lake campground.

The first 10.8 kilometres up the old Redearth Fire Road are somewhat tedious, but the grade is gradual and it is easy to make good time. At Kilometre 10.8 the Shadow Lake trail cuts away from the fire road and climbs into a forest of lodgepole pine, Engelmann spruce and alpine fir. From this junction with the fire road it is only 2.6 kilometres to the Shadow Lake campground, located on the edge of a large meadow within sight of the rugged peaks of the Ball Range. (The cabin at the lower edge of the meadow is operated by a Banff outfitter and is not open to hikers.)

The main trail to Shadow Lake continues up-valley from the campground and reaches the lake's eastern shore at a footbridge which spans its outlet stream. Shadow is large compared with most subalpine lakes, stretching for over two kilometres to the base of Mount Ball (3312 m). Carved from Cambrian sedimentary rock and draped with glaciers, the Ball Mountain Group provides a particularly photogenic backdrop for the lake (though the east-facing cliffs are often in shadow).

From the outlet bridge at Shadow Lake a good trail continues around the south shore for a kilometre before breaking away up Haiduk Creek toward Ball Pass and Haiduk Lake.

Ball Pass. Situated on the Great Divide between Alberta and British Columbia, Ball Pass can easily be visited as a day hike from Shadow Lake or traversed as a

Shadow Lake and Mount Ball

through-route into Kootenay Park. The pass is reached by following the trail which continues around the south shore of Shadow Lake. Keep right at the Whistling Valley — Ball Pass trail junction and climb to the pass in another 2.7 kilometres of steady uphill slogging. From the pass the trail continues down the Hawk Creek valley another 9.7 kilometres to reach the Banff-Radium Highway at the Floe Lake trail head. (See *Hawk Creek — Ball Pass* trail description in Kootenay Park chapter.)

Gibbon Pass. This trail makes a fine half-day jaunt from Shadow Lake or it can be hiked as part of an extended trip to Twin Lakes. The trail strikes off from the Shadow Lake campground and climbs north through subalpine forest and larch-fringed meadowland to the treeless summit of the pass—a total distance of only 3.1 kilometres. Beyond the pass the trail continues its northerly journey, descending to Lower Twin Lake in another 2.9 kilometres. (See *Twin Lakes* trail description.)

Ball Glacier Ice Cave. This is a short trip following rough and sometimes indistinct trail to an ice cave in a small glacier beneath the northeast face of Mount Ball— a fine outing for those who like to explore beyond the more popular routes. The trail branches from the main Shadow Lake trail just before the outlet bridge and follows around the north shore for 1.9 kilometres to the lake's west end. From there, climb an obvious draw to the northwest for another 2.7 kilometres to the glacier. (One of the glacier's ice caves collapsed a few years ago, so the future of the remaining cave is tenuous.)

Haiduk Lake. This beautiful lake at the foot of Whistling Pass is only 8.4 kilometres from the Shadow Lake campground. Follow the Ball Pass trail to the junction 4.3 kilometres beyond the Shadow Lake outlet bridge, turn left and climb the Whistling Valley trail for 3.2 kilometres to the lake. This trail is also popular with backpackers as the scenic highline route to Egypt Lake via Whistling Pass (see *Whistling Valley* trail description).

63

Twin Lakes

Altrude Creek to Lower Twin Lake—8.1 kilometres (5.0 miles)
Altrude Creek to Gibbon Pass—10.8 kilometres (6.7 miles)

Day trip or backpack

Allow 2½ - 3 hours one way

Elevation gain: 605 metres (2,000 feet)

Maximum elevation: 2055 metres (6,750 feet)

Topo maps: Banff 82 O/4
Castle Mountain 82 O/5

Point of Departure: Follow the Trans-Canada Highway to the Altrude Creek Picnic Area, just 400 metres east of the Castle Junction overpass (30 kilometres west of Banff townsite). After turning onto the gravel access road to the picnic area, turn left immediately onto another gravel road and follow it for 300 metres to a small parking area on the left hand side (where the road bends sharply to the right).

0.0—Parking area and trail sign (1450 m).

—Follow old rock quarry road.

0.2—Junction. Smith Lake trail cuts off to left. Stay on old road.

0.5—Old quarry.

—Road reverts to trail. Enter forest.

0.8—Bridge over Altrude Creek.

2.4—Uphill grade steepens.

4.0—Grade moderates, trail becomes rocky and rooty with boggy sections.

6.3—Trail opens out into meadow.

—Path sometimes faint following near major stream.

7.9—Junction (2055 m). Lower Twin Lake straight ahead 0.2 km. Upper Twin Lake and campground to right 0.8 km. Keep left and cross stream for Gibbon Pass.

—Steady ascent through subalpine forest.

10.8—Gibbon Pass (2300 m).

—Steep descent through dense forest.

13.9—Junction and campground (1830 m). Intersection with *Shadow Lake* trail at Km 13.4.

"The Twin Lakes lie at the base of the scarped and nearly vertical front of the watershed range, which rises above them in stupendous cliffs, in the rifts and hollows of which, snow remains throughout the year."

So wrote government geologist George M. Dawson, following a visit to the lakes with a Silver City prospector named Joe Healy on August 5, 1884. His description should serve today's hiker in good stead—an apt introduction to a very dramatic subalpine area on the southwest slope of the Bow Valley.

Two trails of equal length provide the day hiker with access to the Twin Lakes: one starting from near the Altrude Creek Picnic Area on the Trans-Canada Highway and the other originating at the Vista Lake viewpoint on the Banff-Radium Highway (Hwy 93). Though the trail from Highway 93 via Arnica Lake is considerably more open and scenic, it gains nearly 600 metres elevation in 4.4 kilometres, while the path leading up from the Trans-Canada Highway spreads the same elevation gain over the full 8.1 kilometres to Lower Twin Lake.

The trail which climbs from an old rock quarry near the Altrude Creek Picnic Area can only be termed uninspiring. After a half-kilometre it enters the firest and begins its steady ascent toward the Twin Lakes and the Great Divide. Not until the 6.3 kilometre mark does it emerge into open meadows which provide views ahead to Dawson's "stupendous cliffs." In these meadows the track becomes very boggy and somewhat indistinct as it follows near the outlet stream from Lower Twin Lake.

Just 200 metres from the shores of Lower Twin Lake an important junction is encountered. The right hand trail climbs to Upper Twin Lake and campground in 0.8 kilometre. The left branch crosses the creek and begins a 2.9 kilometre ascent to

Lower Twin Lake

the summit of Gibbon Pass. From this point most hikers will continue straight ahead to spend some time at Lower Twin, but they will have to return to this junction if they wish to extend the journey either north or south.

Lower Twin Lake is about as scenic a spot as you will find along the escarpment of the Great Divide. Its rocky north shore and adjacent meadow provide a wonderful foreground to the sheer cliffs beyond.

Regardless of your itinerary, you will probably want to pay a visit to Upper Twin Lake—a lake with an almost identical setting. A well designed campground with private sites is located in the forest just south of the lake's outlet meadow. Beyond Upper Twin the trail climbs over a forested summit to Arnica Lake—a route which serves as an optional exit as well as

approach to the Twin Lakes. If you continue on this trail you will eventually emerge on the Banff-Radium Highway and will have to walk or hitchhike back to your car (see *Arnica Lake* trail description).

Gibbon Pass Option. From the junction at Lower Twin Lake, the trail to Gibbon Pass makes a steady ascent through the forest to this 2300 metre summit. The pass is an exceptional viewpoint for this area of the Rockies in that there are no nearby mountains to block the view to either the north or south. As a result views extend from Mount Hector near Lake Louise to Mount Assiniboine.

From Gibbon Pass you can continue on another 3.1 kilometres to reach the Shadow Lake trail just below Shadow Lake (see *Shadow Lake-Ball Pass* trail description).

65

Arnica Lake

Banff-Radium Highway to Arnica Lake—5.0 kilometres (3.1 miles)
Banff-Radium Highway to Lower Twin Lake—8.2 kilometres (5.1 miles)

Day trip or backpack

Allow 1½ - 3 hours to Arnica Lake

Elevation loss: 120 metres (400 feet)
gain: 580 metres (1,900 feet)

Maximum elevation: 2150 metres (7,050 feet)

Topo maps: Mount Goodsir 82 N/1
Banff 82 O/4

Point of Departure: Follow the Banff—Radium Highway to the Vista Lake viewpoint, 8 kilometres (5 miles) west of Castle Junction and 2 kilometres (1 mile) east of the Banff—Kootenay Park Boundary at Vermilion Pass. The viewpoint is a broad pull-off on the south side of the highway overlooking Vista Lake, the Altrude Creek valley, and the old Vermilion Pass burn.

0.0—Trail sign (1690 m).
—Moderate steady downhill through old burn.

1.4—Vista Lake outlet and bridge (1570 m).
—Steady uphill at moderate grade.

2.6—Junction. Trail from Storm Mountain Lodge intersects from left (2.9 kms to Hwy 93 at lodge). Keep right and uphill for Arnica Lake.
—Steep steady uphill.

4.0—Trail leaves burn, enters forest.

4.2—Small unnamed pond.
—Steady climb.

4.6—Trail levels off.

5.0—Arnica Lake (2150 m).
—Steep uphill.

5.8—Arnica Summit (2285 m).
—Steady downhill.

7.2—Upper Twin Lake (2090 m). Campground.
—Gradual downhill.

8.0—Junction. Intersection with *Twin Lakes— Gibbon Pass* trail at Km 7.9. Lower Twin Lake to right 0.2 km.

The hike to Arnica Lake is somewhat arduous, dropping over 100 metres to the shores of Vista Lake then climbing another 600 metres to reach this small cirque in just 5.0 kilometres. But even with all its downs-and-ups, this tiny tarn nestled against the imposing east face of Storm Mountain is one of the most popular hikes in the Vermilion Pass vicinity. This is probably because it is the shortest trail to any of the Bow Valley's high lakes, and because the trip provides more variety and interest than any other in this area of the park. Additionally, it is frequently the option of choice for those travelling to Twin Lakes, and in autumn it is a speedy route to the golden groves of alpine larch.

At Kilometre 1.4 the steadily descending trail from the viewpoint reaches the lowest elevation on the hike alongside the shores of Vista Lake. This quiet, green-hued lake is a pleasant destination in and of itself for nature hikers, and you will certainly want to spend some time here relaxing and enjoying the scene in preparation for the steep climb ahead.

From the outlet bridge at the east end of Vista Lake, the trail begins its ascent by contouring up across the lower slopes of Storm Mountain. A small grove of trees left unscathed by the fire of '68 contains the unmarked junction of the old trail from Storm Mountain Lodge and the new route. While this old trail is no longer maintained by the park's trail crew, it is still in good shape and is a worthwhile alternative for those who may be staying at the lodge or doing a loop trip from the Altrude Creek Picnic Area via Twin Lake.

From the junction with the lodge trail it is a steady, steep climb to the forest at the edge of the burn, but improving views and fresh breezes blowing across the slope from Vermilion Pass usually distract hikers from the drudgery. Once you have entered the unburned forest, it is a half-hour or less of steady climbing through

Arnica Lake

the Engelmann spruce and alpine fir to the shores of Arnica Lake.

Arnica is backed up against the sheer cliffs of Storm Mountain, and it is enclosed by a typical forest of the upper subalpine zone laced with stands of alpine larch. It is a popular destination for fishermen and apparently supports a fair stock of cutthroat trout.

From the lake's outlet the trail continues to climb for another 800 metres to the summit of a forested ridge jutting out from the Storm Mountain cliffs. By leaving the trail on this summit and climbing along the ridge to the southwest, the hiker is rewarded with extensive views to the north and south along the Bow Valley.

Twin Lakes Option. The trail to Arnica Lake is a popular route for hikers coming from or going to Twin Lakes. The distance to the lakes via this option is identical to that of the alternate route from the Trans-Canada Highway at Altrude Creek. Since the latter trail is more direct and more evenly graded, it is usually the preferred route of access to the lakes, but strong hikers who have made it as far as Arnica Summit will find little hardship in descending the 1.4 kilometres of trail leading to Upper Twin Lake. (See *Twin Lakes* trail description.)

67

Boom Lake

Half-day trip

Allow 1½ - 2 hours one way

Elevation gain: 175 metres (575 feet)

Maximum elevation: 1895 metres (6,210 feet)

Topo maps: Mount Goodsir 82 N/1
        Lake Louise 82 N/8

Point of Departure: Follow the Banff—Radium Highway to the Boom Creek Picnic Area, located beside Boom Creek on the north side of the highway 7 kilometres (4½ miles) west of Castle Junction. The trail strikes off from the Boom Creek bridge at the rear of the picnic area.

0.0—Bridge and trail sign (1720 m).

—Steady uphill at gradual to moderate grades on broad track.

2.3—Junction. Taylor Lake—Panorama Ridge trail cuts up to right. Stay straight ahead on main trail.

5.0—Trail narrows to foot path.

5.1—Boom Lake (1895 m).

The Boom Lake trail is an easy five kilometre trek to a beautifully formed and exceptionally clear body of water lying nearly 1900 metres above sea level. The lake is backed to the south by a massive 600 metre limestone wall and to the west by a glacier-mantled mountain—features which contribute to the dramatic appeal of the area. The hike is particularly pleasant early in the season when the snowpack on Boom Mountain's heights is breaking up, and on a sunny spring day a lucky visitor will see numerous avalanches cascade down the north face of the mountain.

For most of its length the trail is a wide, bulldozed track which, after crossing Boom Creek at the Boom Creek Picnic Area, climbs at a moderate grade well above the creek through a typical subalpine forest of Engelmann spruce and alpine fir. In the spring many small streams make the trail a bit boggy, but the runoff redeems itself by offering an opportunity for many fine drinking stops—something the late season hiker will miss.

Just before the trail reaches the lake it narrows down to a traditional footpath, and 100 metres farther on the path ends abruptly at a rockslide which has tumbled down from the slope to the north and into the eastern end of the lake. A bit of rock hopping takes the hiker to the water's edge.

Across the lake soars the broad north face of Boom Mountain, and the glaciated spires of Mount Quadra (3173 m) and Bident Mountain (3084 m) rise beyond the far end of the lake to the northwest. Consolation Pass, which lies to the east of Bident Mountain, has long intrigued adventurous souls who see it as a quick and easy route to Consolation Lakes, but be forewarned, it is a journey of amazing toil and trouble that has brought seasoned mountaineers to the verge of exhaustion; it is not recommended.

The lake was undoubted visited as early

Boom Lake

as 1884 when the mining town of Silver City was flourishing in the nearby Bow Valley and by 1910 all the peaks surrounding it had been climbed. In 1912 the Alpine Club of Canada held its annual camp in Vermilion Pass and thoroughly crisscrossed the entire area, and the source of Boom Lake's name was documented in the club's journal the following year:

"Boom Lake is so called from the fact that near its eastern extremity an old moraine, at one time the bounding wall of the lake, now just touches the surface which has overflowed it. It spans the lake in a crescent, some distance from the eastern end, and intercepts the drift wood floating down the lake. The appearance created is that of a lumber boom, and hence the name."

69

Taylor Lake

Trans-Canada Highway to Taylor Lake—6.3 kilometres (3.9 miles)

Day trip

Allow 2 - 3 hours one way

Elevation gain: 585 metres (1,920 feet)

Maximum elevation: 2065 metres (6,780 feet)

Topo maps: Lake Louise 82 N/8

Point of Departure: Follow the Trans-Canada Highway to the Taylor Creek Picnic Area, situated on the southwest side of the highway 8 kilometres (5 miles) west of Castle Junction or 17 kilometres (10½ miles) east of the Lake Louise Junction. Walk across the bridge at the rear of the parking area and turn right onto the trail.

0.0—Taylor Creek Picnic Area (1480 m).

—Gradual to moderate uphill grade.

1.0—Bridge across Taylor Creek.

—Steady uphill.

5.8—Bridge across Taylor Creek.

6.1—Junction. Intersection with *Panorama Ridge* trail at Km 9.8. O'Brien Lake to left 2.1 kms. Taylor Lake straight ahead.

6.3—Taylor Lake (2065 m). Campground. Trail to Panorama Ridge cuts uphill from rear of campground.

Of the many high, hanging valley lakes set into the west side of the Bow Valley between Banff and Lake Louise, Taylor Lake is one of the easiest to reach. And in addition to being every bit as pleasant as its sister lakes, it offers the added attraction of two short and scenic side trips, either of which can make the outing a very full and enjoyable one.

The trail to Taylor Lake is straightforward and not overly inspiring, consisting of little more than an old cat track which switchbacks steadily upwards. Views beyond the forest canopy of lodgepole pine and spruce are nonexistant.

The goal is well worth the drudgery of the climb, however, as the trail suddenly emerges into the open meadow near the lake's outlet—an area carpeted with western anemone, marsh marigold, buttercups, and mountain laurel through much of the summer. Fringing the meadow and much of the lakeshore is a typical forest of the upper subalpine zone—a dense, cool cover of alpine fir and Engelmann spruce dotted with the pale green foliage of alpine larch.

The north face of Mount Bell rises abruptly from the south shore of the lake to form a wall over 750 metres high. The low notch of Taylor Pass to the west separates Mount Bell from Panorama Ridge and serves as a rock scrambler's route to the Consolation Valley and Moraine Lake. Beneath the pass, at the far end of the lake, a lacy waterfall flows over ancient Precambrian rock.

The Panorama Ridge trail, a long and rugged highline route running from Boom Creek to Moraine Lake, intersects at Taylor Lake and provides the path to other scenic features a short distance south and north of the lake.

O'Brien Lake. O'Brien Lake is located in a smaller cirque 2.1 kilometres to the south, and with a more lavish display of wildflowers along its shore and a heavier growth of alpine larch in the surrounding

Taylor Lake

forest, it is even more charming than Taylor. To reach it ford Taylor Creek at the trail sign 200 metres below the lake and follow the rocky but well travelled track which drops below the Mount Bell cliffs and then rises back up to the mouth of the O'Brien cirque. The 500 metre-long trail that leads up to O'Brien from the Panorama Ridge trail all but disappears in boggy meadows, but by staying along the left hand side of the lake's outlet stream the route is obvious.

Panorama Ridge. Following the Panorama Ridge trail north from the rear of the Taylor Lake Campground, a brief 0.5 kilometre climb brings the hiker out into one of the great wildflower meadows of

the Rockies. The snowstreaked cliffs of Panorama Ridge serve as a backdrop to the colourful, kilometre-long garden which is fringed by an almost pure forest of alpine larch. Though the trail disappears at the lower edge of the meadow, one can wander and explore for several hours in this high amphitheatre.

While it is possible to continue further in either direction along the Panorama Ridge trail, trail conditions deteriorate rapidly south of the O'Brien cirque and north of the first meadow on Panorama Ridge. For further information on these problems, see the *Panorama Ridge* trail description.

71

Panorama Ridge

Banff-Radium Highway to Moraine Lake—23.2 kilometres (14.4 miles)

Day trip or backpack

Allow 8 - 9 hours

Elevation gain: 650 metres (2,150 feet)

     loss: 485 metres (1,600 feet)

Maximum elevation: 2255 metres (7,400 feet)

Topo maps: Lake Louise 82 N/8

Point of Departure: Northbound hikers begin at the Boom Creek Picnic Area on the Banff—Radium Highway, 7 kilometres (4½ miles) west of Castle Junction (see *Boom Lake* trail). Southbound travellers begin from the Consolation Lakes trail head at Moraine Lake (see *Consolation Lakes* trail).

0.0—Boom Creek Picnic Area (1720 m).

2.3—Junction. Taylor Lake—Panorama Ridge trail cuts up to right from Boom Lake trail.

—Steep uphill on tight switchbacks.

3.9—Forested summit ridge (2180 m).

—Trail descends, contours to northwest.

8.2—Junction. O'Brien Lake uphill to left 500 metres.

9.8—Taylor Creek crossing and junction. Intersection with *Taylor Lake* trail at Km 6.1.

10.1—Taylor Lake (2065 m). Campground. Panorama Ridge trail continues from rear of campground.

—Steady, forested climb.

10.6—Large, meadow. Trail disappears.

11.7—Trail reappears in forest on right side of meadow.

11.9—Old prospector cabins.

16.6—Trail descends, begins swing to west.

—Rough, wet trail conditions.

21.2—Large meadow with shallow lake to right of trail.

21.6—Babel Creek bridge and junction. Intersection with *Consolation Lakes* trail at Km 1.6. Turn right to Moraine Lake.

23.2—Moraine Lake Picnic Area (1885 m).

This is a scenic highline trail running from Boom Creek to Moraine Lake via Taylor Lake. It passes through numerous meadows fringed with alpine larch and occasionally opens out to permit expansive views over the Bow Valley. Unfortunately, the route has received little attention or maintenance since it was first blazed by the Banff outfitter Claude Brewster in 1938. As of this writing (1985) Parks Canada intends to upgrade the trail, and flagging hangs from trees where the track disappears, but you should expect the worst and plan on rough, boggy trail coupled with periods of tedious route-finding.

While it is usually referred to as the Panorama Ridge trail, the southern half of the route is well south of that peak, crossing a southern spur of Mount Bell on its way from Boom Creek to Taylor Lake. It is on this summit ridge, as the trail begins its contour northward toward Taylor Lake, that the problems begin. In several meadows the path disappears entirely, and hikers must search on the opposite side for the point where the trail reappears (usually flagged).

Taylor Lake makes an excellent lunch stop for day hikers, and there is a campsite at the east end of the lake for backpackers. From the rear of the Taylor Lake campsite, the trail climbs onto Panorama Ridge proper and, 500 metres from the lake, disappears into a huge, flower-filled meadow backdropped by the cliffs of Panorama Ridge. The trail reappears one kilometre up-meadow on the right hand side, but soon encounters more meadows and more route-finding headaches. Once the trail loses elevation to contour around the north end of Panorama Ridge, the track is well defined albeit rough and boggy.

Note: Southbound hikers seem to be more inclined to get lost on this trail than do northbound hikers.

Hillsdale

Hillsdale Meadows to Johnston Canyon—14.1 kilometres (8.8 miles)

Day trip

Allow 2½ hours to Ink Pots

Elevation gain: 460 metres (1,500 feet)
loss: 215 metres (700 feet)

Maximum elevation: 1860 metres (6,100 feet)

Topo maps: Banff 82 O/4
Castle Mountain 82 O/5

Point of Departure: Follow the Bow Valley Parkway to the Hillsdale Meadows parking area, situated on the northeast side of the highway 12½ kilometres (7½ miles) west from the parkway's eastern junction with the Trans-Canada Highway and 5½ kilometres (3½ miles) east of the Johnston's Canyon Resort. This parking area is 100 metres west and on the opposite side of the highway from the Hillsdale Meadows interpretive exhibit.

0.0—Hillsdale Meadows parking area (1400 m).

—Follow old vehicle track through meadow.

0.1—Follow vehicle track to right across stream.

—Follow faint track to upper edge of meadow.

0.5—Forest margin. Foot trail begins.

—Steady climb at gradual to moderate grades.

5.0—Hillsdale Slide Summit (1860 m).

5.6—Open meadow.

—Trail descends.

8.0—Junction (1645 m). Intersection with *Johnston Creek—Pulsatilla Pass* trail at Km 5.7. Cross bridge for Ink Pots (0.3 km).

The Hillsdale Meadows used to serve as a pasture for both dairy cattle and horses, and the trail that leads from the meadows to Johnston Creek provided direct access to the Pulsatilla and Badger Pass areas for early outfitters and wardens who used this grazing area. Today the trail is used mainly by hikers who want to make an extended day trip between the Hillsdale Meadows and Johnston Canyon. Though the trail runs through forest for much of the way, it does offer some open views to the steeply tilted limestone slabs of Mount Ishbel and a chance to climb over the tumbled terrain created by the Hillsdale Slide—a great landslip which geologists believe slumped from the Sawback Range some 8,000 years ago during the last retreat of the Bow Valley Glacier.

Hiking from Johnston Canyon to Hillsdale Meadows is quite straightforward as hikers pickup the Hillsdale trail at its junction with the Johnston Creek trail just 300 metres beyond the Ink Pots. Starting at Hillsdale Meadows can be a bit more confusing, however, since there are many trails winding across the 500 metre-long meadow to its upper margin. From the gate which closes off the old access road into the meadows, follow the vehicle track that cuts right across the meadow's central stream and ascend directly to the upper edge of the meadow. An old trail sign may still be in place to mark where good trail begins in the forest, otherwise a few minutes of searching along the forest edge may be required.

Once into the forest the track is well defined as it climbs steadily to the summit of the ancient landslip. Beyond this crest, the trail runs through a small open meadow that allows good views to Mount Ishbel and the Sawback Range. From there the trail reenters the forest and makes a steady descent to the large meadow on Johnston Creek containing the Ink Pots and the junction with the Johnston Creek trail.

73

Johnston Canyon

Bow Valley Parkway to Upper Falls—2.7 kilometres (1.7 miles)
Bow Valley Parkway to Ink Pots—5.8 kilometres (3.6 miles)

Half-day trip

Allow 2 hours to Ink Pots

Elevation gain: 215 metres (700 feet)

Maximum elevation: 1645 metres (5,400 feet)

Topo maps: Banff 82 O/4
　　　　　Castle Mountain 82 O/5

Point of Departure: Follow the Bow Valley Parkway to Johnston Canyon, 17½ kilometres (11 miles) west from its eastern junction with the Trans-Canada Highway or 6½ kilometres (4 miles) east from Castle Junction. The parking area for hikers is on the opposite side of Johnston Creek from the lodge complex and directly opposite the campground entrance. From the trail sign on the northwest side of the parking area, the trail crosses the creek via a hiker's bridge and turns to the right up the canyon.

　0.0—Trail sign and bridge (1430 m).

　1.1—Lower Falls.

　2.7—Upper Falls.

　3.2—Junction. Intersection with *Johnston Creek—Pulsatilla Pass* trail at Km 2.7. Keep right for Ink Pots.

　5.3—Road narrows to trail width.

　　　—Gradual descent to Johnston Creek meadows.

　5.8—Ink Pots (1645 m).

The hike to the Ink Pots via Johnston Canyon is one of the most popular day trips in Banff Park. The first 1.1 kilometres follows a lavishly constructed nature trail to the canyon's Lower Falls, and while the additional kilometres to the Upper Falls and Ink Pots are not as smooth and well manicured, they are hardly demanding by mountain trail standards. The hike ends in an open meadow alongside Johnston Creek where the seven cold water springs of the Ink Pots bubble to the surface.

The path to the Lower Falls stays close to Johnston Creek, hanging to the canyon walls in several places on sturdy iron catwalks. Along this section of canyon dippers can often be seen flitting from rock to rock at the water's edge, and the rare black swift nests on the canyon walls in late summer. Beyond the thundering cataract of the Lower Falls the trail winds through a forest of lodgepole pine, spruce and Douglas fir, and several smaller falls may be seen from the trail before the spectacular 30 metre-high Upper Falls is reached.

Above the Upper Falls the trail climbs to join the old access road from the Moose Meadows trail head. Two kilometres further along the road reverts to footpath and descends to the Johnston Creek meadows where the Ink Pots are encountered on the right side of the trail. These springs issue forth at a constant temperature near 4 degrees Celsius, and the pools' bottoms are composed of quicksand.

The Johnston Creek trail continues beyond the Ink Pots, and the Hillsdale trail intersects it just 300 metres farther along. Continuing on the latter trail makes an interesting day hike option for those who can arrange transportation between the Hillsdale Meadows and Johnston Canyon trail heads. (See *Hillsdale* and *Johnston Creek—Pulsatilla Pass* trail descriptions.)

Castle Crags

Half-day trip

Allow 1½ - 2 hours one way

Elevation gain: 520 metres (1,700 feet)

Maximum elevation: 1980 metres (6,500 feet)

Topo maps: Castle Mountain 82 O/5

Point of Departure: Follow either the Trans-Canada Highway or the Bow Valley Parkway to Castle Junction (30 kilometres west of Banff townsite). If on the Trans-Canada Highway, cross over to the Bow Valley Parkway via the one kilometre-long road that bridges the Bow River and connects the two highways. Follow the Bow Valley Parkway west from Castle Junction 5 kilometres (3 miles) to a paved parking area on the north side of the highway. The trail strikes off as an old access road from the barrier rocks at the upper edge of the parking area.

0.0—Trail head parking area (1460 m).

—Road ascends through closed forest.

1.4—Old cabin.

2.1—Access road reverts to trail.

—Switchback ascent of open slopes.

3.7—Eisenhower Lookout site (1980 m).

This relatively short but steep trail up the slopes of Castle Mountain leads to the site of the old Mount Eisenhower fire lookout and an outstanding panorama of the Bow Valley stretching from the grey limestone peaks near Banff townsite to the glacier-capped summits surrounding Lake Louise. And because it climbs along an open slope with a southwesterly exposure, the trail is one of the earliest to be free of snow in the spring and the latest to close in autumn.

From the roadside parking area the route follows a steep, wide pathway upward through forest of lodgepole pine and spruce. Only a few glimpses are afforded beyond the forest canopy during the first two kilometres, but an old cabin offers a stop of interest at Kilometre 1.4, its dilapidated remains possibly a relic of the short-lived mining boom in this part of the Bow Valley circa 1884.

The fire road eventually reverts to foot trail not far beyond the cabin, and the path traverses out onto the steep, open slopes below overlooking the Bow Valley. From mid-June until August, these meadows rank among the finest of wildflower gardens in the Rockies, overflowing with yellow columbine, heart-leaved arnica, Indian paintbrush and many other colourful species.

With increasing altitude the views up and down the Bow Valley become increasingly impressive. Finally the trail twists up through a cliff, enters a stand of whitebark pine, and contours above the precipice for 100 metres or so to the old lookout site. The lookout cabin which once stood here was constructed by labourers from the local conscientious objector camps in the autumn of 1942. In the mid-1970s Parks Canada ceased manning this and other fire lookouts in the park, preferring to patrol from the highways and by helicopter. In 1983 the lookout cabin was burnt to the ground by some unknown visitors.

Rockbound Lake

Day trip

Allow 2½ - 3 hours one way

Elevation gain: 760 metres (2,500 feet)

Maximum elevation: 2210 metres (7,250 feet)

Topo maps: Castle Mountain 82 O/5

Point of Departure: Follow either the Trans-Canada Highway or the Bow Valley Parkway to Castle Junction (30 kilometres west of Banff townsite). If on the Trans-Canada Highway, cross over to the Bow Valley Parkway via the one kilometre-long road that bridges the Bow River and connects the two highways. The paved parking area for the trail is located on the north side of the Bow Valley Parkway just 200 metres east of Castle Junction, next to the warden's residence and across the road from the Youth Hostel cabins.

0.0—Trail head parking area (1450 m).

—Follows old access road track.

0.3—Junction. Right hand spur trail leads to Silverton Falls (0.8 km). Keep straight ahead on main trail.

—Gradual to moderate uphill grades.

5.0—Access road narrows to single path.

5.3—Boggy and wet conditions during early season and rainy periods.

7.7—Tower Lake (2120 m).

—Trail skirts to right of lake, then switchbacks up headwall.

8.4—Rockbound Lake (2210 m).

The Tower and Rockbound Lakes trip is a rather rigorous 8.4 kilometre hike carrying the trekker high behind the ramparts of Castle Mountain to the snow-fed waters of two distinctly different tarns: one a placid and green mirror fringed by a pleasantly open subalpine forest and meadowland; the other a cold, grey sheet of water contained within a basin of steep scree slopes and massive, tumbled boulders. Much of the trail to the lakes is quite steep access road, and the early season traveller must be prepared to face short sections of boggy terrain in order to reach the lakes and enjoy the scenery found there—the lakes, the Eisenhower Tower, and an extensive view down the Sawback Range and the Bow Valley.

The trail begins as an old access road and is scenically modest for 2.4 kilometres as it gradually climbs up and across the southern flank of Castle Mountain. However, a bit beyond Kilometre 2.4 the trail gains sufficient elevation to grant glimpses of the Bow Valley and the mountains to the west. Prominent are Copper Mountain, rising like a great pyramid above the valley floor, and, to the south a bit, Pilot Mountain, an early landmark in the area. The trail, still access road, continues its traverse around Castle, eventually gaining entrance to the long narrow valley running northwest between the ramparts and Helena Ridge.

At the 5.3 kilometre mark the trail narrows to single file width and, just a bit farther on, views open up to the Eisenhower Tower on Castle Mountain, a 2752 metre mass of Cambrian limestone well-known to local rock climbers. The trail beyond this point can be rather messy, particularly in early season when the entire area is soggy from the melting snow.

The first lake reached is Tower, a small body of water located in a semicircle of rock which would seemingly indicate the end of the trail. However, the track does continue to the right of the lake and climbs steeply up the headwall beyond.

Tower Lake

At the top of the wall one first sees Rockbound Lake and immediately appreciates the lake's name, for it is totally enclosed by rock. Limestone of the Cathedral Formation contains the immediate bed of the lake, while limestones of the Stephen and Eldon formations constitute the high walls of the cirque. The geological position of the lake is also most interesting as it lies precisely in the centre of a great syncline, or downfold in the strata, which runs from Rockbound Lake to Mount Kerkeslin in Jasper Park, some 260 kilometres to the northwest. The syncline is evidenced by the easterly dip in the strata of Castle Mountain and the westerly dip in the bedding of Helena Ridge.

From the scattered forest of spruce, fir and larch at the top of the Tower Lake headwall one can spend an entire day exploring the Rockbound amphitheatre: huge boulders on the open slope leading to the lake's southern shore provide a fine playground for fledgling rock climbers; the slopes of Helena Ridge to the east can be easily ascended for a better perspective of the basin; and mountaineers with a limited amount of experience can ascend the main peak of Castle Mountain from the slopes beyond the lake's north shore.

Mystic Lake

Mount Norquay to Mystic Lake—19.6 kilometres (12.2 miles)
Mount Norquay to Johnston Canyon—36.8 kilometres (22.9 miles)

Backpack

Allow 6 - 8 hours to Mystic Lake

Elevation loss: 90 metres (300 feet)
    gain: 395 metres (1,300 feet)

Maximum elevation: 2010 metres (6,590 feet)

Topo maps: Banff 82 O/4
    Castle Mountain 82 O/5

Point of Departure: Follow the Mount Norquay Road north from the Trans-Canada Highway at Banff townsite's west interchange, climbing 6 kilometres (3½ miles) of twisting switchbacks to the Mount Norquay Ski Area. Turn into the first parking lot on the right (Lot #3) and drive to the far end.

0.0—Trail sign (1705 m).

—Follow access road down through ski area.

1.1—Junction. Cascade Amphitheatre—Elk Lake to right. Keep left for Mystic Lake.

4.0—Forty Mile Creek bridge (1615 m).

—Trail follows close to creek's east bank.

6.0—Junction. Left fork crosses creek to Edith Pass (2.3 km). Keep right for Mystic Lake.

8.2—Campground.

13.5—Junction. Two trails branch left to outfitter camps. Keep high to right.

15.9—Junction (1830 m). Campground (0.3 km) and Forty Mile Summit straight ahead. Turn left for Mystic Lake.

16.0—Mystic Warden Cabin.

18.6—Campground.

19.1—Junction. Mystic Lake 0.5 km to left. Keep right for Mystic Pass.

22.7—Mystic Pass (2285 m).

29.3—Junction (1675 m). Intersection with *Johnston Creek—Pulsatilla Pass* trail at Km 7.4.

31.5—Ink Pots.

36.8—Johnston Canyon Lodge (1430 m).

The Mystic Lake trail offers a classic backpack into the heart of the Rocky Mountain Front Ranges. Fast-running streams, forest-ringed lakes and a nearby alpine pass can all be enjoyed during the course of the hike. And beyond Mystic Lake lies the option of a 36.8 kilometre arrangement trip emerging at Johnston Canyon or an even more demanding loop trip via Mystic, Badger and Forty Mile Passes.

While Mystic Lake and its nearby campground can be reached in a day, most backpackers will probably prefer a more leisurely approach, spending the first night on the trail at the 8.2 kilometre or Mystic junction campgrounds. The 15.9 kilometres of trail from Mount Norquay to Mystic junction are heavily travelled by a horse outfitter and trail conditions are far from ideal, particularly between the 8.0 kilometre mark and the junction. Beyond the junction, however, the trail to the lake is in fairly good shape, as is the trail over Mystic Pass and beyond.

The first portion of the hike involves a gently graded traverse of the northern flank of Mount Norquay, the trail rising and falling through a forest of lodgepole pine and spruce. At the 4.0 kilometre mark Forty Mile Creek is crossed, and the trail proceeds along its eastern bank, with Mount Brewster to the east and, across the valley to the west, some of the more striking peaks in the Sawback Range: Mount Louis, Mount Fifi and Mount Cockscomb. Although much of this section of trail is forested, avalanche paths and willow flats give the hiker frequent chances to examine the valley.

A trail junction at Kilometre 15.9 and a second crossing of Forty Mile Creek move the hiker into the side valley that leads to Mystic Lake. Passing the Mystic Warden Cabin, the trail, plagued by rocks and roots, alternately climbs and levels out, and at the 18.6 kilometre mark it crosses

Mystic Pass

the creek below a large avalanche path. The Mystic Lake campground lies on a low ridge immediately above. A few minutes further effort brings hikers to the Mystic Pass junction, from which it is a scant 500 metres to the shores of Mystic Lake, a serene body of water settled in the bottom of a massive rock cirque.

Though the origin of the lake's name is somewhat obscure, it probably harks back to the day in 1891 when the Stoney Indian William Twin guided 11 year old Bill Brewster and his nine year old brother Jim to the lake. The Banff boys, who later grew up to create an outfitting and tourist transportation empire in the mountain parks, are reputed to be the first whites to visit the lake.

From Mystic Lake junction, the 2285 metre summit of Mystic Pass is a short 3.6 kilometre climb away. The pass itself is 1.5 kilometres in length, running through beautiful alpine meadows flanked by the gnarled and twisted Devonian limestone strata of the Front Ranges.

Johnston Creek Option. For people wishing to go beyond Mystic Lake and Pass to emerge at Johnston Canyon or Moose Meadows, the next day's hike is a full one. Beyond the pass the trail drops through some spectacular rockslide and avalanche paths, bypassing delicate waterfalls, to meet the Johnston Creek trail and just over two kilometres above the Ink Pots. The total distance from the Mystic Lake campground to Johnston Canyon is 18.2 kilometres, and for those who find the distance more than they can handle, there is a campground near the Ink Pots just 5.5 kilometres from the Bow Valley Parkway. (See *Johnston Creek-Pulsatilla Pass* trail description.)

Mystic-Badger-Forty Mile Passes Loop. This wilderness loop trip utilizes three passes in the Sawback Range to make a 90 kilometre-long trip starting and ending at Mount Norquay. But be forewarned, the route loops through prime grizzly territory and much of the trail is heavily used by a commercial horse outfitter. (See *Johnston Creek-Pulsatilla Pass, Badger Pass-Flint's Park*, and *Forty Mile Summit* trail descriptions.)

79

Forty Mile Summit

Mystic Pass Junction to Forty Mile Summit—6.0 kilometres (3.5 miles)*
Mystic Pass Junction to Flint's Park—13.6 kilometres (8.5 miles)

Backpack

Allow 5 hours one way

Elevation gain: 320 metres (1,050 feet)
    loss: 320 metres (1,050 feet)

Maximum elevation: 2150 metres (7,050 feet)

Topo maps: Castle Mountain 82 O/5

Point of Departure: Hike the *Mystic Lake* trail north from Mount Norquay to the Mystic Lake Junction (Km 15.9). Keep right at this junction to begin the Forty Mile Summit—Flint's Park trip. Southbound backpackers can reach the north end of this backcountry trail via the *Johnston Creek* and *Badger Pass* trails or the *Cascade Fire Road* and the old Flint's Park access road.

0.0—Mystic Lake Junction (1830 m). Mystic Lake and Pass to the left. Forty Mile Summit straight ahead.

0.3—Campground and junction. Mystic Lake cutoff to left. Keep straight ahead.

—Steady uphill at gradual to moderate grades.

6.0—Forty Mile Summit (2150 m).

8.0—Sawback Lake viewpoint.

—Trail drops steeply into old burn.

9.0—Creek crossing and junction. Cut left for Sawback Lake (2.2 km) and campground (1.4 km). Flint's Park straight ahead.

—Gradual to moderate downhill on old fire road trace.

13.5—Cascade River bridge.

13.6—Junction and Flint's Park Warden Cabin. Intersection with *Badger Pass—Flint's Park* trail at Km 17.5. Turn right for campground (0.2 km), North Fork Pass and the Cascade Fire Road. Turn left for Badger Pass.

*All distances approximate.

The trail leading to the headwaters of Forty Mile Creek is a primary route into Banff's remote Flint's Park region. This route is most often used by Sawback Trail travellers seeking an alternative to the more heavily hiked Mystic Pass and Johnston Creek trails. For all its wilderness and beauty, the trail does present some drawbacks to the hiker: The route is used by a commercial horse outfitter and trail conditions can be poor during wet weather; and the Flint's Park region is set within the very heart of Banff Park's grizzly country—an area where backpackers must travel alertly and keep a tidy camp.

From the junction with the Mystic Lake trail at Kilometre 15.9, the ascent to Forty Mile Summit is straightforward and moderately graded. In 1985 a hiking trail was completed up the east side of the drainage above the horse trail to provide a drier approach to the summit; the trails diverge just beyond the Mystic Lake Junction and reunite near the pass.

At 2150 metres above sea level, Forty Mile Summit is still below timberline and hardly one of Banff Park's spectacular alpine passes. But the pass is composed of a long, pleasant meadowland fringed with alpine larch and at its north end there is an outstanding view of Sawback Lake. The trail plunges down from this overlook to a junction with the Sawback Lake trail—a 2.2 kilometre side trip that is worth including in your itinerary.

The trail descending Sawback Creek from the Sawback Lake junction follows the overgrown track of an old fire road and passes through the silver spars of a 1936 forest fire which swept much of the Flint's Park region. At Kilometre 13.5 the trail crosses the Cascade River and reaches the Badger Pass-Flint's Park trail and the Flint's Park Warden Cabin. (See also *Badger Pass-Flint's Park* and *North Fork Pass* trail descriptions.)

Badger Pass

Backpack

Allow 2 hours to Badger Pass

Elevation gain: 520 metres (1,700 feet)

Maximum elevation: 2545 metres (8,350 feet)

Topo maps: Castle Mountain 82 O/5

Point of Departure: Hike the *Johnston Creek—Pulsatilla Pass* trail to the junction at Km 21.4. The trail to Badger Pass and points east cuts uphill to the right. Westbound hikers can reach the east end of the trail from the *Cascade Fire Road* or intersect from the south via the *Forty Mile Summit* trail.

0.0—Johnston Creek Junction (2025 m). Pulsatilla Pass straight ahead. Turn right for Badger Pass.

—Moderate to steep uphill through open meadows.

5.0—Badger Pass (2545 m).

—Steep descent.

8.6—Grade moderates as trail joins Cascade River west fork.

—Gradual to moderate downhill grades.

12.0—Campground and junction. Climber's trail to Block Lakes branches south across river.

17.5—Junction and Flint's Park Warden Cabin (1830 m). Forty Mile Summit and Sawback Lake to right. Keep straight ahead for Flint's Park and Cascade Fire Road.

17.6—Junction. North Fork Pass to left. Keep straight ahead for Cascade Fire Road.

17.7—Cascade River north fork bridge and campground.

—Level travel due east on old fire road.

21.0—Junction. Outfitter's camp to right. Keep straight ahead.

25.5—Junction (1740 m). Intersection with *Cascade Fire Road* at Km 23.1. Turn left for Wigmore Summit, Red Deer River and points north. Turn right for Stony Creek, Lake Minnewanka Road and points south.

*All distances approximate.

Badger Pass is one of the highest trail-accessible passes in Banff Park, but because of its remoteness, it is the least visited of these 2500 metre-plus summits. Yet, its solitude combined with extensive flower meadows on its western slope make it a worthy objective for experienced backpackers.

The most direct and gradual ascent to this lofty notch is from the west via Johnston Creek (see *Pulsatilla Pass* trail description). From its junction with the Johnston Creek trail, the sometimes faint path makes a steady ascent eastward to Badger Pass. Much of the moderately graded climb is made beside sparkling streams and through meadows which are covered with wildflowers from mid-July to mid-August.

The eastern lip of the narrow, rocky gap which comprises Badger Pass is often blocked by a cornice of snow until late July or early August. This is quite an effective barrier, and anyone planning on crossing the pass should check out trail conditions with Parks Canada in advance.

Continuing eastward, the trail descends to the headwaters of the Cascade River, a dramatic drop which contains some very steep pitches. At Kilometre 12.0, where two tributary valleys intersect from Bonnet Peak to the north and Block Mountain to the south, there is a campground. The spur trail to the Block Lakes crosses the river at this point, but this side trip should only be attempted by experienced rock climbers since a major cliff guards the final approach to the lakes.

Travel eastward along the north side of the Cascade River to the Cascade Fire Road is quite straightforward and uneventful, following the track of an old fire road through Flint's Park and the remnants of the 1936 forest fire which swept this valley. But stay alert—this here is grizzly country!

81

Johnston Creek—Pulsatilla Pass

Bow Valley Parkway to Luellen Lake—17.1 kilometres (10.6 miles)
Bow Valley Parkway to Pulsatilla Pass—25.3 kilometres (15.7 miles)

Backpack

Allow 6 hours to Luellen Lake

Elevation gain: 915 metres (3,000 feet)

Maximum elevation: 2345 metres (7,700 feet)

Topo maps: Castle Mountain 82 O/5

Point of Departure: Follow the Bow Valley Parkway to the Moose Meadows parking area, located on the north side of the highway 2.3 kilometres (1.4 miles) west of Johnston Canyon Lodge or 4 kilometres (2½ miles) east of Castle Junction. The parking area is situated approximately 100 metres off the highway and is marked by a prominent sign.

0.0—Moose Meadows parking area (1430 m).

2.7—Junction. Johnston Canyon trail intersects from right.

5.3—Ink Pots.

5.5—Campground.

5.6—Johnston Creek bridge to east bank.

5.7—Junction. Hillsdale Meadows to right.

7.4—Junction and bridge. Mystic Pass to right. Keep straight ahead.

11.1—Johnston Creek Warden Cabin.

15.9—Junction. Horse trail continues up valley. Hiker's trail and Luellen Lake trail cut left down to creek.

16.0—Johnston Creek bridge to west bank.

16.1—Junction. Trail to Luellen Lake and campground (1.0 km) continues straight uphill to west. Pulsatilla Pass to right.

17.5—Johnston Creek ford (calf deep) to east bank.

21.4—Junction. Badger Pass to right.

21.9—Campground.

25.3—Pulsatilla Pass (2345 m).

26.4—Pulsatilla Lake.

—Steep descent of Wildflower Creek valley.

31.7—Junction and campground (1830 m). Intersection with *Baker Creek* trail at Km 13.9.

Luellen Lake has long been a popular destination for backcountry fishermen, but with each passing year more and more backpackers are finding their way to the headwaters of Johnston Creek and the lofty summit of Pulsatilla Pass as well. Once into this high, open country, the options for side trips and exploration are numerous as seldom visited passes, glaciers and lakes beckon from every side. In addition, this trail can be used as a segment for an even longer journey through the Front Ranges (see *The Sawback Trail*) or as part of a loop trip via Badger Pass, Flint's Park, Forty Mile Summit, and Mystic Pass.

While backpackers bound for the upper reaches of Johnston Creek can start their journey on the popular Johnston Canyon nature trail (see *Johnston Canyon-Ink Pots* trail description), a more peaceful departure can be made from the Moose Meadows trail head which lies 2.3 kilometres west of the canyon resort complex on the Bow Valley Parkway. This trail intersects with the canyon trail after 2.7 kilometres. You will miss the spectacular Lower and Upper Falls of Johnston Canyon on this option, but you will avoid elbowing your way through the hordes of idle strollers who frequent the canyon trail.

Above the Ink Pots, the trail is less travelled but straightforward as it ascends the Johnston Creek valley at a steady but moderate grade. The creek, bordered by open willow flats, is never far away and there are many pleasant forest glades in which to stop and rest.

At Kilometre 16.0 the hiker's trail branches left from the old horse trail to cross to the west bank of the creek. Less than 100 metres beyond this bridged crossing, the one kilometre-long side trail to Luellen Lake cuts uphill to the left.

Luellen is a long, thin lake back-dropped by the rugged cliffs of Helena Ridge and bordered by a forest of Engel-

Wildflower Valley from Pulsatilla Pass

mann spruce and alpine fir. While it hasn't been stocked for many years, the lake still provides trout fishermen and a resident osprey family with sporadic success. There is a campground at the lake's east end.

Continuing up the Johnston Creek valley, the hiker's trail soon rejoins the horse trail and, a short distance beyond, fords the creek to its east side. Following this calf-deep ford, the trail enters beautiful, open meadows with fine views of the jagged limestone peaks of the Sawback Range to the east.

At Kilometre 21.4 the Badger Pass junction is reached. A campsite just 500 metres further along makes a good base for a side trip to this lofty alpine gap which is one of the highest trail-accessible passes in the Canadian Rockies. The pass also serves as a gateway to the remote headwaters region of the Cascade River (see *Badger Pass-Flint's Park* trail description).

Just 1.4 kilometres beyond the Badger Pass junction the trail swings across the creek one last time (an easy ford) and

begins its ascent to Pulsatilla Pass. Unless you want to explore the large alpine cirque just east of the pass, stay left beneath the glacier-draped cliffs of Pulsatilla Mountain and pick up the trail which climbs to the obvious low notch above. (A more obvious horse trail pulls many hikers across the slope to the east and adds a kilometre of strenuous climbing.)

The view beyond the 2345 metre summit is one of the classic wilderness scenes in the Canadian Rockies—the sparkling waters of Pulsatilla Lake perfectly framed between two rugged mountain chains which march away to the north. Pulsatilla is an old genus name for the white-flowered western anemone, just one of a myriad of wildflowers which spread over the alpine tundra in July and August.

The trail continues northward from the pass another 6.4 kilometres, descending Wildflower Creek to an intersection with the Baker Creek trail. From the Baker Creek junction you may either climb to the Baker Lake-Skoki Valley region or exit to the Bow Valley Parkway (see *Baker Creek* trail description).

Baker Creek

Backpack

Allow 7 - 9 hours to Baker Lake

Elevation gain: 715 metres (2,350 feet)

Maximum elevation: 2210 metres (7,250 feet)

Topo maps: Lake Louise 82 N/8

Point of Departure: Follow the Bow Valley Parkway to the Baker Creek Picnic Area, located 10 kilometres (6 miles) east of the parkway's junction with the Trans-Canada Highway near Lake Louise or 14 kilometres (8½ miles) west of Castle Junction. The picnic area is situated on the northeast side of the highway opposite Baker Creek Lodge, and the trail head is just inside the entrance to the picnic area on the left hand side.

0.0—Baker Creek Picnic Area (1495 m).

—Ascent through forest.

2.4—Junction. Trail to old warden cabin cuts right. Keep straight ahead.

3.5—Descent to Baker Creek.

5.6—Bridge to east side of Baker Creek. (Trails parallel both sides of creek for next 4.5 kms. Stay on west side.)

—Wet, boggy meadows. Trail often indistinct.

10.1—Junction and campground. East side trail crosses creek (bridged) to rejoin west side trail.

10.5—Outfitter's camp.

13.1—Trail crosses to east side of creek (ford.).

13.9—Junction and campground. Pulsatilla Pass to right. Baker Lake straight ahead.

—Steep uphill sections, wet and boggy.

19.3—Junction. Red Deer Lake straight ahead. Baker Lake to left.

20.0—Campground.

20.3—Baker Lake (2210 m).

Scenically Baker Creek is rather mundane, and few people use it as a destination trip. More often the lower valley is hiked as an optional exit from Pulsatilla Pass or Baker Lake, while the upper one-third of the trail is most frequently used as a connecting link between the Pulsatilla Pass and Skoki Valley environs.

From the Baker Creek Picnic Area, the trail climbs over a low ridge covered by 'dog-hair' stands of lodgepole pine, reaching the willow-covered Baker Creek flats again at Kilometre 3.5. At Kilometre 5.6 the trail splits and you have a choice of continuing your journey on the west side of the creek or crossing a nearby log bridge and proceeding up the east side. While the eastern option is a more recent attempt to route the trail onto drier ground, most hikers consider it a failure. You're probably better off staying on the west side.

The 4.5 kilometres beyond the trail split are pretty messy: Boggy willow flats where the track frequently disappears. It is particularly confusing for hikers descending the valley; many people wander up into the forest west of the flats following old tree blazes that lead to nowhere. Keep the creek within sight, persevere, and hope for the best.

Just beyond the 10 kilometre campground the east side trail recrosses the creek to link up with the west route. The trail is running on drier ground now and is better defined. At Kilometre 13.1 the trail fords the creek to the east side (rockhop and wade) and, 800 metres beyond, intersects with the Pulsatilla Pass trail descending Wildflower Creek.

Less than two kilometres above the Wildflower Creek junction, the trail enters a boggy meadow where it becomes indistinct at times. Above the meadow the trail makes a steep, direct ascent through closed forest. The open, flower-filled meadows surrounding Baker Lake are the reward for a rather long, grim ascent of the Baker Valley.

The Sawback Trail

Mount Norquay to Lake Louise Ski Area—73.1 kilometres (45.4 miles)

Backpack

Allow 4 - 6 days

Maximum elevation: 2345 metres (7,700 feet)

Minimum elevation: 1675 metres (5,500 feet)

Topo maps: Banff 82 O/4

    Castle Mountain 82 O/5

    Lake Louise 82 N/8

Point of Departure: Travelling from south to north, start at the Mount Norquay Ski Area (see *Mystic Lake* description). Travelling from north to south, start at the Lake Louise Ski Area (see *Boulder Pass—Skoki Valley* description).

0.0—Mount Norquay Ski Area (1705 m).

4.0—Forty Mile Creek (1615 m).

8.2—Campground.

15.9—Junction and campground. Forty Mile Summit-Badger Pass option straight ahead. Mystic Pass to left.

18.6—Campground.

19.1—Mystic Lake (2010 m).

22.7—Mystic Pass (2285 m).

29.3—Junction (1675 m). Intersection with *Johnston Creek—Pulsatilla Pass* trail at Km 7.4.

37.8—Luellen Lake (1965 m). Campground.

43.3—Junction. Forty Mile Summit-Badger Pass option intersects from right.

43.8—Campground.

47.2—Pulsatilla Pass (2345 m).

53.6—Junction (1830 m). Campground.

58.9—Junction. Keep left for Baker Lake.

59.6—Campground.

59.9—Baker Lake (2210 m).

61.2—Junction. Intersection with *Boulder Lake— Skoki Valley* trail at Km 10.5.

64.5—Boulder Pass (2345 m).

66.0—Halfway Hut. Campground.

69.2—Temple Lodge.

73.1—Fish Creek Parking Lot (1675 m).

The Sawback Trail is a name we have given to an extended backpack which runs from Banff to Lake Louise through the jagged limestone peaks of the Sawback Range and over three 2300 metre-high passes. This route utilizes all or part of previously described trails—Mystic Lake, Pulsatilla Pass, Baker Creek, Boulder Pass—to create an exceptional wilderness trip of some four to five days duration. In recent years it has become one of the most popular backpacking trips in Banff Park.

Most hikers seem to prefer to start this trip from Banff since there is a steady improvement in scenery travelling toward Lake Louise. The journey starts from the Mount Norquay Ski Area and follows the Mystic Lake trail up the Forty Mile Valley to Mystic Pass. The first night's camp is usually pitched at one of the Forty Mile Creek campgrounds or at the Kilometre 18.6 campsite near Mystic Lake.

From Mystic Pass the trail drops down into the Johnston Creek valley where it links up with the Pulsatilla Pass trail. Campgrounds located at Luellen Lake and the open meadows near the Badger Pass junction are excellent sites for the second or third night on this trek.

Climbing from the subalpine meadows at the head of Johnston Creek, the trail crosses the scenic alpine notch of Pulsatilla Pass and plunges down Wildflower Creek to intersect with the Baker Creek trail.

From Baker Lake you have a number of options: Complete the trek by strolling out over Boulder Pass to the Lake Louise Ski Area; make a detour to the Skoki Valley area for a day or two of pleasant wandering; or, if you are a strong, experienced wilderness traveller, extend the journey by continuing north from Skoki to Pipestone Pass and eventually emerge on the Icefields Parkway via Dolomite Pass or the David Thompson Highway via the Siffleur River.

Lake Louise — Moraine Lake

There are few day hiking areas in all of North America comparable to the Lake Louise—Moraine Lake region. Compressed within 100 square kilometres are seven major hikes and a variety of spur options—a total of over 70 kilometres of trail that wend their way through some of the most rugged alpine scenery on the continent.

The Lake Louise-Moraine Lake environs were the birthplace of recreational hiking in the Canadian Rockies. Shortly after the completion of the Canadian Pacific Railway in 1885, tourists began making their way to the area. One of the first high trails cut in the region was to Lake Agnes—named in honour of an early visitor, Susan Agnes, wife of Prime Minister John A. Macdonald, who travelled through the Rockies with her husband in 1886. A small chalet was constructed on the shore of Lake Louise in 1890 by the CPR, and its manager, Willoughby Astley, directed the clearing of many of the early trails in the immediate vicinity of the lake.

In 1893, a pair of young adventurers from the eastern United States, Walter Wilcox and Samuel Allen, began a systematic exploration of the region. The following summer, accompanied by three of their Yale University classmates, they discovered and explored Paradise Valley, the Valley of the Ten Peaks and Consolation Valley. They also made first ascents of many of the surrounding peaks including Mount Temple.

As the adjoining valleys and scenic wonders were discovered, CPR employees constructed trails from the chalet at Lake Louise, providing access for less adventuresome travellers. The trails became increasingly popular, and teahouses and shelters were built at strategic locations. Hotel staff, in fact, maintained much of the trail system through the middle of the twentieth century.

Today these trails are the most heavily used in the Canadian Rockies. On a warm, sunny day hikers are in continual contact with like-minded souls—just a few of the 50,000 plus who use the trails every summer. Still, these trips are some of the most spectacular to be found, and in the autumn, when the crowds have thinned somewhat, the Lake Louise-Moraine Lake area is as fine a place to be as any in the mountains.

The trails to Lake Agnes, Plain of the Six Glaciers and Saddleback all start from the lakeshore in front of the Chateau Lake Louise. A 5.5 kilometre long access road leads from the Trans-Canada Highway, through the Lake Louise service centre, and up along the west slope of the Bow Valley to Lake Louise. Parking is provided in one of several lots just south of the Chateau, and it is a short walk through the forest via connecting walkways to the lakeshore.

Moraine Lake serves as the departure point for hikes to Consolation Lakes, Eiffel Lake-Wenkchemna Pass and Larch Valley-Sentinel Pass. The Moraine Lake Road branches south from the Lake Louise access road 3 kilometres beyond the Lake Louise service centre. The road contours south along the west side of the Bow Valley and into the Valley of the Ten Peaks to reach the parking area at Moraine Lake in just over 12 kilometres. The trail head parking area for the Paradise Valley hike is situated on the right-hand side of the Moraine Lake Road at Kilometre 3.5.

Located on the floor of the Bow Valley below Lake Louise, the Lake Louise service centre is a small village that serves as the base of operations for most of the area's visitors. A large campground is located just over a kilometre south of the service centre proper. Gas stations, a grocery store, park information bureau, warden office and RCMP station are located on the main thoroughfare. Several hotels with restaurants are situated nearby.

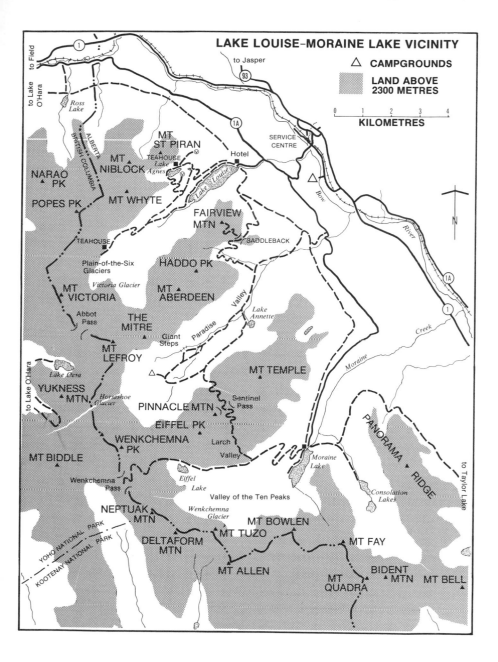

LAKE LOUISE–MORAINE LAKE VICINITY

△ CAMPGROUNDS

LAND ABOVE 2300 METRES

0 1 2 3 4
KILOMETRES

to Field

to Jasper

(1)

(93)

(1A)

to Lake O'Hara

Ross Lake

ALBERTA
BRITISH COLUMBIA

MT ST PIRAN

SERVICE CENTRE

TEAHOUSE *Lake Agnes*

Hotel

MT NIBLOCK

NARAO PK

Lake Louise

Bow

POPES PK

MT WHYTE

N

FAIRVIEW MTN

SADDLEBACK

TEAHOUSE

River

HADDO PK

Plain-of-the-Six Glaciers

Victoria Glacier

MT VICTORIA

MT ABERDEEN

Lake Annette

Valley

(1A)

Abbot Pass

THE MITRE

Paradise

Giant Steps

(1)

MT LEFROY

Creek

to Lake O'Hara

Lake Oesa

MT TEMPLE

Moraine

YUKNESS MTN

Horseshoe Glacier

PINNACLE MTN

Sentinel Pass

EIFFEL PK

PANORAMA RIDGE

MT BIDDLE

WENKCHEMNA PK

Larch Valley

Moraine Lake

to Taylor Lake

Wenkchemna Pass

Eiffel Lake

Valley of the Ten Peaks

Consolation Lakes

NEPTUAK MTN

Wenkchemna Glacier

MT BOWLEN

YOHO NATIONAL PARK

DELTAFORM MTN

MT TUZO

MT FAY

KOOTENAY NATIONAL PARK

MT ALLEN

BIDENT MTN

MT BELL

MT QUADRA

Lake Agnes

Lake Louise to Lake Agnes—3.4 kilometres (2.1 miles)
Lake Louise to Big Beehive—5.0 kilometres (3.1 miles)

Day trip

Allow 1 - 2 hours to Lake Agnes

Elevation gain: 400 metres (1,300 feet)

Maximum elevation: 2135 metres (7,000 feet)

Topo maps: Lake Louise 82 N/8

Point of Departure: Follow the 5½ kilometre (3½ mile) access road that leads up from the Trans-Canada Highway to Lake Louise. A large, multi-level parking area is located on the left hand side of Louise Creek 200 metres from the Chateau Lake Louise. Walk to the lakeshore in front of the Chateau and continue around to the north shore where the trail begins.

0.0—Trail sign and junction (1735 m). Lake Agnes uphill to right.

—Steady uphill climb.

1.6—Switchback and viewpoint.

2.4—Junction with horse trail.

2.6—Mirror Lake and junction (2025 m). Left hand branch contours along south slope of Big Beehive to Plain-of-the-Six Glaciers. Keep right for Lake Agnes.

—Trail continues to switchback upwards.

3.1—Junction. Shortcut trail to Little Beehive and Mount St. Piran branches uphill to right. Lake Agnes straight ahead.

3.4—Lake Agnes, teahouse, junction (2135 m). Trail to Little Beehive (1.0 km) branches uphill immediately above teahouse. Stay on lakeshore trail for Big Beehive.

4.2—West (inlet) end of Lake Agnes.

—Steep switchbacking ascent.

4.7—Summit ridge of Big Beehive and junction. Straight ahead and downhill for Plain-of-the-Six Glaciers highline trail. Keep left along ridge to Big Beehive Lookout.

5.0—Big Beehive Lookout (2255 m).

Hidden in a small cirque above Lake Louise, Lake Agnes has long been the most hiked-to area in the mountain parks. In addition to its own charms, the lake and its adjacent "Beehives" provide breathtaking views of Lake Louise and the Bow Valley.

The first half hour of ascent from the hotel is through a dense subalpine forest of Engelmann spruce and alpine fir, and not until the 1.6 kilometre mark does a break in the trees allow a clear view down to the pale, glacier-fed waters of Lake Louise.

At Kilometre 2.6 the hiker emerges at Mirror Lake—a small body of water that receives its name from its round looking-glass appearance. Above loom the dark cliffs of the Big Beehive, and in the gap to the right, the roof of the Lake Agnes Teahouse is visible—still a steep 800 metres away.

Arriving at the narrow opening where Lake Agnes tumbles from its basin, the entire length of the lake can be seen stretching westward to the foot of Mounts Whyte (2983 m) and Niblock (2976 m). The lake, contained on the south by the long flank of the Big Beehive, is often ice-covered into mid-June.

The area surrounding Lake Agnes abounds in the wildlife and flora of the upper subalpine forest zone. Garbage-debauched chipmunks, ground squirrels, nutcrackers and whiskey jacks beg crumbs from hikers on the teahouse porch, while hoary marmots and pikas whistle and cheep from the rocky slopes above. One early hiker who visited the lake before the turn of the century, quickly retreated to Lake Louise when he heard the shrill whistle of a marmot "which he thought must be the signal of robbers or Indians about to commence an attack."

Big Beehive. The most popular viewpoint above Lake Agnes is the Big Beehive. The trail to this high lookout con-

tinues around the far end of the lake, climbs a short, steep incline, then traverses eastward along the summit ridge to the viewpoint gazebo. A vista across the Bow Valley and the sight of Lake Louise over 500 vertical metres beneath your feet are the rewards for the effort.

Little Beehive—Mount St. Piran. Though not quite so high as the Big Beehive, the Little Beehive is just as scenic. The one kilometre-long trail leaves from behind the teahouse and climbs to the northeast along a partially forested ridge to an old fire lookout cabin overlooking the Bow Valley. The views are quite impressive and include a panorama of the Bow Valley from near its headwaters to the north to the mountains surrounding Banff to the south.

Just over halfway to the Little Beehive lookout from the teahouse, a branch trail cuts left toward Mount St. Piran. For strong hikers who would like to escape the crowds on the more popular routes and who don't mind a good stiff climb, this is an excellent option. The trail runs across a small, subalpine basin, then switchbacks up steep, open slopes to the summit of Mount St. Piran. At 2650 metres above sea level, the peak is nearly as lofty as nearby Fairview Mountain, but not nearly so heavily visited. The views are an improvement on everything visible from the Beehives with the addition of the glacier-clad summit of Mount Lefroy looming above the Devil's Thumb to the south.

Plain-of-the-Six Glaciers Option. Strong hikers who wish a full day of activity can include the Plain-of-the-Six Glaciers in their itinerary after visiting Lake Agnes and the Big Beehive. From the Big Beehive viewpoint, return to the saddle between that peak and the Devil's Thumb. Follow the trail that descends steeply to the south. Not far below you will reach the highline trail running upvalley from Mirror Lake. Turn right and eventually intersect the Plain-of-the-Six Glaciers trail at Kilometre 3.2. (See *Plain-of-the-Six Glaciers* trail.)

89

Plain of the Six Glaciers

Lake Louise to Plain of the Six Glaciers Teahouse—5.3 kilometres (3.3 miles)

Day trip

Allow 1½ - 2 hours one way

Elevation gain: 365 metres (1,200 feet)

Maximum elevation: 2100 metres (6,900 feet)

Topo maps: Lake Louise 82 N/8

Point of Departure: Follow the 5½ kilometre (3½ mile) access road that leads up from the Trans-Canada Highway to Lake Louise. A large, multi-level parking area is located on the left hand side of Louise Creek 200 metres from the Chateau Lake Louise. Walk to the lakeshore in front of the Chateau and continue around to the north shore where the trail begins.

0.0—Trail sign and junction (1735 m). Keep left on lakeshore trail for Plain-of-the-Six Glaciers.

1.9—West (inlet) end of Lake Louise.

2.4—Uphill grades begin.

3.2—Junction. Big Beehive—Mirror Lake highline trail intersects from right.

—Grades become steep through glacial moraine.

5.3—Teahouse (2100 m).

The Plain-of-the-Six Glaciers trail, rising from Lake Louise to a spectacular viewpoint at the base of Mount Victoria, passes through some of the most interesting glaciated scenery in Banff Park. Unfortunately for those seeking solitude, it is also one of the park's busiest trails.

Starting from the trail sign just west of the Chateau, the hiker spends the first 30 minutes walking along the shore of Lake Louise. Away from the crowds and confusion surrounding the hotel, he might better appreciate the description given the lake by the British mountaineer James Outram shortly after the turn of the century: "At every season, every hour, it is wonderful.... As a gem of composition and of colouring it is perhaps unrivalled anywhere."

At the lakehead, a trail-side cliff exposes the Lower Cambrian quartz sandstone which comprises the lower reaches of the surrounding mountains. A short distance beyond, the trail begins to climb, entering a forest arm of spruce and alpine fir.

At Kilometre 3.9 the trail enters into the wasteland produced by the advance and retreat of the Victoria Glacier. All around, beyond and below, ridges of rock and gravel bear mute testimony to the forces that have passed this way. Farther on the trail passes along the top of a morainal ridge, where views improve toward Mount Victoria, Mount Lefroy, the Lefroy Glacier and The Mitre.

The Plain-of-the-Six Glaciers Teahouse, surrounded by a stunted forest typical of the altitude, is an ideal resting spot where lunch and refreshments can be purchased during the summer months. In a boulder field just beyond the teahouse the hiker should watch for the whistling marmots and pikas that make their home in these rough surroundings.

From the teahouse the trail soon leaves the last trees behind, emerging onto the narrow ridge of a lateral moraine. This steep ridge of debris was formed over

The Mitre from Plain of the Six Glaciers trail

many centuries as the Victoria Glacier retreated into the valley. (The last 300 metres of trail along this ridge are very exposed and precarious.)

Mount Victoria (3464 m) and Mount Lefroy (3441 m) dominate the scene from the viewpoint. The gap between Victoria and Lefroy is Abbot's Pass (2922 m), named for Philip Stanley Abbot who died climbing Mount Lefroy in 1896—the first alpinist to perish in the Rockies. Looking closely at the skyline of the pass it is possible to see the alpine hut—a rather substantial stone structure constructed by Swiss guides in the early 1920s.

Big Beehive — Lake Agnes Option. Strong hikers desiring a full day outing can take the highline route back to Lake Louise, keeping left at the junction 1.4 kilometres below the teahouse. By turning left at the next junction on the highline route, you can climb over the crest of the Big Beehive and descend past Lake Agnes and Mirror Lake on the other side. This option adds approximately five kilometres to the normal 13 kilometre round trip to the Plain-of-the-Six Glaciers viewpoint and includes a very strenuous climb to the 2268 metre elevation of the Big Beehive. Views, however, are spectacular indeed. (See *Lake Agnes* trail description.)

Saddleback

Lake Louise to Saddleback—3.7 kilometres (2.3 miles)

Day trip

Allow 1 - 2 hours to Saddleback

Elevation gain: 595 metres (1,950 feet)

Maximum elevation: 2330 metres (7,650 feet)

Topo maps: Lake Louise 82 N/8

Point of Departure: Follow the 5½ kilometre (3½ mile) access road that leads up from the Trans-Canada Highway to Lake Louise. A large, multi-level parking area is located on the left hand side of Louise Creek 200 metres from the Chateau Lake Louise. The trail starts immediately behind the boathouse at the southeast corner of the lake.

0.0—Trail sign (1735 m).

0.3—Junction. Spur trail to Fairview Lookout cuts right. Keep left.

0.4—Junction. Moraine Lake trail branches to left. Keep right.

1.1—Avalanche slope.

—Steady uphill at moderate to steep grades.

3.7—Saddleback (2330 m). Trail to Fairview Mtn. branches right. Sheol Valley straight ahead.

—Trail descends steeply into Sheol Valley.

7.9—Junction (1830 m). Intersection with *Paradise Valley* trail at Km 4.2.

"To see Mount Temple in its noblest grandeur I would take you to the Sadddleback. This is a broad green alp, nearly 2000 feet above Lake Louise, a very favourite hour's ascent by trail, between Mount Fairview and the projecting 'horn' of the Saddle Peak. Crossing the plateau to the tree-fringed brink of the abyss beyond, our gaze is carried straight across the chasm, 1500 feet in depth, to the huge peak . . ."

James Outram, British mountaineer and explorer, wrote those words over 80 years ago, providing an apt description of the 3.7 kilometre hike from the shore of Lake Louise to this beautiful little pass set among the larches. But for many hikers, the lure of Saddleback is its proximity to one of the region's most accessible peaks and breathtaking viewpoints—Fairview Mountain.

In its early stages the trail travels steadily upward at a moderate to steep incline, passing through a closed forest of spruce and alpine fir. Beneath the steep slopes of Fairview Mountain, the route traverses the first of many avalanche paths which serve as excellent viewpoints for the Bow Valley. Openings continue and views improve with elevation, finally culminating beneath the Saddle with an exceptional panorama down the Bow Valley to the mountains near Banff.

As Outram noted, the summit of the Saddleback is a pleasant upland meadow, fringed by stands of alpine larch and, in early summer, covered with buttercups, western anemone, alpine speedwell and many other wildflowers. The broad peak of Mount Temple (3544 m) dominates the view from the summit of the pass, displaying its awesome 1200 metre north wall topped by a cap of ice and corniced snow.

Saddleback is actually a pass situated between two peaks—Fairview Mountain on the northwest and Saddle Mountain to the southeast. Both are easily ascended by strong hikers from the pass. At an elevation of 2745 metres above sea level,

Mount Temple from Fairview Mountain

the summit of Fairview offers the better views—a true alpine experience with the glacier-clad summits of Mount Victoria, Mount Temple and Sheol Mountain close at hand and the blue-green waters of Lake Louise over a vertical kilometre below. While one may scramble straight up to the summit (skirting steep snowbanks early in the year), a discernible trail switchbacks up the southeast slopes of the peak, leading off from the upper margin of alpine larch trees just above the Saddle's crest. Scratched into the rocky slope by early CPR trail builders, it probably qualifies as the Canadian Rockies' highest trail.

Sheol Valley Option. For hikers desiring a full day trip, an interesting extension of the Saddleback trail can be made by continuing down into the Sheol Valley. Lying directly beneath the brooding cliffs of Sheol Mountain, the valley was named in 1894 by the mountaineer S. E. S. Allen, who fancied its resemblance to the "abode of the dead" in Hebrew mythology. Despite its gruesome name, the valley contains many pleasant glades which abound in wildflowers during July and August. The trail finally emerges in Paradise Valley. From there the hiker may swing back around Saddle Mountain to Lake Louise via the Paradise Valley and Moraine Lake trails. Total distance for the loop trip is 14.9 kilometres.

Paradise Valley

Moraine Lake Road to Lake Annette—5.7 kilometres (3.5 miles)

Paradise Valley Circuit—18.1 kilometres (11.2 miles)

Day trip or backpack

Allow 2 hours to Lake Annette

    3 hours to Upper Meadows Campground

Elevation gain: 385 metres (1,250 feet)

Maximum elevation: 2105 metres (6,900 feet)

Topo maps: Lake Louise 82 N/8

Point of Departure: Follow the access road that leads up from the Trans-Canada Highway to Lake Louise. At the 3½ kilometre (2 mile) mark on this road, the Moraine Lake Road branches to the left. Follow the Moraine Lake Road for 2½ kilometres (1½ miles) to the parking area for the Paradise Valley trail, located in the forest on the right hand side of the road.

0.0—Parking area (1720 m).

1.1—Junction. Turn right.

1.3—Junction. Lake Louise straight ahead 4.0 km. Turn left.

4.2—Junction. Sheol Valley—Saddleback to right. Keep straight ahead.

5.1—Junction. Giant Steps and campsite via valley trail straight ahead. Turn left for Lake Annette and highline route.

—Trail crosses bridge over Paradise Creek, begins ascent to Lake Annette.

5.7—Lake Annette (1965 m).

—Trail follows west along lakeshore, then climbs into forest.

6.5—Summit of highline route along rockslide (2105 m).

8.8—Junction. Sentinel Pass uphill to left (2.3 kms). Keep straight ahead for campsite and Giant Steps.

9.4—Junction (2090 m). Campground to left 0.3 km. Giant Steps to right.

9.6—Junction. Upper branch to Giant Steps, left 0.9 km to falls.

9.9—Junction. Lower branch to Giant Steps, left 0.8 km to falls.

13.0—Upper valley loop intersects back at Lake Annette Jct.

18.1—Trail head parking area (1720 m).

When the mountaineer Walter Wilcox and his companions climbed to the summit of Mitre Pass in 1894, they looked into "a valley of surpassing beauty, wide and beautiful, with alternating open meadows and rich forests." They immediately named it Paradise Valley.

Today a trail ascends the valley from the Moraine Lake Road, branching halfway up to create a loop which passes by the shores of Lake Annette on its left arm or the terraced falls of the Giant Steps on its right. Both arms of this upper valley loop meet just below the Horseshoe Glacier headwall in an exquisite open meadow.

The first three kilometres of travel are rather uneventful as the trail is mainly enclosed within a forest of spruce and alpine fir, but at the first bridge across Paradise Creek views begin to open to Mount Temple and the valley headwall.

The trail to Lake Annette branches left from the main valley trail at the five kilometre mark. If you stay right on the main trail, you will continue up along Paradise Creek to the Giant Steps and Horseshoe Meadow in a straightforward if somewhat uneventful manner. However, the Lake Annette option is higher and a lot more scenic, and the distance to the head of the valley is virtually the same.

The British mountaineer James Outram called Lake Annette "a tiny bit of sky dropped from the heavens and almost lost in the depths of the sombre firs." The lake was named for Mrs. Annette Astley, the wife of the first manager of the Lake Louise Chalet. In its immediate surroundings, Annette is rather typical of many subalpine lakes, but its backdrop, the ice-capped 1200 metre north face of Mount Temple, is certainly extraordinary. It is by far the most impressive view of Banff's third highest mountain. Long considered one of the most difficult faces to climb in the Canadian Rockies, the rugged wall

Paradise Valley

was first ascended in 1966.

For those continuing beyond Lake Annette to the head of the valley, the trail climbs to a major rockslide in just over one kilometre. At nearly 2000 metres above sea level, the slide is the highest and best viewpoint on the trail. (Keep a close watch on the nearby boulders where hoary marmots and pikas are often seen.)

After passing the Sentinel Pass junction at Kilometre 8.8, the highline route descends gradually to the beautiful Horseshoe Meadow. In the meadow the highline route is reunited with the main valley trail. Though this meadow is as far as you can go by trail, rock scramblers can continue overland to the Horseshoe Glacier or due south to lofty Wastach Pass. Overnighters will find the only campground in the valley just inside the open forest at the northwest corner of the meadow (a 300 metre-long branch trail leads there from the meadow's double-bridged stream crossing).

The Giant Steps—a pretty series of waterfalls on the north fork of Paradise Creek—are another highlight of the valley. A large number of shortcut trails and intersecting branches makes travel in the Giant Steps area somewhat confusing. Coming back downvalley from Horseshoe Meadow simply keep left on the most obvious trail until you reach the falls. From the bottom of the falls you can follow through a meadow on a rough, boggy hiker's trail for 600 metres and intersect back in with the main valley trail at the 10.8 kilometre bridge. Coming up the main valley trail the side trip to the Giant Steps is more obvious, marked by a signed junction just below the Horseshoe Meadow.

Sentinel Pass Option. An excellent day trip can be completed from Paradise Valley by climbing the steep Sentinel Pass trail from its junction with the highline route. You can either hike to the pass and back from the Horseshoe Meadows campground or continue on through to Moraine Lake. (See *Larch Valley—Sentinel Pass* trail description.)

95

Larch Valley—Sentinel Pass

Moraine Lake to Larch Valley—2.4 kilometres (1.5 miles)
Moraine Lake to Sentinel Pass—5.8 kilometres (3.5 miles)

Day trip

Allow 3 hours to Sentinel Pass

Elevation gain: 720 metres (2,360 feet)

Maximum elevation: 2605 metres (8,550 feet)

Topo maps: Lake Louise 82 N/8

Point of Departure: Follow the access road that leads up from the Trans-Canada Highway to Lake Louise. At the 3½ kilometre (2 mile) mark on this road, the Moraine Lake Road branches to the left. Follow the Moraine Lake Road 12½ kilometres (7½ miles) to its termination at the Moraine Lake parking area. From the parking area, walk down to the lakeshore and continue past the lodge to the trail sign.

0.0—Trail sign (1885 m). Larch Valley—Sentinel Pass trail branches up to right from lakeshore trail.

1.1—Switchbacks begin.

—Steady uphill climb.

2.4—Junction. Eiffel Lake—Wenkchemna Pass straight ahead. Turn right for Larch Valley—Sentinel Pass.

—Trail climbs into open meadows of Larch Valley.

4.7—Switchbacks up steep talus slope.

5.8—Sentinel Pass (2605 m).

—Trail descends north side of pass sharply into Paradise Valley.

8.1—Junction (2100 m). Intersection with *Paradise Valley* trail at Km 8.8.

Larch Valley is one of the most heavily visited areas in the mountain parks during the summer and on weekends in the fall. And no wonder. This meadowland above Moraine Lake, with its thick stands of alpine larch and panoramic backdrop of the Ten Peaks, is exquisite. And beyond the valley, amid stark pinnacles of rock, stands lofty Sentinel Pass—at 2605 metres above sea level, the highest point reached by a major trail in the mountain parks.

From Moraine Lake the trail switchbacks up through a forest of Engelmann spruce and alpine fir, splitting from the Eiffel Lake trail at Kilometre 2.4 and entering the meadows of Larch Valley. This high valley is the main focal point for most hikers who walk this trail. Particularly in autumn, when the needles on the larch have turned to gold, it becomes the most visited area in Banff Park. In midsummer, however, the larch needles are a pale green and the meadows are carpeted with the more showy varieties of wildflowers associated with a snowbed plant community.

As the trail emerges above the last of the trees, there are fine views back to the rugged Wenkchemna Peaks, the ice-draped summit of Mount Fay (3235 m) being the most prominent and striking. The small pools which dot the upper Larch Valley meadows were named the Minnestimma Lakes by the early mountaineer S. E. S. Allen. An Indian word meaning 'sleeping water,' this wonderful name has been all but forgotten by contemporary hikers and map makers.

Ahead, between the vertical walls of Pinnacle Mountain (3607 m) on the left and Mount Temple (3544 m) on the right, is the rugged summit of Sentinel Pass. While still over a kilometre away, the trail begins a switchbacking climb of an open scree slope to the pass—a vertical rise of nearly 200 metres that weeds out many of the Larch Valley hikers.

Located near the axis of a syncline (a

Mount Fay from the Larch Valley meadows

trough or downfold in the strata), the rock formations surrounding Sentinel Pass lie nearly horizontal. Erosion of these layers has created the weird spires immediately north of the summit. The pass receives its name from these towers, and the tallest is known as the Grand Sentinel.

The pass was first ascended, from Paradise Valley, in 1894 by S. E. S. Allen and Yandell Henderson, both members of a group of American mountaineers from Yale University which did much exploration in the region. Mount Temple, the third highest peak in Banff Park, was also climbed the same year by the Yale alpinists—the first ascent of a Canadian peak above 11,000 feet.

Paradise Valley Option. Strong hikers may wish to make a full day outing by continuing over Sentinel Pass and descending into Paradise Valley. The trail drops steeply from the pass (heavy snowdrifts often obscure the track down this rocky gully into July) and connects into the Paradise Valley circuit 2.3 kilometres below. At this junction you can turn right to Lake Annette or left to the head of the valley and the Giant Steps. Both trails join again lower in the valley and follow Paradise Creek to the Moraine Lake Road. Total distance for this option, from Moraine Lake to the Moraine Lake Road at Paradise Creek via Lake Annette, is 16.9 kilometres. It is advisable to arrange transportation for the hike or else be prepared to hitchhike the ten kilometres back to Moraine Lake. (See *Paradise Valley* trail description.)

97

Eiffel Lake—Wenkchemna Pass

Moraine Lake to Eiffel Lake—5.6 kilometres (3.5 miles)

Moraine Lake to Wenkchemna Pass—9.7 kilometres (6.0 miles)

Day trip

Allow 2 - 3 hours to Eiffel Lake

Elevation gain: 720 metres (2,360 feet)

Maximum elevation: 2605 metres (8,550 feet)

Topo maps: Lake Louise 82 N/8

Point of Departure: Follow the access road that leads up from the Trans-Canada Highway to Lake Louise. At the 3½ kilometre (2 mile) mark on this road, the Moraine Lake Road branches to the left. Follow the Moraine Lake Road 12½ kilometres (7½ miles) to its termination at the Moraine Lake parking area. From the parking area, walk down to the lakeshore and continue past the lodge to the trail sign.

0.0—Trail sign (1885 m). Eiffel Lake—Wenkchemna Pass trail branches up to the right from lakeshore trail.

1.1—Switchbacks begin.

—Steady uphill climb.

2.4—Junction. Larch Valley—Sentinel Pass trail branches to right. Stay straight ahead for Eiffel Lake—Wenkchemna Pass.

—Trail levels out contouring open slopes.

5.6—Eiffel Lake (2255 m). Trail runs across talus slope 200 metres above the lake.

—Moderate but steady uphill over alpine tundra and talus slopes.

9.7—Wenkchemna Pass (2605 m).

Exploring above Moraine Lake in 1899, Walter Wilcox and his companions were so impressed by the stark glaciated landscape they named the area Desolation Valley. In its deepest and most desolate heart lies Eiffel Lake.

The Eiffel Lake trail follows the same course as the Larch Valley trail for the first 2.4 kilometres, switchbacking upward through a closed, mature subalpine forest. Splitting near the lower edge of Larch Valley, the Eiffel Lake route continues on alone, emerging onto open slopes that reveal all summits in the Valley of the Ten Peaks as well as the brilliant blue waters of Moraine Lake.

As the trail continues through these flower-filled meadows the Wenkchemna Glacier can be seen stretching down-valley at the foot of the Ten Peaks. Heavy talus deposits from the cliffs above have completely covered most of the glacier's surface, shielding the ice from the sun's rays and accounting in part for the relatively small recession in the past century.

At the 5.6 kilometre mark, the trail passes across a steep scree slope and skirts above the frigid waters of Eiffel Lake. Reflecting upon one of his first visits to the lake, Walter Wilcox wrote: "It would be difficult to find another lake of small size in a wilder setting, the shores being of great angular stones, perfectly in harmony with the wild range of mountains beyond. Except in one place where a green and inviting slope comes down to the water, this rough ground is utterly unsuitable for vegetation and nearly devoid of trees."

The main reason for Eiffel's rugged surroundings is that it was not created as most alpine lakes are. Instead of lying in a basin carved and dammed by the action of glaciers over many centuries, Eiffel is situated in a depression formed by a massive rockslide which broke away from Neptuak Mountain. Large boulders and piles of rock debris which spread across the valley from the base of the mountain

Valley of the Ten Peaks from the Eiffel Lake trail

provide mute testimony to the grand catastrophe which once shook this region.

Immediately above the lake and to the north is Eiffel Peak (3085 m), so named because of a huge rock pinnacle rising near its summit which is suggestive of the Parisian làndmark. Looking at the peak from this angle the hiker can easily see the striking contrast between the light grey limestone composing the summit and the orangish quartz sandstone of the lower cliffs.

A very scenic extension to the hike can be made by continuing on to the summit of Wenkchemna Pass. The trail works its way due west from the lake across rolling alpine tundra, climbing glacial moraine and rockslides, to reach the windswept gap between Wenkchemna Peak and Neptuak Mountain in four more kilometres (much of this last section of trail may be obscured by snowfields before late July). Standing at an elevation of 2605 metres above sea level, this high summit is an excellent viewpoint down the length of the Valley of the Ten Peaks as well as for the Eagle's Eyrie region of Yoho Park and the Prospector's Valley in Kootenay Park. At virtually the same elevation as nearby Sentinel Pass, Wenkchemna is one of the highest points serviced by trail in the Canadian Rockies.

Consolation Lakes

Moraine Lake to Lower Consolation Lake—2.9 kilometres (1.8 miles)

Half-day trip

Allow 1 hour one way

Elevation gain: 65 metres (215 feet)

Maximum elevation: 1950 metres (6,400 feet)

Topo maps: Lake Louise 82 N/8

Point of Departure: Follow the access road that leads up from the Trans-Canada Highway to Lake Louise. At the 3½ kilometre (2 mile) mark on this road, the Moraine Lake Road branches to the left. Follow the Moraine Lake Road 12½ kilometres (7½ miles) to its termination at the Moraine Lake parking area. From the parking area, walk down through the picnic area to the bridge over Moraine Creek just below the lake outlet.

0.0—Trail sign and bridge (1885 m).

—Trail crosses boulder field (stay left at rockslide branch trail junctions), then climbs into forest.

1.6—Junction. Panorama Ridge trail to Taylor Lake branches down to left. Consolation Lakes lie straight ahead.

2.3—Open meadow.

2.9—Lower Consolation Lake (1950 m).

While it is the shortest of the many popular hikes in the Moraine Lake area, the outstanding alpine scenery surrounding the Consolation Lakes makes the trip well worth a half-day of modest effort.

The first 300 metres of trail beyond the Moraine Lake Picnic Area pass over a substantial rockslide which descended from the Tower of Babel to create a natural dam for Moraine Lake. From this region of tumbled rock the trail rises into a pleasant forest of fir and spruce, levelling out along an open meadow just before reaching the lower lake.

Scramble onto one of the many prominent boulders for a relaxed view of the lake and Bident Mountain and Mount Quadra beyond. Back to the north stands Mount Temple (3544 m), the third highest peak in Banff Park and the highest in the Lake Louise—Moraine Lake vicinity.

If you wish to spend a little more time in the area and are well shod, you can visit Upper Consolation Lake. Cross Babel Creek below the outlet of Lower Consolation (on rickety log booms) then follow a rough, wet track which runs along the lake's eastern shore. Climb over a low, narrow ridge of rock debris which separates the two lakes.

Walter Wilcox and Ross Peacock, two American mountaineers, first explored the valley in 1899. Wilcox later wrote: "We are very much pleased with the place, and Ross suggested that, since the other was called Desolation Valley [Valley of the Ten Peaks] we might call this 'Consolation Valley,' a name that seems quite appropriate."

Today the valley offers consolation for those overwhelmed by the hordes of tourists at nearby Moraine Lake. But if you find the trail a bit too worn and overcrowded as well, you may be consoled by the knowledge that hikers have actually lost their way on this straightforward little trip and have had to be "rescued" by the Warden Service.

Bident Mountain and Mount Quadra from Lower Consolation Lake

Boulder Pass—Skoki Valley

Lake Louise Ski Area to Boulder Pass—8.6 kilometres (5.3 miles)
Lake Louise Ski Area to Skoki Lodge—14.4 kilometres (8.9 miles)

Day trip or backpack

Allow 2½ - 4 hours to Boulder Pass
    5 - 6 hours to Skoki Valley

Elevation gain: 770 metres (2,525 feet)

Maximum elevation: 2475 metres (8,120 feet)

Topo maps: Lake Louise 82 N/8
    Hector Lake 82 N/9

Point of Departure: Follow the Trans-Canada Highway to the Lake Louise Ski Area, located on the northeast side of the highway between the Lake Louise east and west exits. Follow the gravel access road which branches right just inside the ski area entrance 2.0 kilometres (1.2 miles) to the right-hand junction with the Temple Lodge Road. Follow the Temple Lodge Road for 1.1 kilometres (0.7 mile) to the Fish Creek parking area just below an access gate.

0.0—Fish Creek parking area (1705 m).

—Follow the Temple Lodge Road.

3.9—Temple Lodge (2010 m).

—Trail ascends open ski slope 200 metres, then crosses into forest.

6.3—Opens into meadow.

7.1—Junction. Turn left for campground (0.1 km) and Hidden Lake (1.3 kms). Halfway Hut hiker's shelter to right (0.1 km). Boulder Pass straight ahead.

—Steady uphill.

8.6—Boulder Pass and junction (2345 m). Trail to Redoubt Lake (1.1 kms) skirts through boulder fields to right. Keep left for Deception Pass.

10.5—Junction. Baker Lake straight ahead (1.3 kms). Keep left for Skoki Valley.

—Steep uphill.

11.0—Deception Pass (2485 m).

—Steady downhill.

13.9—Junction. Red Deer Lakes to right (5.3 kms). Skoki Lodge straight ahead.

14.4—Skoki Lodge (2165 m).

15.6—Campground.

Hidden away behind the Lake Louise Ski Area, the high valleys, passes and lakes of the Slate Range create one of the exceptional hiking areas in Banff Park. And though the trip to Skoki Valley and return is popular as a weekend outing and Boulder Pass is often visited in a long day, one can only begin to explore the more than 200 square kilometres of rugged scenery in this region during an extended visit of several days.

While the initial four kilometres of slogging up the Temple Lodge access road will not bring joy to the hiker's heart, the drudgery of this section is a necessary prerequisite to the sublime countryside beyond. Once the Temple Lodge and ski lift complex is passed, things improve rapidly: the road reverts to trail, albeit wide and often muddy, and the hiker enters a pleasant forest containing Engelmann spruce, alpine fir and the first scattered alpine larch.

Just 2.4 kilometres beyond Temple the trail opens into meadow with views ahead to Boulder Pass and the rugged summits of Mount Richardson (3086 m), Pika Peak (3033 m) and Ptarmigan Peak (3059 m)—the mountains that serve as the apex of the Slate Range. Over 15 kilometres away to the southwest stands glacier-topped Mount Temple (3544 m), the third highest peak in Banff Park. The meadow itself is filled with a wide variety of colourful wildflowers during the summer months and slate-coloured dippers are often seen flying from rock to rock along the creek.

The Halfway Hut is reached a short way into the meadow. A log cabin set on a low bluff above Corral Creek, the hut received its name during the early days of skiing in the Rockies when it served as accommodation for skiers travelling from the Lake Louise railway station to Skoki Lodge. In recent years it has been used as a shelter by hikers.

From Halfway Hut the trail continues

Redoubt Mountain and Ptarmigan Valley from Deception Pass

through relatively open country to the summit of Boulder Pass and the shore of Ptarmigan Lake, an ascending pathway fringed with giant tufts of blue forget-me-nots. Located at 2345 metres above sea level, just above the timberline, the broad tundra-carpeted pass is the home of the hoary marmot, pika, ptarmigan and Columbian ground squirrel.

The trail travels along the slopes above the north shore of Ptarmigan Lake, then cuts up to Deception Pass—named by ski pioneer Cyril Paris for its elusive summit. From the pass, the hiker can look back across the Ptarmigan Valley and beyond Boulder Pass to the jagged summits near Lake Louise.

From Deception Pass the trail drops steadily downward toward the Skoki Valley. Beneath Ptarmigan Peak to the west appear the milky blue waters of the Skoki Lakes—also known as Myosotis and Zigadenus, the genus names for the forget-me-not and the camas lily. Passing through a scattering of alpine larch as it re-enters the timber, the trail eventually

descends into a more defined subalpine forest of spruce and fir as it nears Skoki Lodge.

The name Skoki is supposedly an Indian word meaning "marsh" or "swamp." Like many of the names found in the immediate area, it originates with the first party of mountaineers who visited the valley in 1911, one of the leaders being from the Skokie, Illinois vicinity.

The first lodge in the valley was constructed in 1930 and served as the centre of one of western Canada's first ski resorts. Of course, skiing was of the do-it-yourself variety then—without lifts. In recent years the lodge has experienced a resurgence in popularity with both hikers and cross-country skiers. (Information concerning lodge reservations and rates is available through the ski area office in Lake Louise, or call 403-522-3555.)

Hidden Lake. Lying in a pocket of alpine tundra beneath Mount Richardson and Pika Peak, Hidden Lake is only 1.3 kilometres north of Halfway Hut. The trail cuts away from the Boulder Pass

103

route 100 metres north of the cabin, immediately passes a campground, and ascends through gradually diminishing forest to the lakeshore. The wildflower meadows surrounding the lake are among the finest anywhere in the Rockies.

Redoubt Lake. This easy 1.1 kilometre side-trip starts from the west end of Ptarmigan Lake on the summit of Boulder Pass. The trail is not well-defined, but follow along the south shore of Ptarmigan Lake for 800 metres or so, then cut straight up over open slopes toward the pocket at the foot of Redoubt Mountain. The lake supports a population of cutthroat and brook trout and is one of the highest fishing lakes in Banff Park.

Baker Lake. At a trail junction on the south side of Deception Pass, take the right fork and continue on for 1.3 kilometres to the shore of Baker Lake. There is a campground just east of Baker Lake, and hikers can either continue on around the east side of Fossil Mountain to reach the Red Deer Lakes and campground or turn south to descend the Baker Creek valley (see *Baker Creek* trail description).

Merlin Lake. Set between the exotically-named Wall of Jericho and Merlin's Castle, Merlin Lake is one of the little known gems of the Rockies. The high route to the lake is only 3.1 kilometres long and starts at the footbridge in front of Skoki Lodge. The first kilometre of trail is beautifully designed, constructed by the mountaineer and trail builder Lawrence Grassi. It traverses high onto the side of the Wall of Jericho and then, without ceremony, disappears. Unfortunately Grassi never had an opportunity to complete his work, so the remaining 2.1 kilometres to the lake are for cairn-followers. The route drops to the shore of Castilleja Lake, then climbs to the steep cliff immediately below the Merlin cirque. From here, pick the line of least resistance via the scree chute to the left of the cliff.

A horse trail also traverses the north side of the Merlin Valley, starting from the large, open meadow just below the campground. Total distance from the lodge to the lake via this route is 4.5 kilometres, but the trail is rough in many places. Both routes are for good pathfinders, but the reward is one of the most beautiful lakes in the mountain parks.

Red Deer Lakes. The Red Deer Lakes and campground can be reached over good trail that cuts east from the Skoki Valley trail 500 metres before the lodge. The trail runs between Skoki and Fossil Mountains and emerges to join the trail running north from Baker Creek and Lake. Keep left at all intersections to reach the Red Deer Lakes campground 4.6 kilometres beyond the Skoki Valley junction. The low, swampy Red Deer Lakes are scattered in the forest just beyond.

The most compelling reason to visit the Red Deer Lakes is the opportunity to day hike onto the upper Red Deer River. The Natural Bridge and Douglas Lake are both popular destinations which can be reached in a day from the Red Deer Lakes campground, though fords of the river are required. (See *Red Deer River* trail description.)

Little Pipestone Creek. This valley of forest and meadows can be descended using trails from either the Red Deer Lakes or the Skoki Valley. From the campground below Skoki Lodge, the trail runs north through meadowland and then drops steeply for 800 metres to come abreast of the creek's south fork. At an old trail sign 2.9 kilometres below the campground, cut right away from the trail, ford Little Pipestone Creek, and cross 500 metres of pathless, boggy meadow to intersect the main trail running down from the Red Deer Lakes. From this junction it is possible to turn right to make a loop of Skoki Mountain via the Red Deer Lakes or to turn left and descend to the Pipestone River. The latter is an optional route for backpackers continuing on into the Upper Pipestone Valley (see *Pipestone River* trail description). Total distance from the Skoki Valley campground to Pipestone River is approximately 8.0 kilometres.

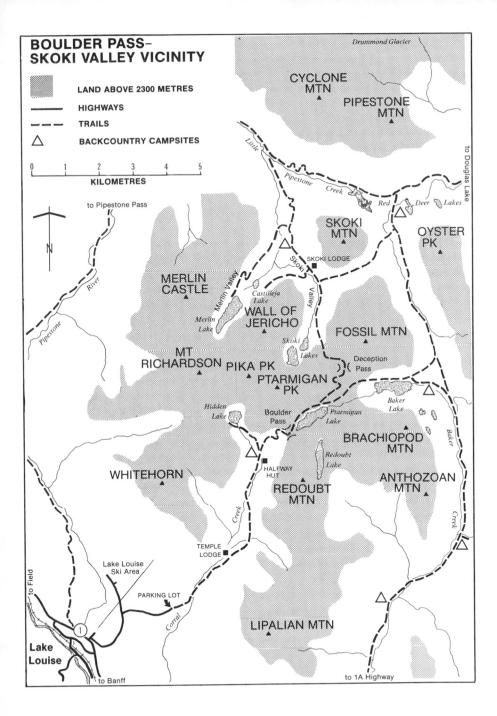

BOULDER PASS–
SKOKI VALLEY VICINITY

LAND ABOVE 2300 METRES

——— HIGHWAYS

– – – TRAILS

△ BACKCOUNTRY CAMPSITES

0 1 2 3 4 5
KILOMETRES

N

to Pipestone Pass

Drummond Glacier

CYCLONE MTN ▲

PIPESTONE MTN ▲

Little *Pipestone* *Creek*

to Douglas Lake

Red *Deer* *Lakes*

SKOKI MTN ▲

OYSTER PK ▲

Skoki SKOKI LODGE ■

MERLIN CASTLE ▲

River

Pipestone

Castilleja Lake

WALL OF JERICHO

Merlin Lake

Merlin Valley

Skoki Lakes

Skoki Valley

FOSSIL MTN ▲

MT RICHARDSON ▲

PIKA PK ▲

PTARMIGAN PK ▲

Deception Pass

Baker Lake

Hidden Lake

Boulder Pass

Ptarmigan Lake

BRACHIOPOD MTN ▲

Baker

△

WHITEHORN ▲

HALFWAY HUT ■

Redoubt Lake

REDOUBT MTN

ANTHOZOAN MTN ▲

△

Creek

Creek

TEMPLE LODGE ■

Lake Louise Ski Area

PARKING LOT →

Corral

①

Lake Louise

△

LIPALIAN MTN ▲

to Field

to Banff

to 1A Highway

105

Red Deer River

Red Deer Lakes to Cascade Fire Road—26.7 kilometres (16.6 miles)

Backpack

Allow 1-2 days one way

Elevation loss: 365 metres (1,200 feet)

Maximum elevation: 2105 metres (6,900 feet)

Topo maps: Hector Lake 82 N/9
　　　　　　Barrier Mountain 82 0/12

Point of Departure: Eastbound travellers can reach the west end of the trail at Red Deer Lakes via the *Boulder Pass-Skoki Valley* trail and the cutoff to the Red Deer Lakes. Westbound back-packers can reach the east end of the trail by hiking the *Cascade Fire Road*, reaching the trail head at Km 58.4, just 200 metres north of the Red Deer River bridge.

0.0—Cyclone Warden Cabin (2105 m).

　　—Gradual to rolling descent along the valley's north side.

1.8—Junction. Natural Bridge to right (2.5 km) via ford of Red Deer River. Keep left.

4.5—Drummond Creek ford (calf-deep).

6.4—Junction. Douglas Lake to right (3.0 km) via ford of Red Deer River. Keep left.

12.2—Red Deer Warden Cabin.

12.6—Tributary creek crossing (on logjam).

14.4—Red Deer River gorge and waterfall.

16.3—Junction. Horseshoe Lake to right (1.0 km) via ford of Red Deer River. Keep left.

20.6—McConnell Creek ford (calf-deep).

25.1—Junction. Divide Creek trail branches uphill to left. Keep right.

25.3—Divide Creek crossing (rock-hop or ankle-deep ford).

　　—Route follows old road bed.

26.7—Cascade Fire Road (1740 m). Trail inter-sects *Cascade Fire Road* at Km 58.4.

The Red Deer Valley is one of the great wilderness valleys in the park, and one of the few untouched by forest fire in over 100 years. Most hikers only know the upper end of the valley, since the Red Deer Lakes and the Natural Bridge are popular day trip destinations from the Skoki Valley. Yet the entire valley offers fine scenery, interesting side trips, and lots of solitude. It also serves as an impor-tant link for extended trips into Banff's northern Front Ranges.

Unlike most of the Front Range val-leys, the Red Deer is quite passable for hikers; the two major fords encountered along the way are seldom a problem (usu-ally below the knees). Most of the side trips—the Natural Bridge, Douglas Lake and Horseshoe Lake — do require cross-ings of the Red Deer River.

From the Cyclone Warden Cabin at the Red Deer Lakes, the trail begins its steady, gradual descent of the valley. At Kilometre 1.8 the trail to the Natural Bridge branches right; a ford of the Red Deer River followed by just over two kilometres of hiking will bring you to a natural arch carved into the strata of a narrow side canyon.

Just two kilometres beyond the Drum-mond Creek ford, the trail runs out onto open flats along the Red Deer River. A signed junction indicates where the trail to Douglas Lake branches south and works its way across the braided river channels to the entrance of the Valley of the Hidden Lakes. The trail reaches Doug-las Lake in approximately three kilome-tres. Beyond the lake there is no trail, but experienced cross country travellers can work their way to the head of this beauti-ful alpine valley which was first explored by Walter Wilcox, A. L. Castle and the guide Fred Stephens in 1921.

The trail continues its descent of the valley as the Red Deer River bends north, running through mature spruce forest and along open meadows. The only other

Drummond Glacier from Red Deer Valley

side trip along the trail occurs at Kilometre 16.3 where a short branch trail to Horseshoe Lake—marked "Skeleton Lake"
on the map—swings east across the river
(this ford is more difficult than those
further upstream, particularly during
periods of high water); the lake has a
good reputation for its trout fishing.

With the exception of a ford of McConnell Creek at Kilometre 20.6, the remainder of the journey to the Cascade
Fire Road is uneventful. From the east
end of the trail the backpacker has the
option of continuing down the Red Deer
Valley on the fire road, turning south
toward Snow Creek Summit, or, from the
junction at Kilometre 25.1, heading north
to the Clearwater Valley via the Divide
Creek-Peters Creek trail.

Fish Lakes

Icefields Parkway to North Molar Pass—11.5 kilometres (7.1 miles)
Icefields Parkway to Upper Fish Lake—14.8 kilometres (9.2 miles)

Day trip or backpack

Allow 5 - 6 hours to Fish Lakes

Elevation gain: 760 metres (2,500 feet)
loss: 365 metres (1,200 feet)

Maximum elevation: 2590 metres (8,500 feet)

Topo maps: Hector Lake 82 N/9

Point of Departure: Follow the Icefields Parkway to the Mosquito Creek Campground, 24 kilometres (15 miles) north of the parkway's junction with the Trans-Canada Highway near Lake Louise. The trail starts directly across the highway from the campground, at the north end of the Mosquito Creek bridge. Parking is available on the west side of the highway, just below the bridge beside the youth hostel entrance road.

0.0—Trail sign (1830 m).

—Gradual uphill with many small side streams.

6.4—Campground.

6.9—Junction. Molar Pass to right 2.9 kms. Keep left for North Molar Pass.

8.0—Trail climbs above trees and levels out into alpine tundra.

8.8—Mosquito Lake.

10.5—Steep climb to North Molar Pass begins.

11.5—North Molar Pass (2590 m).

—Short steep descent levelling out into alpine tundra.

14.8—Upper Fish Lake (2225 m). Campground.

15.7—Lower Fish Lake.

—Rough, steep trail descends slope below lake. Wet and muddy.

17.6—Pipestone River ford.

17.8—Junction (1980 m).

The trail running up Mosquito Creek from the Icefields Parkway leads to one of the most extensive alpine meadowlands in Banff Park. While it is possible to visit the best of these meadows and lofty North Molar Pass and return to the highway in a long day, most hikers prefer to pack-in to the Fish Lakes where it is possible to spend days in exploration. In addition, the trail provides the easiest and most direct route to the Pipestone Pass—Clearwater Pass region.

Through its first seven kilometres, the trail rises gradually through the open, subalpine forest of the Mosquito Creek drainage, then it branches left from the Molar Pass route and climbs onto the alpine meadowlands leading to North Molar Pass. Travel through the Mosquito Creek valley and the higher alplands is usually wet and boggy throughout the summer, and crossing some of the small tributary streams can be troublesome (every stream of note is bridged, but expect wet boots anyway).

The alpine meadows below North Molar Pass are exceptionally beautiful—a wildflower garden dominated by the showy purple blooms of fleabane throughout late July and early August. Sharp fingers of rock and steep talus slopes form a huge amphitheatre enclosing this treeless terrain, while back to the west the glacier-clad ramparts of Mount Hector create a spectacular backdrop for tiny Mosquito Lake.

Beyond the ten kilometre mark, the gentle meadows are left behind and the stiff climb to North Molar Pass commences. Views westward from the summit of this narrow notch are extensive, stretching to the mountains of the Bow Valley and beyond. (The pass is one of the highest traversed by a trail in Banff Park, and the prevailing westerlies create a snowdrift on the east side of the summit which usually blocks the route until late July.)

Upper Fish Lake

The drop to Upper Fish Lake from the pass is quick and steep, the trail descending through a more constricted and rolling alpine landscape enclosed by vertical walls and rockslide debris. The lake can be seen long before it is reached, cradled in a pretty basin amid open stands of Engelmann spruce and alpine fir. At the 14.8 kilometre mark, the trail finally reaches the lake's open shoreline and campground—a peaceful spot but for the continual cascade of rock falling from rotten cliffs on the opposite shore.

The Upper Fish Lake campground is an excellent base for wandering and exploration. Lower Fish is only a kilometre away—a much smaller body of water fringed by what is possibly the most northerly stand of alpine larch in North America. By contouring south from the lower lake along the slope of Molar Mountain it is possible to reach another small lake in approximately two kilometres of trail-less hiking. Nearly three kilometres of open meadow-walking to the north is Moose Lake which, like the Fish Lakes, is noted for its cutthroat trout fishing.

Pipestone Pass. One of the most popular destinations beyond the Fish Lakes is the Pipestone Pass region. It can be reached as a day trip from the Fish Lakes campground or, more commonly, as an extension of your backpacking trip. From Lower Fish Lake a steep, muddy trail descends to the Pipestone River in just two kilometres, where you must ford the river to reach the Pipestone Valley trail on the opposite side. From this junction it is just over eight kilometres to the summit of Pipestone Pass. (See *Pipestone Pass* trail description.)

Experienced backpackers capable of navigating moderately difficult fords can make a 75 kilometre circuit back to the Icefields Parkway via Pipestone and Dolomite Passes from the Fish Lakes. The itinerary for this five-to-seven day trip includes the traverse of Pipestone Pass, a side-trip to Clearwater Pass, the descent of the Siffleur River to its confluence with Dolomite Creek, and the ascent of Dolomite Creek to Dolomite Pass. (See *Pipestone Pass, Siffleur River, Dolomite Creek,* and *Dolomite Pass* trail descriptions.)

109

Molar Pass

Icefields Parkway to Molar Pass—9.8 kilometres (6.1 miles)

Day trip or backpack

Allow 3 - 4 hours to Molar Pass

Elevation gain: 535 metres (1,750 feet)

Maximum elevation: 2365 metres (7,750 feet)

Topo maps: Hector Lake 82 N/9

Point of Departure: Follow the Icefields Parkway to the Mosquito Creek Campground, 24 kilometres (15 miles) north of the parkway's junction with the Trans-Canada Highway near Lake Louise. The trail starts directly across the highway from the campground at the north end of the Mosquito Creek bridge. Parking is available on the west side of the highway, just below the bridge beside the youth hostel entrance road.

0.0—Trail sign (1830 m).

—Gradual uphill with many small side streams..

6.4—Campground.

6.9—Junction. North Molar Pass—Fish Lakes trail cuts up to left. Keep right for Molar Pass.

9.4—Steep climb up scree slope to pass.

9.8—Molar Pass (2365 m).

—Open, flat alpine for next km.

12.7—Trail begins steep descent into Molar Creek valley.

—Wet, boggy trail conditions begin.

14.2—Creek crossing (rock hop).

16.7—Re-enter forest.

17.0—Numerous stream crossings.

18.9—Trail indistinct and very wet as it crosses and recrosses stream channels.

20.0—Campsite.

22.6—Trail climbs forested ridge away from Molar Creek.

24.2—Junction (1815 m). Intersection with *Pipestone River* trail at Km 18.0.

Molar Pass is an optional destination for those hiking the Mosquito Creek valley. While backpackers usually prefer to branch east over North Molar Pass to the Fish Lakes, day hikers will find the summit of Molar Pass more accessible and just as scenic. Beyond the pass, the trail continues down the Molar Creek valley to provide backpackers with an optional, if somewhat lacklustre, route to the Pipestone River trail.

After following the trail up Mosquito Creek for 6.9 kilometres, the route to Molar Pass branches right from the more heavily travelled North Molar Pass option (this junction has been poorly marked in the past and the trail toward Molar is faint in its early stages). In another three kilometres the trail climbs out of the trees and onto the crest of the pass.

The alpine meadows on Molar Pass are just as impressive if not as extensive as those beneath North Molar. The pass also offers a much better view of Molar Mountain (3022 m) and the glaciated summits leading southward to the main peak of Mount Hector.

On your way back from Molar, you can visit Mosquito Lake and the meadows beneath North Molar Pass by hiking up that branch for three kilometres or so; this would make a rather strenuous day trip totalling some 25 kilometres. Setting up a base camp at the 6.4 kilometre campground and day tripping the two passes from there would be a far more relaxing option. (See *North Molar Pass-Fish Lakes* trail description.)

Molar Creek. Running southeast from the summit of Molar Pass, the Molar Creek trail continues for another 15 kilometres to the Pipestone River trail. From that junction you can either ford the Pipestone and ascend Little Pipestone Creek to Skoki Valley or turn left toward Pipestone Pass. Be forewarned, however, that the trail down Molar Creek is rough, very wet, and has been a disappointment to most people who have tried it.

Pipestone River

Backpack

Allow 2-3 days to Pipestone Pass

Elevation gain: 915 metres (3,000 feet)

Maximum elevation: 2470 metres (8,100 feet)

Topo maps: Lake Louise 82 N/8
          Hector Lake 82 N/9

Point of Departure: Follow the Trans-Canada Highway to the Lake Louise Service Centre west exit, located 56½ kilometres (35 miles) west of Banff townsite and 1.5 kilometres (0.9 mile) east of the Icefields Parkway junction. Instead of turning south into the service centre, turn north onto the access road leading to the area's residential district. Keep right at the road split 100 metres from the junction and drive another 200 metres to the trail sign and parking area situated on opposite sides of the road.

0.0—Trail sign (1555 m).

—Trail climbs over forested ridge.

0.8—Junction. Mud Lake to right (0.5 km). Pipestone River straight ahead.

3.0—Trail descends to west bank of Pipestone River.

—Level to rolling trail along river.

14.5—Pipestone River ford. Major crossing to east bank.

17.5—Little Pipestone River ford.

18.0—Little Pipestone Warden Cabin (1815 m). Junction. Red Deer Lakes and Skoki Valley to right. Pipestone River trail fords river to west bank.

18.1—Junction. Molar Pass trail branches left. Keep right for Pipestone Pass.

—Gradual ascent through meadows and forest.

27.0—Singing Meadows campsite and ford to river's east bank.

28.0—Junction (1980 m). Intersection with the *Pipestone Pass* trail at Km 17.8.

36.2—Pipestone Summit (2470 m).

*all distances approximate

For backpackers the trail up the lower Pipestone Valley from Lake Louise is of limited interest. This section of the valley is a long, flat trudge over heavily used horse trail, and a serious ford of the Pipestone River near Kilometre 14.5 makes all of this tedium rather silly. The best way to get to the best scenery in the upper half of the valley is to join the trail farther up via either the North Molar Pass, Molar Pass, or Skoki Valley trails.

The trail head for the Pipestone is situated on the north side of the Trans-Canada Highway approximately one kilometre west of the Lake Louise Ski Area entrance. The trail climbs over a low forested ridge and then descends to join the Pipestone River at Kilometre 3.0. From there it is flat, straightforward walking upvalley over well constructed horse trail. Approximately 14.5 kilometres from the trail head, the track swings across the river channels to the east bank. While it has been navigated by hikers in the past, this ford could prove to be a difficult obstacle during periods of high runoff.

Farther upstream there are two more fords: one on the Little Pipestone and another, at the Little Pipestone Warden Cabin, recrossing the Pipestone to its west bank. The latter ford is usually mid-calf to thigh deep over a rocky river bottom and it can be tricky at high water. Two main access trails intersect at this crossing: the Little Pipestone trail on the east side and the Molar Creek trail on the west.

The remainder of the hike to Pipestone Pass is relatively uneventful but quite scenic. The Singing Meadows are entered around Kilometre 24, and at the north end of the meadows is a primitive campsite and a relatively easy ford to the east side of the Pipestone. Just above this crossing is the junction with the trail from Fish Lakes—the main route to the upper valley and Pipestone Pass (see *Pipestone Pass* trail description).

Pipestone Pass

Icefields Parkway to Pipestone Pass—26.0 kilometres (16.2 miles)

Backpack

Allow 2 days to Pipestone Pass

Maximum elevation: 2590 metres (8,500 feet)

Minimum elevation: 1800 metres (5,900 feet)

Topo maps: Hector Lake 82 N/9
 Siffleur River 82 N/16

Point of Departure: Follow the Icefields Parkway to the Mosquito Creek Campground, 24 kilometres (15 miles) north of the parkway's junction with the Trans-Canada Highway near Lake Louise. The trail starts directly across the highway from the campground, at the north end of the Mosquito Creek bridge. Parking is available on the west side of the highway, just below the bridge beside the youth hostel entrance road.

0.0—Trail sign (1830 m). See *North Molar Pass-Fish Lakes* trail description.

11.5—North Molar Pass (2590 m).

14.8—Upper Fish Lake and campground (2225 m).

15.7—Lower Fish Lake.

17.8—Junction (1980 m). Intersection with the *Pipestone River* trail at Km 28.0.

20.8—Upper Pipestone Warden Cabin site.

—Steep uphill climb over last km to pass.

26.0—Pipestone Summit (2470 m). Trail crosses high gap northeast of true pass.

29.0—Junction. Clearwater Pass 1.0 km to right. Siffleur Valley straight ahead.

36.3—Old Siffleur Warden Cabin (abandoned).

38.2—Old campsite.

41.4—Siffleur River ford. Mid-calf to knee deep crossing to west bank.

—Cross over low, forested ridge.

45.2—Dolomite Creek ford. Calf to thigh deep crossing to west bank (treacherous during high water).

45.3—Junction (1800 m). Intersection with the *Dolomite Creek* trail at Km 25.6. Dolomite Pass and Icefields Parkway to left. Siffleur River trail to park boundary (1.5 km) and North Saskatchewan River bridge at Kootenay Plains (29 kms) to right.

Historically, the trail through Pipestone Pass may well be the most important north-south route in the Canadian Rockies: Before the arrival of the European fur traders Kootenay and Stoney Indians used the pass as a corridor through the Front Ranges; in the late 1850s Dr. James Hector traversed the pass during his landmark exploration of the Rockies; and at the turn of the century homesteaders and early guides used the trail as a primary route from the CPR line at Lake Louise to the Kootenay Plains and points north. Today the pass is visited by more adventurous backpackers looking for wild alpine scenery and solitude.

The most popular and easiest route to Pipestone Pass is via the North Molar Pass—Fish Lakes trail. Many backpackers camp at the Fish Lakes and day hike to Pipestone Pass, while others pack through the pass into the Siffleur or Clearwater valleys beyond. (See *North Molar Pass* trail description.)

From Lower Fish Lake, follow the rough but passable two kilometre-long trail down to the Pipestone River crossing—normally a knee deep ford. On the other side of the crossing the trail intersects with the main valley trail running northwest toward Pipestone Pass.

The upper Pipestone Valley trail climbs beside the river at a gradual grade and eventually ascends through open subalpine forest interspersed with wildflower meadows. Looking back, two narrow necks of ice can be seen descending from the Drummond Glacier, and as soon as the last trees are passed, the view extends south to the Slate Range of the Skoki Valley region.

The trail crests Pipestone Pass via a rocky, windswept gap. Views immediately open out to the northwest, carrying the eye down the Siffleur Valley nearly as far as the Kootenay Plains. This is a very high and exposed viewpoint, a long way from the nearest trees, and a frightening

Kootenay Plains homesteaders crossing Pipestone Pass in 1906

Whyte Museum of the Canadian Rockies

place to be during stormy weather.

A more direct but trackless approach to Pipestone Pass can be made from Fish Lakes by following the 7200 foot contour line north from the lakes. This cross-country route reaches Moose Lake (unnamed on the map) in 2.5 kilometres, then continues in a northwesterly direction, more or less along the aforementioned contour, to eventually intersect with the Pipestone Valley trail approximately three kilometres below the pass. The route, which saves several kilometres and a lot of elevation loss and gain, should be obvious to experienced cross-country travellers armed with a map.

From Pipestone Pass the trail continues into the Siffleur Valley. Three kilometres north of the pass the Clearwater River trail intersects from the right—a poorly defined track that is pretty much lost in the high, rocky alpine terrain. The route to Clearwater Pass is quite obvious, however, and the short side trip is definately worthwhile if the weather is reasonable.

Beyond the Clearwater junction the trail drops down a glacial staircase and into heavy forest where conditions are often boggy. Lower down the trail runs onto willow meadows where the views are open and conditions drier.

Approximately 15 kilometres north of Pipestone Pass, the trail fords the Siffleur to its west bank (usually straightforward). Nearly four kilometres farther along, after the trail crosses a low, forested ridge, there is yet another ford—a far more difficult wade of Dolomite Creek. On the opposite side of this crossing, the Dolomite Creek trail intersects from the south—a trail that can be used as an exit route to the Icefields Parkway (see *Dolomite Creek* trail description).

The Siffleur Valley trail continues northward into the Siffleur Wilderness Area from this junction and eventually reaches the Kootenay Plains in 29 kilometres. The route follows old seismic lines much of the way and passes through the remains of a 1974 fire. A sometimes treacherous ford of the Porcupine Creek cascades adds little to this seemingly endless and scenically limited trek which finally ends at a suspension bridge over the North Saskatchewan River not far from the David Thompson Highway.

113

Helen Lake—Dolomite Pass

Icefields Parkway to Helen Lake—6.0 kilometres (3.7 miles)

Icefields Parkway to Dolomite Pass—8.9 kilometres (5.0 miles)

Day trip

Allow 3 - 4 hours to Dolomite Pass

Elevation gain: 550 metres (1,800 feet)
      loss: 125 metres (410 feet)

Maximum elevation: 2500 metres (8,200 feet)

Topo maps: Hector Lake 82 N/9

Point of Departure: Follow the Icefields Parkway to the Crowfoot Glacier Viewpoint, 33 kilometres (20½ miles) north of the parkway's junction with the Trans-Canada Highway near Lake Louise and 7½ kilometres (4½ miles) south of Bow Summit. The short road leading into the trail head parking lot is on the opposite side of the highway from the viewpoint.

0.0—Trail sign (1950 m).

—Moderate climb through subalpine forest.

2.4—Avalanche slope. First good viewpoint.

2.9—Open terrain for remainder of hike.

3.4—Switchback on southeast end of Cirque Peak ridge.

—Grade moderates and trail begins contour toward Helen Lake.

4.5—Rockslide.

5.0—Helen Creek crossing.

6.0—Helen Lake (2405 m).

—Steep switchbacks.

6.9—Trail summit on high ridge (2500 m).

—Steep descent.

8.1—Katherine Lake (2375 m).

8.9—Dolomite Pass (2395 m). Connects with *Dolomite Creek* trail.

Forest, meadow, lake and snowpeak provide a constant change of scene, drawing the hiker onward toward Dolomite Pass. In addition to being one of the most extensive alpine regions in Banff Park, the Helen Lake-Dolomite Pass environs have, in seasons past, boasted a large colony of hoary marmots and the occasional family of golden eagles—living in a state of not-too-peaceful coexistence. But, for all its glories, it is best to avoid this trip when weather conditions are deteriorating; when it is miserable in the Bow Valley, it is absolutely vile on this exposed tundra plateau.

Climbing from the parking area opposite the Crowfoot Glacier viewpoint, the trail traverses the west-facing slopes of the Bow Valley. At the end of three kilometres of steady ascent, it emerges from the forest of Engelmann spruce and alpine fir and onto steep, mountainside meadows. From this vantage point the Bow Valley falls away below with Crowfoot Mountain and Glacier visible to the southwest, Bow Peak (2869 m) next in line to the south, and the sharp peak of Mount Hector (3394 m) to the southeast.

Once the trail finally attains the shoulder of Cirque Peak, it switches around 180 degrees and contours into the amphitheatre containing Helen Lake. A few stunted whitebark pine are scattered along the ridge at this switchback, indicators of the upper limits of tree growth.

At Kilometre 4.5 the trail drops around the toe of a relatively recent rockslide. In dipping below this pile of tumbled boulders, the route passes through a lush snowbed plant community which is filled with the colourful blooms of fleabane, paintbrush, ragwort and valerian in late July and early August. From here the trail climbs above the last trees and remains above timberline for the duration of the trip to Dolomite Pass.

Helen Lake makes a pleasant resting

Dolomite Pass

spot in these harsh alpine surroundings. Near the shore and on the talus slopes above, hoary marmots whistle and romp. This large grey rodent is related to the eastern woodchuck. Because of a shrill whistle issued as a call of alarm, it is also known as the whistling marmot.

After a visit with the Helen Lake marmots, the hiker can continue up a steep series of switchbacks to the unnamed ridge which serves as the summit of the hike. At nearly 2500 metres above sea level, this spot provides views down to Katherine Lake and Dolomite Pass and back to a sea of peaks which compose the Waputik Mountains. For most day hikers this windswept vantage point is a good spot to stop and turn for home.

Beyond the ridge, the trail drops nearly 100 vertical metres to the level of Katherine Lake. The lake stretches beneath the castellate cliffs of Dolomite Peak to an opening that serves as a splendid window on the southern half of Banff Park. On a clear day the sharp horn of Mount Assiniboine can be seen nearly 100 kilometres away.

Though the trail is not well-defined beyond the north end of Katherine Lake, it is easy to climb over the spongy tundra to the crest of Dolomite Pass. A small lake near the summit provides an excellent resting spot.

Though an old Indian trail is said to have traversed this desolate landscape, the first reported crossing of the pass was made in 1898 by a party of American mountaineers led by the pioneer guide Ralph Edwards. Searching for the Saskatchewan River, the party mistakenly ascended Dolomite Creek and crossed over Dolomite Pass. The wayward mountaineers named lakes Helen and Katherine for the two daughters of one of their company, while the light grey limestone in the surrounding cliffs reminded them of the Swiss Dolomites.

It is possible to continue on through Dolomite Pass and down Dolomite Creek to Isabella Lake and the Siffleur River, but this is rugged trail reserved for experienced backpackers who don't mind fording swift-flowing streams. (See *Dolomite Creek* trail description.)

Dolomite Creek

Icefields Parkway to Isabella Lake—22.3 kilometres (13.9 miles)

Backpack

Allow 9 - 10 hours to Isabella Lake

Elevation gain: 550 metres (1,800 feet)
    loss: 700 metres (2,300 feet)

Maximum elevation: 2500 metres (8,200 feet)

Topo maps: Hector Lake 82 N/9
    Siffleur River 82 N/16

Point of Departure: Follow the Icefields Parkway to the Crowfoot Glacier Viewpoint, 33 kilometres (20½ miles) north of the parkway's junction with the Trans-Canada Highway near Lake Louise and 7½ kilometres (4½ miles) south of Bow Summit. The short road leading into the trail head parking lot is on the opposite side of the highway from the viewpoint.

0.0—Trail sign (1950 m).

8.9—Dolomite Pass (2395 m).

—Faint trail descends tundra slope to upper Dolomite Creek.

11.6—Rockslide. Faint track and cairns.

12.4—Falls on Dolomite Creek.

—Timberline. Steep descent on numerous switchbacks.

13.7—Cross Dolomite Creek to east bank (knee to thigh deep ford).

—Switchbacks.

14.5—Old campsite.

15.5—Mudslide.

17.0—Cross Dolomite Creek to west bank (knee to thigh deep ford).

17.1—Tributary stream crossing (rock hop).

18.6—Extensive mudflats. Trail stays along west side.

22.3—Isabella Lake and campsite (1830 m).

22.4—Warden cabin.

25.2—Old warden cabin (abandoned).

25.6—Junction (1800 m). Intersection with *Pipestone Pass* trail at Km 37.5. Siffleur River trail continues down-valley to park boundary (1.6 km) and North Saskatchewan River bridge at the Kootenay Plains (29.0 km).

The Dolomite Creek trail is a rugged path reserved for experienced backpackers who are willing to ford streams. Yet, despite its difficulties, it provides access to Isabella Lake and the most direct route to the remote Siffleur Valley.

From the summit of Dolomite Pass (see *Helen Lake—Dolomite Pass* trail description), angle left across trail-less tundra and then descend to the west bank of upper Dolomite Creek. The trail reappears along the creek and begins the descent of the Dolomite Valley. Less than three kilometres below the pass, the trail descends a steep landslide (follow cairns) and passes below a fine waterfall.

Once the trail reaches timberline, it switchbacks downhill steeply and, 4.8 kilometres beyond Dolomite Pass, makes the first crossing of the creek—a swift knee to thigh-deep ford. The trail continues its switchbacking descent of the narrow valley, negotiates a mudslide, and then recrosses Dolomite Creek to the west side. Less than two kilometres beyond this second ford, the trail comes abreast of the extensive, braided-stream mudflats south of Isabella Lake. The track is erratic here and does not swing across the flats to the right as shown on the topo sheet. Follow the forest margin on the west side and watch for the trail's reappearance, and in an hour or less you will arrive at a primitive campground and warden cabin near the south end of Isabella Lake.

The trail beyond Isabella is straightforward, passing an abandoned warden cabin three kilometres below the lake and arriving at the Siffleur River trail junction a short distance beyond. From this intersection it is possible to continue north beyond the park boundary into the Siffleur Wilderness Area or to turn right and ascend the Siffleur Valley to Pipestone Pass. (See *Pipestone Pass* trail description.)

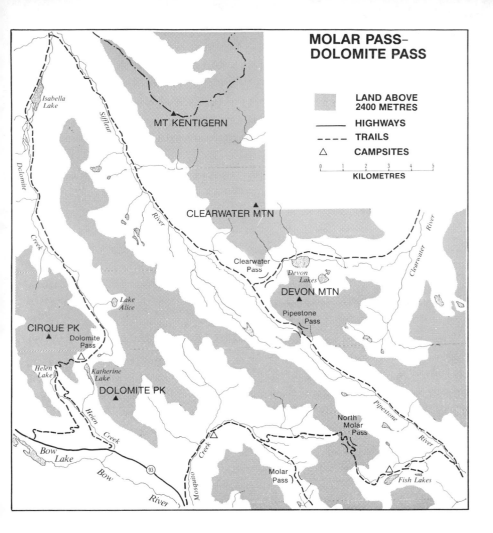

MOLAR PASS–
DOLOMITE PASS

LAND ABOVE
2400 METRES

——— HIGHWAYS

- - - - TRAILS

△ CAMPSITES

0 1 2 3 4 5
KILOMETRES

Isabella
Lake

Siffleur

MT KENTIGERN

Dolomite

River

Creek

CLEARWATER MTN

Clearwater
Pass

*Devon
Lakes*

DEVON MTN

Pipestone
Pass

Lake
Alice

CIRQUE PK
Dolomite
Pass

Helen
Lake

Katherine
Lake

DOLOMITE PK

Clearwater River

Helen Creek

North
Molar
Pass

Pipestone

River

Bow
Lake

93

Bow River

Mosbuo Creek

Molar
Pass

Fish Lakes

117

Bow Glacier Falls

Num-ti-jah Lodge to Bow Glacier Falls—4.3 kilometres (2.7 miles)

Half-day trip

Allow 1 - 2 hours one way

Elevation gain: 155 metres (500 feet)

Maximum elevation: 2105 metres (6,900 feet)

Topo maps: Hector Lake 82 N/9

Point of Departure: Follow the Icefields Parkway to the Num-ti-jah Lodge access road junction at Bow Lake, 36 kilometres (22½ miles) north of the parkway's junction with the Trans-Canada Highway near Lake Louise and 5 kilometres (3 miles) south of Bow Summit. The parking area for hikers is on the left hand side immediately following the entrance to this gravel access road. Walk the 0.6 km long gravel access road or the somewhat brushy lakeshore trail to Num-ti-jah Lodge. The trail begins from the parking area behind the lodge (reserved for lodge patrons).

0.0—Trail sign (1950 m).

—Trail angles across willow flats and crosses small stream, then follows lakeshore for 1.5 kms.

2.4—Broad gravel flats.

—Trail stays to right of river to the mouth of a narrow canyon, then climbs steeply along right edge of canyon (treacherous when wet).

3.2—Natural bridge.

3.4—Viewpoint on moraine.

—Pick route across outwash to falls.

4.3—Bow Glacier Falls (2105 m).

The Bow Glacier Falls trail presents an interesting half-day walk to the foot of an awesome cliff and waterfall at the literal headwaters of the Bow River. Featured along the way are the placid waters of Bow Lake, the gravel flats and moraines of the Bow Glacier outwash plain, and a narrow gorge spanned by a natural bridge.

Because of limited parking at Num-ti-jah Lodge, hikers should leave their vehicles at the parking area beside the Icefields Parkway and walk the 600 metre-long access road to the lodge. From behind the lodge the trail leads off across willow flats and along the shore of Bow Lake, offering reflected views of Crowfoot Mountain on the opposite side of the lake. Ahead the Bow Glacier lies amidst a sea of jagged peaks, the leaning spire of Saint Nicholas Peak rising most prominently on its southern edge.

After leaving the lakeshore near its inlet and travelling over outwash flats, the trail reaches a narrow gorge and begins a steep climb along its rim (this section of trail can be hazardous when wet or snowcovered). Walter Wilcox noted the canyon during his exploration of 1895: "Where the canyon is deepest an immense block of limestone about twenty-five feet long has fallen down, and with either end resting on the canyon walls, it affords a natural bridge over the gloomy chasm. As probably no human being had ever crossed the bridge, we felt a slight hesitation in making the attempt."

Today's route does not cross the bridge, however, but continues upwards along the gorge, emerging onto the crest of a glacial moraine. Here lies the main outwash area for the Bow Glacier with the thundering Bow Glacier Falls beyond—the headwaters of the Bow River and the South Saskatchewan River system. This rocky plain was actually covered with ice during the last glacial

Bow Glacier Falls

advance, but the glacier has since retreated out of sight above the falls and
cliff.

The base of the waterfall may be
reached by picking a route across the 800
metres of outwash and ground moraine
(ptarmigan often seen along the way).
The falls itself, tumbling through a break
in the cliff, is the outlet for a small meltwater lake hidden above at the toe of the
Bow Glacier.

Chephren Lake

Waterfowl Lakes Campground to Chephren Lake—3.5 kilometres (2.2 miles)
Waterfowl Lakes Campground to Cirque Lake—4.2 kilometres (2.6 miles)

Half-day or day trip

Allow 1 - 2 hours to Chephren Lake

Elevation gain: 80 metres (250 feet)
loss: 35 metres (100 feet)

Maximum elevation: 1755 metres (5,750 feet)

Topo maps: Mistaya Lake 82 N/15

Point of Departure: Follow the Icefields Parkway to the Waterfowl Lake Campground, 57½ kilometres (35½ miles) north of the parkway's junction with the Trans-Canada Highway near Lake Louise and 19½ kilometres (12 miles) south of the Saskatchewan River Crossing service centre. Drive through the campground to its western edge and follow along the Mistaya River to a parking area near the footbridge that spans the river and marks the beginning of the trail.

0.0—Mistaya River bridge (1675 m).

　—Moderate uphill grade through subalpine forest.

1.3—Junction. Cirque Lake trail forks sharply to left (2.9 km). Keep right for Chephren Lake.

1.6—Meadow to left of trail with views to Howse Peak (1755 m).

3.5—Chephren Lake (1720 m).

Hidden a short distance from the mainstream of traffic on the Icefields Parkway, beneath the sheer limestone walls of the Great Divide, Chephren and Cirque Lakes offer spectacular scenery and a restful quiet that can be reached with a minimum expenditure of time and energy.

From the rear of the Waterfowl Lakes Campground, the trail crosses the Mistaya River on a sturdy bridge and begins a gradual climb of the west slope of the Mistaya Valley. A junction is passed at Kilometre 1.3—the point where most hikers keep right on the route to the more popular Chephren Lake. Just 400 metres beyond the junction the forest thins, allowing occasional views of Howse Peak and Mount Chephren.

Despite its relatively low altitude, Chephren Lake gives the appearance of a higher alpine tarn. Howse Peak, the rugged, glacier-draped mountain which serves as the lake's backdrop, is named for the Hudson's Bay fur trader Joseph Howse, who crossed the Rockies in 1810. Mount Chephren (pronounced kefren) forms the lake's west shore and is named for the second of the three great pyramids of Egypt.

Cirque Lake. Because the lake is a bit smaller and the trail a bit longer and steeper, Cirque Lake is less frequently visited than Chephren. The trail to the lake branches left at the Kilometre 1.3 junction and soon joins a major stream to climb through open glades and subalpine forest. The lake itself is backed by an 800 metre-high wall created by Midway, Stairway, and Aries Peaks and is noted for its rainbow and brook trout fishing.

By hiking to Chephren Lake in the morning and backtracking to Cirque in the afternoon, both lakes can be visited in one day. Total round trip distance for the twin lake excursion would be 12.8 kilometres.

Chephren Lake and Howse Peak

Mount Sarbach

Day trip

Allow 2 - 3 hours one way

Elevation loss: 35 metres (115 feet)
gain: 590 metres (1,920 feet)

Maximum elevation: 2075 metres (6,800 feet)

Topo maps: Mistaya Lake 82 N/15

Point of Departure: Follow the Icefields Parkway to the Mistaya Canyon parking area, located on the west side of the highway 31 kilometres (19 miles) north of Bow Summit and 5½ kilometres (3½ miles) south of the Saskatchewan River Crossing service centre. This roadside pull-off is approximately halfway along on the steep, long grade that takes the highway south out of the North Saskatchewan River valley. The trail starts at the lower end of the parking area.

0.0—Trail sign (1520 m).

—Trail descends on old road bed.

0.3—Mistaya Canyon and bridge (1485 m). Climb uphill to right after crossing bridge.

0.5—Junction. Howse Pass trail continues straight ahead. Cut sharply back to left for Sarbach Lookout.

—Gradual ascent.

3.1—Grade steepens.

5.2—Sarbach Lookout site (2075 m).

The trail to the old Sarbach Lookout site climbs steeply through a forest of spruce, alpine fir and lodgepole pine and does not begin to emerge into the open until the last 200 metres or so. But from the slopes just above trail's end, views encompass the confluence of three major rivers and a sea of massive peaks.

From the Icefields Parkway, the trail descends to cross the Mistaya Canyon—a spectacular, potholed gorge that compares favourably with the better known canyons of Maligne and Marble—then begins its climb through the forest. The last two kilometres to the lookout site are steep and switchbacking, but the ordeal is nearly over when the cool smell of alpine fir and the bushy, five-needled whitebark pine are encountered—indicators of the upper subalpine forest.

Though trees surround the spot where Banff's only wooden fire tower and a small cabin once stood, views encompassing an arc of 180 degrees may be obtained with a minor amount of scrambling up the mountainside. Looming above to the east, directly across the Mistaya Valley, is Mount Murchison (3333 m), which local Indians once believed was the highest mountain in the Rockies.

In the valley to the north lies Saskatchewan River Crossing and the junction of three rivers—the Howse and Mistaya feeding the North Saskatchewan which turns from its southerly course to flow eastward through an obvious gap in the mountains. The earliest fur traders used the valleys of the North Saskatchewan and Howse as passages across the Rockies between 1807 and 1810. Beyond the rivers' confluence, the North Saskatchewan Valley stretches northward toward its source in the Columbia Icefield, a long corridor of high peaks containing it within a narrow valley.

Mount Sarbach is named for Peter Sarbach, the first Swiss guide to climb in the Canadian Rockies.

Howse Pass

Backpack

Allow 2 days to Howse Pass

Elevation loss: 85 metres (280 feet)
gain: 150 metres (500 feet)

Maximum elevation: 1585 metres (5,200 feet)

Topo maps: Mistaya Lake 82 N/15

Point of Departure: Follow the Icefields Parkway to the Mistaya Canyon parking area, located on the west side of the highway 31 kilometres (19 miles) north of Bow Summit and 5½ kilometres (3½ miles) south of the Saskatchewan River Crossing service centre. This roadside pull-off is approximately halfway along on the steep, long grade that takes the highway south out of the North Saskatchewan River valley. The trail starts at the lower end of the parking area.

0.0—Trail sign (1520 m)

—Trail descends on old road bed.

0.3—Mistaya Canyon and bridge (1485 m). Climb uphill to right after crossing bridge.

0.5—Junction. Sarbach Lookout trail cuts back to left. Keep straight ahead for Howse Pass.

—Gradual descent through forest.

4.0—Junction. Horse trail from Saskatchewan River Crossing intersects from right. Keep left.

4.2—Howse River flats (1435 m).

—Gentle rolling to flat hiking.

7.7—Campsite and stream crossing.

14.0—Trail crosses broad dryas flats.

15.5—Trail climbs back into forest and away from river.

—Boggy, rooty and rolling.

19.0—Junction. Spur trail to Howse River Warden Cabin (0.5 km) and Lagoon Lake to right. Howse Pass straight ahead.

23.0—Junction. Forbes Brook trail to Freshfield Glacier branches right. Keep left.

25.6—Major tributary stream crossing (ford).

25.8—Howse Pass (1527 m).

The Howse Pass trail is significant in that it served as the first regular fur trade route across the Rocky Mountains, and the valley is just about as wild today as it was when David Thompson passed this way in 1807. Yet, despite its colourful history, many hikers find this 26 kilometre hike up a broad low-lying valley somewhat tedious.

After crossing Mistaya Canyon and descending to the Howse River flats just west of Saskatchewan River Crossing, the trail begins its very gradual ascent of the valley, swinging in and out of dense spruce forest with the river never more than 400 metres distant to the hiker's right. At Kilometre 9.0 the trail dips down to the edge of the river to afford an excellent view across the valley to a notch revealing the tumbled blue glaciers of the Lyell Icefield.

After one more visit to the broad, dryas-covered river flats at Kilometre 14.0, the trail climbs into the forest, never to see the light of day again—at least until the last two kilometres leading to the pass. The way is rough and rooty and rather depressing. The large marshy meadow surrounding the warden cabin and primitive campsite near Lagoon Lake does offer some respite, however, and is a good base from which to explore the upper valley.

While more open than much of the upper valley, views from the pass are rather unexceptional. A fair trail continues into British Columbia, descending the west side of the Blaeberry River for 10 kilometres or so to the logging road that runs downvalley to the Trans-Canada Highway just north of Golden.

Freshfield Glacier. An ill-defined, 8.7 kilometre-long track branches from the Howse Pass trail at Kilometre 23.0, fords Conway Creek, and follows along the south side of Freshfield Creek to a point just over a kilometre from the toe of the Freshfield Glacier. For explorers only!

Glacier Lake

Day trip or backpack

Allow 3 hours one way

Elevation gain: 210 metres (700 feet)
loss: 225 metres (750 feet)

Maximum elevation: 1660 metres (5,450 feet)

Topo maps: Mistaya Lake 82 N/15

Point of Departure: Follow the Icefields Parkway to the trail head parking area, located in an old roadside gravel pit on the west side of the highway just one kilometre (½ mile) north of the Saskatchewan River Crossing service centre.

0.0—Trail sign (1450 m).

1.1—North Saskatchewan River footbridge.

2.3—Viewpoint overlooking Howse River.

—Trail climbs over forested ridge (1660 m).

8.9—Glacier Lake (1435 m).

9.2—Campground.

—Trail follows north shore of lake.

12.6—Western end (inlet) of Glacier Lake.

14.4—Trail becomes indistinct along glacial outwash stream.

In June of 1807, David Thompson and a party of North West Company fur traders entered the Howse Valley on their way across the Rockies to build the first trading post on the Columbia River. While camped on the Howse, Thompson wandered into a side valley where he discovered a large lake and marvelled that "all the Mountains in sight from the end of the Lake are seemingly of Ice." The lake was named Glacier 51 years later when Dr. James Hector, geologist with the Palliser Expedition, camped by its shores.

The trail to Glacier Lake begins on an old access road running southwest through a young forest of lodgepole pine— the regrowth following Banff Park's last major forest fire, the Survey Peak burn of 1940. The forest is still very open, allowing good views to the five major mountains that ring this broad section of valley — starting with the predominant peak to the southeast and running clockwise, Mount Murchison, Mount Sarbach, Mount Outram, Mount Erasmus, and Mount Wilson. The main composition of all these mountains is Cambrian and Ordovician limestone and quartz sandstone.

The North Saskatchewan River is crossed on a deluxe footbridge at Kilometre 1.1, and just over a kilometre beyond the trail skirts the edge of a bluff overlooking the Howse River—an outstanding viewpoint for the valley leading to historic Howse Pass. Dropping off the bluff, the trail stays to the northwest side of the river and eventually cuts inland away from the braided flats to begin the climb over a forested ridge to Glacier Lake.

Glacier Lake lies at 1435 metres above sea level and, at approximately three kilometres in length and nearly one kilometre in width, is one of the largest backcountry lakes in Banff Park. The trail continues along the north shore and

Glacier Lake

reaches the brushy flats at the lake's inlet at Kilometre 12.6. The Glacier River, the lake's major tributary, can be followed for another four kilometres toward the Southeast Lyell Glacier, but the trail soon becomes indistinct among the meanders and shifting gravels of the outwash stream.

A primitive campsite at Kilometre 9.2, on the shore of the lake, provides a good springboard for backpackers wishing to do some exploring in the upper end of the valley, and the flats at the west end of the lake are also a good place to camp. The area is frequently visited by black bear, however, so campers should be fastidious with the storage of food and garbage.

Sunset Pass

Icefields Parkway to Sunset Pass—8.2 kilometres (5.1 miles)
Icefields Parkway to Pinto Lake—13.7 kilometes (8.5 miles)

Day trip or backpack

Allow 3 - 4 hours to Sunset Pass

Elevation gain: 725 metres (2,380 feet)

Maximum elevation: 2165 metres (7,100 feet)

Topo maps: Cline River 83 C/2†

†Sunset Lookout trail not shown

Point of Departure: Follow the Icefields Parkway to the Norman Creek bridge, 16½ kilometres (10½ miles) north of the Saskatchewan River Crossing service centre and 28½ kilometres (17½ miles) south of the Banff—Jasper park boundary at Sunwapta Pass. The trail head parking area is located on the open flat to the east of the highway just below the Norman Creek bridge.

0.0—Trail sign at edge of forest (1440 m).

—Moderate uphill grade.

0.6—Grade becomes steep.

1.0—Norman Creek gorge viewpoint.

—Steady uphill with switchbacks.

2.9—Junction. Old Sunset Lookout site to left (1.6 km). Sunset Pass straight ahead.

4.0—Trail levels out into open meadowland.

4.2—Campground.

8.2—Sunset Pass and park boundary (2165 m).

—Steep descent.

13.7—Pinto Lake (1750 m).

Located in the northern region of Banff Park, the Sunset Pass trail travels through extensive meadowlands beneath the cliffs of Mount Coleman to an exceptional viewpoint overlooking Pinto Lake, the remote Cline River valley, and the sea of peaks comprising Alberta's White Goat Wilderness Area. For backpackers the trail extends beyond the pass and the park boundary to the shores of Pinto Lake, while day hikers will find the side trip to the old Sunset Lookout site and its expansive panorama of the North Saskatchewan and Alexandra River valleys an attractive option.

A steep climb from the Icefields Parkway makes any itinerary an arduous one, the first three kilometres of trail rising at an excruciating grade. The path is forest-enclosed and dry (make sure to pack water for the first hour or so of the trip), and the only respite is a brief glimpse of the Norman Creek gorge.

Once the Sunset Lookout junction is passed, the grade moderates somewhat, and a kilometre farther on the trail finally emerges onto flat, open meadows which extend unbroken for over four kilometres to the pass and the park boundary. Mount Coleman, its nearly horizontal strata set within the axis of the Castle Mountain Syncline, stands on the left side of the meadow, while three lesser peaks in the 2800 metre range dominate the right. The massive summits of Mount Amery and Mount Saskatchewan arise beyond the plateau and the North Saskatchewan Valley to the west.

The park boundary is reached in an open subalpine area at the eastern lip of Sunset Pass, and views continue to improve over the next kilometre of hiking until the waters of Pinto Lake are revealed far below. The trail from the pass to the lakeshore campground is a deceptively long and steep 5.5 kilometres.

Many of the features along the Sunset

Sunset Pass

Pass trail commemorate the first visitor to the area A. P. Coleman, geologist, mountaineer and explorer, who travelled over the summit in 1893. Mount Coleman was named in his honour in 1903, and Pinto Lake immortalizes one of the expedition's more troublesome packhorses.

From Pinto Lake two extended wilderness trips are available to backpackers willing to arrange transportation. A very straightforward descent of the Cline Valley can be made by crossing to the south bank of the river just below the lake then following good horse trail 30 kilometres to a junction with the David Thompson Highway.

Another trail runs up Cataract Creek's east bank to the foot of Cataract Pass (stay on the north side of Cline River below Pinto Lake and ford Cataract Creek just above its confluence with the river). While no trail traverses the pass from the Cataract Creek headwaters, experienced wilderness travellers armed with topo maps can easily make their own route through the rocky gap to Nigel Pass—a total distance of around 26 kilom-

etres from Pinto Lake. (See *Nigel Pass* trail description.)

Sunset Lookout. The trail to the old Sunset Lookout site branches left from the main track at Kilometre 2.9 and climbs northwestward along the slopes of Mount Coleman to a spectacular overlook perched on the edge of a sheer limestone cliff. From this vantage point it is more than 450 vertical metres down to the Icefields Parkway and the North Saskatchewan River.

The small, one room Sunset Lookout cabin was built on this location during the summer of 1944 and was demolished in 1977 after Parks Canada abandoned its fire lookouts. In addition to the looming summits of Mount Amery (3329 m) and Mount Saskatchewan (3342 m), the lookout commanded a view directly up the Alexandra River to the ice-covered peaks of the Great Divide over 18 kilometres away.

The trail to the lookout site from the highway is 4.5 kilometres long and totally devoid of water, so remember to pack enough to quench your thirst for the day.

Castleguard Meadows

Backpack

Allow 2 days to Castleguard Meadows

Elevation gain: 610 metres (2,000 feet)

Maximum elevation: 2135 metres (7,000 feet)

Topo maps: Cline River 83 C/2
Columbia Icefield 83 C/3†
†last 25 kms of trail not shown

Point of Departure: Follow the Icefields Parkway to the junction with the Alexandra River Fire Road, 26 kilometres (16 miles) north of the Saskatchewan River Crossing service centre and 2 kilometres (1.2 miles) south of Cirrus Mountain Campground. The fire road and the wooden bridge across the North Saskatchewan River, which serves as the trail head, are virtually invisible from the highway. Watch for a pull-out viewpoint on the west side of the road overlooking the narrow canyon.

0.0—North Saskatchewan River bridge (1525 m).

—Mainly flat fire road walking.

5.8—Road bends west up Alexandra Valley.

10.9—Road comes abreast of extensive river flats.

11.7—Old bridge spans major stream channel, road runs out onto flats.

—Road washouts, inundated by channels during high water (thigh deep fords or worse may be required).

13.5—Terrace Creek bridge and campsite.

20.5—Old trail sign. Road reverts to trail, enters forest.

20.9—Castleguard Warden Cabin (1555 m).

21.4—Campsite.

—Gradual to moderate climb up Castleguard Valley.

30.6—Major stream crossing (log bridge).

31.9—Outram's Shower Bath waterfalls.

—Steep uphill climb.

35.1—Campsite on lower edge of Castleguard Meadows (2135 m).

The Castleguard Meadows comprise a lofty timberline environment where, as described by Dalton Muir and Derek Ford in their wonderful book *Castleguard,* "so many natural features compete for attention that the senses become saturated . . . ."

For experienced mountain travellers who understand the hazards of glacier travel, the easiest route to the Castleguard Meadows follows up the long and relatively level tongue of the Saskatchewan Glacier. This journey entails a seven kilometre hike to the toe of the glacier (see *Saskatchewan Glacier* trail description) followed by a five kilometre walk up this river of ice to a point where the hiker can traverse across to the northern edge of the meadows.

While it may not seem as imposing as the ascent of a major glacier, the approach to the meadows via the Alexandra and Castleguard Valleys is far more gruelling and possesses its own unique set of inconveniences. This trip begins by following twenty kilometres of fire road along the North Saskatchewan and Alexandra Rivers. All is quite straightforward until the road descends onto the Alexandra River flats at Kilometre 11.7. Here the braided multi-channels of the river have washed out the road in many places, and periods of warm weather can bring high water and difficult fords.

From the Castleguard Warden Cabin, the road reverts to a rock and root-filled trail which ascends for just over ten kilometres along the northeast bank of he Castleguard River (tributary streams will have to be waded if log bridges are not in place). This is topped off by a final three kilometres of steep climbing to a campsite on the southern lip of the meadows, situated at just over 2100 metres above sea level. Here the trail ends and the Castleguard Meadows are yours to explore at your leisure.

Saskatchewan Glacier

Icefields Parkway to Saskatchewan Glacier—7.3 kilometres (4.5 miles)

Half-day trip

Allow 2 hours one way

Elevation gain: 155 metres (500 feet)

Maximum elevation: 1800 metres (5,900 feet)

Topo maps: Columbia Icefield 83 C/3

Point of Departure: Follow the Icefields Parkway to the "Big Bend" switchback, located on extensive gravel flats 34 kilometres (12 miles) north of the Saskatchewan River Crossing service centre and 11 kilometres (7 miles) south of the Banff—Jasper park boundary at Sunwapta Pass. Just 0.7 kilometre (0.4 mile) south of this dramatic curve in the highway, just below the road, is an old concrete bridge and a section of the former Banff—Jasper Highway leading down into the gorge. Park on this side of the bridge—the trail head for the hike.

0.0—Old highway bridge (1645 m).

—Follow old roadway downhill.

0.2—Junction. Turn right off old road onto trail.

0.5—Trail joins old access road.

1.3—Begin climb over forested ridge.

2.1—Crest of ridge.

—Gradual downhill to glacier outwash flats.

2.6—Road follows south edge of outwash flats.

2.9—Sections of road washed out by river.

—Contour along cut-bank.

3.9—Route crosses untracked outwash flats to toe of glacier.

7.3—Saskatchewan Glacier toe (1800 m).

The Saskatchewan Glacier trail offers an unusual day's outing for hikers interested in the justly celebrated glaciers of the Canadian Rockies. It is a short trail, easily accessible from the Icefields Parkway, and runs up an open valley floor to the terminus of the largest outlet glacier of the Columbia Icefield.

The day's intrigues begin at the trail head—an old concrete bridge over the North Saskatchewan River. The bridge spans a narrow, deep, undercut gorge of the sort that compels young people to drop rocks into its maw. The trail proper begins just beyond the gorge, where it forks to the right as a rough track disappearing into the forest. Its character abruptly changes within several hundred metres, however, as it joins an old access road.

The old road rises over a low, forested ridge (which hides the glacier from tourists travelling the Icefields Parkway) and drops into the valley of the Saskatchewan Glacier. At the bottom of the ridge, the road emerges onto open flats where it has been washed out by the changing channels of the North Saskatchewan River, and the route upvalley continues as trail along the south bank of the river.

As you approach the glacier terminus, the terrain becomes increasingly rough. The final push can be deceptively long, for you have to cross a number of low recessional moraines and the glacier always appears closer than it actually is.

The toe of the glacier is worthy of exploration. In good years, it is possible to step directly from rock to ice, but more frequently glacial meltwater and fine mud (which can suck laced boots off the unwary's feet) will discourage most from scrambling up on the glacier toe. It is not, however, necessary to attempt the glacier to enjoy its environs.

Experienced glacier travellers often use the Saskatchewan Glacier as a short, fair weather access to the Castleguard Meadows.

Nigel Pass

Icefields Parkway to Nigel Pass—7.2 kilometres (4.5 miles)

Day trip

Allow 2 - 3 hours one way

Elevation gain: 365 metres (1,200 feet)

Maximum elevation: 2195 metres (7,200 feet)

Topo maps: Columbia Icefield 83 C/3

Point of Departure: Follow the Icefields Parkway to the parking area for the Nigel Pass trail, located on the northeast side of the highway 8½ kilometres (5½ miles) south of the Banff—Jasper park boundary at Sunwapta Pass or 2½ kilometers (1½ miles) north of the "Big Bend" switchback on the long grade up to Sunwapta Pass. A gravel side road leads 200 metres to a locked access gate. Park above the gate and walk downhill past it to the trail sign.

0.0—Trail sign (1830 m).

—Trail crosses to northeast side of Nigel Creek via footbridge. Contours northwest above creek, crossing brushy avalanche paths.

2.1—Old Camp Parker.

—Begin ascent up east side of Nigel Creek valley.

5.1—Trail gradually emerges into open meadowland.

—Steady ascent to pass.

7.2—Nigel Pass (2195 m). Banff—Jasper park boundary. Trail descends into Brazeau Valley (see *Brazeau Lake via Nigel Pass* description, Jasper Park chapter).

Nigel Pass is an excellent choice for anyone travelling in the Columbia Icefield vicinity and who would like to spend a day wandering through open subalpine meadows. Not only does the hike provide views of some of the more rugged peaks on the eastern edge of the Icefield and a glimpse into the remote southern wilderness of Jasper Park, but it does so with a minimal amount of effort, climbing less than 400 vertical metres in seven kilometres of travel.

From the parking area just off the Icefields Parkway, the trail immediately crosses Nigel Creek and contours up along the east side of the valley through open avalanche paths. At Kilometre 2.1 the site of old Camp Parker is passed in a stand of large Engelmann spruce and alpine fir. This area was used as a campsite by Indian hunting parties before the arrival of the white man, and early mountaineers exploring the Columbia Icefield around the turn of the century continued the Indian tradition. The carvings on the surrounding trees record the visits of many of these early campers, though most date to the period following the opening of the Banff-Jasper Highway in 1940.

At Camp Parker the trail bends to the north and begins the ascent of the upper Nigel Valley. Throughout this section there are good views back to Parker's Ridge and the 'horn' sub-peak of Mount Athabasca, and Nigel Pass is seldom out of sight ahead.

The trail climbs steadily for the last kilometre to the pass, levelling out where a cairn marks the boundary between Banff and Jasper Parks. Forest cover is very sparse and stunted at the pass, indicting that 2195 metres above sea level is the approximate elevation of timberline at this latitude.

Back downvalley to the south, the ice-clad summit of Mount Saskatchewan (3342 m) is visible beyond Parker's Ridge.

Mount Saskatchewan and Nigel Creek valley from Nigel Pass

To the north is the wild Brazeau River valley and the maze of peaks that comprise the southern edge of Jasper Park. Directly west of the pass, rising above a large cirque, is Nigel Peak (3211 m), named in 1898 by the British mountaineers Hugh Stutfield and Norman Collie for their guide Nigel Vavasour (it was this expedition which discovered the Columbia Icefield).

By continuing beyond the pass a short distance, you can cross the south fork of the Brazeau River (rock hop) to an open talus slope where there are exceptional views down the main Brazeau Valley and back to the north side of Nigel Pass—a fine rock wall featuring several small waterfalls. In fact, strong day hikers would find a descent of the valley as far as Boulder Creek Campground quite rewarding (see *Brazeau Lake* trail description in Jasper Park chapter).

Cataract Pass. Lying some six kilometres southeast of Nigel Pass are the headwaters of the south fork of the Brazeau River. While no defined trail leads in this direction, energetic explorers with a topo map can strike out from Nigel summit and pick a route through the rocky, open terrain to a small lake at the foot of Cataract Pass—a fine area for wandering away an afternoon.

Strong, experienced backpackers can make an interesting trip from Nigel Pass to Pinto Lake by crossing Cataract Pass (2485 m) and descending Cataract Creek (trail appears near timberline on the east side of the creek) to its junction with the Cline River trail just below Pinto Lake. This is a trip best reserved until late in the year since snowbanks often cover the very steep approaches to Cataract Pass into August, and there are also fords of Cataract Creek (just above its confluence with Cline River) and Huntington Creek which may present some difficulty. The distance from Nigel Pass to Pinto Lake is approximately 26 kilometres. (See also *Sunset Pass* trail description.)

131

The Front Ranges

While Banff boasts more kilometres of trail and heavier backcountry visitation than any other park in the Canadian Rockies, one section of the park receives relatively light travel—that rather large territory to the north and east of the Trans-Canada Highway contained within the steeply tilted limestone mountains of the Front Ranges. This section of park encompasses an area of more than 2,000 square kilometres and can be considered a true wilderness in every sense of the word.

There are two main reasons why this part of Banff Park is seldom visited: it is so vast and remote that anyone wishing to penetrate into the heart of the region must plan a trip of a week or more; and many of the more interesting trails are rendered difficult and dangerous by unbridged streams and rivers (unlike Jasper Park which has made most of its remote trails accessible to hikers with bridges and trail upgrading, Banff Park has chosen to leave its wilderness regions in a more primitive state).

In previous editions of this book we provided limited information on the more than 250 kilometres of trail in Banff's eastern wilderness, primarily out of deference to the relatively large grizzly bear population which inhabits the region. But after many years of personal experience and due consideration, we can see little reason to treat this section of Banff Park any differently than the remote reaches of the other mountain parks; wilderness grizzlies are generally less aggressive than those which turn up in heavily travelled areas, and as long as backpackers travel alertly and keep a clean camp, bear-human encounters should be no more frequent or serious here than in other districts.

The only other hazard which travellers in this region should consider is the afore-mentioned unbridged stream crossings. Generally, the streams and rivers in the Front Ranges are less imposing than those in the Main Ranges which are fed by large glaciers and icefields. But these watercourses can run strong and high, particularly during periods of heavy rainfall (glacier-fed rivers in the Main Ranges are usually highest during hot, dry spells). While all of the streams and rivers in this region are forded at appropriate points every summer by backpackers, experience in making river cross-ings is a prerequisite to hiking in this part of the park.

Backpackers should also be aware that the eastern section of Banff Park is the centre of activity for the largest commercial horse outfitter in the Canadian Rockies. The operation has major campsites in Flint's Park and near the Cascade River-Stoney Creek confluence, and horse parties frequent Elk Summit, Forty Mile Summit, Badger Pass, Dormer Pass, and Panther Valley. With the exception of a couple of access trails which get churned up during rainy weather, this activity should cause little inconven-ience to backpackers; the outfitter has been very sympathetic to hikers in the past, and the annual passage of horses over these trails plays a major role in their remaining open and passable.

Nearly every major valley in these eastern ranges has a trail running through it. Most of these trails developed during the early decades of this century when Banff outfitters led excursions and hunting parties out into this game-rich country.

The most important and dependable track through the Front Ranges is the Cascade Fire Road, which runs just over 75 kilometres from the Lake Minnewanka Road near

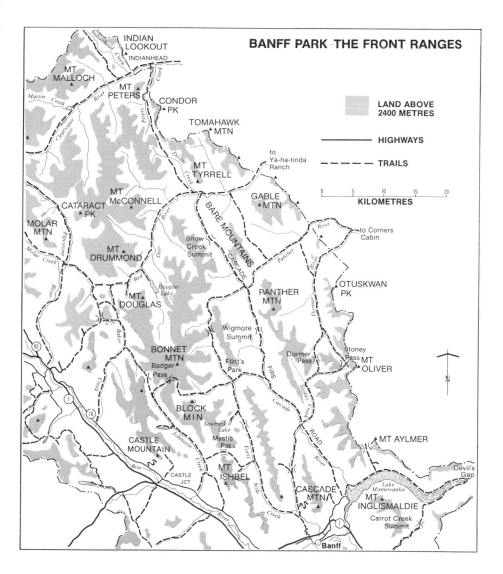

BANFF PARK–THE FRONT RANGES

LAND ABOVE
2400 METRES

——————— HIGHWAYS

– – – – – – TRAILS

0   5   10   15   20
KILOMETRES

Banff to the government ranch at Ya-Ha-Tinda beyond the park's eastern boundary. The road travels through the heartland of the Front Ranges wilderness, has bridges over all streams and rivers, and serves as a terminus for most of the region's trails—Elk Summit, Dormer Pass, Flint's Park, Panther River, North Fork Pass, and Red Deer River.

The only major trails which don't intersect with the Cascade Fire Road are those in the remote northern part of this district—Divide Creek-Peters Creek, Clearwater River, and Indianhead Creek. These areas are usually reached via the Red Deer River or Pipestone Pass-Siffleur River trails.

133

Cascade Fire Road

Lake Minnewanka Road to Park Boundary—69.3 kilometres (43.0 miles)

Backpack

Allow 3 - 5 days one way

Maximum elevation: 2255 metres (7,400 feet)

Minimum elevation: 1465 metres (4,800 feet)

Topo maps: Banff 82 O/4

Castle Mountain 82 O/5

Barrier Mountain 82 O/12

Point of Departure: Northbound backpackers will begin from the junction of the Lake Minnewanka Road and Cascade Fire Road just 6½ kilometres (4 miles) north of Banff townsite. The Upper Bankhead Picnic Area, 800 metres south of the actual road junction, serves as the official trail head and parking area.

0.0—Upper Bankhead Picnic Area (1465 m). Follow the 800 metre-long footpath which connects the picnic area to the fire road.

5.6—Cascade River bridge (1555 m). Campground.

13.8—Stony Creek (1645 m).

14.0—Junction. Dormer Pass to right.

23.1—Junction. Flint's Park and Badger Pass to left.

30.1—Junction. Big Horn Lake 4.5 km to right.

33.0—Wigmore Summit (2010 m).

39.1—Windy Warden Cabin. Lower Panther River trail runs east from meadow behind cabin.

39.3—Junction. Upper Panther River and North Fork Pass to left.

39.4—Panther River bridge (1885 m). Panther Falls 0.4 km to right from north end of bridge.

42.8—Junction. Harrison Lake 4.0 km to left.

46.8—Junction. Grouse Lake 1.2 km to right.

49.3—Snow Creek Summit (2255 m).

49.5—Junction. Snowflake Lake 2.0 km to left.

58.2—Red Deer River bridge (1740 m).

58.4—Junction. Red Deer River trail to left.

62.9—Tyrrell Creek bridge.

69.3—Park boundary and access gate (1660 m).

This well-graded dirt road provides one of the primary means of access to the Front Ranges of Banff Park. Though a fire road does not yield the most aesthetic of hiking experiences, this is the one route in the park's eastern wilderness which guarantees the backpacker dry feet and a well-defined path. It also intersects with most of the region's more interesting trails.

The fire road was developed in the late 1930s and 1940s in response to a number of large conflagrations which swept this region and other areas of the Rockies. Up until 1984 the road was frequently travelled by park warden vehicles, but when the Stony Creek and Cascade River bridges collapsed that summer, it was decided the road should revert to a foot and horse trail.

Running north from the Lake Minnewanka Road, the Cascade trail bisects the Front Ranges district. It follows the Cascade River for nearly 25 kilometres, crosses Wigmore Summit, descends to the Panther River, climbs again to Snow Creek Summit (2255 m) and finally joins the Red Deer River for the remainder of its journey to the park's east boundary.

In addition to a half-dozen short side trips to alpine lakes in the vicinity of Wigmore and Snow Creek Summits, a number of major access trails branch from the fire road throughout its length— Elk Summit, Dormer Pass, Flint's Park, Panther River, North Fork Pass, and Red Deer River. Utilizing other trail descriptions in this section, 1:50,000 topo maps, and a little imagination, the backpacker should have little trouble making extended loop trips which provide outstanding scenery and lots of solitude.

At present the only unbridged stream crossing on the Cascade Fire Road is Stony Creek (Kilometre 13.8). For those who are reluctant to just slosh on through, there is a footbridge 600 metres downstream which allows for a dry passage.

Dormer Pass

Backpack

Allow 4 - 6 hours to Dormer Pass

Elevation gain: 730 metres (2,400 feet)

Maximum elevation: 2375 metres (7,800 feet)

Topo maps: Castle Mountain 82 O/5
Barrier Mountain 82 O/12

Point of Departure: Hike the *Cascade Fire Road* or the *Elk Pass* trail to Stony Creek, Km 13.8 on the Cascade Fire Road. Just 200 metres north of the Stony Creek crossing, the Dormer Pass trail cuts right away from the fire road.

0.0—Cascade Fire Road (1645 m).

0.5—Campsite.

1.3—Stony Creek ford. Knee to thigh deep crossing to east bank.

—Gradual to moderate uphill grades.

6.5—Stony Creek ford to west bank.

6.8—Stony Creek ford to east bank.

9.0—Junction. Stony Pass to right. Keep left and ford creek for Dormer Pass.

—Steep uphill.

12.5—Dormer Pass (2375 m).

—Steep switchbacking descent.

17.0—Grade moderates near junction of west and east branches of Dormer River.

18.5—Dormer River ford to east bank. Dormer Warden Cabin 0.2 km below ford on west bank.

24.5—Junction (1770 m). Park boundary via Dormer River trail to right (6.0 km). Keep left and ford river for Panther River.

—Steady uphill grade.

28.5—Panther—Dormer Divide (2055 m).

—Moderate downhill over rough, boggy trail.

32.0—Panther River ford and junction (1770 m). Mid-calf to knee deep crossing to intersect *Panther River* trail at Km 12.0. Park boundary to right. Cascade Fire Road to left.

*All distances approximate.

The trail running up Stony Creek to Dormer Pass is one of the most attractive options branching from the Cascade Fire Road. In addition to the pass itself, which breaks through the limestone walls of the Palliser Range at 2375 metres above sea level, the trip offers the options of a visit to nearby Stony Pass or an extended journey to the Panther River.

Thanks to heavy horse travel, the trail is well-defined through its entire length, but there are a number of streams along the way which must be waded. The first of these is at Kilometre 1.3 where the trail swings to the east side of Stony Creek—a troublesome ford during periods of high runoff; three fords of the creek further upvalley are less demanding.

At Kilometre 9.0 the trail to Stony Pass stays right while the Dormer Pass trail branches left, crosses Stony Creek and makes a 3.5 kilometre ascent to the pass. The pass is a long, narrow corridor which is frequented by large flocks of mountain sheep.

From Dormer Pass, the trail switchbacks down steeply to the meadows of the upper Dormer Valley. Just above the Dormer Warden Cabin, the trail crosses to the east side of the river. It remains there for the next six kilometres, passing through open meadows which allow fine views of the surrounding mountains.

At Kilometre 24.5 a major junction is reached. The right branch continues down the Dormer to the park boundary; the left branch fords the river, crosses over the Dormer-Panther Divide and descends to the Panther River. (See *Panther River* trail description.)

Stony Pass. This branch trail runs eastward from the Dormer Pass trail at Kilometre 9.0, loops over Stony Pass (2330 m), and finally rejoins the main trail just above the Dormer Warden Cabin. The trail, which is marked on the map, disappears in a number of places, but the route is obvious.

Panther River

Backpack

Allow 5 - 6 hours one way

Elevation loss: 140 metres (450 feet)

Maximum elevation: 1875 metres (6,150 feet)

Topo maps: Barrier Mountain 82 O/12

Point of Departure: Eastbound backpackers can reach the west end of the trail by hiking the *Cascade Fire Road* to the Windy Warden Cabin at Km 39.1 (the trail departs from the meadow behind the cabin). Westbound travellers usually approach from the south via the *Dormer Pass* trail and the Panther—Dormer Divide shortcut, intersecting with the Panther River trail at Km 12.0, approximately 3.0 kms west of the park boundary.

0.0—Windy Warden Cabin (1875 m).

1.5—Panther River ford to north bank (mid-calf to knee deep).

1.8—Panther River ford to south bank.

2.2—Panther River ford to north bank.

—Flat to rolling walk downvalley above north side of river.

5.7—Old warden cabin.

6.0—Junction. Bare Range shortcut from Red Deer River intersects from north (poorly marked junction).

8.0—Cold sulphur spring.

12.0—Junction (1770 m). Intersection with the *Dormer Pass* trail (Panther-Dormer divide shortcut) at Km 32.0. Panther Valley trail continues east to park boundary (3.0 km).

*All distances approximate.

The Panther River is one of the least visited of the major valleys in the eastern part of Banff Park. While it does not contain the spectacular mountains and views of other parts of the Front Ranges, it does have a certain quiet and haunting beauty that lingers in a hiker's memory.

The horse trail down the lower Panther River branches east from the Cascade Fire Road at the Windy Warden Cabin (Kilometre 39.1). The trail immediately enters the Panther River gorge where narrow canyon walls force it to cross the river three times in the space of a kilometre; however, all three fords are simple calf-deep wades across a smoothly flowing stream. Once through this cleft in the Bare Range, good trail leads all the way downvalley along the north side of the river to the eastern park boundary.

At Kilometre 5.7 an old dilapidated warden cabin is passed, and just beyond there is an excellent campsite beside a creek. The shortcut trail which runs along the foot of the Bare Range to Red Deer River branches north from the Panther trail on the east side of this stream.

The junction with the Dormer Pass trail (Panther-Dormer Divide shortcut) at Kilometre 12.0 marks the end of the Panther River trail for most hikers. This junction is only three kilometres or so short of the park boundary, and the trail leading back toward Dormer Pass is the usual option. (See *Dormer Pass* trail description.)

Bare Range. This 13.5 kilometre trail serves as a shortcut between the Red Deer River valley and the Panther River. The junction on the east side of the tributary stream at Kilometre 6.0 is not easy to find; while at least one hiker claims to have travelled the length of the trail with little difficulty, expect the track to be faint and the ford of the Red Deer River at the north end to be demanding.

North Fork Pass

Cascade Fire Road to North Fork Pass—12.0 kilometres (7.5 miles)*
Cascade Fire Road to Flint's Park—20.5 kilometres (12.5 miles)

Backpack

Allow 5 hours to North Fork Pass

Elevation gain: 540 metres (1,770 feet)

Maximum elevation: 2425 metres (7,950 feet)

Topo maps: Barrier Mountain 82 O/12
  Castle Mountain 82 O/5

Point of Departure: Southbound backpackers will begin from the Panther River bridge at Km 39.4 on the *Cascade Fire Road*, the trail cutting west from the fire road less than 100 metres south of the bridge. Northbound travellers can begin from the junction at Km 17.6 on the *Badger Pass—Flint's Park* trail, an intersection which is just a few metres from the Flint's Park Warden Cabin. Access to this southern terminus can be made by either the *Badger Pass—Flint's Park* or the *Forty Mile Summit* trails.

0.0—Cascade Fire Road (1885 m).

0.4—Panther River ford to north bank (mid-calf deep).

—Flat valley bottom trail.

5.2—Panther River ford to south bank.

—Trail climbs over shoulder then swings due south toward Panther River headwaters.

10.7—Trail begins steep climb up left side of bowl toward pass.

12.0—North Fork Pass (2425 m).

—Steep descent down south side of pass.

14.0—Grade moderates. Trail intermittant, disappears in deadfall.

16.3—Good trail reappears on east side of creek.

18.0—Cross to west side of creek.

—Steady downhill on gradual grade.

20.5—Junction (1830 m). Intersection with *Badger Pass—Flint's Park* trail at Km 17.6. Cascade River north fork bridge and campsite to left (0.1 km).

*All distances approximate.

Situated at an elevation of 2425 metres above sea level, between the headwaters of the Panther River and North Fork of the Cascade River, North Fork Pass is probably one of the least hiked areas in Banff Park. Accessible from either Flint's Park or the Cascade Fire Road, this 20.5 kilometre trek provides an excellent side trip for experienced backpackers who are on extended trips through the Front Ranges.

Running west from the Panther River bridge at Kilometre 39.3 on the Cascade Fire Road, the trail soon fords the Panther to its north bank and then works its way upvalley at a flat to gently rolling grade. Near the five kilometre mark the trail recrosses the Panther to its south bank, climbs up and over the shoulder of a mountain, and then turns south into a narrow valley to begin its ascent of North Fork Pass. The trail gains 380 metres of elevation over the last five kilometres to the summit.

The narrow gap of North Fork Pass gives an excellent view due south across Forty Mile Summit to Mounts Edith, Louis and Fifi and the peaks south of Banff townsite. All around rise the steeply tilted limestone summits of the Sawback Range.

From the pass the trail drops steeply away to the south, descending to the North Fork of the Cascade River. Here the track enters the silver forest remains of a major forest fire which swept this region in 1936 and promptly disappears into the deadfall. For the next two kilometres or so, the trail is intermittent and difficult to find, but by persevering down the east side of the North Fork, you should come upon it again where it reappears as a well defined track. The trail soon swings to the west side of the stream and completes the rest of the descent to the Flint's Park trail junction over a broad, obvious path. (See *Badger Pass—Flint's Park* trail description.)

Divide Creek — Peters Creek

Red Deer River to Clearwater River—25.7 kilometres (16.0 miles)

Backpack

Allow 2 days one way

Elevation gain: 625 metres (2,050 feet)
     loss: 655 metres (2,150 feet)

Maximum elevation: 2395 metres (7,850 feet)

Topo maps: Barrier Mountain 82 0/12
     Forbidden Creek 82 0/13†

     †trail not shown

Point of Departure: Northbound backpackers can reach the south end of the trail from either the *Cascade Fire Road* or the *Red Deer River* trail; the junction which serves as the southern trail head is at Km 25.1 of the *Red Deer River* trail, just 200 metres west of the Divide Creek ford. Southbound hikers can begin from the east end of the *Clearwater River* trail.

0.0—Red Deer River Junction (1770 m).

—Steady climb on slopes above Divide Creek canyon.

6.6—Trail begins sharp descent.

8.0—Divide Creek ford (ankle-deep).

8.4—Divide Warden Cabin.

—Trail climbs through upper subalpine forest and into alpine.

11.6—Divide Summit (2395 m).

—Trail descends north side of pass.

13.0—Cross to east side of Peters Creek.

—Valley narrows with numerous side scree slopes.

18.8—Peters Creek ford to west bank (calf-deep).

18.9—Peters Creek ford to east bank.

19.2—Peters Creek ford to west bank.

20.8—Steep climb away from creek begins.

22.4—Steep descent to Clearwater Valley.

24.0—Clearwater Valley floor, meadows.

24.9—Old outfitter's camp.

25.3—Clearwater River ford to north bank (swift, thigh-deep).

25.7—Junction (1740 m). Connects with *Clearwater River* trail at Km 0.0.

Branching north from the Red Deer River trail less than two kilometres west of the Cascade Fire Road, this horse trail serves as the main connecting link between the Red Deer Valley and the Clearwater River to the north.

From the junction with the Red Deer River trail, the trail climbs a steep, grassy bluff and then begins a slow, steady climb along a mountainside above and to the west of the tight, precipitous canyon of Divide Creek. After reaching an elevation of nearly 2285 metres above sea level on the shoulder of an unnamed mountain, the trail plunges down some 150 vertical metres in less than two kilometres to a crossing of Divide Creek just below the Divide Warden Cabin.

From the warden cabin the trail eases its way up through open meadows to reach the exceptionally scenic Divide Summit at Kilometre 11.6. This 2395 metre pass, which is inhabited by a large marmot colony, provides fine views south across the Red Deer Valley to Mount White and the sawtooth peaks of the Bare Range.

The trail descends north from the pass keeping to an excellent outfitter's trail along the right (east) side of Peters Creek. This trail runs all the way to the base of Mount Peters where it makes three fords in rapid succession. It then passes along a series of difficult scree slopes on the lower slopes of Mount Peters before making a final climb over the northeast shoulder of the mountain and descending to an old outfitter's camp in a meadow close to the Clearwater River.

The ford of the Clearwater is straightforward in periods of low water, and the Clearwater Valley trail is joined on the opposite shore. From this junction most backpackers turn west and follow the Clearwater River trail back into Banff Park (see *Clearwater River* trail description).

Clearwater River

Backpack

Allow 2 -3 days one way

Elevation gain: 590 metres (1,950 feet)

Maximum elevation: 2330 metres (7,650 feet)

Topo maps: Forbidden Creek 82 0/13
　　　　　Siffleur River 82 N/16
　　　　　Hector Lake 82 N/9

Point of Departure: Westbound backpackers can reach the east end of the Clearwater Valley near the park boundary by hiking the *Divide Creek— Peters Creek* trail north from the Red Deer River. The junction of this trail with the Clearwater Valley trail just 2.5 kms east of the park boundary serves as the start of the trip. Eastbound backpackers can reach the western end of the trail by hiking to Km 21.2 on the *Pipestone Pass* trail— an ill-defined junction just 3.0 kms north of the Pipestone Pass summit.

0.0—Divide Creek—Peters Creek Junction (1740 m).

　　—Follow west along old road track.

2.4—Park boundary. Wide track reverts to trail width.

3.4—Indianhead Lodge Warden Cabin.

3.5—Indianhead Creek crossing (ankle-deep).

4.2—Junction. Trail to Indianhead Creek— Whiterabbit Pass branches right.

7.5—Malloch Creek crossing (rock-hop or calf-deep ford).

13.1—Trident Lake.

14.4—Junction. Short branch trail left to Martin Creek waterfalls.

14.6—Martin Lake. Ford Martin Creek at lake outlet (70 metres wide, knee to thigh deep crossing).

17.1—Clearwater Lake (1905 m).

19.6—Clearwater Lakes Warden Cabin.

　　—Steady climb to pass, moderate grades.

28.9—Upper Devon Lake.

30.5—Clearwater Pass (2330 m).

31.6—Junction. Intersection with *Pipestone Pass* trail at Km 21.2.

The Clearwater is the most remote valley in Banff Park. Just getting to either end of the trail takes a minimum of two days. Yet this isolation preserves it as one of the last great unspoiled regions in the Rockies.

The Clearwater River trail can be reached from the west via Pipestone Pass and the headwaters of the Siffleur River (see *Pipestone Pass* trail description), but the valley unfolds far more dramatically when it is ascended from the park's eastern boundary at Indianhead to its scenic climax on lofty Clearwater Pass.

The most common approach to the Indianhead area is made from the Red Deer Valley utilizing the Divide Creek— Peters Creek trail; this route intersects the Clearwater trail at a point just 2.4 kilometres east of the park boundary. Just one kilometre west of the park boundary is Indianhead Lodge—one of the most isolated warden cabins in Banff Park.

From Indianhead the ascent of the valley is forested and somewhat monotonous. As the trail skirts north of Trident Lake, two waterfalls can be heard—one across the valley on Roaring Creek and the other ahead just below the outlet of Martin Lake (a short spur trail leads to an overlook for the latter falls).

Martin Lake can only be seen from the trail at the lake's outlet. Martin Creek must be forded at this point, a task best accomplished by wading into the shallows of the lake itself where the current is less swift. From this soggy crossing, the trail continues its level way to Clearwater Lake and then begins the climb to Clearwater Pass, an easy 425 vertical metres spread over the next 12 kilometres.

Clearwater Pass is a long, curving tundra summit where the sparkling Devon Lakes offset the harsh rock faces of the surrounding mountains. From the summit the trail descends for one kilometre to a junction with the Pipestone Pass— Siffleur Valley trail.

Whiterabbit Pass

Clearwater River to Whiterabbit Pass—12.7 kilometres (7.9 miles)

Backpack

Allow 4 hours to pass

Elevation gain: 470 metres (1,550 feet)

Maximum elevation: 2270 metres (7,450 feet)

Topo maps: Siffleur River 82 N/16

Point of Departure: Hike to the junction at Km 4.2 on the *Clearwater River* trail, just 0.7 km west of the Indianhead Creek ford. The Indianhead Creek trail angles off to the northwest from the main Clearwater Valley trail.

0.0—Clearwater River Junction (1800 m).

—Gradual to moderate uphill to northwest.

3.4—Trail bends due north, begins steep climb.

6.1—Summit (2165 m). Begin descent to Indianhead Creek.

7.9—Trail levels off above Indianhead Creek, begins ascent toward pass.

10.7—Cross to east side of Indianhead Creek (rock-hop).

12.7—Whiterabbit Pass (2270 m). Park boundary. Trail descends to Headwaters Cabin (6.0 km) and Whiterabbit Creek, emerging at the North Saskatchewan River suspension bridge at Kootenay Plains 36.8 kilometres from pass.

The Whiterabbit Trail is an old outfitter's route connecting the Clearwater Valley with the Kootenay Plains to the north. It is still commonly used by horse parties, but seldom by backpackers, even though it is quite passable and scenic.

From its junction with the Clearwater River trail, 800 metres west of Indianhead Lodge, the trail climbs over a 2165 metre summit before descending into the Indianhead Creek drainage. Much of the ascent of Indianhead Creek is made through open meadows, and Whiterabbit Pass is a broad, grassy pass which allows good views north into the Ram River valley.

While Whiterabbit Pass is a worthwhile side trip for backpackers camped in the Clearwater Valley, most hikers continue the journey north into the Clearwater Provincial Forest and onwards to the Kootenay Plains. From the pass the trail makes an easy descent to the south branch of the Ram River. The river is forded to its west bank 4.7 kilometres from the pass.

Just over a kilometre beyond the Ram River ford is the old Headwaters Cabin— a dilapidated forest ranger cabin situated on a bluff which provides one of the most scenic viewpoints in all of the Front Ranges. The trail runs northwest from the cabin over a low divide and descends onto the headwaters of Whiterabbit Creek. The Whiterabbit is a long, straight valley filled with heavy forest and large areas of deadfall (an erratic trail is maintained primarily by passing horse parties).

When Whiterabbit Creek runs out onto the floor of the North Saskatchewan Valley, the trail enters an area of old logging roads. Keep left at all junctions until the Siffleur River bridge is crossed. From this junction it is a short walk to the suspension bridge across the North Saskatchewan River and the trail head parking lot.

Short Hikes and Nature Trails

TUNNEL MOUNTAIN — 1.8 kilometres

The Tunnel Mountain trail provides a short, easy and readily accessible hike from downtown Banff. The mountaintop, just 300 vertical metres above the town, offers excellent viewing of the Banff environs, and, in particular, an impressive vista of the north ridge of Mount Rundle and a 30 kilometre section of the Bow Valley stretching from the Massive Range on the west to the Canmore vicinity on the east. The trail is one of the oldest in the park and probably is hiked more than any other near Banff.

To reach the trail head, follow Wolf Street east from Banff Avenue to where it ends at the foot of Tunnel Mountain. Turn right onto St. Julien Road and follow it 350 metres, watching for the trail sign and parking area on the left (uphill) side of the road. For those with a vehicle, 0.3 kilometre of uphill hiking can be saved by continuing up St. Julien Road 0.5 kilometre to the Tunnel Mountain Road (St. Julien turns left at the entrance to the Banff Centre campus). Turn left onto Tunnel Mountain Road and continue uphill another 0.5 kilometre to a parking area where the Tunnel Mountain trail crosses the road on its way to the summit.

The trail gradually ascends the western flank of Tunnel Mountain via a series of sweeping switchbacks, climbing through a thick forest of lodgepole pine and Douglas fir. After passing a couple of fine viewpoints on the mountain's summit ridge, the trail eventually ends on a small promontory which was once the site of the Tunnel Mountain fire lookout tower. *Topo map: Banff 82 0/4.*

FENLAND TRAIL — 2.1 kilometres

This short loop trail can be reached quite easily on foot from downtown Banff, and it offers a pleasant walk through an environment which most visitors would not associate with the mountains.

By walking or driving out of Banff on the Mount Norquay Road, one crosses the railroad tracks just south of the CPR station and immediately encounters the Fenland trail sign on the left-hand side of the road. Approximately 100 metres into the forest the trail splits, making an elongated loop through the forest via a level pathway and returning to the junction in just under two kilometres.

The main feature of this walk is the way in which a pond-marsh environment is slowly transforming into a mature, valley bottom spruce forest. At various points along the trail hikers will encounter open swamps, streams where beaver have been at work, willow and shrub communities which have been pruned by browsing deer and elk, and stands of towering spruce trees—the last stage of fenland succession. Along with the adjacent Vermilion Lakes, the Fenland is one of the prime birding areas of Banff Park. *Topo map: Banff 82 0/4.*

STONEY SQUAW — 2.1 kilometres

One of the highest viewpoints in the Banff townsite vicinity, the summit of Stoney Squaw offers an excellent survey of the many interesting features in the Bow Valley. An alternate trail along the mountain's north slope offers the option of a loop trip, returning to the trail head via a very different forest environment than what was encountered on the ascent.

Follow the Mount Norquay Road north from the Trans-Canada Highway at Banff townsite's west interchange, climbing six kilometres of twisting switchbacks to the Mount Norquay Ski Area. Turn into the first parking lot on the right (Lot #3) and watch for the trail sign just inside the entrance on the right-hand side.

The trail is enclosed in a dense forest of lodgepole pine and spruce for much of its length, but within 200 metres of the mountain's 1884 metre summit the hiker begins to catch glimpses of the Banff environs to the south and east. Spread out below are Banff townsite, Tunnel Mountain and the Bow Valley. Mount Rundle, the Spray Valley, Sulphur Mountain and the Sundance Valley are all visible, while the towering south face of Cascade Mountain (2998 m) looms above the viewpoint at trail's end.

By descending northwest from the summit along a little rib of forest-covered rock for a few metres, you will pick up good trail. This trail drops down through dense forest along the cool north side of the mountain and eventually intersects at the top of a ski run. Walk down this run to a dirt ski area access road, turn left and follow the road back to Parking Lot #3. *Topo map: Banff 82 0/4.*

MULESHOE — 1.1 kilometres

This short trail climbs up the steep, southwest slope of Mount Cory above the Muleshoe (a horseshoe shaped arm of the Bow River). The trip gives hikers an excellent tour of a montane forest—an arid life zone forested with lodgepole pine. aspen and old Douglas fir. The meadows near the top of the trail, which provide a good overview of the Bow Valley, are coloured by prairie anemone, bluebells, gaillardia, blue flax, and other dryland wildflowers throughout much of the summer.

The trail head is located on the north side of the Bow Valley Parkway, directly across from the Muleshoe Picnic Area. This picnic area, which serves as a parking lot for the trail, is reached by following the Parkway west 5.5 kilometres from its eastern junction with the Trans-Canada Highway near Banff.

Though the nature trail only travels 1.1 kilometres to a semi-open viewpoint overlooking the Muleshoe, a steep but well defined track continues up the slope to an expansive meadow with an unobstructed panorama of the Bow Valley from Castle Mountain to the peaks near Banff. For hikers with lots of stamina, it is possible to follow this trail upwards into subalpine forest for nearly two kilometres more, finally topping the west ridge of Mount Cory at an elevation of nearly 2200 metres above sea level.

While this trail makes an ideal spring hike (often open in mid-May), the slope is infested with wood ticks early in the season: Be sure to check yourself over carefully for these sneaky critters following any outing on the Muleshoe. *Topo map: Banff 82 0/4.*

SMITH LAKE — 1.5 kilometres

Smith Lake is a quiet pool nestled into the south slope of the Bow Valley and surrounded by a forest of lodgepole pine and white spruce. The trail is of moderate grade—just long enough to stifle the sounds of the Trans-Canada Highway, but short enough to be visited in less than an hour.

To reach the lake, follow the Trans-Canada Highway to the Altrude Creek Picnic Area, just 400 metres east of Castle Junction (30 kilometres west of Banff). After turning south onto the gravel access road to the picnic area, turn left immediately onto another gravel road and follow it for 300 metres. A small parking area just off this road to the left marks the start of the trail—an old rock quarry access road. Just 100 metres down this road, the Smith Lake trail branches uphill to the left. *Topo maps: Castle Mountain 82 0/5 and Banff 82 0/4.*

MUD LAKE — 1.2 kilometres

For anyone in search of a little peace and quiet in the very busy tourist area surrounding the lower Lake Louise village, Mud Lake is an attractive if not overly spectacular destination. The lake is just over a half-kilometre in length and is encircled by a dense forest composed primarily of fire succession lodgepole pine, but the lakeshore remains open enough to allow views out to the peaks which surround this section of valley.

To reach the Mud Lake trail, follow the Trans-Canada Highway to the Lake Louise Service Centre west exit, located 56 kilometres west of Banff townsite and 1.5 kilometres east of the Icefields Parkway junction. Instead of turning south into the service centre district, turn north onto the access road leading to the area's residential district. Keep right at the road split 100 metres beyond the junction and drive another 200 metres to the trail sign and parking area situated on opposite sides of the road.

The trail climbs from the valley bottom and soon intersects with the broad Pipestone River horse trail. At Kilometre 0.7 the trail to Mud Lake branches right from the Pipestone route and reaches the lakeshore 500 metres beyond. *Topo map: Lake Louise 82 N/8.*

HECTOR LAKE — 2.1 kilometres

The Hector Lake hike, a short, downhill excursion off the Icefields Parkway, is of limited use to casual hikers owing to the necessity of fording the Bow River before the lakeshore is reached. It is primarily used by fishermen who hike the first half of the trail to gain access to the river.

The trail head is located on the west side of the Icefields Parkway 18 kilometres north of its junction with the Trans-Canada Highway. A sign marks the trail head (there is no parking area) one kilometre north of the Hector Lake viewpoint.

Initially, the trail travels due west to the floor of the Bow Valley through closed forest, reaching the Bow River at the 1.1 kilometre mark. While the ford is not difficult at low water (late in the season), it can be treacherous when water levels are high. The trail begins anew on the opposite side of the river and reaches the shore of Hector Lake in another kilometre of easy walking, emerging at the site of an old cabin camp once operated by pioneer guide and outfitter Jimmy Simpson. *Topo map: Hector Lake 82 N/9.*

PEYTO LAKE — 2.4 kilometres

Though many travellers stop to admire the turquoise beauty of Peyto Lake from the high overlook at Bow Summit, few ever walk to its shore. And that, for most, is fortunate, since the 2.4 kilometre trail connecting the viewpoint to the lakeshore drops some 275 vertical metres—a formidable hole that might prove the undoing of many idle tourists.

There are actually two trails leading to the waters of Peyto Lake. The trail descending from the viewpoint, while being the most arduous, is probably the most interesting for most hikers since it allows the option of continuing on to the toe of the Peyto Glacier.

To reach the trail head at the Peyto Lake viewpoint, follow the Icefields Parkway to Bow Summit, 41 kilometres north of the Trans-Canada Highway (just 4.8 kilometres north of Numtijah Lodge at Bow Lake). Follow the access road which branches west from the Parkway to the main parking area below the viewpoint. A paved nature trail runs 400 metres to the viewpoint. The trail down to the lake begins uphill from the main viewpoint platform.

From the viewpoint, the path dives down into a lush subalpine forest, switchbacking madly to the broad, gravel outwash flats at the head of Peyto Lake. From this point hikers can either roam at their leisure along the lakeshore or head off in the direction of Peyto Glacier to the south. For the latter option, walk across the flats parallel to the lake's main tributary stream to a point about 100 metres left of where the stream cuts through a forested morainal ridge. Find the trail which crosses this ridge, then follow cairns upstream through rocky terrain toward the toe of the glacier. The trail gets steeper and more treacherous near the glacier, and anyone venturing onto the ice should be experienced and equipped with rope and ice axe.

A shorter, less arduous trail reaches Peyto Lake from the Icefields Parkway just 2.7 kilometres north of Bow Summit. The trail, a scant 1.4 kilometres long, leads to a pleasant little beach on the east shore of Peyto Lake (travel along the lake from this tiny beach is not easy since there is heavy bush and no lakeshore trail). *Topo maps: Hector Lake 82 N/9 and Blaeberry River 82 N/10.*

WARDEN LAKE — 2.2 kilometres

For anyone who is camping or lodging near Saskatchewan River Crossing, the trail to Warden Lake makes a nice after-dinner stroll. The trail is flat and totally undemanding, and the tiny lake itself is quite peaceful—a shallow body of water where moose are often seen feeding against the spectacular backdrop of Mount Murchison (3333 m).

The Warden Lake trail strikes off from the south side of the Saskatchewan River Crossing Warden Station. Follow the Icefields Parkway to this warden complex, located 75 kilometres north of the Trans-Canada Highway and two kilometres south of the Parkway's junction with the David Thompson Highway (Hwy #11) and the Saskatchewan River Crossing resort. Park alongside the dirt access road opposite the warden station and start the hike at the trail sign on the east side of the highway.

Once past the warden station, the trail becomes a wide, gravelly road for most of its distance to the lake (avoid foot trails which branch from the road). After passing a small pond and crossing a log bridge at Kilometre 1.9, the road reverts to trail. From this point it is only 300 metres to the shores of the lake. A rough trail runs along the northeast shoreline, and a smaller pond situated just beyond the lake's eastern tip can be visited by following this track for a few more minutes. *Topo map: Mistaya Lake 82 N/15.*

PANTHER FALLS — 1.0 kilometre

This short trail leads to one of the more spectacular falls in Banff Park—a thundering cascade on Nigel Creek that plunges some 180 metres. Yet because the waterfall cannot be seen from the Icefields Parkway and the trail is unmarked, it is seldom visited.

To reach Panther Falls, follow the Icefields Parkway to a large roadside parking area on the "Big Hill" (the long grade which climbs from the North Saskatchewan Valley to Sunwapta Pass). This pulloff is located on the east side of the highway 113 kilometres north of the Trans-Canada Highway and nine kilometres south of Sunwapta Pass (the Banff-Jasper boundary).

The unmarked beginning of this one kilometre-long trail is located at the lower end of the parking area, hidden just below its eastern edge. This roaring falls, whose base is shrouded in mist, received its name from a party of early explorers who thought the water's leap from the lip of the cliff resembled that of a panther.

While the lip of Panther Falls is located only a few metres from the roadside parking area, it is a very dangerous area which should be avoided by one and all; accidents involving people who lose their balance and tumble over waterfalls are common in the Rocky Mountains. *Topo map: Columbia Icefield 83 C/3.*

PARKER'S RIDGE — 2.4 kilometres

The Parker's Ridge hike constitutes a short, spectacular excursion into the alpine life zone. Beginning at the marked parking area alongside the Icefields Parkway near the northern end of Banff Park, the trail winds up and over a high, treeless ridge to a prospect overlooking the 12 kilometre-long tongue of the Saskatchewan Glacier. Parker's Ridge is home to a small population of mountain goats and supports a limited plant life of stunted willows, mosses, heather and several species of tiny wildflowers.

The trail head parking area is located on the west side of the Icefields Parkway 41 kilometres north of Saskatchewan River Crossing and 4.2 kilometres south of the Banff-Jasper boundary at Sunwapta Pass. The lower reaches of the trail climb through open meadows and scattered stands of alpine fir. About halfway up the north-facing slope, however, at an elevation of 2130 metres, the stunted fir give way to the low clinging ground cover typical of alpine tundra.

Beyond the ridge summit, the trail gradually descends another half kilometre to the Saskatchewan Glacier viewpoint. Here the hiker has a panoramic view of the uppermost limits of the North Saskatchewan River valley, dominated by the Saskatchewan Glacier—a spur of ice flowing down from the Columbia Icefield on the continental divide.

While returning from the ridge summit, please refrain from shortcutting across the tundra. Summer lasts but a few short weeks at this elevation and life is a tenuous affair for the native flora, so stay on the trail and save this area for the enjoyment of others. *Topo map: Columbia Icefield 83 C/3.*

Jasper National Park

With an area of 10,878 square kilometres, Jasper is the largest of Canada's Rocky Mountain national parks. Lying along the eastern slope of the Rockies in western Alberta, the park is bordered on the west by the continental divide and Mount Robson Provincial Park, while to the south it shares a common boundary with Banff National Park.

Jasper contains close to 1,000 kilometres of trail, many of which run through areas of historical significance dating to the early fur trade days. Day hiking opportunities in Jasper are somewhat limited and scattered as compared to other mountain parks. The largest concentration of day and half-day trips is in the Jasper townsite vicinity, but these are basically low level hikes to forest encircled lakes. The best day trips in the park are the Cavell Meadows at the foot of Mount Edith Cavell, Bald Hills and Opal Hills at the northwest end of Maligne Lake, the Sulphur Skyline above Miette Hot Springs, and Wilcox Pass overlooking the Athabasca Glacier.

Jasper's main glory, however, is its backpacking trail system. Thanks to a program of trail upgrading and bridge building started in the 1970s, it may well be the premier area for remote wilderness hiking in North America. Routes such as the North and South Boundary Trails offer solitary rambles of over 160 kilometres each, while shorter trail segments like Jonas Pass, Maligne Pass and the popular Skyline Trail can be linked together to form hikes ranging from three to nine days duration. Other areas, notably the Tonquin Valley and the Fryatt Valley, offer 'objective' hikes where a base camp can be established for further day hike exploration.

In an attempt to protect some environmentally sensitive areas and to insure a wilderness experience for backcountry visitors, park officials have set a quota for each of Jasper's trails, and anyone planning an overnight trip in the park must obtain a park use permit. Quotas in popular areas can fill rapidly during the months of July and August (Tonquin Valley, the Skyline Trail, and the Fryatt Hut are by far the most popular), and hikers should come to the park with several options in mind. For hikers devoted to the idea of a specific trail, it is possible to reserve a spot up to three weeks in advance (the park will pre-book to 30 percent of each trail's quota) by writing the Superintendent, Jasper National Park, P.O. Box 10, Jasper, Alberta T0E 1E0. The requests should include the name of the leader, the number of hikers, the route, destination and the dates of the days to be spent hiking.

Restrictions concerning open wood fires apply to certain areas, and hikers should check with park information staff concerning the use of fire at their destination campgrounds. (The use of small camp stoves is encouraged.) Park use permits and trail information can be obtained year around from the Jasper Townsite Information Centre on Connaught Drive and at the Columbia Icefield Centre during the summer months.

The town of Jasper provides the full gamut of visitor services, ranging from motels, gas stations and grocery stores to hiking and climbing specialty shops. Gas, food and accommodation are also available at the Columbia Icefield, Sunwapta Falls, and Miette Junction (Pocahontas) during the summer months.

JASPER NATIONAL PARK

◇ INFORMATION BUREAU
▲ CAMPGROUNDS
—— HIGHWAYS

0   10   20   30   40
KILOMETRES

Access: The primary route of access to Jasper Park from the east and west is Highway #16 (the Yellowhead Highway), and the town of Jasper is situated 362 kilometres west of Edmonton, Alberta, and 440 kilometres northeast of Kamloops, B.C., on this route. Many travellers enter the park from the south via the 230 kilometre-long Icefields Parkway (beginning just west of Lake Louise on the Trans-Canada Highway).

Jasper is well served by public transport. East and westbound VIA Rail trains stop in Jasper townsite each day. All Greyhound buses travelling between British Columbia cities and Edmonton, Alberta, stop at Jasper townsite, and flag stops can be arranged for Miette Junction (Pocahontas). Brewster Transportation operates a daily bus service between Calgary International Airport and Jasper, travelling via Banff, Lake Louise and the Icefields Parkway (backpackers have the option of buying tickets to trail head drop-off points anywhere along the way).

147

Cavell Meadows

Half-day trip

Allow 1 hour one way

Elevation gain: 370 metres (1,200 feet)

Maximum elevation: 2135 metres (7,000 feet)

Topo maps: Amethyst Lakes 83 D/9†
†trail not shown

Point of Departure: Follow the Icefields Parkway (Hwy 93) south from Jasper townsite 7½ kilometres (4½ miles) to the junction with the 93-A Highway. Turn right onto the 93-A and follow south for 5½ kilometres (3½ miles) to the junction with the Mount Edith Cavell Road. Follow the Cavell Road 14½ kilometres (9 miles) to its terminus at the parking area beneath Mount Edith Cavell. The trail head for Cavell Meadows and Angel Glacier is at the south edge of the parking area.

0.0—Trail sign (1765 m).

—Follow paved trail across glacial moraine.

0.6—Junction. Nature trail to lake at toe of Angel Glacier straight ahead. Switchback up to left for Cavell Meadows.

—Steady uphill along moraine and into forest.

3.2—Junction. Trail splits into alpine meadows loop—keep right for more gradual ascent.

—Trail climbs into open alpine meadows.

3.8—Cavell Meadows Summit (2135 m). Trail descends from this point to connect back into approach trail at Km 3.2.

The Cavell Meadows trail offers a short ramble through a beautiful alpine meadow lying high above the standard tourist viewpoint for the Angel Glacier. The meadow is lovely in its own right, but it further provides an outstanding perspective of the hanging glacier and the north wall of Mount Edith Cavell. The trail is a popular one, and hikers should approach it more with scenery than solitude in mind.

The trip begins from the parking area on the paved Path of the Glacier which runs to a small lake at the toe of Angel Glacier (a short side trip and worth a visit). Hikers bound for the Cavell Meadows should catch the left hand trail fork at the half-kilometre mark to switchback up and over a sharp ridge of a lateral moraine.

After climbing through a subalpine forest of spruce and fir, the trail emerges near timberline to face the magnificent Mount Edith Cavell and Angel Glacier. With an elevation of 3363 metres, the peak is the highest in this section of the park. It is composed of a combination of Pre-Cambrian sandstones and shales and Cambrian quartz sandstones, and is considered one of the classic mountains of the Canadian Rockies. The Angel Glacier, the head of which is slowly grinding a huge amphitheatre into the uppermost reaches of the great rock wall, adds much to the glory of its northern aspect. The toe of the glacier, cascading over a 300-metre cliff in a spectacular series of icefalls, is its most visible part from this angle.

From the first overlook, the trail continues to the south, then loops upward to even higher viewpoints in the flower-filled alpine meadows above. The loop is finally closed by dropping back down to join the approach trail near the first viewpoint. Hikers should stay on the trail in the upper meadows; indiscriminate wandering by the large numbers of people who visit here could quickly make a hash of this beautiful but fragile landscape.

Angel Glacier from Cavell Meadows

Tonquin Valley

Dr. J. Monroe Thorington, a well known mountaineer and historian who devoted many years of his life to rambling about the Canadian Rockies, wrote eloquently of the Tonquin Valley and how its "unique combination of lake, precipice, and ice . . . presents itself with a singular beauty almost unequalled in alpine regions of North America." For anyone who has visited this area during a spell of good weather, and particularly late in the year when the crowds have dispersed and the air is crisp and clear, it would be hard to dispute that this is one of the truly spectacular hiking areas in the mountain west. But in the midst of summer, when the rains are pelting down, the mosquitoes, black flies and no-see-ums are swarming, the campgrounds are all filled to capacity, and the trails have been churned to mush by heavy horse use, this lovely area comes very close to a backpacker's definition of hell; at such times it is better to forget the Tonquin's reputation and to go in search of less travelled ways.

The Tonquin Valley more closely resembles a high, five kilometre-long pass than a true valley. Its broad crest cradles the Amethyst Lakes, a pair of beautiful interconnected lakes which lie at the base of a 1000 metre wall of Precambrian quartz sandstone called The Ramparts. The wall is actually composed of ten spectacular castellate peaks which are certainly worthy of names such as Bastion, Drawbridge, Redoubt, Dungeon and Paragon — a glowering collection of towers and turrets which the Indians once thought to be inhabited by huge and horrible beasts possessed of supernatural powers. A few kilometres west of the northern Amethyst Lake are Moat Lake and the twin passes of Moat and Tonquin, while Chrome Lake and the heavily glaciated spires of the Eremite Valley lie just south of the Tonquin Valley (both areas are prime day trip destinations for those camped in the valley).

Two trails of almost equal length lead into the valley — one running up the Astoria River from near the base of Mount Edith Cavell, the other travelling via Portal Creek and Maccarib Pass from the Marmot Basin Road. Generally, the Maccarib Pass approach is considered the most scenic, while the Astoria River trail is the quickest route to the campgrounds at the south end of Amethyst Lake and the Wates-Gibson Hut at Outpost Lake.

In addition to the four campgrounds in the valley, there is a lodge located at the Narrows and a cabin camp at the end of the north lake, but as of this writing both operations are oriented to horse parties (information on these lodges can be obtained from the Jasper Chamber of Commerce, Jasper, Alberta T0E 1E0). While there is no camping permitted in the Eremite Valley region, the Wates-Gibson Hut on the shores of Outpost Lake can accommodate up to 40 people; the hut is staffed with a custodian throughout the summer and information concerning booking and rates is available from the Alpine Club of Canada, Box 1026, Banff, Alberta T0L 0C0 or by phoning 403-762-4481.

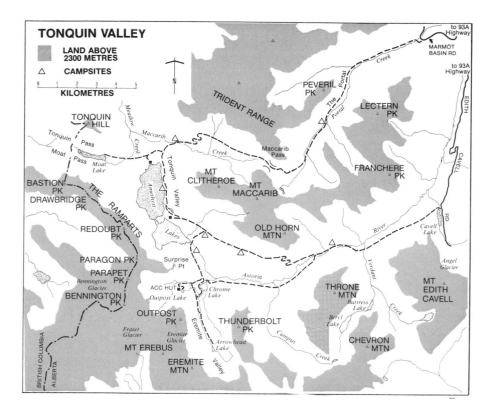

Maccarib Pass

Backpack

Allow 7 - 9 hours to Amethyst Lakes

Elevation gain: 730 metres (2,400 feet)
    loss: 235 metres (770 feet)

Maximum elevation: 2210 metres (7,250 feet)

Topo maps: Jasper 83 D/16
    Amethyst Lakes 83 D/9

Point of Departure: Follow the Icefields Parkway (Hwy 93) south from Jasper townsite 7½ kilometres (4½ miles) to the junction with the 93-A Highway. Turn right onto the 93-A and follow south for 2½ kilometres (1½ miles) to the junction with the Marmot Basin Ski Area access road. Follow the Marmot Basin Road for 6½ kilometres (4 miles) to the point where it crosses Portal Creek. Park in the parking area on the south side of the creek.

0.0—Trail sign (1480 m).

0.5—Portal Creek bridge to north side of creek.

—Ascend Portal Creek canyon.

4.0—Circus Creek bridge.

5.0—Trail emerges into open rockslides.

7.7—Portal Creek Campground.

10.1—Grade steepens on climb to pass.

12.4—Maccarib Pass (2210 m).

12.9—First views into Tonquin Valley. Gradual descent toward valley.

18.5—Tonquin Valley viewpoint.

19.5—Maccarib Campground and Maccarib Creek bridge.

20.4—Junction. Moat Lake straight ahead 3.0 kms. Turn left for Amethyst Lakes.

—Flat valley bottom trail running due south.

21.3—Amethyst Lakes (north end).

22.9—Amethyst Campground.

24.0—Tonquin Valley Lodge (1975 m).

—Trail climbs east from lodge junction.

26.2—Junction. Intersection with *Tonquin Valley via Astoria River* trail at Km 16.8.

Of the two main trails into the Tonquin Valley, Maccarib Pass is slightly longer and more arduous, yet it holds a definite scenic advantage over the Astoria River trail: from the lofty heights of Maccarib Pass, the trail descends a six kilometre-long meadow which discloses ever-improving views of one of the most sublime scenes in the Canadian Rockies — the sheer cliffs of The Ramparts rising from the placid waters of the Amethyst Lakes.

Striking off from the Marmot Basin Road, the trail over Maccarib ascends the narrow canyon of The Portal, and by climbing high onto the north side of the valley and traversing rockslides below Peveril Peak, it soon provides excellent views to the head of the valley and the peaks surrounding the pass. After descending back to the valley floor, the trail makes a five kilometre-long climb through an open subalpine forest of Engelmann spruce and alpine fir. The trail finally emerges above the last of the trees less than two kilometres from the pass.

While the approach to Maccarib Pass offers some fine views, particularly to the jagged summit of Old Horn Mountain rising above a col to the south, the trail's true reward lies on the western slope of the pass. From the first glimpse of The Ramparts and Moat Pass obtained near the summit, each succeeding kilometre across the open alpine tundra brings an ever-broadening perspective of the Tonquin Valley and its surrounding peaks.

After passing a fine campground at Kilometre 19.5, the trail drops to the floor of the Tonquin Valley near the north end of the Amethyst Lakes. Here the path forks, the right branch leading to Moat Lake and the left running south along the east shore of the Amethyst Lakes. From this junction a well defined trail skirts the shore of the northern-most lake, but south of Tonquin Valley Lodge and the Narrows the shoreline becomes extremely marshy. The only good trail climbs well

Amethyst Lakes and The Ramparts from Maccarib Pass trail

up onto the east side of the valley to the Clitheroe Campground junction before descending to the south end of the lakes at Surprise Point (see *Astoria River* trail description).

In addition to all the usual wildlife one would expect to find in the upper subalpine life zone, the Tonquin is also home to a herd of mountain caribou; these shy animals are usually seen on the open slopes above timberline, and because of their nervous disposition they should never be approached or harrassed. Grizzly bears also travel through the area from time to time.

Moat Lake. This is a short side trip branching from the Maccarib Pass trail just beyond the north end of Amethyst Lakes. From the junction, the trail runs across rocky, open meadows and enters the trees. A spur trail cuts left at Kilometre 1.3 and leads to a cabin camp and the north end of the Amethyst Lakes — a very pretty viewpoint. Moat Lake is reached less than two kilometres beyond the cabin camp junction. The perpendicular cliffs of the northern Ramparts rise above the lake's southern shoreline, while its waters stretch for more than a kilometre toward the nearby twin passes of Moat and Tonquin on the Alberta-B.C. boundary.

153

Astoria River

Backpack

Allow 6 - 8 hours to Amethyst Lakes

Elevation gain: 445 metres (1,450 feet)
     loss: 130 metres (420 feet)

Maximum elevation: 2105 metres (6,900 feet)

Topo maps: Amethyst Lakes 83 D/9†
    †trail not shown

Point of Departure: Follow the Icefields Parkway (Hwy 93) south from Jasper townsite 7½ kilometres (4½ miles) to the junction with the 93-A Highway. Turn right onto the 93-A and follow south for 5½ kilometres (3½ miles) to the junction with the Mount Edith Cavell Road. Continue on the Cavell Road for 12½ kilometres (8 miles) to the roadside parking area above Cavell Lake. Leave your vehicle in one of the pulloff parking areas and hike down to the Astoria River trail head at the outlet to Cavell Lake.

0.0—Cavell Lake and bridge (1720 m).

    —Contour through forest along north slope of Mt. Edith Cavell.

5.0—Astoria River bridge to north side (1660 m).

6.8—Astoria Campground.

8.2—Junction. Shortcut to Chrome Lake—Eremite Valley cuts left across river via log bridge (6.5 kms to Chrome Lake).

    —Steep switchbacks up slopes of Old Horn Mtn.

12.9—Maximum elevation (2105 m). High subalpine meadows.

13.3—Switchback Campground.

16.8—Junction. Intersection with *Tonquin Valley via Maccarib Pass* trail at Km 26.2. Tonquin Valley Lodge, Amethyst Campground, and north end of Amethyst Lakes to right. Keep left for Clitheroe and Surprise Point Campgrounds and south end of Amethyst Lakes.

16.9—Clitheroe Campground.

18.7—Amethyst Lakes south end (1975 m). Bridge across outlet stream.

19.1—Surprise Point Campground.

The Astoria River trail should be considered the express route to the Tonquin Valley. While the distance to the Amethyst Lakes is not all that much shorter via the Astoria than Maccarib Pass, the elevation gain is markedly less, and you can reach the Clitheroe Campground with its panoramic view of the valley in just 16.9 kilometres. And if you are bound for the Alpine Club of Canada hut at Outpost Lake, the Chrome Lake-Eremite Valley shortcut up the south side of the river is by far the quickest option.

The trail begins from the Mount Edith Cavell Road and immediately descends to cross the bridge at the outlet to Cavell Lake. The next five kilometres consist of a long, gradually descending traverse through the forest on Mount Edith Cavell's north slope. The trail eventually reaches the Astoria River and crosses to the north side to begin its ascent of the valley.

At Kilometre 8.2 the branch trail to Chrome Lake and Eremite Valley cuts left to cross the Astoria on a log bridge. The main trail continues along the north side of the river and soon begins a strenuous switchbacking climb up the south slope of Old Horn Mountain. You reach the maximum elevation on the trail near the thirteen kilometre mark, and then level off across the west slope of Old Horn. Here you are greeted with the first views of The Ramparts and Amethyst Lakes.

It was from the slopes of nearby Mount Clitheroe that the topographical surveyor Morrison P. Bridgland first photographed the valley in 1915 and subsequently revealed its glories to the world. The area drew a steady procession of visitors over the ensuing years, particularly photographers. In 1918 the Banff photographer Byron Harmon shot the first motion picture footage of the valley from the slopes of Clitheroe, and in 1928 Ansel Adams visited the valley with members of

The Ramparts from near Surprise Point

California's Sierra Club, his first outing as the club's official photographer.

At Kilometre 16.8 the trail splits, the right hand branch descending to Tonquin Valley Lodge and the northern Amethyst Lake (see *Maccarib Pass* trail description), the left running downhill to the outlet for the southern lake beneath Surprise Point; the Clitheroe Campground lies just 100 metres below this junction within the scattered fir and spruce trees of the upper subalpine forest.

Most backpackers who reach the Tonquin Valley via Astoria River stay at Clitheroe or Surprise Point Campgrounds. Both have good views of The Ramparts, and they are good jumping-off points for day trips into the Eremite Val-

ley region to the south (see *Chrome Lake-Eremite Valley* trail description).

Chrome Lake via Astoria Valley. This trail branches from the Astoria River trail at Kilometre 8.2, crosses the river, and runs up the south side of the valley to reach Chrome Lake in 6.5 kilometres. This is an old access trail and is not well maintained. The track tends to be narrow, rough and, with the exception of a few meadowy areas, forest-enclosed. Once you reach Chrome Lake, stay on the trail leading around the north side of the lake for 0.3 kilometre to an intersection with the Chrome Lake-Eremite Valley trail, 1.9 kilometres south of the Surprise Point Campground.

155

Eremite Valley

Surprise Point Campground to Arrowhead Lake—6.6 kilometres (4.1 miles)

Backpack

Allow 2 - 3 hours one way

Elevation loss: 135 metres (450 feet)

Elevation gain: 180 metres (600 feet)

Maximum elevation: 2010 metres (6,600 feet)

Topo maps: Amethyst Lakes 83 D/9†
†trail not shown

Point of Departure: Hike to the Surprise Point Campground at the south end of Amethyst Lakes using either the *Maccarib Pass* or *Astoria River* trails.

0.0—Surprise Point Campground (1965 m).

—Trail runs south from campground, descending steadily via rocky, rough track.

1.9—Junction (1830 m). Branch trail leads left to north shore of Chrome Lake (0.3 km) and the junction with the Astoria River trail at Km 8.2 (7.6 kms). Keep right for Outpost Lake and Eremite Valley.

2.4—Junction. Branch trail right to Outpost Lake and Wates—Gibson Hut (1.1 kms). Keep left for Eremite Valley.

—Trail runs through open meadows west of Chrome Lake.

3.2—Junction. Branch trail left to south shore of Chrome Lake. Eremite Valley straight ahead.

4.5—Old Alpine Club of Canada campground (no camping).

—Trail climbs onto old rockslide and ascends valley along its crest. Track becomes vague and intermittent.

6.6—Arrowhead Lake (2010 m). Area of extensive rockslides and moraines near head of Eremite Valley.

While Amethyst Lakes and The Ramparts serve as the scenic focal point of the Tonquin Valley region, the valley is open-ended with trails running both north and south to lakes and views of equal grandeur. The most popular of these day trips from campgrounds in the Tonquin runs south from the Surprise Point Campground to Chrome Lake and the Eremite Valley, While the distance is not far, you will want to reserve a full day for the trip so you can explore the upper end of the Eremite Valley and still have time for a side trip to Outpost Lake.

From the Surprise Point Campground a rough and rocky trail descends due south to the extensive meadowland containing Chrome Lake and Penstock Creek. From the first junction encountered in this meadow, it is a short, 300 metre walk down to the shore of Chrome Lake—a small but beautiful sheet of turquoise water which reflects the mountains surrounding the head of the Eremite Valley to the south.

The main trail runs west 500 metres to another junction just a short distance above Penstock Creek. The right hand branch follows Penstock Creek upstream, crosses to the true right bank of the creek at the foot of a steep forested slope, and then climbs to the shores of tiny Outpost Lake—a total distance of only 1.1 kilometres from the junction with the Eremite Valley trail. While the lake is ringed by forest, the sharp prow of Outpost Peak does provide a spectacular backdrop. The Wates—Gibson Hut, operated by the Alpine Club of Canada, is located on the lake's north shore. (Check with the Alpine Club's main office in Banff or with the hut custodian concerning accommodation.)

The main trail continues south to reach the head of the Eremite Valley in another four kilometres. The track is rough and vague over the last two kilometres, but the route is obvious and the destination well worth the effort. The Eremite is a

Chrome Lake and the Eremite Valley

spectacular alpine region where glaciers crown almost every peak and which has been a popular haunt of climbers ever since the first Alpine Club camps were held in the Tonquin Valley (1926) and at Chrome Lake (1934). The valley surrounding tiny Arrowhead Lake is a tumbled area of rockslides and glacial moraines which offers unlimited opportunities for scrambling and exploration.

Chrome Lake via Astoria River. The Chrome Lake—Eremite Valley region can be reached directly without the need of detouring through the Tonquin Valley. At Kilometre 8.2 on the Astoria River route to Amethyst Lakes, a trail branches left to the south side of the river and ascends to Chrome Lake and the junction with the Eremite Valley trail in another 7.6 kilometres. There is no camping permitted in the Eremite Valley region, however, so this approach will be of primary interest to those who have reserved overnight accommodation at the Alpine Club's hut on Outpost Lake.

Athabasca Pass

Moab Lake to Athabasca Pass—49.1 kilometres (30.5 miles)

Backpack

Allow 3 days to Athabasca Pass

Elevation gain: 545 metres (1,780 feet)

Maximum elevation: 1755 metres (5,750 feet)

Topo maps: Athabasca Falls 83 C/12
Amethyst Lakes 83 D/9†
Athabasca Pass 83 D/8†
†last 36 kms not shown

Point of Departure: From the junction of the Ice-fields Parkway and Highway 93-A at Athabasca Falls, follow the 93-A north for 9 kilometres (5½ miles) to the Moab Lake access road junction. Follow the Moab Lake Road southwest 7 kilometres (4½ miles) to the parking area for the short lake trail. The rock barriers at the left hand corner of the parking area mark the beginning of the Athabasca Pass trail.

0.0—Moab Lake parking area (1210 m).

—Trail begins on restored fire road and passes above and to the east of Moab Lake. Rolls along on old fire road grade for next 8.5 kms.

6.6—Whirlpool Campground.

8.6—Tie Camp Warden Cabin (1245 m).

—Horse trail continues south along west side of Whirlpool, flat to rolling.

11.2—Tie Camp Campground.

15.0—Simon Creek Campground.

20.3—Middle Forks Warden Cabin (1325 m).

21.1—Middle Forks Campground.

25.8—Trail crosses channel of Whirlpool (ford).

—Scott Gravel Flats.

30.9—Scott Camp Campground.

38.8—Whirlpool River footbridge to east side.

41.0—Kane Meadows Campground (1585 m).

—Trail crosses Kane Meadows then bends south-southwest to begin ascent to pass.

48.5—Committee's Punchbowl Campground.

49.1—Athabasca Pass (1755 m). Historical marker and park boundary near north shore of Committee's Punchbowl.

During the winter of 1811, David Thompson, Canada's foremost fur trade explorer, made the first recorded crossing of Athabasca Pass. For the next forty years, the pass became the main fur trade route across the Canadian Rockies. Today the long trail up the Whirlpool River to the pass is about as lonely as it was during the first half of the last century — a great place to commune with the spirits of long dead fur traders and to imagine their awe as they first wandered through this corridor of ice-clad peaks.

The first 8.5 kilometres of trail beyond Moab Lake follows the old Whirlpool Fire Road along the west side of the river. At the Tie Camp Warden Cabin the road reverts to horse trail. Just 3.8 kilometres farther on you pass the remains of the old Tie Camp. (In the early part of this century, timber was cut here and floated down the Whirlpool and Athabasca Rivers to the Jackladder near Jasper to be made into railway ties.)

On the Scott Gravel Flats there is a fine view due south to the Scott Glacier — a tongue of the Hooker Icefield. The trail to this point is fairly straightforward, but from here to the pass the track is less defined as it swings back and forth from gravel flats to forest, and hiking conditions are less reliable. As of this writing there is a footbridge which takes the trail to the east side of the Whirlpool just below the Kane Meadows, but this bridge has been subject to washout during high runoff; at the meadows there is a crossing of a tributary stream from the Kane Glacier that could also cause problems during hot weather.

Above the Kane Meadows the trail makes its final gradual climb to the pass, but the track is poorly defined and usually quite boggy. The route is obvious, however, staying along the east side of the Whirlpool all the way to the summit. At the pass there is a historical marker commemorating this important fur trade route and a small pond called The Committee's Punchbowl (named by Hudson's Bay company governor George Simpson in 1824); here, on the crest of the continent, fur traders would stop and drink a toast to the officers of the company.

As yet, no trail has been developed down the western slope of the pass, though bits and pieces of the old fur trade track can still be found. The fur trade route down *Le Grande Côte* followed Pacific Creek for approximately seven kilometres then, utilizing the obvious low depression in the forested ridge which runs southeast from Mount Brown, crossed over to Jeffrey Creek. The trail descended Jeffrey Creek to the Wood River and followed the latter stream, with much difficulty, to the Big Bend of the Columbia River at Boat Encampment. Today the waters of Kinbasket Lake, created by the Mica Dam, back up into the Wood Valley, and the Mica Creek area at the end of the road running from Revelstoke, B.C. can only be reached by boat. This trip is seldom hiked, and then only by experienced bushwhackers who have arranged transportation across the reservoir.

Geraldine Lakes

Geraldine Road to Second Geraldine Lake—5.0 kilometres (3.1 miles)

Day trip or backpack

Allow 2 - 3 hours one way

Elevation gain: 410 metres (1,340 feet)

Maximum elevation: 1890 metres (6,200 feet)

Topo maps: Athabasca Falls 83 C/12†
   †trail not shown

Point of Departure: From the junction of the Icefields Parkway and Highway 93-A at Athabasca Falls (31 kilometres south of Jasper townsite), follow the 93-A north for 1.1 kilometres (0.7 miles) to the junction with the Geraldine Fire Road—a dirt road which cuts left into the forest from the 93-A. Follow this gravel road for 5½ kilometres (3½ miles) through the forest and up a series of switchbacks to its termination at a locked access gate. The parking area and trail head for Geraldine Lakes lie 50 metres below the gate at the last bend in the road.

0.0—Trail sign (1480 m).

   —Moderate uphill climb.

1.8—Lower Geraldine Lake (1610 m).

   —Trail skirts west shore of lake.

2.7—Southern end of Lower Geraldine Lake.

   —Steep 90 metre climb, followed by level trail through rockslides angling toward left side of valley.

4.2—Base of waterfall.

   —Very steep 150 metre climb.

5.0—Viewpoint on ridge overlooking Second Geraldine Lake.

   —Trail skirts above east shore of lake.

6.2—Campground (1890 m). Second Geraldine Lake inlet.

Lying high between the steep slopes of Mount Fryatt and Whirlpool Peak, the four Geraldine Lakes offer hiking options that range from a few hours' stroll to several days of rock scrambling and exploring. The first lake is an easy 45 minute trek from the trail head; and the third and fourth lakes are for adventurers who need no trail and are well-accustomed to the rigours of bushwhacking. The upper three lakes are situated in wild rocky environs and give an impression of remote wilderness, even though they lie only a few kilometres from the trail head.

The initial two kilometres of trail to the lowest lake are well-travelled. The lake is serene, enclosed by a thick forest of lodgepole pine and spruce, and reflects the flanks of Mount Fryatt (3361 m) to the south.

From the north end of the lake the trail continues along the west shore, reaching the far end of the lake at Kilometre 1.7. From here it climbs steeply for 300 metres, paralleling a 90 metre waterfall that cascades over rock steps to the lake below. The trail here is quite rough, filled with rocks and roots, and good boots (and legs) are recommended.

At the top of the falls the trail enters a short valley and angles off to the left side, crossing a large boulder field and bypassing a diminutive tarn at Kilometre 3.8. Much of the trail over the boulder field is marked only by cairns, and you should watch closely for them to pick up the trail on the opposite side. At the end of the valley the trail climbs steeply to the left of a waterfall that is even more spectacular than the first (and the climb is steeper and longer than the first).

A rocky ridge at the top of the climb is a good viewpoint. From here the hiker can best appreciate the geological nature of the Geraldine Lakes as he sees the way the higher lakes feed into the lower. Known as *pater noster* lakes, the Geraldine Lakes form a chain of small tarns occupying

Falls below Second Geraldine Lake

depressions in a glacially-carved stairway. The rocks rising on either side are Cambrian in age, with strata dipping to the southwest at an angle of ten to twenty-five degrees. An outstanding view of the second Geraldine Lake lies just a short distance beyond.

Although the ridge will probably represent the culmination of the day's efforts for many hikers, the trail does continue around the east shore of the second lake. It ends at a campground at the southern end of the lake. For particularly ambitious hikers, well-experienced in route-finding, a third and fourth lake lie beyond the second. No trail has been cut to either.

161

Fryatt Valley

Backpack

Allow 2 days to Upper Fryatt Valley

Elevation gain: 820 metres (2,700 feet)

Maximum elevation: 2040 metres (6,700 feet)

Topo maps: Athabasca Falls 83 C/12†
         Fortress Lake 83 C/5†
         †last 3.7 kms not shown

Point of Departure: From the junction of the Ice-fields Parkway and Highway 93-A at Athabasca Falls (31 kilometres south of Jasper townsite), follow the 93-A north for 1.1 kilometres (0.7 miles) to the junction with the Geraldine Fire Road—a dirt road which cuts left into the forest from the 93-A. Follow this gravel road for 2.1 kilometres (1.3 miles) to a trail sign and small parking area on the left side of the road.

0.0—Trail sign (1220 m).

—Route follows old fire road track.

1.9—Bridges across stream channels.

7.2—Trail comes abreast of Athabasca River at site of old cable car crossing.

—Trail climbs away from river.

11.6—Lower Fryatt Campground (1280 m). Fryatt Creek bridge to east bank.

—Trail climbs east side of Fryatt Valley.

15.9—Fryatt Creek bridge to west bank.

17.7—Brussels Campground.

—Trail climbs over major rockslide.

18.7—Fryatt Lake (1715 m).

—Trail follows along west shore of lake.

19.5—West end of Fryatt Lake.

—Trail winds and climbs through dense forest.

21.1—Headwall Campground (1780 m). Foot of Headwall Falls.

—Steep scramble up Headwall.

21.9—Trail emerges at top of Headwall.

22.0—Fryatt Hut (2000 m).

—Trail continues through meadows then climbs forested moraine.

23.2—Unnamed lake (2040 m).

The Fryatt Valley trail is something of a long, tedious grunt, and the final climb up the Headwall to the level of the upper valley is one you will long remember. But this tiny, one kilometre-long vale tucked away deep within the heart of one of Jasper's great mountain ranges is a jewel that will reward all your efforts. The valley is best visited as a three day trip: one day to hike in and set a base camp, one day for exploration in the upper valley, and one day to hike out.

The first seven kilometres of walking from the Geraldine access road is flat and forest-enclosed. The trail finally comes abreast of the Athabasca River near the site of an old cable car crossing, and you will have the dubious pleasure of seeing the Icefields Parkway two hundred metres away on the opposite side. From this point the trail veers south and begins its climb to the mouth of the Fryatt Valley.

The trail crosses Fryatt Creek at the Lower Fryatt Campground and enters the valley proper — a narrow gorge descending between the towering peaks of Mounts Fryatt and Christie. The climb up the east side of the valley is steady through heavy forest for the next four kilometres. At Kilometre 15.9 the track crosses to the west side of the creek and works its way up along relatively flat, open gravel flats; here the first views open up to the sharp, glaciated peaks at the head of the valley.

You are forced to climb over a major slide at Kilometre 17.7, but the summit of this rock pile provides a fine view of Fryatt Lake. The trail is rocky and rooty as it runs along the west shore of the lake, then it ascends through subalpine forest to the foot of the Headwall. Here, at the foot of the spectacular Headwall Falls, the last act in the Fryatt Valley drama unfolds in the form of an excruciatingly steep scramble — over 200 metres of vertical spread over just 0.8 kilometres of trail.

Upper Fryatt Valley

The top of the Headwall will silence your curses. Suddenly the upper valley opens into view — ice-clad peaks and subalpine meadowland. Back to the north the lower Fryatt Valley stretches out beneath you like a map and the peaks of the Maligne Range rise up beyond the broad Athabasca Valley. A small waterfall dropping into a large pool near the lip of the Headwall makes a fine place to rest on a warm day, and the Fryatt Hut lies less than 100 metres farther along.

The hike to the lake at the head of the upper valley is short and very scenic. The trail, which is wet and not always well defined, travels through wildflower meadows, climbs a rocky, sparsely forested moraine where the creek plunges briefly into an underground passage, and finally descends through the last stunted alpine fir and Engelmann spruce to the shore of a small lake fed by the meltwaters of the nearby Belanger Glacier. On the shore of this alpine lake there is nothing to obstruct the view except a crowd of sharp peaks which all but encircle the head of this fine hanging valley. From this point it is possible to do much off-trail exploration, particularly onto the slopes to the north, and experienced rock scramblers can even ascend to the high col between Mounts Fryatt and Belanger.

There is no camping allowed in the upper Fryatt Valley, but the Fryatt Hut does provide overnight accommodation there. While the hut makes an ideal base camp for exploration, it is small and cramped and usually booked solid throughout the hiking season. A better alternative is to set your camp at one of the campgrounds below the Headwall and commute to the upper valley without the burden of a full pack.

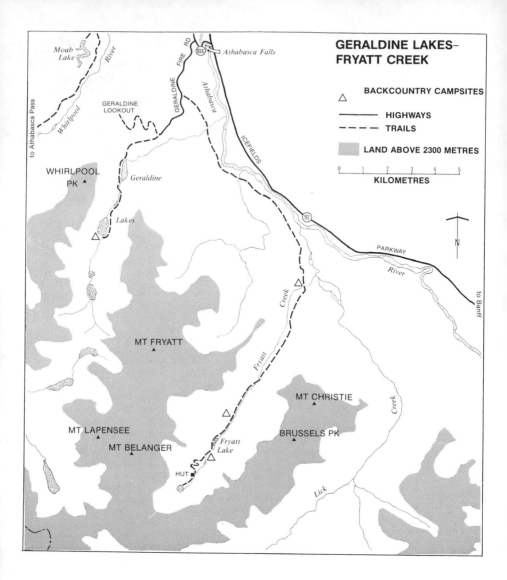

GERALDINE LAKES–
FRYATT CREEK

△ BACKCOUNTRY CAMPSITES

━━━━ HIGHWAYS

▬ ▬ ▬ TRAILS

▓▓▓ LAND ABOVE 2300 METRES

0　1　2　3　4　5
KILOMETRES

Moab
Lake

River

Athabasca Falls

to Athabasca Pass

Whirlpool

GERALDINE
LOOKOUT

GERALDINE FIRE RD

93A

Athabasca

ICEFIELDS

WHIRLPOOL
PK ▲

Geraldine

Lakes

△

93

PARKWAY

River

N

to Banff

Creek

△

MT FRYATT
▲

Fryatt

MT CHRISTIE
▲

Creek

△

MT LAPENSEE

MT BELANGER
▲

Fryatt
Lake

BRUSSELS PK
▲

△

HUT ▪

Lick

Fortress Lake

Sunwapta Falls to Fortress Lake—24 kilometres (15 miles)*

Backpack

Allow 8 - 10 hours one way

Elevation loss: 60 metres (200 feet)

Maximum elevation: 1400 metres (4,600 feet)

Topo maps: Athabasca Falls 83 C/12
        Fortress Lake 83 C/5†
        †last 10 kms not shown

Point of Departure: Follow the Icefields Parkway (Hwy 93) to the Sunwapta Falls junction, 54½ kilometres (34 miles) south of Jasper townsite and 49 kilometres (30½ miles) north of the Columbia Icefield Information Centre. The Sunwapta Falls access road leads 0.6 kilometre to the falls parking area. The trail begins on the opposite side of the footbridge which crosses the Sunwapta River at the falls viewpoint.

0.0—Sunwapta Falls bridge (1400 m).

    —Trail begins gradual descent to Athabasca River.

7.8—Big Bend Campground.

    —Mainly flat travel on east side of Athabasca River.

14.2—Athabasca Crossing Campground.

15.2—Athabasca River bridge.

    —Trail runs south along Chaba River.

17.7—Chaba River ford (calf to thigh deep crossing to west side).

    —Sketchy trail along west side of river flats.

24.0—Fortress Pass (1340 m). Park boundary and east end of Fortress Lake.

* All distances approximate.

As one of the largest natural lakes on the crest of the Great Divide, Fortress Lake should be one of the most popular trails in Jasper Park, but because of river fords and the lack of a good trail around the lakeshore, it is seldom hiked. However, in 1985 Parks Canada constructed a bridge across the Athabasca River which eliminated one of the most harrowing fords in the Rockies. Now, despite some lesser crossings on the Chaba River, the trail is a viable option for experienced wilderness travellers in search of a truly unique destination.

The first fifteen kilometres of trail running south from Sunwapta Falls follows relatively flat, easygoing terrain along the east side of the Athabasca River. One kilometre beyond the Athabasca Crossing Campground the trail bridges the Athabasca just upstream from its confluence with the Chaba River. The trail continues due south along the east side of the Chaba, and then, approximately 2.5 kilometres beyond the Athabasca River bridge, works its way across this multi-channeled river (usually calf to thigh deep) to the west side. The track is very sketchy along the west side of the Chaba, but the way to Fortress Lake is obvious.

Once you reach the east end of Fortress Lake on the crest of Fortress Pass, you are entering British Columbia's Hamber Provincial Park. But since there is no lakeshore trail worth mentioning, it is not an easy park to enter. Any further exploration along the shoreline will have to be made by bushwhacking through mature spruce forest. There is a small, rundown cabin just over halfway down the north side of the lake, but this is used primarily by fly-in fishermen. For those content to camp at the east end of the lake, the scenery is still quite exciting, particularly to the ice-clad slopes of Serenity Mountain to the west.

Wilcox Pass

Wilcox Creek Campground to Wilcox Pass—4.0 kilometres (2.5 miles)

Day trip

Allow 2 hours to pass

Elevation gain: 335 metres (1,100 feet)

Maximum elevation: 2375 metres (7,800 feet)

Topo maps: Columbia Icefield 83 C/3
Sunwapta Peak 83 C/6†
†trail not shown

Point of Departure: Follow the Icefields Parkway (Hwy 93) to the Wilcox Creek Campground, located on the east side of the highway 2.8 kilometres (1.7 miles) south of the Columbia Icefield Information Centre or 1.9 kilometres (1.2 miles) north of the Banff—Jasper park boundary at Sunwapta Pass. The trail head is located just inside the entrance to the campground on the left hand side of the access road.

0.0—Wilcox Creek Campground (2040 m).

—Trail climbs steeply through dense sub-alpine forest.

1.8—Grade moderates as trail emerges at tree-line.

2.5—Athabasca Glacier viewpoint.

—Gradual ascent through alpine tundra.

4.0—Wilcox Pass Summit (2375 m).

—Route follows north through hummocky, rock-ribbed pass. Track often vague.

7.2—North edge of pass (watch for markers or cairns).

—Trail drops steeply into forest. Track vague (watch for flagging).

8.8—Trail crosses to true left side of creek, track becomes more defined.

—Moderate to steep descent on slope to south of Tangle Creek.

11.2—Tangle Creek trail head (1860 m). Intersects with Hwy 93 200 metres south of Tangle Falls and 10 kms north of Wilcox Creek Campground trail head.

On a clear summer's day, the meadows of Wilcox Pass offer much of what is best about hiking in the Canadian Rockies. The pass is a broad, rolling alpine valley lying above and running parallel to the Icefields Parkway, and at the end of the last century, when the ice of the Athabasca Glacier choked off the valley below, outfitters followed a route over its summit to reach the wild regions north of the Columbia Icefield. Beginning close to timberline, the trail quickly delivers hikers to flower-carpeted meadows punctuated by small reflective tarns, cut by a clear, racing stream, and surrounded by some of the finest alpine scenery in the entire mountain range. For the effort required, the reward is a bargain hard to beat.

From its head at the Wilcox Creek Campground, the trail immediately enters a heavy, mature 400-year old forest of alpine fir and Engelmann spruce. The initial portion of trail is steep, climbing some 120 vertical metres within the first three-quarters of a kilometre. The rigour of the ascent is broken, however, less than a kilometre into the hike as you abruptly emerge from the forest to find yourself on a ridge overlooking the Icefields Parkway and, to the southwest, the panorama of Mounts Athabasca (3491 m) and Andromeda (3442 m), Athabasca Glacier, Snow Dome (3460 m), Dome Glacier, and Mount Kitchener (3511 m).

The trail moderates in grade once on the ridge and follows it for a half kilometre to the edge of a steep gully occupied by a cascading mountain stream. There the trail veers to the north and begins a gradual ascent of the valley, eventually working to a position on the northeast margin of the meadows.

The meadows are an open invitation to wander, and many hikers happily spend an entire day without reaching the pass proper. The stream distracts some; the small tarns in the meadow bottoms catch others; some hike back across the mead-

Mount Athabasca from Wilcox Pass

ows to scramble along the ridge of Mount
Wilcox and settle in for an hour or two of
glacier watching; and a few energetic souls
will work their way over the ridge to the
northeast to find the lake and glacier
nestled at the foot of Nigel Peak. Those
who do stray from the trail, however,
should recognize the fragility of the meadow environment by treading lightly—
avoiding wet marshy areas and spreading
the party abreast of one another rather
than following single file. It is often possible to see bighorn sheep in the pass environs, and, occasionally, moose and coy-
ote.

For those with extra time, energy, and
curiosity, it is possible to follow the pass
beyond its broad, rolling summit and descend Tangle Creek back to the Icefields
Parkway, another four kilometres distant.
Though the trail often disappears in the
alpine tundra near the northern edge of
the pass, a marker indicates where the
descent to the Tangle Creek valley begins.
In the forest below a well defined trail
gradually takes shape. Emerging at Tangle Falls, hikers are 10.1 parkway kilometres north of the original trail head.

167

Brazeau Lake

Icefields Parkway to Brazeau Lake—32.3 kilometres (20.1 miles)

Backpack

Allow 2 days to Brazeau Lake

Elevation gain: 455 metres (1,500 feet)
loss: 475 metres (1,550 feet)

Maximum elevation: 2195 metres (7,200 feet)

Topo maps: Columbia Icefield 83 C/3
Sunwapta Peak 83 C/6
Job Creek 83 C/7

Point of Departure: Follow the Icefields Parkway to the parking area for the Nigel Pass trail, located on the northeast side of the highway 8½ kilometres (5½ miles) south of the Banff—Jasper park boundary at Sunwapta Pass or 2½ kilometres (1½ miles) north of the "Big Bend" switchback on the long grade up to Sunwapta Pass. A gravel side road leads 200 metres to a locked access gate. Park above the gate and walk downhill past it to the trail sign.

0.0—Trail sign (1830 m).

7.2—Nigel Pass (2195 m).

7.6—Ford south fork of Brazeau River.

—Steep descent through rocky terrain to marshy river flats.

10.6—Brazeau River bridge to west bank.

10.7—Boulder Creek Campground.

11.4—Boulder Creek bridge.

13.8—Four Point Campground.

14.0—Junction (1915 m). Jonas Pass trail branches left.

14.8—Four Point Creek crossing.

18.5—Brazeau River bridge to east side.

20.8—Wolverine South Campground.

26.1—Brazeau River bridge to west side.

29.3—Brazeau Campground (1720 m). Bridge across north fork of Brazeau River to junction. South Boundary Trail to right. Turn left for Brazeau Lake.

31.4—Junction. Intersection with *Poboktan Pass* trail at Km 36.6. Brazeau Lake and Brazeau River Bridge Campground to right.

32.3—Brazeau Lake (1810 m).

The five kilometre-long Brazeau Lake is one of the largest wilderness lakes in Jasper Park, but because it lies over thirty kilometres from the nearest highway, its nearby campgrounds are relatively peaceful and uncrowded. In addition to being a prime destination for anyone in search of solitude, it is a stop on one of the finest backpacks in the Canadian Rockies — the Brazeau Lake-Poboktan Pass-Jonas Pass loop trip.

The most direct route to the lake follows the Nigel Pass trail out of the northern end of Banff Park and down onto the headwaters of the Brazeau River along Jasper's southern boundary (see *Nigel Pass* trail description, Banff Park chapter). While Nigel Pass provides an extraordinary beginning to this lengthy journey, the descent into the upper Brazeau Valley is very scenic in its own right. After hopping across the river's headwaters, the hiker makes a steep descent through old rockslides to the first of several lush meadows encountered in the valley — a marshy vale fed by a waterfall at its upper end and fringed with the white tufted heads of cottongrass.

After crossing to the west side of the Brazeau at the lower end of the meadow and descending through a three kilometre-long stretch of subalpine forest, the trail reaches another plateau in the valley and a long stretch of open meadowland. At Kilometre 14.0, just beyond the Four Point Campground, the junction with the Jonas Pass trail is passed — an important intersection for those contemplating the Brazeau-Poboktan-Jonas loop trip.

The trail switches back to the right side of the river at Kilometre 18.5 and, just over two kilometres beyond, passes the very pretty Wolverine South Campground, nestled in a grove of trees beside the river. Below the campground the trail makes a steady drop through the forest, crosses back to the left side of the river, and finally emerges onto yet another level of the valley.

Brazeau Lake

At Kilometre 29.3 the hiker comes abreast of the Brazeau Campground opposite the bridge which spans the north fork of the Brazeau River — the main outlet stream from Brazeau Lake. This is not a particularly pleasant campground, and most backpackers prefer to ascend the two kilometre-long valley to camp at the Brazeau River Bridge site 500 metres below the end of the lake.

Oddly enough, the Brazeau Lake area was one of the first mountain valleys to be visited by the fur trade explorers of the North West Company. In the autumn of 1800, Duncan McGillivray and a small party of men accidentally stumbled up this valley in an attempt to find a route through the mountains. After climbing one of the ridges to the west of Brazeau Lake, they abandoned the reconnaissance and returned to their trading post at Rocky Mountain House.

Brazeau Lake via Poboktan Pass. Brazeau Lake can also be reached from the Sunwapta Warden Station on the Icefields Parkway by traversing Poboktan Creek and Pass. This route is five kilometres longer than the Nigel Pass-Brazeau River approach, but it has its own scenic rewards. (See *Poboktan Pass* trail description.)

Brazeau Lake-Poboktan Pass—Jonas Pass. While it is possible to visit Poboktan Pass as a day trip from the campground on Brazeau Lake, most backpackers prefer to continue north through the pass to other lands. The most popular of these extended journeys crosses Poboktan to the headwaters of Poboktan Creek, then doubles back over Jonas Shoulder and Pass to rejoin the Brazeau River trail near the Four Point Campground. Total distance for this loop trip, starting and ending at the Nigel Pass trail head, is 80 kilometres. Generally the trip is done over four or five days. (See *Poboktan Pass* and *Jonas Pass* trail descriptions.)

169

Poboktan Pass

Icefields Parkway to Poboktan Pass—24.3 kilometres (15.1 miles)
Icefields Parkway to Brazeau Lake—37.5 kilometres (23.3 miles)

Backpack

Allow 2 - 3 days to Brazeau Lake

Elevation gain: 760 metres (2,500 feet)
loss: 580 metres (1,900 feet)

Maximum elevation: 2300 metres (7,550 feet)

Topo maps: Sunwapta Peak 83 C/6

Point of Departure: Follow the Icefields Parkway (Hwy 93) to the Sunwapta Warden Station, located 31½ kilometres (19½ miles) north of the Columbia Icefield Information Centre or 71½ kilometres (44½ miles) south of Jasper townsite. Just 200 metres south of the warden station, on the opposite side of Poboktan Creek, is the parking area for the trail.

0.0—Sunwapta Warden Station (1540 m).

0.1—Poboktan Creek footbridge.

6.2—Junction (1760 m). Maligne Pass to left. Keep right for Poboktan Pass.

6.4—Poligne Creek bridge.

7.5—Poboktan Creek Campground.

12.0—Waterfalls Campground.

21.3—Jonas Cutoff Campground and junction (2120 m). Turn right and cross creek for Jonas Pass. Poboktan Pass ahead.

24.3—Poboktan Pass (2300 m).

28.6—John-John Creek Campground.

32.8—John-John Creek bridge.

36.5—Brazeau River north fork bridge.

36.6—Brazeau Lake Junction (1810 m). Intersection with *Brazeau Lake* trail at Km. 31.4. Brazeau River Bridge Campground and Brazeau Lake to left 0.9 km.

Poboktan Pass has long served as an important link between the Saskatchewan and Athabasca watersheds: Iroquois trappers working for the North West Company undoubtedly utilized the pass in the early 1800s when travelling to and from Rocky Mountain House; the geologist A. P. Coleman made the first recorded crossing of the pass in 1892 as he travelled north from the Brazeau country in search of two mythical 16,000 foot mountains on Athabasca Pass; and Mary Schaffer and her companions traversed Poboktan sixteen years later on their explorations north from Lake Louise to Maligne Lake. Today Poboktan remains an important north-south passageway for backpackers, and its extensive alpine meadows offer the bonus of being one of the best places in Jasper Park to see the elusive mountain caribou.

The quickest route to Poboktan Pass is the 24.3 kilometre trail leading up Poboktan Creek from the Sunwapta Warden Station on the Icefields Parkway. The trail continues beyond the pass to reach Brazeau Lake in another 12.3 kilometres, making this route only five kilometres longer than the normal approach to the lake via Nigel Pass and the Brazeau River. But few people hike this trail entire as described herein. Rather, sections of the Poboktan Pass trail are normally utilized in conjunction with other intersecting trails to create extended wilderness outings — trips such as The Glacier Trail and the Brazeau Lake-Poboktan Pass-Jonas Pass loop.

From the parking lot on the south side of Poboktan Creek, opposite the Sunwapta Warden Station, the trail immediately crosses the creek and follows it east for a little more than six kilometres to its junction with the Maligne Pass trail. From there it arcs to the southeast, following the creek upstream, along the foot of Le Grand Brazeau range of mountains.

Poboktan Valley from Poboktan Pass

Beyond the Maligne Pass junction, the trail is damp to the point of boggy in several places, but corduroy sections, bridges, and alternate horse and hiker trails help the traveller through and over the worst spots. The cataract at the Waterfalls Campground and the waterfall two kilometres farther upvalley provide welcome changes of scene from the spruce and pine forest.

In a pleasant little ravine at Kilometre 21.3, the hiker comes upon the Jonas Cutoff Campground. This is the point where the Jonas Pass trail intersects from the south, an important junction for backpackers who are including this very scenic option in their itinerary (see *Jonas Pass* trail description). Beyond the campground, the trail begins its steady climb to Poboktan Summit, gradually emerging from the timbered valley onto the alpine meadows of the pass over the next three kilometres.

The pass and valley were named by A.P. Coleman in 1892, Poboktan being the Stoney name for the owls the party saw in this area. The pass is frequently visited by caribou that roam through the Front Ranges of Jasper Park, and on occasion a grizzly bear can be spotted at a distance across the open tundra.

From Poboktan Pass the trail drops sharply into the John-John Creek drainage — a narrow valley composed of rockslides and open gravel flats. At the mouth of the valley, the trail emerges onto a large slide overlooking Brazeau Lake. From this point it is a hike of just over three kilometres to the campground at the east end of the lake and the intersection with the trail from Brazeau Valley (see *Brazeau Lake* trail description).

Brazeau Lake-Poboktan Pass-Jonas Pass. The 15.3 kilometre section of trail running between Brazeau Lake and the Jonas Cutoff Campground via Poboktan Pass is a part of one of the most popular loop trips in Jasper Park. The trip starts and ends at the Nigel Pass trail head on the Icefields Parkway and runs a total distance of 80 kilometres. (For this and other options, see descriptions for *Brazeau Lake, Jonas Pass,* and *The Glacier Trail.*)

171

Jonas Pass

Brazeau River to Poboktan Creek—18.9 kilometres (11.7 miles)

Backpack

Allow 6 - 8 hours one way

Elevation gain: 555 metres (1,820 feet)
    loss: 350 metres (1,150 feet)

Maximum elevation: 2470 metres (8,100 feet)

Topo maps: Sunwapta Peak 83 C/6

Point of Departure: Hike the *Brazeau Lake* trail to the junction at Km 14.0, just 0.2 km beyond the Four Point Campsite. The Jonas Pass trail branches northwest from this intersection. Southbound hikers can reach the north end of the trail from the *Poboktan Pass* trail.

0.0—Brazeau River Junction (1915 m). Brazeau Lake and South Boundary Trail straight ahead. Turn left for Jonas Pass.

—Trail climbs steeply up west side of Four Point Valley.

4.4—Trail emerges above timberline.

9.8—Jonas Pass Summit (2320 m).

—Trail continues north through pass environs.

13.0—Trail passes beneath rockslide then begins steep climb to Jonas Shoulder.

15.6—Jonas Shoulder Summit (2470 m).

—Trail descends from summit (track indistinct) swinging to east side of tributary gorge.

18.8—Poboktan Creek crossing.

18.9—Jonas Cutoff Campground and junction (2120 m). Intersection with the *Poboktan Pass* trail at Km 21.3.

The 18.9 kilometre trail from the Brazeau Valley to Poboktan Creek via Jonas Pass includes one of the most impressive alpine traverses in the mountain parks — a thirteen kilometre section of trail that never drops below timberline. Along the way there is an assortment of glaciated peaks, long stretches of wildflower meadow, a variety of alpine wildlife ranging from hoary marmots to mountain caribou, and a 2470 metre viewpoint which looks out over much of Jasper Park's southern wilderness. However, there are no campgrounds on the Jonas Pass trail, so backpackers must be prepared to make the entire journey in one day.

From its junction with the Brazeau River trail, just beyond the Four Point Campground, the trail starts its vigorous climb toward Jonas Pass. The trail rises through a beautiful open forest, climbing over 200 vertical metres in less than two kilometres. A series of small streams coming down from the left heralds the approach of timberline, and within a few minutes hiking the trail levels off, leaving the last of the alpine fir and Engelmann spruce behind. Ahead the trail works gradually up the southwest side of the long, narrow vale that constitutes the pass, staying just above the small creek that flows down the valley bottom. The pass is as long as it is beautiful, and it isn't until the 9.8 kilometre mark that its crest is reached.

Beyond the summit the trail maintains its altitude for about 1.5 kilometres, bypassing a small alpine tarn, and then gradually descends a similar distance, angling off toward the north. Just beyond a large, distinctive rockslide the trail swings to the right and begins its ascent of Jonas Shoulder, the high ridge that separates the Jonas and Poboktan drainages. The first portion of the climb is steep and the trail is sketchy in places, but the track becomes more distinct with altitude.

The scenery along the Jonas Shoulder

Caribou above Jonas Pass

climb is spectacular, and frequent rest stops with map and camera are highly rewarding. Hoary marmots and pikas inhabit the trailside rockslides, and there is always a chance of sighting some of the caribou that make the Jonas-Poboktan area their summer residence. (If you do come across one or more of these animals, please give them room, since they are very shy and easily disturbed.) Mountain goat and grizzly bear also frequent the region.

From the Jonas Shoulder crest, barren, desolate and beautiful at 2470 metres above sea level, views open out over the vast meadows of Poboktan Pass and the forested Poboktan Valley stretching away to the northwest. On the north side of the summit, the trail descends a steep talus slope and spongy meadows, then angles off to the east side of a major gully. Less than a kilometre after reaching timberline, you will emerge at the Jonas Cutoff Campground and the intersection with the Poboktan Pass trail. At this point you can continue north down the Poboktan Valley or turn southeast to ascend nearby Poboktan Pass (for either option, see *Poboktan Pass* trail description).

Because it is the second highest trail in Jasper Park, sections of the Jonas Pass trail are often covered by snowbanks into early August, particularly on the leeward side of Jonas Shoulder. Be aware that such conditions could cause route-finding difficulties.

Brazeau Lake-Poboktan Pass-Jonas Pass. The Jonas Pass trail is the highlight section of a 80 kilometre loop trip originating and ending at the Nigel Pass trail head in Banff Park. This hike descends the Brazeau Valley to Brazeau Lake, traverses Poboktan Pass, and then doubles back over Jonas Shoulder and Pass to the upper Brazeau Valley. The trip, which is one of the most popular extended backpacks in Jasper Park, divides itself nicely into five days of hiking, though it can be done in less. (See *Brazeau Lake* and *Poboktan Pass* trail descriptions.)

Jonas Pass is also an important segment on the 90 kilometre Glacier Trail which runs from Maligne Lake to Nigel Pass. (See description for *The Glacier Trail.*)

Maligne Pass

Icefields Parkway to Maligne Pass—15.2 kilometres (9.4 miles)
Icefields Parkway to Maligne Lake—47.9 kilometres (29.8 miles)

Backpack

Allow 2 - 3 days to Maligne Lake

Elevation gain: 700 metres (2,300 feet)
    loss: 550 metres (1,800 feet)

Maximum elevation: 2240 metres (7,350 feet)

Topo maps: Sunwapta Peak 83 C/6
    Southesk Lake 83 C/11
    Athabasca Falls 83 C/12

Point of Departure: Follow the Icefields Parkway (Hwy 93) to the Sunwapta Warden Station, located 31½ kilometres (19½ miles) north of the Columbia Icefield Information Centre or 71½ kilometres (44½ miles) south of Jasper townsite. Just 200 metres south of the warden station, on the opposite side of Poboktan Creek, is the parking area for the trail. Southbound hikers can start from the *Bald Hills* trail at the end of the Maligne Lake Road.

0.0—Sunwapta Warden Station (1540 m).

0.1—Poboktan Creek footbridge.

6.2—Junction (1760 m). Poboktan Pass straight ahead. Turn left for Maligne Pass.

11.2—Avalanche Campground.

13.5—Trail reaches maximum elevation, contours into pass.

15.2—Maligne Pass (2240 m).

17.8—Maligne River ford.

18.6—Mary Vaux Campground.

23.7—Old outfitter's camp.

29.0—Mary Schaffer Campground.

37.4—Maligne River suspension bridge.

43.1—Trapper Creek Campground and bridge.

46.6—Junction. Moose Lake to right (0.1 km). Keep straight ahead.

47.6—Junction. Bald Hills Fire Road. Turn right.

47.9—Maligne Lake parking area (1690 m).

The Maligne Pass trail is a challenging 48 kilometres of mountain track that can be hiked either by itself or in combination with the Poboktan Pass—Jonas Pass trails to the south and the Skyline Trail to the north. While not as spectacular or easy to travel as the Poboktan—Jonas and Skyline routes, Maligne Pass does offer much in the way of beautiful scenery, especially in the alpine meadows stretching out from the pass. The entire distance is prime habitat for the larger mammals of the Canadian Rockies, and with luck hikers might spot elk, moose, mountain goat, caribou or grizzly bear.

Like its companion trails to the north and south, Maligne Pass often lies buried under deep snow until the latter part of July, and hikers should inquire about snow conditions and water runoff before starting the trek. In fact, since the trail features a number of unbridged stream crossings and several kilometres of boggy meadows, it is recommended that the hike be made only in August or early September when most creeks are low.

From the parking area across the creek from the Sunwapta Warden Station, the trail immediately crosses Poboktan Creek via a footbridge and ascends the north side of the valley, gaining 210 metres of altitude in the 6.2 kilometres to the Poboktan Creek—Maligne Pass junction. The trail cuts north at the junction and begins what can be a long wet climb toward the Maligne Pass meadows.

Working through heavy spruce and pine forest the trail crosses and recrosses Poligne Creek six times in less than five kilometres. While bridges may be in place on the early crossings, expect to do some serious wading further along. Beyond Avalanche Campsite the trail reaches timberline and follows a more gradual grade toward the pass, working through boggy meadows and making another ford of Poligne Creek before finally heading for

Maligne Pass from Poligne Creek

higher, drier ground on the east side of the pass.

At Kilometre 15.2, the trail traces the eastern shore of the small but lovely lake that drains both north and south from the summit of the pass. The pass and the route north into the Maligne Valley have historical importance in that they were first used by two lady explorers, Mary Schäffer and Mary Adams, during their journey of discovery in the summer of 1908. Travelling north from Lake Louise with their guides and a string of horses, they crossed Maligne Pass on July 6th. Looking into the upper Maligne Valley from the pass, Mary Schäffer later wrote: "I think I never saw a fairer valley. From our feet it swept away into an unbroken green carpet as far as the eye could see . . . and then the cavalcade made a quick descent of about a thousand feet, tramping under foot thousands of blossoms of the *trollius* and *pulsatilla* which covered the way." Some of today's campsites in the Maligne Valley are believed to be the same used by this party on its way to the rediscovery and exploration of Maligne Lake.

Beyond the pass the trail drops gradually toward timberline, passing through the magnificent alpine meadows which, as Mary Schäffer described, present a rich variety of wildflowers during the summer months. With timberline comes another series of stream fords and, although less numerous than those on the other side of the pass, they will again constitute a problem for early summer hikers.

After passing the Mary Vaux Campsite, the trail moves through alternate sections of forest and large open willow flats that provide excellent scenic relief for what otherwise would be a very long stretch of enclosed hiking. The Mary Schäffer Campsite is passed at the 29 kilometre mark and the Maligne River is crossed via a sturdy cable suspension bridge at Kilometre 37.4.

Beyond the Maligne River the trail continues as before, a relatively level path through forest and meadows. There is another campsite just before the Trapper Creek footbridge and a rather long 4½ kilometres of hiking to the Bald Hills Fire Road and the Maligne Lake parking area.

175

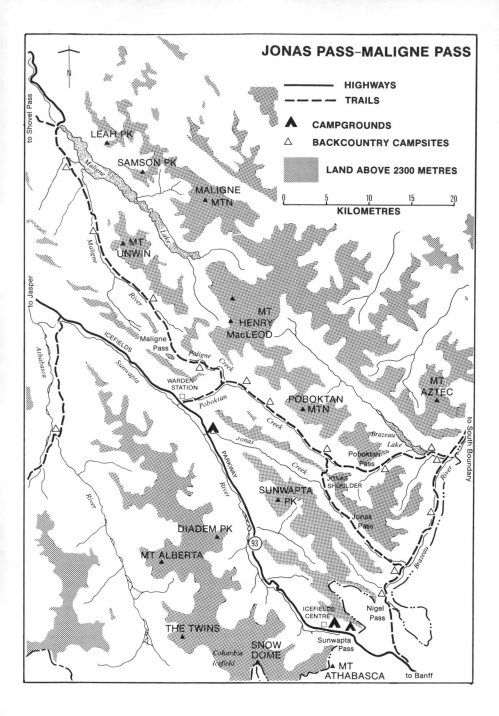

JONAS PASS–MALIGNE PASS

- —— HIGHWAYS
- --- TRAILS
- ▲ CAMPGROUNDS
- △ BACKCOUNTRY CAMPSITES
- ▨ LAND ABOVE 2300 METRES

0   5   10   15   20
KILOMETRES

to Shovel Pass

LEAH PK

SAMSON PK

Maligne

MALIGNE MTN

Lake

MT UNWIN

to Jasper

Maligne

River

ICEFIELDS

Sunwapta

Maligne Pass

Pedigne Creek

WARDEN STATION

Poboktan

MT HENRY MacLEOD

MT AZTEC

POBOKTAN MTN

Creek

Jonas

Creek

Brazeau Lake

Poboktan Pass

to South Boundary

PARKWAY

River

SUNWAPTA PK

JONAS SHOULDER

Jonas Pass

River

Brazeau

DIADEM PK

93

MT ALBERTA

Athabasca

River

ICEFIELDS CENTRE

Nigel Pass

THE TWINS

SNOW DOME

Columbia Icefield

Sunwapta Pass

MT ATHABASCA

to Banff

The Glacier Trail

Maligne Lake to Nigel Creek—89.7 kilometres (55.7 miles)

Backpack

Allow 4 - 7 days

Maximum elevation: 2470 metres (8,100 feet)

Minimum elevation: 1690 metres (5,550 feet)

Topo maps: Athabasca Falls 83 C/12
    Southesk Lake 83 C/11
    Sunwapta Peak 83 C/6
    Columbia Icefield 83 C/3

Point of Departure: Travelling from north to south, start from the parking area on the northwest shore of Maligne Lake (see *Bald Hills* trail). Northbound hikers can start from the *Nigel Pass* trail in northern Banff Park.

0.0—Maligne Lake parking area (1690 m).

4.8—Trapper Creek Campground.

18.9—Mary Schaffer Campground.

29.3—Mary Vaux Campground.

32.7—Maligne Pass (2240 m).

36.7—Avalanche Campground.

41.7—Junction (1760 m). Intersection with *Poboktan Pass* trail at Km 6.2.

43.0—Poboktan Creek Campground.

47.5—Waterfalls Campground.

56.8—Jonas Cutoff Campground and junction (2120 m). Intersection with *Jonas Pass* trail at Km 18.9.

60.1—Jonas Shoulder Summit (2470 m).

65.9—Jonas Pass (2320 m).

75.7—Junction (1915 m). Intersection with *Brazeau Lake* trail at Km 14.0.

75.9—Four Point Campground.

79.0—Boulder Creek Campground.

82.5—Nigel Pass (2195 m).

89.7—Nigel Pass trail head (1830 m).

In 1924, Jasper outfitter Jack Brewster initiated one of the most spectacular pack trips ever in the Canadian Rockies — a three week journey from Jasper to Lake Louise via the Columbia Icefield. Dubbed "The Glacier Trail," Brewster's tour travelled through some of the finest mountain scenery in Jasper and Banff Parks. Though the first 50 kilometres of the trail from Jasper to Maligne Lake has been replaced by the Maligne Lake Road and the southern half of the route from the Columbia Icefield to Lake Louise is now the Icefields Parkway, the section from Maligne Lake to the Icefields is still intact and can be hiked in a week or less.

The Glacier Trail starts at the northwest end of Maligne Lake and runs south to cross three of the most scenic passes in Jasper Park — Maligne, Jonas and Nigel. (It is possible to add the Skyline Trail to the northern end of this trip, thereby extending the journey from 90 to 134 kilometres.) The southern terminus for the trip is at the Nigel Pass trail head in Banff Park, just a few kilometres from the Columbia Icefield.

Working south from Maligne Lake, the trail makes a long ascent of the upper Maligne Valley, and if you get a reasonably early start, your first night's camp will probably be set at the Mary Schäffer Campground (Kilometre 18.9). From the Maligne Valley, the trail traverses Maligne Pass and descends Poligne Creek to an intersection with the Poboktan Creek trail. The route follows up Poboktan Creek to the Jonas Cutoff Campground, then branches south to cross Jonas Pass and drop into the upper Brazeau Valley. The last leg of the trip is out over Nigel Pass to the Icefields Parkway.

Since the Glacier Trail utilizes segments of four trails already presented in this chapter, you can refer to the *Maligne Pass, Poboktan Pass, Jonas Pass* and *Brazeau Lake* trails for a more detailed description of this tour.

177

The Skyline Trail

Backpack

Allow 2 - 3 days

Elevation gain: 820 metres (2,700 feet)
     loss: 1350 metres (4,450 feet)

Maximum elevation: 2510 metres (8,250 feet)

Topo maps: Athabasca Falls 83 C/12
            Medicine Lake 83 C/13

Point of Departure: From its junction with the Yellowhead Highway (Hwy 16) 5 kilometres (3 miles) east of Jasper townsite, follow the Maligne Lake Road 44½ kilometres (27½ miles) to Maligne Lake. Continue past the lodge for 0.5 kilometre, crossing the lake outlet bridge to the picnic area parking lot at road's end. The trail sign for the Skyline Trail lies on the edge of the forest just above the parking lot, 100 metres to the right of the Bald Hills Fire Road gate.

0.0—Maligne Lake Picnic Area (1690 m).

2.1—Junction. Lorraine Lake to left 0.2 km.

2.4—Junction. Mona Lake to right 0.2 km.

4.8—Evelyn Creek bridge. Old Horse Campground.

8.3—Little Shovel Campground.

10.3—Little Shovel Pass (2240 m).

12.2—Snowbowl Campground.

17.5—Big Shovel Pass (2320 m).

17.6—Junction. Trail to Watchtower Basin contours off to right. Skyline Trail descends to left.

19.5—Junction. Intersection with *Wabasso Lake* trail at Km 14.5. Turn left for Curator Campground (0.8 km) and Wabasso Lake. Keep right for Skyline Trail.

20.4—Curator Lake.

22.1—The Notch (2510 m).

28.3—Centre Lakes.

30.4—Tekarra Lake.

30.9—Tekarra Campground (2060 m).

35.6—Junction. Turn right onto Signal Mountain Fire Road.

35.7—Signal Campground.

44.1—Maligne Lake Road (1160 m).

Ambling along the ridges of the Maligne Range, the Skyline is one of the exceptional backpacks in North America. It is the highest trail in Jasper Park, with approximately 25 of its 44 kilometres travelling at or above timberline, and its loftiest summits provide expansive views over a good portion of the park's 10,878 square kilometres. The trail passes through some of the finest wildflower meadows in the Rockies, and the area is home to a variety of alpine mammals, including the mountain caribou. But the hiking season on this popular route is short (if there is snow anywhere in the park, it will be on the Skyline), and because of the fragile nature of the terrain, use is carefully controlled (the trail's limited quota is frequently filled).

The easiest way to take this one way backpack is from Maligne Lake, starting 520 metres higher than the northwest end of the trail near Maligne Canyon. From the sign above the Maligne Lake picnic area, the trail strikes off through a fire succession forest of lodgepole pine, and throughout the first five kilometres the grade remains gentle.

At Kilometre 4.8 the trail crosses Evelyn Creek (an excellent spot to rest and fill water bottles), then begins to switchback upward to Little Shovel Pass. Views continue to improve, particularly back to the fine peaks surrounding Maligne Lake, as the trail climbs into open subalpine terrain.

From the treeless summit of Little Shovel Pass the trail descends into the beautiful subalpine meadowland of the Snowbowl. Alpine fir and Engelmann spruce finger out into the tundra vegetation of the bowl, and even during the driest summers fresh streams tumble through from the heights above, a factor which adds to the general sogginess of the area. Ascending from the Snowbowl, the trail reaches the crest of 2320 metre Shovel Pass at Kilometre 17.5.

Queen Elizabeth Ranges from Little Shovel Pass

Shovel Pass gains its name from an incident which occurred in 1911. The Otto brothers, pioneer outfitters in the Jasper area, were building the first trail over the range and attempting to transport a boat to Maligne Lake via this improbable route. Finding the snow so deep their horses could not pass, they ingeniously hacked a pair of shovels out of the native timber below and managed to scratch a trail through the snowbanks. These wooden shovels were erected below the pass, and supposedly stood for many years as a monument to the Ottos' arduous haul.

Not far below the pass the trail from the Watchtower Basin intersects from the right, and a little farther along is the junction with the Wabasso Lake trail. These two trails offer optional routes of access to, or escape from, the Skyline (see *Watchtower Basin* and *Shovel Pass via Wabasso* trail descriptions).

From the Wabasso junction the Skyline climbs past the shores of Curator Lake and begins its steep ascent to The Notch — a narrow passageway onto the summit ridge of Amber Mountain. At an elevation of 2510 metres above sea level,

The Notch is the high point on the Skyline and an extraordinary viewpoint for the Athabasca Valley and nearby Mount Edith Cavell. Even Mount Robson, over 80 kilometres away to the northwest, is visible. For the next five kilometres the hiker remains near the 2500 metre level, wandering along barren ridges with range upon range of mountains for company on either side.

Beyond the summit of Amber Mountain the trail begins a gradual switchbacking descent, levelling off near the Centre Lakes and entering the first scattered alpine fir above Tekarra Lake. Crossing the outlet stream below the lake, the trail traverses around onto the northern slopes of Mount Tekarra. Ahead views slowly open to the Colin Range, Pyramid Mountain and other familiar peaks near Jasper townsite. The hiker finally emerges on the Signal Mountain Fire Road at Kilometre 35.6, just 500 metres below the old Signal Mountain fire lookout site. From this junction 8.5 kilometres of downhill road hiking bring the traveller to the Maligne Lake Road near Maligne Canyon.

179

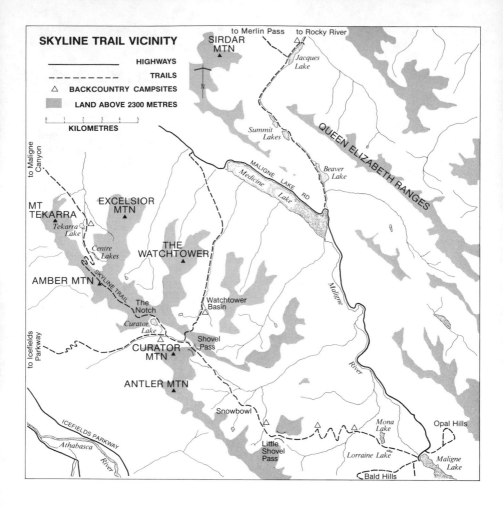

SKYLINE TRAIL VICINITY

HIGHWAYS

TRAILS

△ BACKCOUNTRY CAMPSITES

LAND ABOVE 2300 METRES

0 1 2 3 4 5
KILOMETRES

N

to Merlin Pass   to Rocky River

SIRDAR MTN ▲

Jacques Lake

to Maligne Canyon

Summit Lakes

QUEEN ELIZABETH RANGES

MALIGNE LAKE RD

Medicine *Lake*

Beaver Lake

MT TEKARRA ▲

Tekarra Lake △

EXCELSIOR MTN ▲

Centre Lakes

THE WATCHTOWER ▲

AMBER MTN ▲

SKYLINE TRAIL

The Notch

Watchtower Basin

Maligne

Curator Lake △

CURATOR MTN ▲

Shovel Pass

to Icefields Parkway

ANTLER MTN ▲

Snowbowl

River

ICEFIELDS PARKWAY

Athabasca *River*

Little Shovel Pass

△   △   △

Mona Lake

Opal Hills

Lorraine Lake

Maligne Lake

Bald Hills

180

Shovel Pass via Wabasso

Icefields Parkway to Skyline Trail—14.5 kilometres (9.0 miles)

Backpack

Allow 5 hours to Skyline Trail

Elevation gain: 1100 metres (3,600 feet)

Maximum elevation: 2200 metres (7,200 feet)

Topo maps: Medicine Lake 83 C/13|
  †first 2.7 kms not shown

Point of Departure: Follow the Icefields Parkway (Hwy 93) to the Wabasso Lake parking area, located on east side of the highway 15 kilometres (9½ miles) south of Jasper townsite or 16 kilometres (10 miles) north of the Highway 93-A junction at Athabasca Falls.

0.0—Trail sign (1100 m).

—Rolling, forested terrain.

2.7—Wabasso Lake.

2.9—Junction. Valley of the Five Lakes and Old Fort Point to left. Keep right for Skyline Trail.

—Steep, switchbacking climb up southwest slopes of Maligne Range.

12.5—Grade moderates.

13.7—Curator Campground and outfitter's cabin.

14.5—Junction (2200 m). Intersection with the *Skyline Trail* at Km 19.5.

Only the most masochistic backpackers in the world will want to hike to the Skyline Trail using the Wabasso Lake trail. It is without a doubt the most gruelling, unpleasant trail in the Canadian Rockies as it climbs 800 of its 1100 vertical metres in just under nine kilometres on a muddy, well-churned horse route. In addition, the climb is over a well forested, southwest-facing slope that turns into an oven on a sunny, midsummer's day and is inundated with mosquitoes and horseflies. With the exception of purists who might want to hike directly to the Skyline from downtown Jasper via Old Fort Point and Valley of the Five Lakes, the Wabasso Lake trail's only value is as a quick, downhill escape route from the Skyline Trail.

The first 2.7 kilometres of trail follow the pleasant nature path leading from the Icefields Parkway to Wabasso Lake. Wabasso is a quiet little lake inhabited by muskrat and occasional waterfowl, but its pastoral beauty belies the miseries which lie ahead. From the junction at the lake's northwest corner, the main trail turns right, skirts the north shore, and then veers eastward toward the forested slopes of the Maligne Mountains.

The climb begins in earnest at Kilometre 3.5 as do the mud and bugs. Finally, around Kilometre 12.5, the uphill grade moderates as the trail enters a pleasant but boggy subalpine valley. Near the head of this vale is an outfitter's cabin and the combo horse-hiker Curator Campground. From the campground it is a short climb to the Skyline Trail near Curator Lake and Big Shovel Pass.

Whether climbing or descending this trail, be forewarned that water is scarce on the long, unrelenting slopes between Wabasso Lake and the upper meadow. Carry a good supply of drinking water with you.

Watchtower Basin

Maligne Lake Road to Watchtower Campground—9.8 kilometres (6.1 miles)
Maligne Lake Road to Skyline Trail—13.2 kilometres (8.2 miles)*

Day trip or backpack

Allow 4 hours one way

Elevation gain: 985 metres (3,250 feet)

Maximum elevation: 2375 metres (7,800 feet)

Topo maps: Medicine Lake 83 C/13

Point of Departure: From its junction with the Yellowhead Highway (Hwy 16) 5 kilometres (3 miles) east of Jasper townsite, follow the Maligne Lake Road for 18½ kilometres (11½ miles) to the Watchtower Basin trail head. The parking area is approximately 100 metres to the right of the main road via a gravel access road, situated on an open flat on the north side of the Maligne River.

0.0—Trail sign (1390 m).

—Trail drops down immediately and crosses Maligne River via footbridge. Climbs steeply up opposite slope.

0.5—Trail angles east, climbing at gradual to moderate grade.

5.6—Trail veers south, begins moderate climb along Watchtower drainage.

7.6—Trail opens out into Watchtower Valley.

9.6—Ford to east side of creek.

9.8—Watchtower Campground.

—Route upvalley stays on east side of creek. Trail indistinct.

12.3—Obvious trail climbs scree slope beneath headwall pass.

12.8—Headwall summit (2375 m).

—Trail contours left across open slope toward Big Shovel Pass.

13.2—Junction (2320 m). Intersection with *Skyline Trail* at Km 17.6.

*Distances beyond Km 9.8 approximate.

As a first backpack trip of the season, the ten kilometre trek to the Watchtower Basin is nearly ideal: it is relatively short and of moderate gradient, but long enough and in places steep enough to remind dormant muscles just what backpacking is all about. The upper valley is beautiful and the high meadows and passes visible from the campground offer interesting exploratory possibilities. For more enthusiastic souls, there is the option of continuing the backpack onto the Skyline Trail or making a traverse across the breadth of the Maligne Range.

From the sign at the parking area the trail heads south into a dense forest of pine, spruce and fir. After crossing the Maligne River via a sturdy footbridge, the trail turns south and begins a short but steep climb up the northern flank of The Watchtower. After it has gained enough elevation to leave most hikers slightly winded, the track angles off toward the southeast. The next two kilometres run gradually uphill, traversing numerous marshy areas, most of which are bridged with corduroy walkways of lodgepole pine.

At the 2.5 kilometre mark the trail gradually veers back to the south and begins the major climbing portion of the hike. Just over three kilometres later the trail levels off and enters the meadows of the Watchtower Basin. The trail stays on the west side of the stream that drains the valley for the next four kilometres, finally crossing to the east side to reach the Watchtower Campground at Kilometre 9.8. The campground is on the site of the old Watchtower Cabin, which served as a base for Jasper ski enthusiasts in the early 1930s (the cabin was accidentally destroyed by fire in the late 1970s).

One of the easiest sidetrips from the campground is to a small lake less than a kilometre away to the west and 150 vertical metres up on the lower slopes of The

Watchtower Basin

Watchtower. While there is no trail to this pretty tarn, finding your way up across the meadows should be no problem. The rockslides surrounding the lake are home to pika and white-tailed ptarmigan.

As of this writing, the trail upvalley from the campground is sketchy to non-existent, but the terrain is open and the general route to the head of the valley (staying to the east side) is obvious. As you near the end of the valley, look for defined trail picking up again on the scree slope leading to a high pass on the crest of the Maligne Range. From this lofty col, approximately three kilometres beyond the campground, views open out over the scenic heartland of the range — Shovel Pass, Curator Lake and The Notch; an intersection with the Skyline Trail lies immediately below this summit.

Some of the best features of the Skyline Trail, such as the Snowbowl or The Notch, can be visited as a day trip from a base camp in the Watchtower Basin. In fact, backpackers can complete their journey by following the Skyline or by traversing across the Maligne Range and descending into the Athabasca Valley on the Wabasso Lake trail (see *Skyline Trail* and *Shovel Pass via Wabasso* trail descriptions).

Bald Hills

Maligne Lake to Bald Hills Lookout Site—5.2 kilometres (3.2 miles)

Day trip

Allow 2 hours one way

Elevation gain: 480 metres (1,575 feet)

Maximum elevation: 2170 metres (7,120 feet)

Topo maps: Athabasca Falls 83 C/12

Point of Departure: From its junction with the Yellowhead Highway (Hwy 16) 5 kilometres (3 miles) east of Jasper townsite, follow the Maligne Lake Road 44½ kilometres (27½ miles) to Maligne Lake. Continue past the lodge for 0.5 kilometre, crossing the lake outlet bridge to the picnic area parking lot at road's end. The trail sign for the Bald Hills trail is at the locked access gate opposite the parking area entrance.

0.0—Trail sign (1690 m).

 —Steady uphill on moderately graded fire road.

3.2—Junction. Evelyn Creek cutoff. Stay on fire road.

5.2—Bald Hills Lookout site (2170 m).

Reached by a rather uninspiring trudge over a fire road, the Bald Hills provide an exceptional overview of Maligne Lake and its surrounding peaks. The subalpine meadows on this long, rolling ridgetop are carpeted with wildflowers in July and early August, providing a colourful foreground for the lake and mountains and an ideal environment for aimless wandering.

The fire road runs west from the parking area at Maligne Lake, climbing through a fire succession forest of lodgepole pine. Near Kilometre 2.5, scattered spruce begin to appear and the environment becomes pronouncedly subalpine in character, with pleasant open meadows and stands of stunted alpine fir and Engelmann spruce gradually disappearing into the barren tundra above.

The road ends near the site of the old Bald Hills fire lookout, which was removed in the early 1980s. Views from the open slopes near this summit encompass nearly 360 degrees. Below, the greenish-blue waters of Maligne Lake stretch toward the Narrows, with Leah Peak (2801 m) and Samson Peak (3081 m) rising beyond. The prominent glacier-clad summits that peek above the meadows to the south are Mounts Unwin and Charlton, both well in excess of 3000 metres above sea level.

In 1908, Mary Schäffer, the Rockies' first lady of exploration, and her companions reached Maligne Lake — its first recorded visit since 1875. Describing their journey down the lake and through the Narrows by raft, Mary Schäffer later wrote: "There burst upon us that which, all in our little company agreed, was the finest view any of us had ever beheld in the Rockies . . . Yet there it lay, for the time being all ours — those miles and miles of lake, the unnamed peaks rising above us, one following the other, each more beautiful than the last." Mary Schäffer and her party were responsible for

Maligne Lake from Bald Hills

naming most of the mountains and other features in the valley, including the Bald Hills.

The panorama to the north is no less interesting. To the northwest stand the rounded summits of the Maligne Range, a 45 kilometre-long chain that stretches to Jasper townsite. Due north the Maligne River rolls away to the foot of the Queen Elizabeth Range. The bedding of the range, composed of a light grey Devonian limestone, has been tilted nearly vertical by the forces of mountain building and eroded to form a series of sharp, sawtoothed peaks.

The Bald Hills comprise a seven kilometre-long ridge which extends north from the Maligne Range. The highest summit on this low, rolling ridgeline only reaches 2600 metres, and most of the others are well beneath that elevation. It is easy to work your way south through the open meadows, an area where wildflowers abound through mid-summer and there is always the chance of spotting wildlife, including mountain caribou.

Hikers should be forewarned that there is no reliable water on the Bald Hills trail, so take a supply with you.

185

Opal Hills

Opal Hills Circuit—8.2 kilometres (5.1 miles)

Half-day trip

Allow 4 hours round trip

Elevation gain: 460 metres (1,500 feet)

Maximum elevation: 2160 metres (7,100 feet)

Topo maps: Athabasca Falls 83 C/12†
 †trail not shown

Point of Departure: From its junction with the Yellowhead Highway (Hwy 16) 5 kilometres (3 miles) east of Jasper townsite, follow the Maligne Lake Road 44½ kilometres (27½ miles) to Maligne Lake. Turn left into the main parking area just before the lodge and keep left to the third and uppermost parking lot. The trail sign is at the upper left corner of the parking area.

0.0—Trail sign (1700 m).

0.2—Junction. Maligne Lakeshore trail to right. Keep left.

—Very steep uphill.

1.6—Junction. Trail splits for upper loop. Keep right.

—Steady uphill.

2.6—Trail emerges into meadow.

3.2—Trail summit (2160 m). Trail levels out into meadows behind hills.

4.7—Trail emerges from behind hills, drops back into forest.

6.6—Junction. Connects back to approach trail at Km 1.6.

8.2—Trail sign (1700 m). Parking area.

Despite a steep initial climb, the Opal Hills loop is one of the more pleasant half-day hikes in Jasper Park. A short jaunt to the top of the grassy hillocks near the trail summit offers a fine view of Maligne Lake and the surrounding peaks. Travelling through high subalpine meadowland, the trip allows excellent opportunities for a day of nature-browsing, or just lying back on a hillside and snoozing in the sun.

There is no fooling about on the Opal Hills trail as it heads grimly upward with hardly a switchback, gaining elevation at a heart-pounding rate. The first two kilometres are through a dense forest of lodgepole pine, the creation of some past forest fire. Splitting at Kilometre 1.6, the trail loops up into an open bowl beneath the Opal Hills. Either branch will bring the hiker to the same point, but the right-hand option reaches the objective in far less time.

Keeping to the right at the junction, the trail enters spruce forest for a short stretch, then climbs back into the pine and finally out into the open meadow at Kilometre 2.6. Once into the meadow, the trail levels off, crosses through a draw to the left and circles into a basin behind low hills. Any of these grassy knolls provides an excellent view out across the upper Maligne Valley. Maligne Lake stretches away to the southeast and disappears beneath the twin peaks of Mount Unwin (3268 m) and Mount Charlton (3217 m); across the valley lie the rolling Bald Hills; farther to the northwest are the rounded summits of the Maligne Range.

The first recorded journey to Maligne Lake was made in 1875 by the railroad surveyor Henry MacLeod, who was so disappointed by his long and fruitless slog to this cul de sac that he named it Sorefoot Lake. The Stoney Indians knew of the lake by the name "Chaba Imne," or Great Beaver Lake. In 1908 the lake was explored by an expedition mounted by

Opal Hills

Mary Schäffer, who was responsible for naming most of the mountains in the vicinity.

The trail continues its run through the open basin. The area provides excellent big game habitat, and moose are sometimes seen browsing the scrub willow on the broad flats.

After travelling through the basin for two kilometres, the trail emerges from behind the meadowed knolls and makes a gradual descent through pleasant forest back to the loop junction.

Jacques Lake

Maligne Lake Road to Jacques Lake Campground—12.2 kilometres (7.6 miles)

Day trip or backpack

Allow 4 - 5 hours to Jacques Lake

Elevation gain: 90 metres (300 feet)
loss: 45 metres (150 feet)

Maximum elevation: 1540 metres (5,050 feet)

Topo maps: Medicine Lake 83 C/13

Point of Departure: Drive the Yellowhead Highway (Hwy 16) to its junction with the Maligne Lake Road 5 kilometres (3 miles) east of Jasper townsite. Follow the Maligne Lake Road 28 kilometres (17½ miles) to the Beaver Creek Picnic Area, located on the left side of the highway opposite the south end of Medicine Lake. Park in the picnic area to the left of the locked access gate where the trail begins.

0.0—Trail sign (1450 m).

—Follows flat fire road.

1.6—Beaver Lake.

4.8—First Summit Lake. Follow foot trail into forest to right.

6.0—Second Summit Lake (1540 m). Trail stays in forest to right of lake.

7.4—Trail skirts to left of small lake.

—Area of many stream crossings.

11.2—Junction. Trail to Merlin Pass branches left. Stay straight ahead.

11.6—Jacques Lake (south end).

12.2—Jacques Lake Campground (1495 m).

—Trail crosses outlet stream (north end of lake).

12.5—Jacques Lake Warden Cabin. Connects with *South Boundary Trail* at Km 153.2.

Lying beneath the severely faulted limestone mountains of the Front Ranges and surrounded by a luxuriant forest, Jacques Lake is an excellent destination for either strong day hikers or casual backpackers. The trail to the lake is unusual in that it travels through a narrow mountain valley, past four lakes and over a watershed divide — all within less than twelve kilometres and with little appreciable gain or loss of elevation.

After a pleasant walk of 1.6 kilometres on an old access road, the first point of interest on the hike is reached — Beaver Lake. The lake's still green waters are often visited by loon and other waterfowl, and this is far too pleasant a place to stop so early in the day.

The fire road continues beyond Beaver Lake, entering more open country. The sheer walls of the Queen Elizabeth Range appear to the right, the mountains' light grey slabs of Devonian limestone tilted nearly verticle and eroded to form a jagged sawtooth ridge.

At Kilometre 4.8 the hiker comes upon the first Summit Lake, a small body of water ringed by a forest of spruce, lodgepole pine and cottonwood poplar. Here the fire road reverts to foot trail and continues on past two more small lakes in the next three kilometres. Notice that the first two of these lakes have no visible outlet; lakes of this type are known as "sinks" and generally drain through subterranean passages in the limestone bedrock.

The last four kilometres to Jacques Lake are through a dense forest filled with streams. The main creek running down to the lake is crossed at least three times, while numerous small tributaries tumble in along the way. Needless to say, this is not a dry hike.

Though strong hikers can make the round trip in a day, the peaceful scene at Jacques Lake is not conducive to leaping up and racing back on the return trek. Better to backpack and stay at the small

Jacques Lake

campground near the lake's outlet.

Jacques Lake is named for the mountain range to the northwest which was, in turn, named for Jacques Cardinal, a horse-tender for the Hudson's Bay Company on the Athabasca Trail during the early nineteenth century.

The Jacques Lake trail continues beyond the north end of the lake, crosses the outlet stream to the Jacques Warden Cabin, and then runs northeast down Breccia Creek. This is the route South Boundary Trail travellers should follow, but there is little worthwhile scenery in this direction that can be reached on a day trip from Jacques Lake. (See *South Boundary* trail description.)

Merlin Pass. Near the south end of Jacques Lake, the trail to Merlin Pass branches to the northwest. This trail runs for 30 kilometres to Highway 16. While Merlin Pass can be visited as a day trip from Jacques Lake Campground, most backpackers use the trail as an optional exit from the area. (See *Merlin Pass* trail description).

189

The South Boundary Trail

Maligne Lake Road to Icefields Parkway—165.7 kilometres (103.0 miles)

Backpack

Allow 10-14 days

Maximum elevation: 2255 metres (7,400 feet)

Minimum elevation: 1360 metres (4,450 feet)

Topo maps: Medicine Lake 83 C/13
          Mountain Park 83 C/14
          Southesk Lake 83 C/11
          George Creek 83 C/10
          Job Creek 83 C/7
          Sunwapta Peak 83 C/6
          Columbia Icefield 83 C/3

Point of Departure: Travelling from north to south, start from the *Jacques Lake* trail head on the Maligne Lake Road. Northbound hikers can start from the *Nigel Pass* trail head in northern Banff Park.

0.0—Maligne Lake Road (1450 m). Beaver Creek Picnic Area.

11.2—Junction. Merlin Pass to left. S. Boundary straight ahead.

12.2—Jacques Lake Campground (1495 m).

12.5—Jacques Lake Warden Cabin.

25.0—Grizzly Campground (1360 m).

31.0—Grizzly Warden Cabin.

33.9—Rocky River suspension bridge (1405 m).

37.6—Climax Campground.

39.7—Gretna Lake.

42.6—Rocky Falls.

47.9—Rocky Forks Campground (1590 m).

56.8—Medicine Tent Campground.

57.0—Junction (1700 m). Rocky Pass to left.

60.9—Medicine Tent Warden Cabin.

66.1—Lagrace Campground.

70.5—Medicine Tent Lakes.

74.1—Cairn Pass (2255 m).

76.1—Cairn Pass Campground.

79.1—Cairn River Warden Cabin.

86.2—Cairn River bridge.

88.6—Junction. Southesk Lake to right.

The South Boundary Trail is no spectacular, high country trek — there are only two alpine passes along the entire route, and much of the trail travels rather uneventfully through kilometre after kilometre of lowland forest. But whatever the trail may lack in flashy scenery, it makes up in a feel of total isolation. The trail is long (166 kilometres), there are unbridged river crossings, and some days pass without another human encounter. Once you pass Jacques Lake on the north or the Brazeau Lake junction at the south end, there is a sense of total commitment to the journey, and the only trail which permits "escape" between those two points, Rocky Pass, brings the hiker out onto one of the loneliest roads in western Canada.

There is some disagreement as to which direction the trail should be hiked. There is an elevation advantage to starting from the south, but over a trail this long, such benefits tend to be insignificant. Since the best scenery lies on the southern half of the journey, we have opted to start in the north and take the hiker southwards. But, if an extended period of good weather is predicted when you sign out for this trip, you may want to hike Nigel Pass and the upper Brazeau Valley first.

One could not ask for an easier start to a major trek than the gentle Jacques Lake trail, and the Jacques Lake Campground ˙ at Kilometre 12.2 is one of the nicest along the entire South Boundary (a good excuse to make your first day out a short one). Beyond Jacques Lake the trail does not feel so civilized. The track gets rougher and hikers are scarcer as the trail works its way to the northeast and passes through the narrow Breccia Creek gorge, crossing the stream four times on footbridges. After the final crossing, the trail climbs out of the Breccia Canyon, bends around to the southeast, and descends to the Rocky River at Grizzly Campground. This entire 12.5 kilometre section from

Mount Dalhousie from Cairn River

88.8—Cairn River ford (calf to knee deep).

88.9—Cairn River Campground (1675 m).

93.0—Park boundary.

95.2—Southesk River suspension bridge. Park boundary.

95.9—Junction. Cardinal River to left. S. Boundary to right.

97.5—Southesk Campground (1610 m).

97.8—Junction. Dowling Ford to left. S. Boundary to right.

110.0—Isaac Creek ford (calf deep).

110.2—Isaac Creek Campground (1585 m).

111.3—Junction. Isaac Creek Warden Cabin to left. S. Boundary straight ahead.

123.1—Arete Warden Cabin.

123.7—Arete Campground.

132.4—Big Springs.

135.9—Brazeau Warden Cabin.

136.3—Junction. Brazeau Lake and Poboktan Pass to right. S. Boundary to left.

136.4—Brazeau Campground (1720 m).

144.9—Wolverine South Campground.

151.7—Junction. Jonas Pass to right. S. Boundary straight ahead.

151.9—Four Point Campground.

155.0—Boulder Creek Campground.

158.5—Nigel Pass (2195 m). Banff-Jasper boundary.

165.7—Icefields Parkway (1830 m). Nigel Pass trail head.

Jacques Lake to the Rocky River is forest-enclosed and fairly tedious.

From the pleasant Grizzly Camp-ground, located on a bank above the rushing waters of the Rocky River, the trail carries on upvalley along the southwest side of the river. While the trail is well defined, there is an unexpected calf-deep ford of a side stream at Kilometre 33.4. Views throughout this section of valley are limited until you cross the Rocky River suspension bridge at Kilometre 33.9 and emerge onto the open willow flats on the northeast side of the river. (The suspension bridge is 200 metres upstream from where the horse trail fords the river, so be sure to watch for the hiker's trail that leads off in that direction.)

Continuing upvalley along the northeast side of the river, travel is mainly through forest once again, though there are more glimpses out to the steeply-tilted limestone peaks of Front Ranges than there were back downvalley. At Kilometre 42.6, you suddenly emerge on an overlook immediately above Rocky Falls — a waterfall staircase in the Rocky River which creates a very impressive diversion along this otherwise lacklustre section of valley.

At Kilometre 47.9, just beneath the westward dipping limestone slabs of Mount Lindsay, the trail comes to the Rocky Forks Campground. Just 200 metres beyond the campground, the horse trail to the Rocky Forks Warden Cabin branches down to the right, while the hiker's trail continues straight ahead. This 1.7 kilometre hiker's cutoff is less defined than the horse trail, but it saves two fords of the Medicine Tent River. The hiker's path rejoins the horse trail at Kilometre 49.8 and continues its southeasterly course, but this time upstream along the Medicine Tent.

At Kilometre 53.9 the horse trail fords the Medicine Tent once more. Again, there is a hiker's trail (cutting off to the left 100 metres before the crossing) which stays on northeast side of the river. As of this writing, this 2.9 kilometre path is fairly vague in sections, but the trees along the way have been well blazed. The

Brazeau Valley

horse trail swings back across the river to rejoin the hiker's track at the Medicine Tent Campground.

Just 200 metres beyond the Medicine Tent Campground, the Rocky Pass trail intersects from the north. This is an important junction, since it is the only escape route from the South Boundary along its entire length; this 11.5 kilometre trail, running from the old Coal Branch road, also serves as a speedy access route to the Medicine Tent-Cairn Pass region. (See *Rocky Pass* trail description.)

As the trail continues up the Medicine Tent, the forest becomes more open and views improve. Beyond Lagrace Campground, the trail begins its climb toward the summit of Cairn Pass. The Medicine Tent Lakes are passed in an open alpine meadow at Kilometre 70.5 and, after a short steep climb through the last stands of alpine fir and Engelmann spruce, the pass is crested.

At 2255 metres above sea level, Cairn Pass is the high point of the trip in more ways than one. The view back down the Medicine Tent to the Rocky River valley is spectacular, allowing the first good overview of the country you have been hiking through for the past couple of days. The alpine meadows which stretch out on both sides of the pass, dotted with numerous small lakes, are about as extensive and beautiful as any in Jasper Park. The summit of the pass is also inhabited by a huge colony of hoary marmots.

Immediately above the pass to the west stands the low, cone-shaped peak of Southesk Cairn, and if you look closely, you can see the giant rock cairn which was erected on the summit by James Carnegie, the Earl of Southesk, when he passed this way on a hunting trip in 1859. (Experienced route finders can easily ascend this peak and add a rock or two to this historical edifice.)

Beyond Cairn Pass the trail continues in a southeasterly direction, descending through alpine and subalpine meadows for the next five kilometres. Southesk Cairn and the pass environs remain visible throughout this stretch, all the way to the Cairn River Warden Cabin junction. Bypassing the warden cabin at Kilometre 79.1, the main trail drops down into the forested Cairn River valley and skirts along the northeast bank of the river for the next seven kilometres.

193

At Kilometre 86.2, the trail crosses a bridge to the south side of the Cairn, swings over a forested height of land, and returns to the river in 2.6 kilometres to ford it (normally calf-deep) just above its confluence with the Southesk River. Just 200 metres before this second ford, the 22.4 kilometre trail to Southesk Lake branches to the right (see *Southesk Lake* trail description).

Nearly three kilometres beyond the Cairn River Campground, the horse trail comes abreast of the Southesk River and crosses to the south bank. In order to avoid this demanding ford, the hiker's trail continues east and climbs a forested ridge above the north side of the river. At Kilometre 93.0, the trail crosses the park boundary into provincial forest lands, and just 0.6 kilometre farther along, intersects a broad seismic line cut through the forest. Turn left and follow this cut for 100 metres to where the trail branches right and runs back into the forest. Another seismic line is encountered in another 100 metres. Follow this cut to the left for just over 100 metres and watch for the point where the trail exits to the right again.

Following this brief encounter with provincial forest desecration, the trail switchbacks down steeply to the Southesk River suspension bridge at Kilometre 95.2 and returns to the sanctity of the park. After taking a break on the rock slabs of this pleasant canyon, cross the bridge and climb 300 metres to rejoin the horse trail.

All of this wandering around in the forest actually takes the hiker out of the Front Ranges and into the fringes of the Foothills. From Southesk Campground, on a small point of land overlooking a sink lake, you have your first real perspective of the surrounding countryside — great expanses of flat, forested landscape, broken only by the dramatic peaks of Mount Dalhousie rising on the southwest horizon.

Just beyond Southesk Campground, the trail branches south and begins re-entry into the mountains via the Brazeau Valley. The trail runs through a rocky and rooty forest as it makes its ascent of the valley, but the grade remains flat, as it has been ever since the Southesk suspension bridge. With the exception of some sink lakes at Kilometre 100.4 which allow open views toward Tarpeian Rock, this is a long, tedious section enclosed by a canopy of lodgepole pine.

The scenery in the Brazeau Valley begins to improve at Isaac Creek. Here, on the rocky, dryas-covered flats near the mouth of the Isaac Creek canyon, there are fine views of the mountains across the valley, and most particularly to the sheer 1300 metre face of Tarpeian Rock. Continuing upvalley the trail alternates between sections of forest and large grassy meadows which run down to the Brazeau River. In midsummer these dry, open meadowlands are coloured with wildflowers typical of the montane grasslands — gaillardia, wood lilies, shrubby cinquefoil, bluebells, etc.

At Kilometre 132.4 there is an added surprise in the form of several large springs which gush from the base of a cliff and cascade down to the trail. These springs create a mini-rain forest environment in the midst of an otherwise semi-arid valley, and they provide welcome relief on a hot summer day.

The trail runs through the grounds of the Brazeau Warden station at Kilometre 135.9, and 500 metres farther along reaches the junction with the Brazeau Lake trail. The junction lies just over two kilometres below Brazeau Lake, and hikers may want to take a side trip to the lake — the largest found along the South Boundary route.

At the Brazeau Lake trail junction, the hiker returns to more trampled ways; the loneliness experienced over the past several days is about to disappear, and you can expect to encounter more fellow travellers over this final thirty kilometres of trail. This last leg to the headwaters of the Brazeau River and Nigel Pass is one of the most scenic sections on the entire trip, however, and with decent weather it should provide a fitting climax to the South Boundary Trail. (See *Brazeau Lake* and *Nigel Pass* trail descriptions.)

Southesk Lake

South Boundary Trail to Southesk Lake—22.4 kilometres (13.9 miles)*

Backpack

Allow 5-6 hours one way

Elevation gain: 170 metres (560 feet)

Maximum elevation: 1850 metres (6,070 feet)

Topo maps: George Creek 83 C/10
Southesk Lake 83 C/11

Point of Departure: Hike *The South Boundary Trail* to the Southesk Lake trail junction, 88 kilometres from the Maligne Lake Road at Beaver Creek, 77 kilometres from the Icefields Parkway at Nigel Creek, or 43 kilometres from the Coal Branch road via Rocky Pass.

0.0—Southesk Lake Junction (1680 m).

—Flat to gentle uphill along north side of Southesk River.

8.0—Southesk Falls Campground.

21.7—Southesk Lake (1850 m). Horse campground.

—Trail follows north shore of lake.

22.4—Southesk Campground.

* All distances approximate.

If Southesk Lake isn't the most remote point accessible by trail in Jasper Park, it certainly feels as though it is. Its location is very isolated — tucked away in the heart of the park's southeast wilderness and only accessible via a long trek on the South Boundary Trail plus an extra eighteen kilometres to the head of the Southesk Valley. The lake itself is low and encircled by forest, but the attraction for many of the experienced backpackers who make the journey each season is the chance to explore beyond the lake to the 2300 metre pass which serves as the divide between the Rocky and Southesk Rivers.

The trail to Southesk Lake strikes off from the South Boundary Trail at Kilometre 88.6, just 300 metres west of the Cairn River Campground (see *South Boundary Trail* description). As of this writing, a commercial outfitter is running regular packtrips over this trail, so the track up the north side of the river is well defined, if sometimes a bit muddy; the climb up the valley is quite gradual all the way to the lake. After passing the horse camp at the east end of the lake, the trail follows around the north shore for approximately 0.7 kilometre to the hiker campground.

Using Southesk Lake as a base camp, most backpackers like to explore westward to Glacier Pass at the foot of Maligne Mountain (not to be confused with the pass of the same name on Jasper's north boundary). The distance to this very wild and scenic summit is approximately 19 kilometres, and there is no maintained trail beyond Southesk Lake. However, by using a map and keeping to the north side of the river, the route is obvious.

Some intrepid backpackers continue their explorations northward, descending the Rocky River to the South Boundary Trail at Rocky Forks — a long, rough bushwhack with lots of streams to ford along the way.

Rocky Pass

Coal Branch Road to South Boundary Trail—11.5 kilometres (7.1 miles)

Day trip or backpack

Allow 3-4 hours to Medicine Tent River

Elevation gain: 120 metres (390 feet)
loss: 260 metres (850 feet)

Maximum elevation: 1960 metres (6,430 feet)

Topo maps: Mountain Park 83 C/14†

† trail incorrectly marked

Point of Departure: Follow Highway #16 east from Jasper Park East Gate 22 kilometres (13½ miles) to the intersection with Highway #40 South. Turn right onto Highway #40 and follow it south 48 kilometres (30 miles) to the junction with the Cadomin Road. Turn right and follow the Cadomin Road south, through the village of Cadomin, 23 kilometres (14 miles) to Cardinal River Divide. Continue down the opposite side of the divide for another 1.7 kilometres to where a seismic line intersects the road from the southwest — the beginning of the Rocky Pass trail.

0.0—Seismic line and horse campsite (1840 m).

—Trail follows seismic line southwest.

2.5—Junction. Rocky Pass trail branches left from seismic line.

—Trail fords Cardinal River and climbs to pass.

7.1—Rocky Pass (1960 m).

—Steep descent along east side of tributary stream.

11.5—Junction (1700 m). Intersection with *The South Boundary Trail* at Km 57.0. Medicine Tent Campground to right 0.2 km.

For hikers who want to reach the heart of the South Boundary Trail backcountry quickly (or escape from same), the 11.5 kilometre trail running over Rocky Pass from the old Coal Branch road south of Cadomin is the only option. Rocky Pass itself is very scenic and a worthy objective for a day hike, but few will want to make the long, rough drive to this remote area beyond Jasper's eastern boundary for a simple day trip.

The trail starts out on a seismic line, following it on a southwest compass bearing from the road. Near the 2.5 kilometre mark, you will enter a meadow area. The trail to the pass breaks away to the left from the seismic line in this meadow, but the cut-off is frequently obscured by willow growth (watch for horse tracks veering off the line to the left). Once you have left the seismic line, the horse trail is obvious leading across the meadow. The trail passes an old homestead and two small lakes, then it makes two easy fords of the Cardinal River before climbing steeply to the pass.

Rocky Pass, situated at 1960 metres above sea level, is a treeless, windswept gap which serves as a window to the wild Medicine Tent Valley. A small lake just a few metres east of the park boundary makes a fine turn-around point for day hikers and a good rest stop for backpackers.

From the pass the trail plunges down the east side of a canyon which serves as a tributary of the Medicine Tent River. After passing beneath a series of punchbowl-style waterfalls, it finally reaches the South Boundary Trail at a junction 200 metres south of the Medicine Tent Campground.

Those who use the Rocky Pass trail as an escape route should realize that the mining town of Mountain Park, which shows up near the trail head on many maps, is long defunct. Traffic is sparse on the old Coal Branch road, but those who do travel it are usually sympathetic to hitchhikers.

Merlin Pass

Yellowhead Highway to Jacques Lake Campground—31.0 kilometres (19.3 miles)*

Backpack

Allow 1-2 days one way

Elevation gain: 925 metres (3,050 feet)

Maximum elevation: 1930 metres (6,350 feet)

Topo maps: Snaring 83 E/1
　　　　　Miette 83 F/4
　　　　　Medicine Lake 83 C/13

Point of Departure: Follow the Yellowhead Highway (Hwy #16) north 21 kilometres (13 miles) from the Jasper townsite east exit. The parking area for the trail is on the right (east) side of the highway just 2.8 kilometres north of the Cold Sulphur Spring.

0.0—Trail sign (1005 m).

7.5—Cinquefoil Campground.

11.0—Emir Campground.

11.5—Jacques Pass (1785 m).

15.5—Nashan Campground (1540 m).

20.0—Merlin Pass (1930 m).

23.0—Dromore Campground (1620 m).

26.5—Unnamed summit (1760 m).

30.0—Junction (1495 m). Intersection with *Jacques Lake* and *South Boundary Trail* at Km 11.2.

31.0—Jacques Lakes Campground.

* All distances approximate.

Traversing a series of narrow valleys and three low passes at the foot of the Jacques Range, the Merlin Pass trail offers an optional route to and from Jacques Lake. The track is rough and sketchy in places, there are several unbridged stream crossings, and the scenery is somewhat limited, but the Merlin route does provide far more solitude than the normal trail to Jacques Lake.

Starting from the parking area on the Yellowhead Highway, the Merlin trail crosses a kilometre of shrubby flats and enters the narrow Jacques Creek valley to begin a steady, moderately steep ascent to Jacques Pass. At just 1785 metres above sea level, the pass is well below timberline and offers only limited views to the limestone peaks of the Jacques Range on the north and the Colin Range to the south.

From Jacques Pass the trail drops down into the Nashan Creek valley, crosses the creek, and then climbs to the summit of Merlin Pass — a narrow gap sandwiched between the cliffs of Mounts Merlin and Dromore. This is a rather stiff piece of hiking which rises 380 vertical metres in just over four kilometres.

Beyond Merlin Pass, the hiker plunges downhill once more, this time into the Dromore Valley, and once again, has to regain much of that lost elevation by climbing to an unnamed summit 3.5 kilometres southeast of the Dromore Creek Campground. The roller coaster ends on this forested pass, however, as the trail makes its final descent to a junction with the Jacques Lake trail near the south end of the lake.

The Merlin Pass trail can also serve as an alternate beginning (end) to the South Boundary Trail, an option which brings the total distance for this marathon journey up to 185 kilometres. (See *South Boundary Trail* description.)

Sulphur Skyline

Miette Hot Springs to Sulphur Skyline Summit—4.0 kilometres (2.5 miles)

Half-day trip

Allow 2 hours one way

Elevation gain: 700 metres (2,300 feet)

Maximum elevation: 2070 metres (6,790 feet)

Topo maps: ,Miette 83 F/4†

†last 1.8 km not shown

Point of Departure: From its junction with the Yellowhead Highway (Hwy 16) 7 kilometres (4½ miles) west of Jasper Park East Gate or 41 kilometres (25½ miles) east of Jasper townsite, follow the Miette Hot Springs Road south 17½ kilometres (11 miles) to its termination at the new hot springs pool complex. The trail leads upslope from the hot pool building.

0.0—Trail sign (1370 m).

—Trail climbs at moderate but steady grade on old access road.

0.8—Road narrows to trail width.

—Ascend through old burn dotted with spruce and pine.

2.2—Shuey Pass and junction (1660 m). Trail to Fiddle River and *Mystery Lake* straight ahead. Turn uphill to right for Sulphur Skyline.

—Grade steepens and views open up.

3.4—Trail climbs above last stunted trees.

4.0—Sulphur Skyline Summit (2070 m).

The short but steep trail leading to the summit of Sulphur Ridge is one of the truly fine day hikes in Jasper Park. Not only does it offer excellent close-up views of sawtoothed mountain ranges, but it is also an exceptional vantage point for several remote wilderness valleys—the most prominent being the Fiddle River drainage which snakes southwest for over 24 kilometres to its headwaters on a high rockbound pass. But be forewarned, this is a steep dry hike. Take water along.

Beginning at the new Miette Hot Springs pool complex, the trail climbs steadily to a low pass 2.2 kilometres distant. Immediately upon cresting the pass, the Sulphur Skyline trail branches up and to the right, beginning an even steeper ascent into the alpine environs of this small mountain overlooking the hot springs area. The laboured breathing ends on the highest point of the ridge and expansive views spread out below.

In addition to the southerly vistas of the Fiddle River valley and the rocky pyramid of Utopia Mountain (2563 m), there are equally impressive valleys and mountains stretching away to the north. Just a few kilometres below Miette Hot Springs, beyond the confluence of Sulphur Creek and the lower Fiddle River, are the jagged summits of Ashlar Ridge—the layers of grey limestone having been uplifted and steeply tilted to erode into a typical sawtooth mountain formation. The valleys running on either side of Ashlar Ridge descend to the broad Athabasca Valley, and further north the broad U-shaped Moosehorn Valley disappears into the distant haze.

For those with a little time and energy left to spare, the Skyline Ridge can be traversed along its length toward the hot springs. With some bushwhacking and careful route-finding, hikers can descend near the end of the ridge to the trail just above the pool facility.

Fiddle River from Sulphur Skyline

Mystery Lake

Day trip or backpack

Allow 3 - 4 hours one way

Elevation gain: 475 metres (1,550 feet)
loss: 350 metres (1,150 feet)

Maximum elevation: 1660 metres (5,450 feet)

Topo maps: Miette 83 F/4†
†last 7.2 kms not shown

Point of Departure: From its junction with the Yellowhead Highway (Hwy 16) 7 kilometres (4½ miles) west of Jasper Park East Gate or 41 kilometres (25½ miles) east of Jasper townsite, follow the Miette Hot Springs Road south 17½ kilometres (11 miles) to its termination at the new hot springs pool complex. The trail leads upslope from the hot pool building.

0.0—Trail sign (1370 m).

—Trail climbs at moderate but steady grade on old access road.

0.8—Road narrows to trail width.

—Ascend through old burn dotted with spruce and pine.

2.2—Shuey Pass and junction (1660 m). *Sulphur Skyline* trail cuts uphill to right. Stay straight ahead for Mystery Lake.

—Trail begins steep descent.

4.5—Fiddle River. Keep to west bank, travelling north.

4.8—Fiddle River ford.

6.8—Trail leaves river bank (1310 m). Begin ascent to Mystery Lake.

7.1—Junction. Trail to Fiddle River Cabin branches right. Keep left.

9.8—Park boundary (1495 m).

10.5—Mystery Lake.

11.7—Mystery Lake Campground.

Mystery Lake is a small, peaceful body of water lying just beyond the eastern boundary of Jasper National Park. Below treeline, the lake offers a gentle solitude for backpackers desiring a protected retreat combined with a day or two of trout fishing. The trail to the lake is an interesting one, offering several types of challenge and a variety of terrain. Because of a major ford of the Fiddle River, it is recommended the trail not be hiked until midsummer nor during periods of heavy rainfall.

The trail begins at the new Miette Hot Springs pool complex and gradually climbs to a low pass in 2.2 kilometres. The first section of trail is frequently intersected by smaller trails running in from left and right, but the main route is easily discernible. The trail switchbacks through some willow meadows just before the pass summit is reached, granting the hiker an opportunity to look back down the Sulphur Creek valley.

From the top of the pass the trail begins a gradual descent through coniferous forest to Kilometre 3.9, where a viewpoint reveals the rapids of the Fiddle River 300 metres below. Beyond the viewpoint the trail drops rapidly toward the river and into the narrow canyon of the Fiddle.

At the 4.5 kilometre mark the trail reaches the river's edge and swings to the north, toward a narrow notch in the canyon's high limestone cliffs. You must ford the river before reaching the notch and should watch closely for a likely spot as you move downstream. The ford, nearly impossible in early summer, is usually not difficult after the first week of August.

Once across the river stay on the east bank, even though the horse trail wanders back and forth across the river four or five times in the following 2.3 kilometres. Staying on the east bank will necessitate some bushwhacking and riverside boulder hopping whenever the horse trail is on the opposite side, but it does save several tricky fordings.

Crossing the Fiddle River on the Mystery Lake trail

At Kilometre 6.8 the trail cuts away from the river to the east and begins a short but steep climb to Mystery Lake. Keeping to the left at the 7.1 kilometre trail junction, you walk through alternating sections of forest and willow, the latter often over your head (and thus miserable on a wet day), to the western end of Mystery Lake at Kilometre 10.5. Although there is evidence of a packer's camp at the lakeshore, the designated campsite is at the far end of the lake, reached by following the lake's south shore.

Fiddle River

Miette Hot Springs to Whitehorse Pass—24.6 kilometres (15.3 miles)

Backpack

Allow 2 days to pass

Elevation gain: 1025 metres (3,350 feet)
    loss: 260 metres (850 feet)

Maximum elevation: 2135 metres (7,000 feet)

Topo maps: Miette 83 F/4†
    † trail not shown

Point of Departure: From its junction with the Yellowhead Highway (Hwy 16) 7 kilometres (4½ miles) west of Jasper Park East Gate or 41 kilometres (25½ miles) east of Jasper townsite, follow the Miette Hot Springs Road south 17½ kilometres (11 miles) to its termination at the new hot springs pool complex. Park in the hot pool parking area and walk south on the road 500 metres, down to the site of the old hot pool. The trail leads up the right side of the narrow Sulphur Creek drainage from this site.

0.0—Trail sign (1370 m).

0.2—Miette Hot Springs (source springs).

0.3—Junction. Horse trail intersects from right. Keep left.

2.6—Fiddle Pass (1645 m).

4.3—Fiddle River (1400 m).

5.7—Utopia Creek Campground and ford (ankle to mid-calf).*

8.4—Fiddle River Warden Cabin.*

13.0—Slide Creek Campground.*

20.3—Whitehorse Pass Campground. Tributary ford.*

24.6—Whitehorse Pass (2135 m).

* Distance approximate.

Striking off to the southeast from Miette Hot Springs, the Fiddle River trail runs through remote country which is gradually being discovered by experienced backpackers. While most travellers terminate their journey on the alpine tundra of Whitehorse Pass, it is possible to continue the trip by descending Whitehorse Creek to the old Coal Branch country east of the Jasper Park.

The first 4.3 kilometres of trail running up Sulphur Creek and down to the Fiddle River are quite well developed and frequently hiked as a nature walk from Miette Hot Springs. However, the trail becomes more of a wilderness track as it proceeds upvalley along the southwest side of the Fiddle and forces the hiker to wade Utopia Creek.

Just over a kilometre beyond the Slide Creek Campground, the trail swings across to the northeast side of the Fiddle, making the crossing via an easy rock hop. Farther along the horse trail crosses back to the southwest bank briefly, but hikers can follow a path which stays on the northeast bank. Throughout this section of valley, the trail alternates between rockslides, forest and gravel flats.

At the Whitehorse Pass Campground, the trail branches left up the river's north tributary stream and makes the final climb to the narrow notch of Whitehorse Pass and the park boundary. Called Fiddle Pass on the topo map, this 2135 metre summit provides fine views back down the Fiddle Valley and to the rugged peaks of the Nikanassin Range.

For those willing to arrange transportation, it is possible to continue on through the pass, following horse trail down to Whitehorse Creek and then old access road (heavily used by trail bikers) down the north side of the creek. The trail emerges on the old Coal Branch road at Whitehorse Campground, six kilometres south of Cadomin. Total distance from Whitehorse Pass is approximately 14 kilometres.

Celestine Lake Road

The Celestine Lake Road is a 27 kilometre-long gravel road which runs along the west side of the Athabasca Valley from the Snaring Campground north of Jasper townsite to Celestine Lake and the lower Snake Indian Valley. The road is rough and narrow in spots, and in any other area of the parks it would be closed to the public. But since this road provides access to a number of important trails, such as Devona Lookout, Vine Creek, Moosehorn Creek, and the North Boundary Trail, it remains open, albeit with strict travel restrictions in the form of alternating hours of one-way traffic north and southbound.

To reach the Celestine Lake Road, follow the Yellowhead Highway (Highway #16) to the Snaring Campground junction, 9 kilometres (6 miles) north of the Jasper townsite east exit. Follow this branch road five kilometres to the campground and continue past the entrance on the road which runs north across the Snaring River bridge. Just 1.5 kilometres beyond the campground, the Celestine Lake Road begins in the form of a gravel road which branches to the left.

As of this writing, two way traffic is allowed to Kilometre 7.6 on the Celestine Lake Road. At a point 1.3 kilometres beyond the Snaring Warden Station, there is a limited access sign. from this point northward traffic is one-way, alternating between north and south every two hours. The sign indicates the hours of north and southbound travel, but this information is also available at the Snaring Campground entrance station and the Park Information Centre in Jasper.

At Kilometre 9.2, just after crossing the Vine Creek bridge, the Vine Creek trail branches to the northwest from the road. The road continues along onto the open slopes of the valley, high above the shores of Jasper Lake. At Kilometre 22.5 it drops down to cross the Snake Indian River bridge, and then switchbacks to the northwest. The Moosehorn Creek trail head is passed on the right-hand side of the road at Kilometre 24.0. The Celestine Lake parking area and the end of road are reached at Kilometre 27.0. The trail signs for Devona Lookout and the North Boundary Trail are situated respectively on the east and north edges of the parking area.

While this road can be navigated by most any vehicle, it is narrow and rocky in spots, so extreme caution should be exercised. You should adhere strictly to the times listed on the one-way access instructions, but be wary on blind corners — someone else may not be following the rules. During periods of heavy rainfall, check with the Park Information Centre concerning conditions, since muddy sections and high water at the Corral Creek crossing could cause problems for smaller vehicles. No trailers are permitted on the road.

Devona Lookout

Celestine Lake Road to Devona Lookout Site—4.2 kilometres (2.6 miles)

Half-day trip

Allow 1½ hours one way

Elevation gain: 160 metres (525 feet)

Maximum elevation: 1404 metres (4,605 feet)

Topo maps: Snaring 83 E/1

Point of Departure: Drive to the Devona Lookout trail head at the end of the Celestine Lake Road as described in the *Celestine Lake Road* introduction (see page 203). The trail strikes off from the access gate on the east side of the parking area.

0.0—Access gate (1245 m).

—Route follows old fire road.

1.3—Princess Lake.

1.6—Celestine Lake and campground.

—Gradual uphill grades.

3.5—Road crests open ridge.

4.2—Devona Lookout site (1404 m).

The short trail leading to the old Devona Lookout site makes one of the nicest half-day trips in Jasper Park. In addition to passing two pretty lakes, Princess and Celestine, the summit at the end of the trail looks out over a section of the Athabasca Valley stretching from near Jasper townsite to the hills beyond the park's eastern boundary. The hike will certainly make a welcome break following a rather long and demanding drive to get to it via the Celestine Lake Road.

The Devona Lookout trail strikes off from the east edge of the parking lot at the end of the 27 kilometre Celestine Lake Road (see description for this road on page 203), and follows along an old service road all the way to the lookout site. Princess and Celestine Lakes are passed in the first two kilometres. Both are relatively large bodies of water surrounded by spruce forest and backdropped by the summits of the Beaver Bluffs and the Bosche Range to the north; both are popular spots for fishermen. A campground at the west end of Celestine Lake offers about the easiest backpack to an overnight camp that can be found in the mountain parks.

After a gradual climb through the forest beyond Celestine Lake, the road runs out onto an open ridge where excellent views of the Athabasca Valley begin. The grassy, south-facing slopes are typical of the montane life zone, and they are covered with the blooms of such wildflowers as western wood lilies, Indian paintbrush, camus lilies, shrubby cinquefoil, and purple vetch from mid-June through early July, and gaillardia, bluebells, and purple asters in late July and August.

At Kilometre 4.2 the site of the old Devona fire lookout tower is reached (dismantled in the mid-1980s), and an outstanding viewpoint for the Athabasca Valley lies just 150 metres beyond at the end of the summit ridge. Jasper Lake is

Roche Miette and the Athabasca Valley

directly beneath the viewpoint to the south, while the distinctive outline of Pyramid Mountain can be seen rising in the distance near the town of Jasper. To the northeast the Athabasca River runs out through the last of the Front Ranges into the forested foothills beyond Jasper's eastern boundary.

As you look out over this incredible panorama, you might imagine the valley without the highway and railway, appearing as it did in the first half of the nineteenth century when it served as the main fur trade corridor through the Rockies. The famous fur trade post of Jasper House stood immediately below this ridge, at the north end of Jasper Lake. In 1846, this colourful outpost was described as follows:

"Jasper's House consists of only three miserable log huts. The dwelling-house is composed of two rooms, of about fourteen or fifteen feet square each. One of them is used by all comers and goers: Indians, voyageurs, and traders, men, women, and children being huddled together indiscriminately; the other room being devoted to the exclusive occupation of Colin [the post factor] and his family, consisting of a Cree squaw, and nine interesting half-breed children."

Straight across the valley, rising above the waters of Jasper Lake, stand the impressive walls of Roche Miette. The mountain is composed of the massive, cliff-forming Palliser limestone — a formation of the Upper Devonian period. As an early traveller on the Athabasca Trail noted, Miette's Rock "derives its appellation from a French voyageur, who climbed its summit and sat smoking his pipe with his legs hanging over the fearful abyss."

205

Moosehorn Lakes

Backpack

Allow 2 days to Moosehorn Lakes

Elevation loss: 155 metres (500 feet)
 gain: 580 metres (1,900 feet)

Maximum elevation: 1585 metres (5,200 feet)

Topo maps: Snaring 83 E/1†
 Miette 83 F/4†
 Entrance 83 F/5†
 Rock Lake 83 E/8
 †first 10.5 kms not shown

Point of Departure: Drive the Celestine Lake Road to the Moosehorn Creek trail head as described in the *Celestine Lake Road* introduction (see page 203). The trail strikes off to the right from the Celestine Lake Road at Kilometre 30.5 (Mile 19) in the form of a secondary fire road. Park beside (but not in front of) the locked gate which controls access to this road.

0.0—Access gate (1160 m).

2.3—River flats (1005 m).

—Flat walking through river delta swamp.

7.2—Bridge over side channel.

—Trail climbs onto open hills, contours above Athabasca Valley.

11.6—Junction (1065 m). Moosehorn Creek trail branches uphill to left.

13.7—Ronde Creek Campground.

21.4—Moosehorn Creek ford (knee deep).

22.7—Moosehorn Creek crossing.

24.6—Moosehorn Creek crossing.

25.4—Moosehorn Warden Cabin.

25.6—Moosehorn Campground (1310 m).

25.9—Large meadow. Branch right and ford stream to follow trail in forest above east side of meadow.

29.1—Begin climb to pass.

32.0—Moosehorn Pass (1585 m). Park boundary.

32.3—Upper Moosehorn Lake.

—Trail skirts east side of lake.

33.3—Junction. Intersection with *Wolf Pass* trail.

The Moosehorn Lakes trail is actually two trails in one: the first eleven kilometres follow the west side of the Athabasca Valley, passing through a unique wetland environment and rolling across open, montane grasslands; the final two-thirds of the trail ascend the heavily forested Moosehorn Valley to a pair of low elevation lakes just beyond the park's northeast boundary. The first section follows gentle, well-maintained trail and makes an excellent day trip for amateur botanists, while the Moosehorn portion, fraught with rough, boggy track and unbridged streams, is a more demanding area reserved for the experienced backpacker.

From the trail head on the Celestine Lake Road, the hiker makes a gradual descent to Devona Flats via an old access road. When the road reaches the flats, it turns northeast and runs out onto the Snake Indian River delta — a very special area of backwaters, beaver ponds, and dense swamp vegetation. (And mosquitoes!) Here a multitude of shade-tolerant and moisture-loving plants abound, including such flowers as pink pyrola, butterwort, and yellow and white lady slippers.

The road reverts to trail in the midst of the Snake Indian jungle. After passing a large beaver pond and crossing the Coronach Creek footbridge, the path exits the swamp and quickly climbs onto the dryland hills overlooking the Athabasca Valley. On these semi-arid slopes montane flowers such as western wood lily, gaillardia, bluebell, and wild rose flourish. The trail contours along these open slopes for some four kilometres. Across the Athabasca Valley to the east the buttresses of Roche Miette are in constant view. Finally, at Kilometre 11.6, the trail to the Moosehorn Valley branches uphill to the left. This junction marks the farthest point of worthwhile travel for the day hiker and the beginning of more serious

Moosehorn Valley

labour for the backpacker.

From the grassy slopes overlooking the Athabasca Valley, the trail climbs onto the forested slopes beneath Roche Ronde and drops into the Moosehorn Valley proper. At Kilometre 21.4 it fords the creek to the east side (a wide crossing which could be troublesome during periods of heavy rainfall). The trail crosses the creek two more times in the next 3.2 kilometres, but if improvised log bridges are in place, you can avoid further wading.

After passing the Moosehorn Warden Cabin and Campground, the trail emerges into the southern end of a monstrous meadow. The hiker's trail angles to the right, fords Moosehorn Creek one last time (now a peaceful stream flowing through the willows), and gains the higher ground in the forest along the meadow's eastern margin. The trail stays just above the meadow in the forest for the next three kilometres, then makes its final ascent to the pass and the park boundary.

Moosehorn Pass is an unpretentious summit enclosed by forest, but a short walk down through a grassy meadow soon brings the hiker to the shores of upper Moosehorn Lake — a placid sheet of water reflecting the peaks of the Bosche Range. The trail continues along the east side of the Moosehorn Lakes (primitive campsites are located at the north end of both lakes). Despite the solitude encountered along the Moosehorn Valley, you may not find yourself alone at the lakes, since they are a popular destination for horseback and all-terrain vehicle parties riding south from the Wildhay River.

Wolf Pass. At the north end of lower Moosehorn Lake, the trail to Wolf Pass branches west. By following this route, experienced wilderness travellers can continue their journey into the heart of the Bosche Range and even make a circuit back to the original Moosehorn trail head on the Celestine Lake Road — an extended journey of some five to seven days. Be forewarned, however, the narrow canyon called "The Keyhole," which lies two kilometres west of the Moosehorn Lakes, forces the hiker to wade its stream 32 times! (See *Willow Creek* trail description.)

Vine Creek

Day trip or backpack

Allow 4 hours one way

Elevation gain: 625 metres (2,050 feet)

Maximum elevation: 1660 metres (5,450 feet)

Topo maps: Snaring 83 E/1†
    †trail not shown

Point of Departure: Follow the Celestine Lake Road to the Vine Creek trail head as described in the *Celestine Lake Road* introduction (see page 203). After crossing the Vine Creek bridge at Kilometre 9.2 (Mile 5.7), watch for the trail branching away from the road to the northwest in the form of an old access road track.

0.0—Trail head (1035 m).

    —Follow old access road uphill. Road reverts to trail which follows along east side of creek.

5.8—Vine Creek ford to west side.*

6.3—Vine Creek ford to east side.*

8.3—Vine Creek Campground (1660 m).

8.8—Vine Creek Warden Cabin.

*Distance approximate.

The Vine Creek trail travels up a narrow, forested valley in a very straightforward, uninspiring manner to a campground situated in subalpine meadows at the foot of Roche De Smet. Because it strikes off from the controlled access Celestine Lake Road, the trail is somewhat difficult to reach and of marginal interest once you get there. Yet, for true wilderness lovers who would like to do some exploring beyond the headwaters of this little-used valley, the trip may be worthwhile.

The trail starts up the east side of the valley on an old access road, but this broad track is soon traded for a traditional footpath. The ascent is quite steady over track that is often wet and poorly defined, and with the exception of a brief stint on the west side of the creek near the six kilometre mark, the trail stays on the east side throughout.

A campsite is reached at Kilometre 8.3 and the Vine Creek Warden Cabin lies another 500 metres beyond. Though the hiker has definitely reached the level of true subalpine forest on this 1660 metre divide, the meadows at this elevation remain small and willow covered; views are limited to the peaks in the immediate vicinity — Roche De Smet (2539 m) to the east and the summits of the Grassy Ridge to the southwest.

Though wardens sometimes ride along the foot of the De Smet Range to the Shale Banks and points north, there is no defined trail beyond the warden cabin. While travel is rough, there are numerous exploration opportunities for another ten kilometres or so beyond the Vine Creek headwaters provided by the many low passes and side valleys of the De Smet Range.

Hikers into this valley should be aware that this is prime bear country (you will probably see diggings or scat along the trail).

Willow Creek

Rock Lake to North Boundary Trail—13.9 kilometres (8.6 miles)

Backpack

Allow 4 - 5 hours to North Boundary Trail

Elevation loss: 140 metres (450 feet)

Maximum elevation: 1495 metres (4,900 feet)

Topo maps: Rock Lake 83 E/8

Point of Departure: Follow the Yellowhead Highway (Hwy 16) east from the Jasper Park East Gate for 20 kilometres (12½ miles) to the junction with Highway 40 North. From this junction, which is just 4 kilometres west of Hinton, turn left and follow Highway 40 for 40 kilometres (25 miles) to its junction with the Rock Lake Road. Turn left onto the Rock Lake Road and follow 2 kilometres (1.2 miles) to another junction just beyond the Moberly Creek bridge. Turn left and stay on the most defined road for the next 27 kilometres (16½ miles), keeping right at major intersections, to the Rock Lake Campground. Keep right at the entrance to the campground and at future intersections to climb around and above the north side of Rock Lake for 4.3 kilometres (2.7 miles) to road's end at an access gate and parking area—the start of the *Willow Creek* trail.

0.0—Access gate (1495 m). Willmore Wilderness boundary.

—Follow old access road.

1.8—Junction. Trail to Willow Creek cuts left from road.

—Gradual descent through forest and burn.

4.8—Park boundary.

6.5—Rock Creek crossing (ford two channels).

8.5—Junction. *Wolf Pass* trail cuts off to left. Stay right for Willow Creek.

—Trail follows open valley, across boggy willow flats.

12.0—Willow Creek Warden Cabin.

13.9—Junction (1355 m). Intersection with *North Boundary Trail* at Km 32.2.

The Willow Creek trail is an important access route into Jasper's North Boundary country. As an optional starting point for the North Boundary Trail, it saves eighteen kilometres and a lot of tedious fire road walking. It is a particularly advantageous access trail for those planning loop trips on the trails north of the North Boundary Trail. The trail's only real disadvantages are the rather lengthy drive required beyond Jasper's east boundary to the trail head and a double ford of Rock Creek.

Starting from the locked gate above the west end of Rock Lake, follow the old access road into the Willmore Wilderness Area for 1.8 kilometres to a junction where the Willow Creek trail branches to the left. The trail runs downhill through forest and old burn until, shortly after crossing into Jasper Park, it reaches Rock Creek. There are two channels which must be crossed here, and since keeping bridges in place at this crossing has been a difficult task, you can expect a double ford.

South of Rock Creek, the going is mostly flat, if sometimes boggy, through open willow meadows. The Willow Creek Warden Cabin is passed at Kilometre 12.0, and just two kilometres beyond the trail intersects with the North Boundary Trail near the Willow Creek Campground (see *North Boundary Trail*).

Wolf Pass. Approximately two kilometres south of the Rock Creek crossing, the trail to Wolf Pass branches east from the Willow Creek trail. This trail skirts the north end of the Bosche Range, then turns southeast to ascend a long forested valley to the summit of Wolf Pass. By following this trail beyond the pass and Jasper's eastern boundary, experienced wilderness travellers can make connection with the Moosehorn Lakes trail, the total distance from Willow Creek to Lower Moosehorn Lake being 24.5 kilometres. (See *Moosehorn Lakes* trail description.)

The North Boundary Trail

Celestine Lake Road to Berg Lake Parking Lot—173.4 kilometres (107.7 miles)

Backpack

Allow 8 - 14 days

Maximum elevation: 2020 metres (6,625 feet)

Minimum elevation: 855 metres (2,800 feet)

Topo maps: Snaring 83 E/1
Rock Lake 83 E/8
Blue Creek 83 E/7
Twintree Lake 83 E/6
Mount Robson 83 E/3

Point of Departure: Westbound backpackers can reach the east end of the North Boundary Trail by driving to the end of the Celestine Lake Road as described in the *Celestine Lake Road* introduction (see page 203). The North Boundary Trail begins at the access gate on the north side of the parking area. Eastbound backpackers can reach the west end of the trail by driving the Yellowhead Highway (Hwy 16) west from Jasper townsite 84 kilometres (53 miles) to the Mount Robson service centre. Take the road which cuts off to the north beside the service station-general store and follow it for 2 kilometres to its terminus at the Robson River parking area (see *Berg Lake* trail description).

0.0—Celestine Lake Parking Area (1245 m).

12.1—Shalebanks Campground.

19.8—Seldom Inn Campground.

21.3—Snake Indian Falls (0.2 km to left).

22.1—Junction. Trail branches right from fire road.

30.4—Horseshoe Campground.

32.2—Junction (1355 m). *Willow Creek* trail branches right. Keep left.

32.7—Willow Creek Campground.

34.1—Junction. Rock Creek trail branches right. Keep straight ahead.

38.3—Mud Creek.

40.9—Junction (1395 m). Glacier Pass trail branches right. Keep straight ahead.

41.7—Deer Creek.

45.4—Welbourne Campground and Warden Cabin.

In the summer of 1910, a small party of European alpinists exploring the slopes of Mount Robson heard of an old Indian trail which led down the Smoky River, over a high pass and eastward along the Snake Indian River to its mouth in the Athabasca Valley. Thinking the route might offer a quick exit from the mountains, the group set off down the Smoky under the guidance of outfitter John Yates. With some expert route-finding by this veteran guide, the party made the first recorded traverse of today's North Boundary Trail.

Visits to the northern wilds of Jasper Park were fairly few and sporadic over the next few decades. Even as late as the 1960s the North Boundary country was well known to only a few wardens and a handful of horsemen and adventuresome hikers. But today, probably because it is one of the best maintained wilderness trails in western Canada, the North Boundary is visited by hundreds of backpackers every summer.

Hikers should be forewarned that, except for the country near Mount Robson and a brief interval on Snake Indian Pass, the North Boundary Trail does not offer spectacular alpine scenery. In fact, many travellers find the trail quite tedious, particularly when the weather is wet and the trail has been churned up by horses' hooves. Yet, if one appreciates wild, remote country without river fords and bushwhacking, where pleasant campsites await the weary hiker at the end of the day, then the trail is ideal.

Certainly the North Boundary country possesses its own unique and subdued brand of beauty. It is a wilderness inhabited by moose, bear and one of the largest wolf populations in the mountain parks (as well as porcupines which will munch on your pack at night if you leave it sitting on the ground). We've known many a park warden who would quite

Snake Indian Falls

50.1—Milk Creek.

52.2—Nellie Lake.

56.4—Blue Creek Warden Station.

57.3—Blue Creek Campground.

57.8—Blue Creek Suspension Bridge.

58.1—Junction (1495 m). *Blue Creek* trail branches right. Keep straight ahead.

69.6—Three Slides Warden Cabin.

72.3—Three Slides Campground.

80.5—Hoodoo Warden Cabin (0.2 km to left).

85.0—Oatmeal Camp Campground.

91.3—Snake Indian Pass (2020 m).

97.2—Byng Campground.

97.6—Byng Warden Cabin.

105.5—Twintree Lake (1558 m).

106.7—Twintree Warden Cabin.

108.4—Twintree Campground.

110.6—Twintree Creek bridge.

117.7—Donaldson Creek Campground.

120.3—Smoky River bridge.

120.8—Junction (1385 m). Lower Smoky River trail to right. Keep left.

121.2—Lower Smoky Warden Station.

124.9—Chown Creek Campground and bridge. Bess Pass trail branches right.

132.0—Wolverine Warden Cabin.

133.1—Carcajou Creek.

136.0—Wolverine Campground.

146.1—Junction. *Moose Pass* trail branches left.

148.5—Adolphus Warden Station.

148.9—Adolphus Campground.

150.7—Adolphus Lake.

151.5—Robson Pass (1652 m). Jasper—Mount Robson park boundary. Connects with *Berg Lake* trail at Km 21.9.

173.4—Robson River bridge (855 m). Berg Lake trail parking area.

happily live out his days riding through these wild valleys.

The eastern terminus of this long wilderness trek is at Celestine Lake, just 43 kilometres east of Jasper townsite via the Yellowhead Highway and the Celestine Lake Road. From rather inauspicious beginnings in the forest-enclosed Celestine Lake parking area, the trail follows the Snake Indian River to its source on Snake Indian Pass, descends past Twintree Lake to the Smoky River, ascends the Smoky to its headwaters on the glacier-clad slopes of Mount Robson, and finally emerges at the Berg Lake trail head in Mount Robson Provincial Park, British Columbia. Though popularly known as the 100 Mile North Boundary Trail, the distance from Celestine Lake to Robson Pass measures out to 94 miles; tacking on the last segment of trail through Robson Park, the total trip is 108 miles, or 173 kilometres.

As might be suspected, the hiking options in so vast a country are endless. Many backpackers only penetrate this wilderness for a day or two before retracing their steps, but to most the attraction lies in traversing the entire trail. While some hike the North Boundary Trail from west to east, our preference is from east to west — a choice which allows a gradual improvement in scenery day by day culminating in the spectacular Mount Robson environs near the end of the journey. Elevation gain is spread out over many miles on the east to west option and is hardly noticeable, while eastbound travellers face two long gruelling climbs on the first half of their journey and an uninspiring 22 kilometre fire road walk on the final day.

Starting from the trail head at the end of the Celestine Lake Road, the first 22 kilometres of the trail follow a relatively level, well-graded fire road (no longer used by warden vehicles and currently in the process of regenerating). Travel is fairly tedious along this first section except for the Snake Indian Falls, a most impressive waterfall which thunders over a sheer cliff of limestone.

Just beyond Snake Indian Falls the

Snake Indian Pass

trail branches away from the fire road, and at Kilometre 29.8 it opens out into broad meadowlands as it nears the point where the Snake Indian Valley makes a bend to the west. Willow Creek flows into the Snake Indian from the north at this bend, and the country surrounding this junction is particularly beautiful as the meadows offer expansive views up the course of the river to the west and to the Daybreak Peak country in the north.

From Willow Creek the trail turns westward on its long journey toward the Great Divide. The country remains pleasant and open as the trail winds through stands of aspen and lodgepole pine and skirts along meadows laced with scrub birch, willow and shrubby cinquefoil. Near the Deer Creek-Little Heaven trail junction, you will encounter the destruction of a major windstorm that swept this area around 1980. The tornado-like winds, which struck in the early spring, blew due east and uprooted all but the youngest and slimmest lodgepoles. Trees

were hurled into parallel piles like giant jackstraws, cutting a swath that is approximately three kilometres long and 300 metres in width.

Continuing westward the valley narrows as the hiker draws nearer to the rugged peaks which serve as the gateway to Blue Creek and the upper Snake Indian Valley. At Kilometre 52.2 the trail passes a pretty backwater lake which reflects the jagged summit of 2786 metre Mount Simla — the most inspiring view on this section of trail. From this point there is a true sense of having entered the mountains.

Blue Creek is a significant landmark on the North Boundary Trail for several reasons: it serves as the gateway to some very remote country on the park's northern border; the nearby warden station is an important base for much of the patrol activity in the northern section of the park; and for the westbound hiker it is the beginning of more serious mountain travel. The first six kilometres of hiking

213

west of Blue Creek are quite beautiful as views often stretch across the Snake Indian Valley and its marshy, lake-dotted overflow plain. At Three Slides the first major glacier of the trip can be seen covering the slopes of Upright Mountain at the head of a valley to the south (not Mount Robson as some folks believe). At Kilometre 80.5 the Hoodoo Warden Cabin is passed and the climb to Snake Indian Pass begins, a moderate but steady uphill which breaks out of the trees at Kilometre 86.5 to allow an unobstructed view to the narrow gap of Snake Indian Pass straight ahead.

At 2020 metres above sea level, Snake Indian Pass is set in rolling alpine terrain. Paralleling the pass to the north are steeply tilted slabs of limestone which form the most prominent peaks of the region — Snake Indian Mountain and Monte Cristo Mountain. From this pleasant summit the trail descends Twintree Creek to the shores of Twintree Lake — a silty, forest-enclosed body of water which was named by outfitter John Yates and company in 1910 for two lone pine trees situated on two small islands of rock near the lake's outlet.

From Twintree Lake the trail continues down Twintree Creek for a distance before crossing the stream and climbing over a ridge of Twintree Mountain. Beyond the forested crest of this ridge, a stiff descent of 300 metres is made in eight kilometres to the crossing on the Smoky River. It is a rocky, rooty and often boggy track that is easily the toughest section of trail on the entire hike.

A new world is entered once the traveller reaches the Smoky River. Here are rugged mountains and rocky river flats where glaciers are close at hand and hard at work. The valley of Chown Creek, running away to the west at Kilometre 124.9, is particularly spectacular, dominated as it is by the cold grey ramparts of 3216 metre Mount Bess.

The climb up the Smoky is relatively gradual though rough and rocky in sections, and the scenery continues to improve. At Kilometre 139.3 the trail travels beneath the Mural Glacier as it begins

a somewhat more serious ascent toward Robson Pass. Finally, the long awaited view of Mount Robson (weather permitting) is obtained from the open meadow below Adolphus Lake. The lake lies about 1.5 kilometres into the trees beyond this willow-covered valley, but its western shore opens out onto the broad flats of Robson Pass where the monarch of the Rockies towers in all its majesty.

When the hiker reaches the Robson Park boundary, he might well consider that he has returned to civilization. Within the space of a few kilometres you pass from a relatively peaceful and primitive land into one of the busiest backcountry areas in the mountain parks. The scenery, however, is exceptional. (For a detailed description of the final 22 kilometres of the trip, see *Berg Lake* in the Mount Robson Park chapter.)

Though the North Boundary Trail has been hiked in as little as six or seven days (runners have done it in two), a more comfortable pace suggests doing the trip in 10 days to two weeks; this pace is encouraged by the spacing of campsites at intervals of approximately 10 to 13 kilometres. Finally, cabins situated along the trail are strictly for warden patrol use, and while they are all interconnected by telephone line, they should only be entered in the case of a serious emergency.

While the North Boundary Trail as it is described here is the itinerary of choice for most backpackers, the many trails which branch from the route allow for a great variety of trips. The Willow Creek trail, which runs 13.9 kilometres from Rock Lake to an intersection with the North Boundary at Kilometre 32.2, is an optional point of access to the standard route. Trails leading up Blue Creek, Deer Creek and Mowitch Creek provide optional trips north from the main trail, including loops into the southern valleys of the Willmore Wilderness Area. At Kilometre 146.1, the Moose River trail intersects to furnish an alternate route to or from the Yellowhead Highway via a remote wilderness valley. (See trail descriptions for *Willow Creek, Glacier Pass, Blue Creek,* and *Moose River*.)

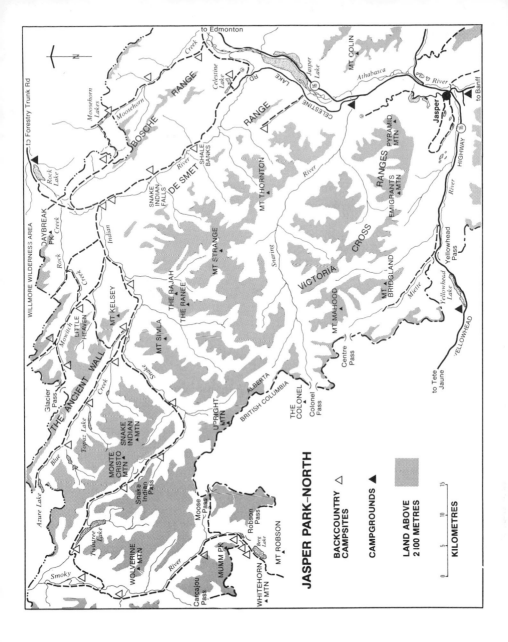

JASPER PARK–NORTH

BACKCOUNTRY
CAMPSITES △

CAMPGROUNDS ▲

LAND ABOVE
2 100 METRES

0   5   10   15
KILOMETRES

215

Blue Creek

North Boundary Trail to Azure Lake—34.5 kilometres (21.4 miles)

Backpack

Allow 2 days one way

Elevation gain: 470 metres (1,550 feet)

Maximum elevation: 1965 metres (6,450 feet)

Topo maps: Blue Creek 83 E/7
 Twintree Lake 83 E/6

Point of Departure: Follow the *North Boundary Trail* to the junction with the Blue Creek trail at Kilometre 58.1, just 300 metres west of the Blue Creek suspension bridge.

0.0—North Boundary Trail Junction (1495 m).

 —Trail crosses dry ridge forested with mature lodgepole pine.

5.9—Upper Blue Creek Campground. Suspension bridge to east side of creek.

 —Enter area of extensive meadows.

15.5—Topaz Warden Cabin.

16.8—Topaz Campground. Topaz Lake 1.7 kilometres to west.

 —Trail crosses and recrosses Blue Creek.

22.4—Natural Arch viewpoint.

25.3—Caribou Inn Campground. Caribou Lakes 2.5 kilometres to west.

 —Short, steep climb through open lodgepole forest to upper meadows. Trail becomes sketchy.

34.5—Azure Lake.

35.7—Park boundary (1965 m).

Blue Creek occupies a broad, thirty kilometre-long valley running northwest from the Snake Indian River to a deep blue lake straddling the park's boundary with the Willmore Wilderness Area. The trip up this exceptionally scenic valley is considered the most worthwhile side trip branching off of the North Boundary Trail. Topaz and Caribou Lakes, on the valley's western slope, provide the bonus of some of the best Dolly Varden and rainbow trout fishing in the Canadian Rockies.

Six kilometres beyond its junction with the North Boundary Trail, the trail reaches Blue Creek proper and crosses to the northeast side via a suspension bridge. Immediately above the crossing, the hiker enters the huge meadows which dominate the remainder of the valley. The limestone peaks of The Ancient Wall march away in an endless procession to the northwest, an outstanding example of a sawtoothed mountain range. Just before Caribou Inn is reached, the hiker passes beneath the only vantage point for the Natural Arch — a huge, hollowed-out upfold in the wall beneath the summit of Mount Perce.

The trail is sketchy in the upper valley, but since the meadows are dry and open, the walk to Azure Lake is quite straightforward and pleasant. You can find your own route up across the open grassy meadows above the lake's north shore and then traverse a series of rock ledges to reach the summit of Hardscrabble Pass and one of the most sublime views in all of Jasper Park.

Glacier Pass. By continuing into the Willmore's Sulphur Valley from Hardscrabble Pass (good trail reappears north of the pass), the hiker can eventually ascend the South Sulphur Valley and return into Jasper via Glacier Pass. The Blue Creek-Glacier Pass-Little Heaven loop creates one of the most rewarding trips in Jasper's northern wilderness. (See *Glacier Pass* trail description.)

Glacier Pass

North Boundary Trail to Glacier Pass—30.3 kilometres (18.8 miles)

Backpack

Allow 2 days to Glacier Pass

Elevation gain: 705 metres (2,300 feet)

Maximum elevation: 2100 metres (6,900 feet)

Topo maps: Rock Lake 83 E/8
　　　　　Blue Creek 83 E/7†

　　　† last 20.5 kms not shown

Point of Departure: Follow the *North Boundary Trail* to its junction with the Glacier Pass trail at Kilometre 40.9 (8.2 kilometres west of the Willow Creek Campground).

0.0—North Boundary Trail Junction (1395 m).

　—Steady ascent through Deer Creek canyon.

9.4—Little Heaven Warden Cabin and junction (1690 m). Trail to McLaren Pass branches southwest.

9.8—Little Heaven Campground.

9.9—Junction. Mowitch Creek trail to Rock Creek branches right.

　—Trail ascends north side of Mowitch Creek.

21.4—Junction. Desolation Pass trail branches right.

23.7—Vega Warden Cabin.

25.1—Glacier Pass (Vega) Campground.

27.1—Trail bends north and begins final ascent to pass.

30.3—Glacier Pass (2100 m).

The Glacier Pass trail branches from the North Boundary Trail at Kilometre 40.9, runs up Deer Creek to the meadows of Little Heaven, and then follows Mowitch Creek to its headwaters on a 2100 metre summit straddling the Jasper Park-Willmore Wilderness boundary. The trail is one of the more attractive options in the North Boundary country, and by utilizing well defined horse trails on the South Sulphur and West Sulphur Rivers in the Willmore Wilderness, experienced backpackers can loop west over Hardscrabble Pass and intersect with the Blue Creek trail at Azure Lake.

From the North Boundary junction, the trail runs north of Deer Creek for nearly five kilometres to the mouth of the Deer Creek canyon. Here it climbs over 150 vertical metres in the canyon before it emerges into the meadows of Little Heaven (traditionally, a heavenly pasture for horses). The warden cabin is found on a promontory overlooking this pastoral scene, and the campground lies beyond and to the right across a small stream.

As the trail exits from the meadows, it crosses to the north side of Mowitch (pronounced MAU-wick) Creek. Following the creek in a westerly direction, the trail enters the Front Ranges and, after passing beneath the south face of Vega Peak, turns north to reach the grassy summit of Glacier Pass at Kilometre 30.3.

Desolation Pass. The six kilometre-long trail to Desolation Pass (2055 m) branches north from the Glacier Pass trail at Kilometre 21.4. The pass, which is frequently visited by caribou, makes an excellent side trip for Mowitch Creek backpackers.

McLaren Pass. The 22 kilometre-long trail from Little Heaven to Blue Creek via McLaren Pass (2120 m) provides a direct connection between these two major valleys. (Once it reaches the Blue Creek Valley, the trail turns south to intersect with the North Boundary Trail just east of the Blue Creek suspension bridge.)

Saturday Night Lake Circuit

Saturday Night Lake Circuit—24.6 kilometres (15.3 miles)

Day trip or backpack

Allow 8-10 hours round trip

Elevation gain: 540 metres (1,800 feet)

Maximum elevation: 1640 metres (5,400 feet)

Topo maps: Jasper 83 D/16

Point of Departure: Follow Connaught Drive (Jasper's main street) to Cedar Avenue. Turn west on Cedar and follow it two blocks to where it becomes Pyramid Avenue. Continue on Pyramid two more blocks to the intersection with Pyramid Lake Drive on the west edge of town. Turn left and follow Pyramid Lake Drive and then Cabin Creek Road for 1.5 kms (keep right at all intersections and follow along the west edge of town). Watch for a dirt road leading uphill from Cabin Creek Road, opposite the mobile home residential district. Follow this dirt road 50 metres to the parking area and trail sign on the left hand side.

0.0—Trail sign (1100 m).

2.3—Marjorie Lake.

2.6—Junction. Hibernia Lake to right 1.0 km.

4.2—Caledonia Lake.

9.2—Junction. Minnow Lake to left 1.0 km.

12.4—Junction. High Lakes to right 200 metres.

12.9—Cascade (1640 m). Trail turns back down-valley.

18.0—Junction. Saturday Night Lake to left 1.0 km.

21.4—Cabin Lake (west end).

22.5—Cabin Lake (east end) and junction. Turn right and cross reservoir landfill.

23.4—Stream crossing.

24.6—Trail sign (1100 m).

The Saturday Night Loop trail provides a long day or overnight trip working out around a number of the small lakes in the hill country west of Jasper townsite. While most of the journey is forest-enclosed and views are limited, the trail makes an excellent area for nature study, and the many lakes allow for tranquil rest stops along the way.

From the trail head at the west edge of town, the pathway immediately crosses Cabin Creek and climbs onto a low bluff with a brief open view up the Athabasca Valley. Marjorie Lake is the first of the many small lakes encountered on this journey, appearing in the forest to the left of the trail at Kilometre 2.3. Just beyond Marjorie Lake, the short branch trail to Hibernia Lake cuts up to the right.

A quick look at a map shows that the lakes and ridges in this rolling country tend to be elongated in an east-west direction — the result of a large glacier which once moved down the Miette to the Athabasca Valley. Large boulders and other glacial debris can be found throughout the area.

At Kilometre 4.2 the trail skirts the north shore of Caledonia Lake where, in early summer, western wood lilies and wild roses bloom. Beyond Caledonia Lake there is a long section of enclosed forest hiking with some steady uphill grades. Many forest wildflowers grow along the trail, including bunchberry, single's delight, arnica, calypso orchids, Labrador tea, and Indian paintbrush. Also, keep an eye out for scattered patches of red columbine, a rare flower on the eastern slope of the Rockies.

After passing the Minnow Lake junction (the lake lies less than a kilometre to the west), the trail climbs along some forested ridges to reach the High Lakes. Just 500 metres farther along, the trail reaches the foot of a large cascade, where it turns back to the east and begins the return journey.

Caledonia Lake

The descent on the north arm of the loop trail is steady through a forest of spring-fed streams and beaver swamps. At Kilometre 18.0 a short trail branches north to Saturday Night Lake. From this junction it is just over three kilometres to the west end of the Cabin Lake reservoir, the largest body of water on the hike.

At the east end of Cabin Lake, cross the landfill dam and follow the access road that leads down through the forest. A stream cuts this road 600 metres below Cabin Lake. Cross the stream on a footbridge just inside the forest margin to the left. A trail on the opposite side runs out onto an open bluff overlooking the Athabasca Valley and then descends through forest back to the trail head parking area.

Backpackers on this circuit should be aware that the area is frequently visited by black bear, so keep a clean camp.

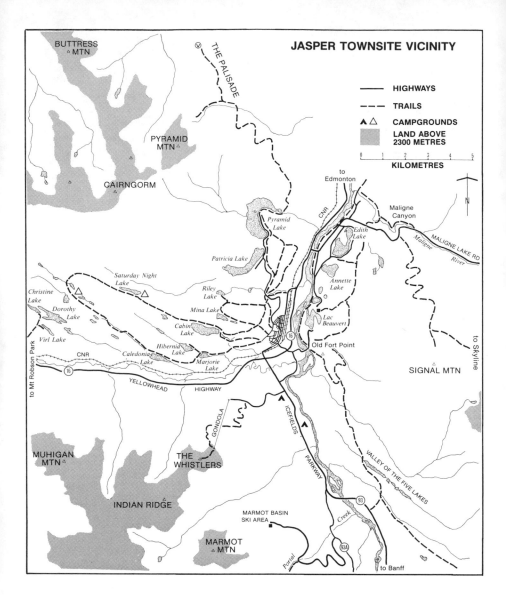

JASPER TOWNSITE VICINITY

HIGHWAYS

--- TRAILS

▲△ CAMPGROUNDS

LAND ABOVE
2300 METRES

0   1   2   3   4   5
KILOMETRES

BUTTRESS
△ MTN

THE PALISADE

PYRAMID
MTN △

CAIRNGORM
△

to
Edmonton

Pyramid
Lake

CNR

Maligne
Canyon

Edith
Lake

MALIGNE LAKE RD

Maligne
River

Patricia Lake

Saturday Night
Lake

Annette
Lake

Christine
Lake

Riley
Lake

Dorothy
Lake

Mina Lake

Lac
Beauvert

Virl Lake

Cabin
Lake

16

to Mt Robson Park

CNR

Caledonia
Lake

Hibernia
Lake

Marjorie
Lake

Old Fort Point

SIGNAL MTN
△

to Skyline

YELLOWHEAD   HIGHWAY

GONDOLA

ICEFIELDS

MUHIGAN
MTN △

THE
WHISTLERS

PARKWAY

VALLEY OF THE FIVE LAKES

INDIAN RIDGE
△

MARMOT BASIN
SKI AREA

93

Creek

MARMOT
△ MTN

Portal

93A

to Banff

N

220

The Palisade

Pyramid Lake to Palisade Lookout Site—10.8 kilometres (6.7 miles)

Day trip

Allow 3½ - 5 hours one way

Elevation gain: 840 metres (2,750 feet)

Maximum elevation: 2020 metres (6,650 feet)

Topo maps: Jasper 83 D/16

Point of Departure: Follow Jasper's main street, Connaught Drive, to the southwest edge of town. Turn right onto Pine Avenue, the last side street before leaving the village. Follow Pine for four blocks to where it bends right onto Pyramid Lake Drive. Follow Pyramid Lake Drive for 0.8 km to where it cuts uphill to the left and leaves the village proper. Follow this road for 6½ kilometres (4 miles) to Pyramid Lake. Continue on around the lake to the right to where the road ends at a locked access gate. Park at the nearby lakeshore picnic area.

0.0—Access gate (1180 m).

—Follow fire road east along lakeshore.

1.1—Pyramid Lake outlet and bridge.

—Fire road climbs away from lake at gradual to moderate grade.

7.6—Junction. Microwave relay station at left. Keep right.

10.8—Palisade Lookout site (2020 m).

The trip to the site where the Palisade Lookout cabin once stood is a long, grim trek over a wide, well-graded fire road that is more highly prized by Jasper's mountain bike enthusiasts than by hikers. Yet, the views from this escarpment are among the most rewarding in the Jasper vicinity, scanning a broad area stretching from Roche Miette and Jasper Lake to the towering summit of Mount Edith Cavell.

From the locked gate at the Pyramid Lake picnic area, the fire road rolls through a forest of spruce, aspen, lodgepole pine, and old Douglas fir, then begins the long, steady climb along the back side of The Palisade. At Kilometre 7.6 the road forks, the right spur leading to the lookout site while the left continues to the Pyramid Mountain telecommunications tram.

Arriving at the old lookout site, views suddenly open to the north and east. Across the Athabasca Valley are the grey limestone mountains of the Colin Range with strata tilted nearly vertical and eroded into a series of sawtooth peaks. The range was named by the explorer-geologist Dr. James Hector for Colin Fraser, an employee of the Hudson's Bay Company who tended the tiny Jasper's House post near the far end of Jasper Lake in the 1830s and 40s. Roche Miette—a butte-like mountain rising to the right of Jasper Lake—dominates the distant opening of the Athabasca Valley to the northeast. A short climb to an open knoll behind the lookout site provides excellent views southward to Pyramid Mountain (2766 m), colourfully comprised of red and orange quartz sandstones and unceremoniously crowned by a telecommunications tower.

Keep a close watch around the site for mountain sheep that visit this open ridge. And remember to pack water on the hike, since there is no dependable supply along the way.

The Whistlers

Whistlers Road to Whistlers Summit—7.9 kilometres (4.9 miles)

Day trip

Allow 3 hours one way

Elevation gain: 1250 metres (4,100 feet)

Maximum elevation: 2470 metres (8,100 feet)

Topo map: Jasper 83 D/16

Point of Departure: Follow the Icefields Parkway (Hwy 93) 1.8 kilometres (1.1 miles) south from its junction with the Yellowhead Highway at the edge of Jasper townsite. Turn right onto the Whistlers Road and follow it for 2.7 kilometres (1.7 miles). Turn left onto a gravel access road 200 metres below the youth hostel and follow it 300 metres to the trail head parking area.

0.0—Trail sign (1220 m).

—Steady uphill through dense, bushy forest.

3.1—Trail passes beneath tram line.

—Trail contours southwest into large gully descending from summit.

5.6—Trail climbs above timberline.

—Climb up slope immediately west of tram terminal.

6.8—Upper tram terminal.

—Trail continues up ridge behind terminal.

7.9—Whistlers Summit (2470 m).

The trail up The Whistlers starts at the edge of the montane life zone in a brushy forest composed of deciduous species such as aspen, white birch and mountain alder, passes up into a cool subalpine forest where the coniferous Engelmann spruce and alpine fir trees dominate, and eventually emerges onto the treeless alpine tundra of the mountain's summit. Spanning a vertical rise of 1250 metres, or 4,100 feet, this trail is almost unique in the Canadian rockies in its ability to display such a wide variety of vegetation in the space of only eight kilometres. While the mountain is serviced by a gondola lift, this sky tram creates very little distraction (the trail only comes in contact with the lift twice along its route). The tram also offers the option of hiking the trail from top to bottom, thereby avoiding one of the most gruelling ascents in the mountain parks.

From the parking area near the base of the mountain, the trail begins its long ascent in heavy bush. After passing beneath the tram line at Kilometre 3.1, the forest becomes more open and subalpine in nature — an area of moist, cool meadows where myriads of wildflowers bloom in July and early August. Soon the trail turns south and begins a steep climb of a major gully which descends the north face of the mountain. Shortly after emerging above timberline, the trail reaches the gondola's upper terminal. The final kilometre to the summit ridge is hiked in the company of the many tourists who ride the lift each day throughout the summer.

There is a 360 degree panoramic view from the summit which takes in most of the mountains and valleys in this section of the park (take a small scale map along to help identify the many features). Only a few hardy plants survive on this windswept ridge, and the animal inhabitants, hoary marmots and pikas, find shelter in the rocks beneath the summit.

Dorothy Lake

Yellowhead Highway to Dorothy Lake—3.9 kilometres (2.4 miles)

Yellowhead Highway to Christine Lake—4.2 kilometres (2.6 miles)

Half-day trip

Allow 1-2 hours one way

Elevation gain: 250 metres (820 feet)

Maximum elevation: 1340 metres (4,400 feet)

Topo map: Jasper 83 D/16†

† trail not shown

Point of Departure: Follow the Yellowhead Highway (Hwy #16) to the Meadow Creek bridge, located 11 kilometres (7 miles) west of the highway's junction with the Icefields Parkway. Turn right onto a gravel access road at the west end of the bridge and park to the left of an access gate. Walk down the road beyond the gate and cross the CNR tracks at the marked crossing point. Continue downhill to a broad footbridge across the Miette River which marks the beginning of the trail.

0.0—Miette River bridge (1090 m).

—Steady uphill through forest.

1.6—Trail descends to Minaga Creek.

2.1—Minaga Creek bridge.

3.5—Junction. Virl Lake to right 0.4 km. Dorothy Lake straight ahead.

3.9—Dorothy Lake (1340 m).

4.2—Christine Lake.

These three peaceful lakes, enclosed by a forest of lodgepole pine, white spruce, Douglas fir and aspen poplar, make a pleasant half-day outing in the rolling country west of Jasper townsite. Though views from their shores are limited, the lakes possess a sense of solitude that is often lacking on the popular alpine trails. In addition, the lakes' low elevation makes them ideal for early and late season hiking.

Climbing over a ridge from its head on the Miette River, the trail drops down to Minaga Creek at Kilometre 2.1. A gradual ascent through the forest for the next 1.4 kilometres brings the hiker to the Virl Lake junction, where a short right-hand spur leads to the shore of this tiny, elongated lake. Slightly more open than Dorothy and Christine Lakes, Virl reflects Indian Ridge and Muhigan Mountain to the south.

Just 0.4 kilometre above the Virl Lake Junction, the main trail reaches Dorothy Lake, the largest of the three sisters. Tightly encircled by forest, Dorothy is quite similar in appearance to Virl. Yet another 0.4 kilometre beyond is Christine Lake with its unique rock peninsulas.

With a map and a good sense of direction, an interesting day of exploration can be spent in the forest beyond the three lakes. Daydreaming back 150 years to the time when the first fur traders bushwhacked their way up the Miette Valley to the Yellowhead Pass, the hiker can strike out to Iris Lake (just a short distance east of Dorothy), or contour around the end of the ridge to the north of Dorothy and intersect the Saturday Night Loop trail near Minnow Lake.

Unlike most of the lakes in the mountain parks where fish stocking was discontinued many years ago, Virl, Dorothy and Christine, along with other lakes in the immediate vicinity of Jasper townsite, are regularly stocked with rainbow trout.

Golden Lake

Yellowhead Highway to Cut Lake—4.0 kilometres (2.5 miles)
Yellowhead Highway to Golden Lake—4.4 kilometres (2.7 miles)

Half-day trip
Allow 1-2 hours one way
Elevation gain: 390 metres (1,280 feet)

Maximum elevation: 1490 metres (4,900 feet)

Topo map: Jasper 83 D/16†

† trail not shown

Point of Departure: Follow the Yellowhead Highway (Hwy #16) to the Clairvaux Creek bridge, located 15½ kilometres (9½ miles) west of the highway's junction with the Icefields Parkway and 5½ kilometres (3½ miles) east of Jasper Park West Gate. Turn north onto the gravel access road at the west end of the bridge. A parking area lies just below the highway on the right. Walk beyond the rock barriers at the east end of the parking area and cross the CNR tracks at the crossing sign. Continue downhill to the Miette River bridge. There is a broad clearing on the opposite side of the bridge, and the trail starts from the north edge of the clearing (look for the trail sign on the forest margin).

0.0—Miette River bridge.

—Gradual to moderate uphill, contouring east along ridge.

1.6—Stream crossing.

—Trail runs northwest through forest.

4.0—Cut Lake (1490 m).

4.4—Golden Lake (1450 m).

Of all the tiny fishing lakes in the rolling forest country west of Jasper townsite, Cut and Golden are the least known and visited. Since the lakes are regularly stocked with rainbow trout, anglers can make this short hike with reasonable hopes of success. Nature lovers will find the trail a pleasant walk through a forest carpeted with wildflowers.

From the edge of the clearing on the north side of the Miette River bridge, the trail climbs through a mixed forest of lodgepole pine, white spruce, aspen and white birch. The trail runs in an easterly direction along this forested ridge for the first kilometre or so, then, after crossing a small stream, it bends back to the northwest and runs up along the drainage toward Cut and Golden Lakes. A wide variety of shade tolerant wildflowers grow beneath the forest canopy, including calypso orchids (in early summer), single's delight, pink pyrola, bog orchids, bunchberry and twinflowers; also, keep an eye out for clumps of red columbine — a rare flower on the eastern slope of the Rockies.

At Kilometre 3.5 the trail crests a ridge and passes through a "dog-hair" stand of lodgepole pine, i.e. trees that seeded so thickly following a forest fire that their growth has stagnated for lack of sunlight. There are limited views south from the summit of this ridge to the peaks of Roche Noire and Muhigan Mountain.

The eastern shore of Cut Lake is reached at the 4.0 kilometre mark, and Golden Lake lies just 400 metres farther along. Both lakes are ringed by dense forest and open views are limited to a few distant peaks to the west.

Neither Cut or Golden Lake is named on the map, but the pair do show up on the 1:50,000 scale sheet on the north side of a low ridge, approximately 2.5 kilometres north of the confluence of Clairvaux Creek and the Miette River.

Miette River

Decoigne Warden Station to Miette Warden Cabin—19.5 kilometres (12.0 miles)*

Backpack

Allow 1-2 days to warden cabin

Elevation gain: 555 metres (1,820 feet)

Maximum elevation: 1675 metres (5,500 feet)

Topo maps: Jasper 83 D/16
Rainbow 83 D/15
Resplendent Creek 83 E/2

Point of Departure: Follow the Yellowhead Highway (Hwy #16) to the junction with the Decoigne Warden Station access road, located 21 kilometres (13 miles) west of Jasper townsite and 0.2 kilometre east of the Jasper West Gate. Follow the paved access road north across the CNR tracks and the Miette River bridge 0.4 kilometre to an intersection with a gravel road. Follow this road left 0.4 kilometre to the Decoigne Warden Station entrance. Keep right at the entrance to a locked gate across the gravel access road.

0.0—Access gate (1120 m).

—Trail follows gravel road (old railway roadbed) due west.

4.4—Junction. Miette trail branches right from gravel road.

—Trail ascends east side of Miette Valley.

19.5—Miette River bridge (1675 m). Trail crosses to west bank and Miette Warden Cabin.*

—Sketchy trail continues north. For experienced route-finders only.

28.0—Centre Pass (1980 m).*

* Distance approximate.

The trail which runs from the Decoigne Warden Station to the headwaters of the Miette River is a low elevation route used primarily by warden patrols. While the trail fizzles well below any scenic rewards, experienced route-finders can forge upwards to some fine alpine meadows on Miette Pass and even bushwhack over Grant and Colonel Passes to the Moose River trail in Mount Robson Provincial Park. For seasoned wilderness travellers who are looking for challenge and solitude, the upper Miette Valley is worthy of consideration.

The first 4.4 kilometres of the trail are far from challenging as they follow along the roadbed of one of the early rail lines constructed through Yellowhead Pass. A flat gravel road passes along the Miette river flats — a marshy area with good views ahead toward Yellowhead Pass. The horse trail up the Miette Valley branches right from this road at Kilometre 4.4, just 100 metres before the road is cut by the Miette River at the site of an old railway bridge.

The trail up the Miette climbs onto the eastern slope of the valley through a forest of lodgepole pine and spruce. Views are limited and travel is somewhat tedious, but the trail is well maintained. Around the 19.5 kilometre mark, just below the slopes of Mount Bridgland, the trail drops down to cross the Miette River to its west bank.

The trail above the Miette Cabin is reported sketchy to nonexistent. Armed with a topo map and a certain amount of perseverance, experienced backcountry travellers can beat a path to the summit of Miette Pass, some nine kilometres farther north. The pass is an extensive alpine region composed of three separate summits and definitely worthy of exploration. The topo map indicates the route to this pass as well as the extension over Grant and Colonel Passes to the Moose River, but don't expect to find anything resembling normal trail.

Short Hikes and Nature Trails

MINA AND RILEY LAKES — 4.3 kilometres

Mina and Riley Lakes can be reached in less than an hour from the western edge of Jasper townsite. Though the lakes are a fairly popular destination, their setting in a mixed forest of lodgepole pine, white spruce, Douglas fir and poplar gives them a feeling of isolation and a certain serene charm. Regular stocking with rainbow trout is an added attraction for fishermen.

To reach the trail head, follow Connaught Drive (Jasper's main street) to Cedar Avenue. Turn west on Cedar and follow it two blocks to where it becomes Pyramid Avenue. Continue on Pyramid two more blocks to the intersection with Pyramid Lake Drive on the west edge of town. Turn left on Pyramid Lake Drive and then right to enter the large parking area opposite the Jasper Activity Centre.

Pickup the trail which runs along the hillside on the west edge of the parking area and follow it to the left (south) up and into the forest. After a steady uphill over the first 0.8 kilometre, the trail crosses the Cabin Lake Road (a limited access gravel road running to the town's water supply reservoir). From this crossing it is a relatively flat walk through the forest to Mina Lake at Kilometre 2.0. The trail continues down along the north side of the lake, then bends north to reach the Riley Lake junction at Kilometre 3.5. Take this branch trail to the left to reach this tiny lake in another 800 metres. While it is possible to make a loop trip by returning to Jasper on the trail which runs due east from the 3.5 kilometre junction, the least confusing route through this maze of branching and interconnecting trails is to return the way you came. *Topo map: Jasper 83 D/16.*

OLD FORT POINT CIRCUIT — 6.5 kilometres

Old Fort Point is a prominent hill which rises to the east across the Athabasca River from Jasper townsite. It is reputed to be the site of the first fur trade post in the Rocky Mountains, Henry's House, which was constructed by the Northwest Company's William Henry during the winter of 1811. While it is likely this cabin was a bit farther downstream, the knoll provides a very fine viewpoint overlooking the confluence of the Athabasca and Miette Rivers — an area which still evokes a lot of history.

To reach Old Fort Point, follow Connaught Drive (Jasper's main street) to its intersection with Hazel Avenue. Turn at this junction and cross the CNR tracks, following this road 0.6 kilometre to its intersection with the Yellowhead Highway (Hwy #16). Cross the Yellowhead and continue 100 metres to a junction with the road to Lac Beauvert. Turn left and follow this road one kilometre, crossing the Athabasca River bridge to the large picnic area parking lot just around the rocky prow of Old Fort Point on the right. The trail strikes off into the forest from the rear of this parking area and runs due east beneath Old Fort Point's north slope. The grade is essentially flat for the first kilometre or so, but then the trail climbs the rear of the knoll to its summit ridge and turns west to make its final run to the true summit. Once you have enjoyed the fine panorama from the top of Old Fort Point, pickup the trail which descends the steep west slope and return to the picnic area parking lot. Total distance for the loop is 6.5 kilometres. *Topo map: Jasper 83 D/16.*

MALIGNE CANYON — 3.7 kilometres

Maligne Canyon is one of the most popular tourist stops in Jasper Park. The upper half of the canyon trail may well be the busiest nature hike in the Canadian Rockies, but few visitors ever hike the entire 3.7 kilometre length of the trail. When this trip is approached from the lower end of the canyon, it is a very special nature hike through the most spectacular limestone slit canyon in the mountain parks.

The trail begins at a peaceful picnic area near the confluence of the Maligne and Athabasca Rivers. To reach this parking area, follow the Yellowhead Highway (Hwy #16) east 1.7 kilometres (1.1 miles) from the Jasper townsite east junction. Turn right onto the Maligne Lake Road and continue for 2.3 kilometres (1.4 miles) to the Warden Office - Sixth Bridge junction. Turn left and follow this access road 0.8 kilometre. Turn left at the Sixth Bridge sign and follow this branch road another 0.8 kilometre to the Sixth Bridge picnic area. Park at the picnic area and walk across the Maligne River bridge to the trail sign on the north side of the river.

The first half-hour or so of hiking is over flat to gradual uphill trail enclosed in a forest of white spruce and lodgepole pine mixed with poplars and birch. At Kilometre 1.6 the Fifth Bridge over the Maligne is passed (100 metres to the right of the main trail). Above Fifth Bridge the trail begins its ascent of the canyon proper and skirts an area where the river flows underground. Fourth Bridge is passed at Kilometre 2.9, and the trail crosses to the south side of the canyon via Third Bridge at Kilometre 3.1. You are now skirting above the deepest and most spectacular part of the canyon. Here you will begin to encounter sightseers who have descended from the parking area at the upper end of the trail. Try to ignore them and enjoy this unique geological feature which has been carved from the bedrock over many thousands of years. The teahouse at the top of the canyon makes a nice place to stop for refreshments before the return journey. *Topo maps: Jasper 83 D/16 and Medicine Lake 83 C/13.*

VALLEY OF THE FIVE LAKES — 2.3 kilometres

The Valley of the Five Lakes is a small, open-forested valley set in the rolling hill country just south of Jasper townsite. The five lakes, all of which are just over pond dimensions and of an exquisite jade green colour, can be visited in an easy two hour stroll. The trip to the lakes makes an excellent half-day family outing. (While the Valley of the Five Lakes shows up quite prominently on most topographical maps, the lakes have been misnamed the Wabasso Lakes on some of these sheets.)

The trail head is located on the east side of the Icefields Parkway 9 kilometres (5½ miles) south of its intersection with the Yellowhead Highway (Hwy #16) at Jasper townsite. The first kilometre of the journey is through open, flat terrain, the predominant forest cover consisting of lodgepole pine. At the 0.8 kilometre mark the trail crosses a small stream and climbs a low ridge where the hiker has a fine view back across the Athabasca Valley to Mount Edith Cavell (3363 m). From the top of the ridge the trail dips into the Valley of the Five Lakes. A recommended route is to proceed north to the largest lake and pickup the trail running back to the south along its eastern shoreline; this trail works down the valley and touches each lake, thus providing a loop circuit of the five. (It is also possible to reach the Valley of the Five Lakes from Old Fort Point near Jasper Park Lodge via a ten kilometre trail, but the route is long, rolling and somewhat tedious.) *Topo map: Jasper 83 D/16.*

WABASSO LAKE — 2.7 kilometres

The 2.7 kilometre trail from the Icefields Parkway to Wabasso Lake makes a very easy trip for hikers in the Jasper vicinity who are looking for a pleasant walk of an hour or so. Though the lake takes its name from the Cree word for rabbit, you are more likely to see muskrat along the marshy shores of this tiny lake. (Wabasso Lake is not named on most topographical maps, and the nearby Valley of the Five Lakes is frequently misnamed Wabasso Lakes.)

The parking area for Wabasso Lake is located on the east side of the Icefields Parkway 14½ kilometres (9 miles) south of its intersection with the Yellowhead Highway (Hwy #16) at Jasper townsite. The trail traverses quite level terrain through stands of lodgepole pine and aspen, crossing a small stream at 1.4 kilometres and running past a pond at 2.4 kilometres. Once it reaches Wabasso, the trail skirts the west shore to the north end of the lake where the approach trail to the Skyline Trail strikes off to the east (see *Shovel Pass via Wabasso* trail description). *Topo map: Medicine Lake 83 C/13.*

GERALDINE LOOKOUT — 2.5 kilometres

Most hikers who take the trouble of driving the rough Geraldine Fire Road are usually bound for the Geraldine Lakes. However, those who are seeking a shorter outing may continue on foot up the fire road from the Geraldine Lakes parking area to the site of an old fire lookout which once surveyed the Athabasca and lower Whirlpool Valleys. While the trip is uphill all the way, the broad, well-graded road should allow you to reach the lookout site in less than an hour.

To reach the Geraldine Lakes parking area, follow the 93-Alternate Highway 1.1 kilometres (0.7 mile) north from its junction with the Icefields Parkway at Athabasca Falls. At the junction with the Geraldine Fire Road, turn left and follow this rocky, dirt roadway 5½ kilometres (3½ miles) through forest and up a series of switchbacks to its termination at the Geraldine Lakes trail head. The locked access gate across the fire road just above the parking area marks the beginning of the Geraldine Lookout hike. The trip to the lookout site is unremarkable as it follows the last 2.4 kilometres of the fire road through an enclosed forest of lodgepole pine, Engelmann spruce and alpine fir. At Kilometre 1.9 the road flattens out, and 600 metres farther along it reaches the open knoll where the fire lookout tower once stood (removed circa 1984). The site, which is situated at 1700 metres above sea level on the north ridge of Geraldine Peak, looks out over a broad stretch of the Athabasca Valley. *Topo map: Athabasca Falls 83 C/12.*

MOOSE LAKE — 1.4 kilometres

For Maligne Lake visitors who would like to escape the crush of motorhomes, tour buses, and snapshot-shooting tourists for an hour or so, the Moose Lake loop trail is a fine nature outing where one can find solitude and sanity. The trip utilizes a short stretch of the Maligne Pass trail before cutting off into the forest to reach this pleasant little tarn surrounded by pine and spruce; on the return trip it skirts along the shoreline of Maligne Lake.

After following the Maligne Lake Road to the north end of the lake, continue past the lodge-boat dock complex and cross the Maligne River bridge to the picnic area at road's end. Follow the Bald Hills trail from the upper edge of the picnic area parking lot and watch for the trail which cuts left from this fire road just 300 metres above the access gate. This is the trail which runs south to Maligne Pass, but you will branch left from this track at Kilometre 1.3. From this second junction it is a mere 100 metres to the shores of Moose Lake — a quiet body of water which reflects the top of Samson Peak across Maligne Lake. Returning to the picnic area, continue along the trail as it loops back to the north and descends to the Maligne Lake shoreline at Kilometre 2.4. This lakeshore trail passes the warden's residence and reaches the picnic area 100 metres beyond. *Topo map: Athabasca Falls 83 C/12.*

LOWER SUNWAPTA FALLS — 1.3 kilometres

While thousands of tourists stop along the Icefields Parkway to view Sunwapta Falls each summer, few ever make the trip to a series of cataracts 1.3 kilometres beyond the main falls. Lower Sunwapta Falls is composed of three major waterfalls spread over some 150 metres of the Sunwapta River. The combination of solitude and open views to the surrounding peaks make this hike a far more rewarding experience than a visit to the upper falls.

To reach Sunwapta Falls, follow the Icefields Parkway (Hwy #93) 54½ kilometres (34 miles) south from its junction with the Yellowhead Highway (Hwy #16) at Jasper townsite, or 49 kilometres (30 miles) north from the Icefields Information Centre. Turn onto the Sunwapta Falls access road and follow it 600 metres to the parking area. From the parking lot, follow the main viewing trail which skirts above the falls to the right. Continue past the falls viewpoint to where the paved trail turns to dirt and begin a gradual descent through lodgepole pine forest to the lower falls. At Kilometre 0.6 the trail emerges from the forest and there are fine views south across the Sunwapta River to the upper Athabasca Valley and the glaciated summit of Mount Quincy. Lower Sunwapta Falls have formed where the river is cutting through a narrow canyon similar to that which contains the upper falls, but the effect is more that of a staircase than a single cataract. *Topo map: Athabasca Falls 83 C/12.*

BEAUTY CREEK — 1.6 kilometres

Before the old Banff-Jasper Highway was rerouted across the Sunwapta River flats at the foot of Tangle Peak, one of the popular stops for highway travellers was the Beauty Creek canyon. Here, a trail climbed past a series of cataracts to eventually emerge at beautiful Stanley Falls. Today this unmarked trail is a bit removed from the new highway, and few tourists even know that there is something special up this rather unremarkable, forested drainage.

To reach the start of the Beauty Creek trail, follow the Icefields Parkway south 87 kilometres (54 miles) from its junction with the Yellowhead Highway (Hwy #16) at Jasper townsite, or north 15½ kilometres (9½ miles) from the Icefields Information Centre. Two kilometres south of the Beauty Creek Youth Hostel, while crossing the broad, braided gravel flats beside the Sunwapta River, watch for a small pull-off on the east side of the highway at the end of a gravel water diversion dike. The trail starts at this roadside parking area and runs along the crest of the dike to an arm of forest. On the opposite side of this narrow grove of trees, the hiker emerges onto the old Banff-Jasper Highway right-of-way. Turn right and follow this old roadbed 600 metres to where Beauty Creek cuts through it. The trail branches left from the road at this point and follows along the north side of a narrow limestone canyon. The path climbs steadily through dense forest, passing a number of small waterfalls. The last and highest of these cataracts, Stanley Falls, is reached at the 1.6 kilometre mark. Beyond this fine waterfall the trail fades and the canyon opens out into a forested valley. *Topo map: Sunwapta Peak 83 C/6.*

Yoho National Park

Yoho National Park lies on the western slope of the Great Divide in British Columbia, bordered by Banff Park on the east and Kootenay Park on the south. Covering 1,313 square kilometres of rugged mountain terrain, Yoho is the smallest of the four contiguous parks.

Yoho's 300 kilometre trail system extends into nearly every corner of the park. While the majority of these trails are well-constructed and maintained, most hiking occurs in the two backcountry recreation areas of Lake O'Hara and the Yoho Valley. The overwhelming popularity of these two areas is a result of spectacular alpine terrain coupled with excellent trail systems that allow backpackers to set up a central camp and range out in many directions on scenic day trips. Needless to say, neither area offers much in the way of solitude.

Emerald Lake is also a much used day hiking hub. Trails radiate from the lake to the lofty heights of Yoho and Burgess Passes as well as beautiful Hamilton Lake. The area's proximity to the Yoho and Little Yoho Valleys makes it a natural extension for hikes to and from that region.

Running directly through the heartland of the park, sharing the valley bottom with the Kicking Horse River and the Canadian Pacific Railroad, the Trans-Canada Highway serves as access to a number of short but scenic day trips, the most popular being Sherbrooke Lake, Paget Lookout and Wapta Falls. Longer, infrequently travelled trails ascend the Amiskwi and the Beaverfoot.

Backpackers must obtain a park use permit, specifying their destination, before setting out on any overnight trip. Since the major campgrounds have quotas, popular areas are often filled to capacity during the peak season and hikers would do well to keep several options in mind. Park use permits are available from the Yoho East Information Centre, 3.5 kilometres east of Field townsite on the Yoho Valley Road, during the summer months, or from the park administration offices in Field during the winter. Registration for hazardous activities is a voluntary option.

Situated 16½ kilometres (10 miles) west of the continental divide, the small railway town of Field is the only service centre in the park. A gas station and a grocery store-restaurant offer the barest of essential services. There is also a small general store adjacent to the Kicking Horse Campground, approximately four kilometres east of Field townsite on the Yoho Valley Road. The Yoho National Park administration offices are found in the townsite.

Access: The only highway access to Yoho Park is the Trans-Canada Highway. The village of Field, in the heart of the park, is situated 82 kilometres west of Banff, Alberta, and 54 kilometres east of Golden, B.C., on this route.

Yoho is also served by public transport. East and westbound VIA Rail trains stop in Field each day. Field is also a flag stop for east and westbound Greyhound buses travelling the Trans-Canada Highway. (This bus stop has the distinction of being only 400 metres from the Burgess Pass-Highline Trail trail head, thereby allowing backpackers to disembark from a transcontinental bus and strike off on one of the park's finest backcountry trail trips.)

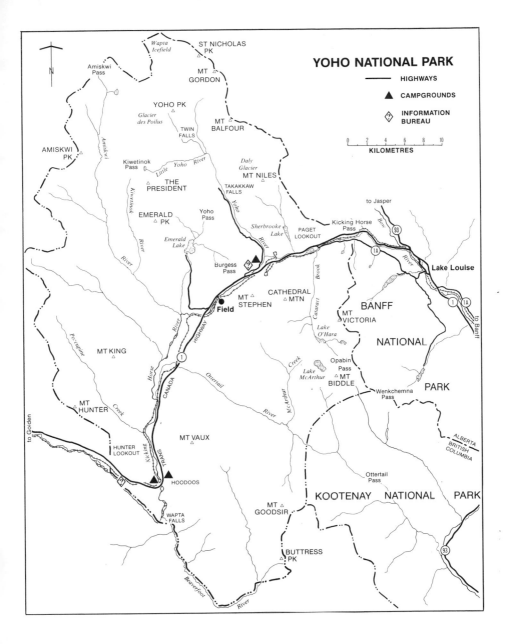

YOHO NATIONAL PARK

HIGHWAYS

▲ CAMPGROUNDS

◈ INFORMATION BUREAU

KILOMETRES

0 2 4 6 8 10

N

Wapta Icefield

ST NICHOLAS PK

Amiskwi Pass

MT GORDON

YOHO PK

Glacier des Poilus

TWIN FALLS

MT BALFOUR

AMISKWI PK

Kiwetinok Pass

Little Yoho River

Daly Glacier

MT NILES

THE PRESIDENT

TAKAKKAW FALLS

EMERALD PK

Yoho Pass

Sherbrooke Lake

PAGET LOOKOUT

Kicking Horse Pass

to Jasper

93

1A

Emerald Lake

River

Burgess Pass

Lake Louise

MT STEPHEN

Field

CATHEDRAL MTN

Cataract Brook

BANFF

MT VICTORIA

1A

to Banff

1

MT KING

Porcupine

Horse River

HIGHWAY

CANADA

1

Ottertail

Lake O'Hara

Creek

Lake McArthur

Opabin Pass

MT BIDDLE

Wenkchemna Pass

NATIONAL

PARK

MT HUNTER

Creek

Kicking

TRANS

MT VAUX

McArthur River

HUNTER LOOKOUT

ALBERTA BRITISH COLUMBIA

1

HOODOOS

Ottertail Pass

WAPTA FALLS

MT GOODSIR

KOOTENAY NATIONAL PARK

to Golden

to Golden

BUTTRESS PK

93

Beaverfoot River

Paget Lookout — Sherbrooke Lake

Trans-Canada Highway to Sherbrooke Lake—3.1 kilometres (1.9 miles)
Trans-Canada Highway to Paget Lookout—3.5 kilometres (2.2 miles)

Half-day trip

Allow 1 - 2 hours one way

Elevation gain: 520 metres (1,700 feet)

Maximum elevation: 2135 metres (7,000 feet)

Topo maps: Lake Louise 82 N/8

Point of Departure: Follow the Trans-Canada Highway to the Wapta Lake Picnic Area, 5½ kilometres (3½ miles) west of the Great Divide (Alta-B.C. boundary) and 11 kilometres (7 miles) east of Field. The picnic area is on the north side of the highway just 400 metres west of Wapta Lodge. The trail sign is just upslope from the picnic shelter.

0.0—Trail sign (1615 m).

0.2—Junction. Trail from lodge intersects from right. Keep left.

—Steady uphill through forest.

1.4—Junction. Sherbrooke Lake straight ahead 1.7 kms. Turn right for Paget Lookout.

—Trail begins steep ascent.

3.5—Paget Lookout (2135 m).

The lookout cabin high on the side of Paget Peak hasn't been manned for many years, but anyone who visits the site will readily understand why it was considered a crucial vantage point in the days when the parks department was developing its forest fire control policy. Not only does the lookout command an expansive view of the historic Kicking Horse Pass and Valley, but it provides an open view directly up the Cataract Valley to the dramatic peaks surrounding Lake O'Hara and even glimpses of the Bow Valley and the Slate Range in Banff Park. Like most trails to fire lookouts, however, the way is steep.

The first half-hour of travel takes the hiker up and across the southern flank of Paget Peak, the trail running through a forest which is predominantly Engelmann spruce and alpine fir with some fire succession stands of lodgepole pine. At the 1.4 kilometre mark the trail splits, the trail to Sherbrooke Lake continuing straight ahead and the one to Paget Lookout cutting right.

Not far beyond the junction the trail gains sufficient altitude to allow an occasional glimpse across the Kicking Horse Valley to Vanguard Peak (2465 m) and Cathedral Mountain (3189 m). At this point the trail is rising into the upper subalpine zone, an area dominated by stunted alpine fir, whitebark pine and, oddly enough at this elevation, even the occasional Douglas fir.

Following a right angle turn around the flank of Paget Peak, the hiker confronts the sheer 750 metre-high east face of Mount Ogden across the Sherbrooke Valley. Far below are the glacier-green waters of Sherbrooke Lake.

The trail ends near timberline at the Paget Lookout after a final 0.8 kilometre of arduous climbing. The lookout is not as high as the 2375 metres above sea level indicated on the topo map, but it is still

Paget Lookout and the Kicking Horse Valley

high enough to allow some pretty dramatic views: due east lie the Bow Valley and the Slate Range, dominated by its highest peak, Mount Richardson (3086 m); to the south, directly across the valley, are the valley of Cataract Brook and the glacier-mantled peaks of the Lake O'Hara region; and to the southwest the braided river flats of the Kicking Horse Valley are framed between Mounts Stephen and Burgess.

From the lookout, strong hikers with good boots can pick an easy route to the 2565 metre summit of Paget Peak, just over a kilometre due north.

Sherbrooke Lake. The trip to Sherbrooke Lake is popular with families and individuals who desire an easy half-day outing to a peaceful subalpine lake, and it is easily visited as a side-trip by stronger hikers bound for or returning from Paget Lookout.

From the junction at Kilometre 1.4 on the Paget Lookout trail, the trail to Sherbrooke Lake climbs steadily for another half kilometre, working through an open forest carpeted with buttercups, arnica,

bunchberry, clintonia and single's delight. Once the trail has levelled out, the south shore of Sherbrooke Lake is just over a kilometre away.

Sherbrooke is one of the largest backcountry lakes in Yoho Park. Its waters are a pale, milky blue, which is typical of glacier-fed lakes, but the lake acts as a settling pond for much of this glacial silt so that the water emerging in Sherbrooke Creek below the lake is remarkably clear compared to that in most streams in this part of the park.

From the lake's outlet, the trail continues along the east shore for another rough and muddy 1.4 kilometres to reach the northern end at the main tributary stream. Climbing beyond the lake's inlet, the trail eventually terminates on the upper plateaus near the valley head, some three kilometres distant. Though this section of trail is infrequently tended and usually covered in deadfall, open meadows and thundering cascades make the journey beyond Sherbrooke Lake well worthwhile.

233

Lake O'Hara

When people who have spent time in the Canadian Rockies get together to reminisce, the name Lake O'Hara comes up early and fondly. It is a special place for those who love the mountains, and it is easy to understand why: within a five kilometre radius of the central campground and lodge at Lake O'Hara are 25 named lakes, some of the highest and most rugged mountains in the entire range, and one of the most extensive and well-maintained trail systems in the mountain parks. The trails, built over a period of nearly 50 summers by Dr. George Link, Carson Simpson and Lawrence Grassi, radiate from Lake O'Hara as spokes from a hub, and vary from a simple stroll around the lake to a challenging expedition around the Alpine Circuit. Hikers can pursue a different trail every day and return to a central camp each evening, making the area an obvious destination for a hiking vacation.

The scenery of the region is dominated by the same two peaks that form the impressive backdrop for Lake Louise, the continental divide summits of Mounts Lefroy (3423 m) and Victoria (3464 m). The two mountains also provide the immediate setting for one of the five distinct hiking "pockets" of Lake O'Hara, the Lake Oesa cirque. A second such pocket is the Opabin Plateau, located between Yukness Mountain (2847 m) and Mount Schäffer (2693 m), while the McArthur Pass-Lake McArthur region to the west of Mount Schäffer makes a third. The Odaray Plateau, high on the eastern flank of Odaray Mountain, constitutes a fourth, and the Duchesnay Basin, cradling Linda Lake and the Morning Glory, Cathedral and Odaray Lakes, offers a fifth. Each of these compact regions merits a full day's exploration.

Lake O'Hara was first charted by J. J. McArthur, a surveyor working the Railway Belt lands south of Hector Siding in 1887. Lieutenant-Colonel Robert O'Hara, an Irishman who heard of the region from McArthur, visited the location shortly thereafter and was so impressed he returned repeatedly to explore its lakes, creeks and mountains. It is to O'Hara's wanderings the region owes its name. The Alpine Club of Canada held one of its early mountaineering camps at Lake O'Hara in 1909, and by 1911 the region was popular enough among alpinists to warrant construction of a mountain hut, the Wiwaxy Lodge — a small cabin still standing in the Alpine Meadows.

Today, a number of facilities support the many tourists, hikers and climbers who flock to the lake each summer. A warden's cabin is located at the west end of the lake and, 200 metres farther east, stands the stately Lake O'Hara Lodge with its scattering of small guest cabins. The Elizabeth Parker Hut, an Alpine Club of Canada cabin with accommodation for twenty-four, lies 0.7 kilometre to the west of the lake in the Alpine Meadows. Of more immediate interest to most hikers is the 30-site campground lying beside the main access road 0.6 kilometre north of the warden cabin. Owing to the area's great popularity, reservations can be made for twenty of these campsites a maximum of two months prior to a Lake O'Hara visit; ten of the sites are left open on a first-come, first-serve basis. Reservations can be made by contacting the park office at 604-343-6324 from mid-April to mid-May, or the Yoho East Information Centre at 604-343-6485 from mid-May to late September. A small daily fee is charged for a campsite.

As might be expected, the summer months see an abundance of hikers and climbers using the area. It is imperative that people visiting Lake O'Hara note the fragile nature of the environment and make a concerted effort to harmonize their activities with the land around them. Hikers can help by staying on the trails, even if it occasionally means wet or muddy boots.

234

While the complete Lake O'Hara topography is covered on the Lake Louise 82 N/8 sheet, only the major trails are marked thereon. The best map of the area is that produced by the Lake O'Hara Trails Club, copies of which may be purchased at the lodge. *The Magic of Lake O'Hara* by Don Beers gives a more detailed look at the area's trails than that afforded here, and Jon Whyte's *Tommy and Lawrence: The Ways and the Trails of Lake O'Hara* provides a fine history of how these marvelous trails developed.

Access: Most O'Hara trips begin from the parking area at the traffic control gate at the foot of the Lake O'Hara access road. The parking lot is reached by turning south off the Trans-Canada Highway onto the 1-A Highway 3.2 kilometres (2 miles) west of the continental divide or 1.6 kilometres (1 mile) east of the lodge at Wapta Lake. Cross the CPR tracks and turn right onto the gravel road leading 800 metres to the Lake O'Hara parking area. A traffic gate restricts entrance to the Lake O'Hara access road. From this point hikers have the option of either hiking the eleven kilometre-long road or taking the Cataract Brook trail that begins at the rear of the small parking area just below the traffic gate (see *Cataract Brook* trail description).

Persons with reservations for Lake O'Hara Lodge, the Abbot Pass climbing hut, the Elizabeth Parker Hut or the O'Hara Campground can ride to the lake on one of the area's buses (a one-way fee is charged). From late June to Labour Day buses leave the lower parking lot at 8:30 a.m., 11:30 a.m., and 4:30 p.m. The buses will also carry day hikers to the lake on the rare occasion when the area's quota of visitors has not been filled. (The Yoho East Information Centre is the clearing house for reservations and current information on the Lake O'Hara area. Always check in at this office or call 604-343-6485.)

Afternoon tea at Lake O'Hara Lodge is available to hikers who make reservations for same at the lodge's front desk; publications on the area are also available for purchase at the lodge. Information on accommodation at the lodge can be obtained during the off-season by writing Lake O'Hara Lodge Ltd., Box 1677, Banff, Alberta T0L 0C0, or by calling 403-762-2118 (be forewarned that the lodge is usually booked-up well in advance of each summer season). Information on accommodation at the Elizabeth Parker Hut or the nearby Abbot Pass Hut can be obtained from the Alpine Club of Canada, Box 1026, Banff, Alberta T0L 0C0, or by calling 403-762-4481.

Cataract Brook

O'Hara Parking Lot to Lake O'Hara Campground—12.9 kilometres (8.0 miles)

Backpack

Allow 4 hours one way

Elevation gain: 410 metres (1,350 feet)

Maximum elevation: 2010 metres (6,600 feet)

Topo map: Lake Louise 82 N/8

Point of Departure: Follow the Trans-Canada Highway to its junction with the 1-A Highway 3.2 kilometres (2 miles) west of the Great Divide (Alta-B.C. boundary), or 1.6 kilometres (1 mile) east of Wapta Lake. Turn onto the 1-A Highway and follow it across the CPR tracks. Turn right onto the gravel road on the opposite side of the railway tracks and follow it 0.8 kilometre to the Lake O'Hara parking lots. The trail strikes off from the rear of the small parking lot immediately below the O'Hara access road.

0.0—Parking area (1600 m).

1.5—Cataract Brook bridge.*

2.5—Junction. Old road from Wapta Lake intersects from right. Follow trail across road.*

3.5—Narao Lakes.*

—Trail climbs along lower slopes of Cathedral Mountain.

9.5—Duchesnay Creek bridge.*

10.2—Junction. Linda Lake to right. Morning Glory Lakes straight ahead. Turn left for O'Hara Campground.

10.5—Morning Glory Creek bridge.

11.0—Junction. Turn right for O'Hara Campground.

12.9—Lake O'Hara Campground (2010 m).

* Distances approximate.

Cataract Brook is the main outlet stream running north from Lake O'Hara, and the trail travelling up the west side of the valley is an alternate route of access to this popular, backcountry hiking area. Of course, if you are overnighting at Lake O'Hara, you can pay your money and ride the bus. If you decide you'd rather walk, you can hike the access road, which is nearly two kilometres shorter than the trail and provides a better surface for fast travel. But, if you'd like a more aesthetic approach to the area, one which climbs gradually through a cool subalpine forest interspersed with meadows, rockslides and avalanche slopes, the trail is definitely the only way to go.

From the parking area at the foot of the O'Hara access road, the trail runs southwest through the forest and then makes a short climb to Hector Gorge and a bridged crossing of Cataract Brook. Near Kilometre 2.5 an old access road from Wapta Lake is crossed (stay on the footpath). Less than a kilometre beyond, the trail passes along the swampy meadows which contain the Narao Lakes, where there are views to the east to the rugged peaks which comprise the Great Divide.

Beyond the Narao Lakes the trail climbs gradually through a major rockslide and then into a forest of lodgepole pine and Engelmann spruce on the lower slopes of Cathedral Mountain. The avalanche slopes along these steep slopes provide good views out over the Cataract Valley.

At the 10.2 kilometre mark, the hiker comes to a four-way junction which is just a kilometre east of Linda Lake and 800 metres north of the Morning Glory Lakes. The route to the campground turns left at this intersection. Keep right at another junction 800 metres farther along and climb through rocky, subalpine forest to the Lake O'Hara Campground.

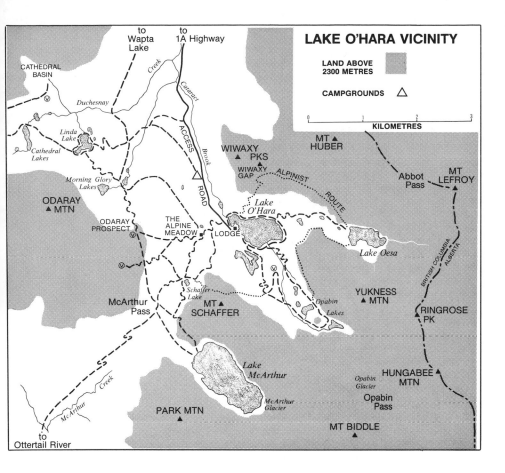

LAKE O'HARA VICINITY

to Wapta Lake
to 1A Highway

LAND ABOVE 2300 METRES

CAMPGROUNDS △

0   1   2   3
KILOMETRES

CATHEDRAL BASIN

Duchesnay

Creek

Cataract

ACCESS

Brook

ROAD

Linda Lake

Cathedral Lakes

Morning Glory Lakes

ODARAY ▲ MTN

ODARAY PROSPECT

THE ALPINE MEADOW

LODGE

WIWAXY ▲ PKS

WIWAXY GAP

ALPINIST

Lake O'Hara

MT ▲ HUBER

Abbot Pass

MT LEFROY

ROUTE

BRITISH COLUMBIA
ALBERTA

Lake Oesa

Schaffer Lake

McArthur Pass

MT ▲ SCHAFFER

Opabin Lakes

YUKNESS ▲ MTN

RINGROSE PK

Creek

McArthur

Lake McArthur

Opabin Glacier

McArthur Glacier

HUNGABEE ▲ MTN

Opabin Pass

to Ottertail River

PARK MTN ▲

MT BIDDLE ▲

237

Lake Oesa

Lake O'Hara to Lake Oesa—3.2 kilometres (2.0 miles)

Half-day trip

Allow 1 - 2 hours one way

Elevation gain: 240 metres (785 feet)

Maximum elevation: 2275 metres (7,460 feet)

Topo maps: Lake Louise 82 N/8

Point of Departure: Travel to Lake O'Hara as described in the *Lake O'Hara* area introduction (see page 234). Walk to the Lake O'Hara Warden Cabin, which is located on the O'Hara Fire Road 0.6 kilometre south of the campground and 0.2 kilometre north of the lodge. To reach the trail head, walk past the warden cabin, pick up the lakeshore trail, and follow it north 150 metres to the lake outlet bridge.

0.0—Lake O'Hara outlet (2035 m).

—Follow around north lakeshore.

0.2—Junction. Wiwaxy Gap trail branches left. Stay on lakeshore trail.

0.8—Junction. Lake Oesa trail branches uphill to left from lakeshore.

—Steep climb followed by steady uphill over rockfall and benchlands.

2.4—Lawrence Grassi memorial plaque.

2.5—Victoria Lake and junction. Shortcut to Yukness Ledge alpine route branches right. Keep straight ahead.

3.0—Junction. Yukness Ledge alpine route branches right, Abbot's Pass—Wiwaxy Gap routes to left.

3.2—Lake Oesa (2275 m).

Set in a high, barren cirque beneath the towering spine of the Great Divide, Oesa is one of the many exquisite turquoise lakes located near Lake O'Hara. It is also the busiest single trail in any of O'Hara's five major hiking areas.

From the warden cabin at the northwest corner of Lake O'Hara, hike east along the lake's north shoreline. At Kilometre 0.8, the trail to Lake Oesa branches left from the lakeshore trail and makes a steep climb to the top of the rock band which rises above the east shore of Lake O'Hara. From the summit of this cliff there is a fine view back over the lake. Beyond this viewpoint, the grade moderates as the trail rises in steps over a series of rock terraces leading to Lake Oesa. Three small lakes are passed along the way — Yukness Lake, Lake Victoria and Lefroy Lake.

At the 2.4 kilometre mark there is a plaque commemorating Lawrence Grassi, one of the grand old men of the mountains. Although Grassi spent most of his life as a coal miner in Canmore, Alberta, he is best remembered for his dedication to mountaineering and trail building in the Rockies. He worked as a warden at Lake O'Hara in the late 1950s, and many of the routes stitching the terrain together owe their existence to Grassi's passion for trail work.

At Kilometre 3.0, the trail reaches its maximum elevation on a slight rise overlooking Lake Oesa, a point which is just 200 metres shy of its western shore. The lake's name is reputed to be the Stoney Indian word meaning "ice," so-called because it is frozen nearly year-round. Guarding the lake are Yukness Mountain (2847 m) to the south and Mount Huber (3368 m) to the north, while hidden in the towering walls at the far end of the lake is Abbot's Pass (2922 m) — the major alpine route between Lake O'Hara and Lake Louise. The lakeshore itself is composed of rockslides, talus slopes and

Lake Oesa

moraines, ideal habitat for the pikas and marmots who make this area their home.

Alpine Circuit. The high level alpine route which contours around the rocky heights of the Lake O'Hara cirque crosses the Oesa trail at its highest point, 200 metres west of the lake. By hiking north on this route you can reach Wiwaxy Gap and then descend back to Lake O'Hara, reaching the lakeshore trail just 500 metres west of the Lake Oesa junction. Following the Alpine Circuit to the south, you can traverse the Yukness Ledge and intersect into the Opabin Plateau trail system. (See *Alpine Circuit* trail description.)

Abbot Pass. The junction of the Alpine Circuit with the Oesa trail also serves as the point of departure for rock scramblers heading to Abbot Pass. After following the track north toward Wiwaxy Gap for a short distance, the Abbot Pass route breaks away to contour across the talus slopes above Oesa's north shore. Near the east end of the lake, the route begins the ascent of the steep couloir leading to the pass. There is no trail as such to the pass, only footprints in the scree. The climb is steep and gruelling, and loose rock dislodged in the couloir is a constant hazard. The Abbot Pass Hut is now being tended by a custodian, and hikers and climbers with reservations can spend the night there for a nominal fee (contact the Alpine Club of Canada office in Banff for reservations).

239

Opabin Plateau

Lake O'Hara to Opabin Lake—3.2 kilometres (2.0 miles)

Half-day trip

Allow 1 - 2 hours one way

Elevation gain: 250 metres (820 feet)

Topo maps: Lake Louise 82 N/8

Point of Departure: Travel to Lake O'Hara as described in the Lake O'Hara area introduction (see page 234). From in front of the Lake O'Hara Lodge or the rear of the lodge's cabin complex, pick up the lakeshore trail running south.

0.0—Lake O'Hara Lodge (2035 m).

—Follow lakeshore trail along southwest shoreline.

0.3—Junction. Opabin Plateau West Circuit cuts uphill to right away from lakeshore.

0.4—Junction. Trail from Alpine Meadow intersects from right.

0.5—Mary Lake.

—Steep uphill beneath Opabin Plateau cliffs.

1.6— Junction. All Souls' alpine route branches right. Opabin Prospect trail branches left 50 metres further along. Stay straight ahead for Opabin Plateau.

—Grade levels out on plateau.

1.9—Junction. Loop trail from Opabin Prospect intersects back into main trail from left. Across stream, 50 metres beyond, Opabin Plateau Highline branches left. Main trail stays right.

2.6—Junction. Opabin Plateau Highline rejoins main trail from left.

—Trail skirts west side of Hungabee Lake, then ascends bench to head of valley.

3.2—Opabin Lake and junction (2285 m). Opabin Pass alpine route cuts up toward pass. Opabin Plateau East Circuit cuts back downvalley to left.

3.6—Junction. Yukness Ledge alpine route cuts uphill to right from east side of Hungabee Lake. East Circuit trail continues downvalley.

4.2—Trail begins descent into forest.

5.3—Junction (2035 m). Opabin Plateau East Circuit intersects with lakeshore trail.

The Opabin Plateau circuit is one of the classic hikes of the Lake O'Hara region, and is a high priority on any list of Lake O'Hara musts. The plateau is only a short distance from Lake O'Hara Lodge, but many hikers spend an entire day rambling among the small meadows, stands of alpine larch and numerous tarns that punctuate this beautiful hanging valley. Such explorations are facilitated by a network of secondary trails that crisscross the plateau.

The circuit is actually an elongated loop trail which runs up the west side of the plateau, then makes a 180 degree turn at the head of the valley to return via its eastern side. The west and east side trails are known respectively as the Opabin Plateau West Circuit and the Opabin Plateau East Circuit. Because it seems the most direct route to most hikers, the West Circuit is usually used on the approach to the plateau, while the East Circuit is utilized to return to the O'Hara lakeshore trail.

The hike starts from the Lake O'Hara Lodge complex and follows the lakeshore trail south. Just 300 metres beyond the lodge, the West Circuit trail branches to the right. After passing Mary Lake at the 0.5 kilometre mark, the trail makes a steep climb through the cliffs which serve as the northern lip of the Opabin Plateau. The trail reaches the top of the cliff at Kilometre 1.6, where a short side trail branches left to Opabin Prospect — an outstanding cliff-top viewpoint which overlooks Lake O'Hara and the Cataract Brook drainage, and a good place to go for a breather after the rather stiff ascent from Mary Lake.

Beyond the Opabin Prospect junction, the trail enters the meadowlands of the plateau, passing along the west shore of Hungabee Lake and ascending a rocky benchland to reach the head of the valley and Opabin Lake at Kilometre 3.2 (A highline route branches left from the

Opabin Lake

West Circuit trail at Kilometre 1.9, traverses the crest of a rocky ridge leading upvalley, and rejoins the trail at Kilometre 2.6.) From the shore of Opabin Lake, there are excellent views of Hungabee Mountain (3492 m), as well as the Opabin Glacier and Opabin Peak. Hungabee means "the chieftain" in the Stoney Indian language, while Opabin means "rocky."

From Opabin Lake, most hikers return to Lake O'Hara via the East Circuit trail. This route descends through flower-filled tundra meadows and skirts along Yukness Mountain rockslides (home to hoary marmots and pikas). The east shore of Hungabee Lake is passed at Kilometre 3.6, and, not far beyond, the trail drops back into forest to start its steep descent back to Lake O'Hara. The East Circuit reaches the lakeshore trail just 300 metres east of the junction with the West Circuit. From this point it is a short walk back to

Lake O'Hara Lodge, or you can choose to continue on around the east side of the lake to eventually emerge on the O'Hara Road near the warden cabin.

Yukness Ledge. This section of the Alpine Circuit branches from the Opabin Plateau East Circuit at Kilometre 3.6. By following this spectacular route along the rockslides and ledges of Yukness Mountain, you can make a highline traverse to Lake Oesa. An Opabin Plateau-Lake Oesa loop trip makes a fine full day's outing.

All Soul's Prospect. The trail which branches from the Opabin Plateau West Circuit at Kilometre 1.6 is the westernmost extension of the Alpine Circuit. This rugged, 1.8 kilometre alpine route traverses the All Souls' Prospect to an intersection with the Lake McArthur trail at Schäffer Lake. (See *Alpine Circuit* trail description.)

241

Lake McArthur

Lake O'Hara to Lake McArthur—3.5 kilometres (2.2 miles)

Half-day trip

Allow 1 - 2 hours one way

Elevation gain: 310 metres (1,025 feet)

Maximum elevation: 2345 metres (7,700 feet)

Topo maps: Lake Louise 82 N/8

Point of Departure: Travel to Lake O'Hara as described in the *Lake O'Hara* area introduction (see page 234). Walk to the Lake O'Hara Warden Cabin, which is located on the O'Hara Fire Road 0.6 kilometres south of the campground and 0.2 kilometres north of the lodge. The trail begins at the trail sign on the west side of the road across from the warden cabin.

0.0—Trail sign (2035 m).

—Trail climbs to Alpine Meadow.

0.3—Junction. Big Larch Route to Schaffer Lake branches left. Keep right.

—Trail enters Alpine Meadow.

0.6—Elizabeth Parker Hut and junction. Odaray Plateau—Linda Lake to right. Keep left for Lake McArthur.

—Moderate to steep uphill.

1.5—Junction. Big Larch Route rejoins main trail from left. Across outlet stream, trail to Odaray Plateau branches right. Main trail stays left.

1.6—Schaffer Lake and junction. McArthur Pass to right. Keep left for high route to Lake McArthur.

—Trail climbs shoulder of Mt. Schaffer, skirts rockslide.

2.4—Junction (2210 m). McArthur Pass to right 0.3 km. Turn left for Lake McArthur via high route.

—Moderate to steep uphill along cliffs and boulder fields.

3.0—Trail summit (2345 m).

—Gradual descent to lake.

3.5—Lake McArthur (2250 m).

Lake McArthur, the largest and deepest of the lakes in the O'Hara environs, lies at an elevation of 2250 metres in a tight cirque carved from the cliffs of Mount Schäffer, Mount Biddle, and Park Mountain. Owing to its 85-metre depth, the lake is a startling deep blue, and its colour, in combination with the rock of the surrounding mountains, the ice of the nearby Biddle Glacier, and the sparse alpine vegetation of the cradling cirque, have made Lake McArthur a prime destination for artists and photographers for many decades. The trip is best reserved for late summer, however, since the lake is often frozen over until mid-July.

Starting from the trail sign opposite the O'Hara Warden Cabin, hike to the Alpine Meadows. At a junction beside the Elizabeth Parker Hut, keep left and begin the ascent of the forested slope behind the meadows. The trail climbs steadily through a heavy, subalpine forest which gradually transmutes from Engelmann spruce and alpine fir to alpine larch by the time Schäffer Lake is reached at Kilometre 1.6.

Fifty metres beyond the Schäffer Lake outlet bridge, the cutoff trail to Lake McArthur branches left from the McArthur Pass trail, skirts around the south shore of the lake, and climbs steeply through stands of larch to a shoulder of Mount Schäffer. Lawrence Grassi, one of the well-known trail builders of O'Hara, is responsible for the stone stairway leading up the cliff. The trail follows the edge of the rock band for a short distance, a vantage point for Cathedral Mountain and points north.

By turning left at the McArthur Pass junction (Kilometre 2.4), you can follow a high, scenic route to the lake. This trail bends around the west ridge of Mount Schäffer and climbs along cliffs and boulder fields to the trail summit and the first view of Lake McArthur at Kilometre 3.0. The last 500 metres of trail descend to

Lake McArthur

the north end of the lake via a series of beautiful alpine meadows interspersed with rock bluffs. (If snow is still lingering on this high trail or weather conditions are poor, you should avoid this steep, exposed route and follow the lower route which branches from the McArthur Creek trail 300 metres west of McArthur Pass.)

Odaray Plateau. The Lake McArthur trail can be hiked in combination with the Odaray Plateau circuit to make a very scenic loop trip. Our favourite itinerary starts with the ascent to Odaray Prospect, then follows the Odaray Plateau trail due south to McArthur Pass and Lake McArthur; finish off the trip by traversing the Lake McArthur cutoff to Schäffer Lake and following the Big Larches trail to the Alpine Meadows and Lake O'Hara.

Total distance for the Odaray Plateau–Lake McArthur loop, starting and ending at Lake O'Hara, is 9.5 kilometres. (See *Odaray Plateau* trail description.)

Big Larches Route. This alternate trail branches south from the Lake McArthur trail at the lower edge of the Alpine Meadows (Km 0.3), climbs along a steep rockslide beneath the Mount Schäffer cliffs and through stands of giant alpine larch, and rejoins the main trail at Schäffer Lake (Km 1.5). The total distance for this option is virtually the same as staying on the main trail, but since the Big Larches trail is steep and rocky in places, it is best hiked as a route of descent. For an excellent after-dinner stroll, hike the Lake McArthur trail to Schäffer Lake and return via the Big Larches route — a loop hike of only three kilometres.

243

Odaray Plateau

Lake O'Hara to Odaray Prospect—2.6 kilometres (1.6 miles)

Half-day trip

Allow 1 hour to Odaray Prospect

Elevation gain: 280 metres (920 feet)

Maximum elevation: 2315 metres (7,600 feet)

Topo maps: Lake Louise 82 N/8

Point of Departure: Travel to Lake O'Hara as described in the *Lake O'Hara* area introduction (see page 234). Walk to the Lake O'Hara Warden Cabin, which is located on the O'Hara Fire Road 0.6 kilometre south of the campground and 0.2 kilometre north of the lodge. The trail begins at the trail sign on the west side of the road across from the warden cabin.

0.0—Trail sign (2035 m).

—Trail climbs to Alpine Meadow.

0.3—Junction. Big Larch Route to Schaffer Lake branches left. Keep right.

—Trail enters Alpine Meadow.

0.6—Elizabeth Parker Hut and junction. Lake McArthur—McArthur Pass trail to left. Turn right and cross meadow stream for Odaray Prospect.

0.7—Junction. Trail to Morning Glory Lakes and Linda Lake to right. Odaray Prospect trail cuts uphill into forest to left.

—Trail switchbacks uphill at moderately steep to steep grades.

1.4—Junction. Direct trail to Odaray Grand-view alpine route cuts uphill to left. Keep right for Odaray Prospect.

—Trail contours through forest to north-west.

2.2—Junction. Trail to Morning Glory Lakes and Linda Lake continues straight ahead. Odaray Prospect uphill to left.

2.6—Odaray Prospect (2285 m).

—Trail cuts back to southeast to traverse across Odaray Plateau.

3.4—Junction. Odaray Grandview alpine route cuts uphill to right.

4.5—McArthur Pass (2210 m). Intersects with *McArthur Creek* trail at Km 2.1.

The Odaray Plateau is one of the more popular Lake O'Hara destinations. The trail, though uniformly steep, is short and rewards the hiker's efforts manifold. From Odaray Prospect, the hiker looks down a 300 metre cliff to the emerald looking-glass of upper Morning Glory Lake and up to the sheer east wall of Odaray Mountain, laced with the silver threads of Odaray and Morning Glory Falls. From the summit of the plateau traverse, there is a 180 degree panorama which centres on Lake O'Hara and spreads across the lake's spectacular back-drop — the wall of peaks which comprises the Great Divide.

Starting from the trail sign opposite the O'Hara Warden Cabin, hike to the Alpine Meadows and keep right at the Alpine Club cabins. After crossing the small stream that runs through the meadows, watch for the Odaray Prospect trail branching left. From the meadows the trail switchbacks up through a cool, sub-alpine forest. At Kilometre 1.4, the trail to Odaray Prospect branches right from the direct route to the plateau and contours to the northwest. Turn left at the 2.2 kilometre junction and reach the Prospect after another 10 minutes or so of climbing.

The Odaray Prospect is one of the finest viewpoints on any of O'Hara's five primary trails. In addition to its views of nearby upper Morning Glory Lake and Odaray Mountain, there is a fine vista to Cathedral Mountain, rising like a medieval castle five kilometres away to the north. It is appropriate that a site just below the Prospect was chosen for a memorial plaque to Dr. George K. K. Link, an American botanist who spent fifty summers exploring, mapping and trail building in the O'Hara area, for Dr. Link and his wife Adeline spent many a summer's afternoon sunbathing and re-laxing on a rock outcrop not far from this overlook.

Cathedral Mountain and Upper Morning Glory Lake from Odaray Prospect

After taking a long break on Odaray Prospect, follow the trail which doubles back to the south and traverses across the meadows of the Odaray Plateau. In a few minutes you will be up high enough to look down through the scattered larches to the turquoise waters of Lake O'Hara. These high meadows are filled with wildflowers from mid-July to mid-August, and in late September the larch trees turn the mountainside to gold.

The branch trail to the Grandview Prospect is passed 800 metres beyond Odaray Prospect, and at Kilometre 4.0 you can look through the gap of McArthur Pass to the double spires of Mount Goodsir, the highest mountain in Yoho Park. The trail finally descends to the forested summit of McArthur Pass where you have the option of visiting Lake McArthur or returning to Lake O'Hara

via Schäffer Lake (see *Lake McArthur* trail description).

Odaray Grandview Prospect. For particularly energetic hikers, there is an option which manages an even more spectacular overview of the region than the Odaray Plateau and Prospect. Just 800 metres south of the Prospect, in the middle of the Plateau traverse, a spur trail branches west and climbs steeply for 1.1 kilometres to a large cairn marking the Odaray Grandview Ridge. At 2530 metres above sea level, the ridge is the only spot on the Lake O'Hara trail network from which all the major lakes of the area can be seen. Those considering the option should be forewarned that this is a tough, dry scramble (not really a trail, but a route frequently marked only by paint marks and cairns), so judge your capabilities accordingly.

245

Linda Lake—Cathedral Basin

Lake O'Hara Campground to Linda Lake—3.7 kilometres (2.3 miles)
Lake O'Hara Campground to Cathedral Basin—7.4 kilometres (4.6 miles)

Day trip

Allow 2 - 3 hours to Cathedral Basin

Elevation gain: 305 metres (1,000 feet)

Maximum elevation: 2315 metres (7,600 feet)

Topo maps: Lake Louise 82 N/8

Point of Departure: Travel to Lake O'Hara as described in the *Lake O'Hara* area introduction (see page 234). The trail strikes off into the forest from the north edge of the O'Hara Campground, just beyond the last site on the campground's lowest level.

0.0—Lake O'Hara Campground (2010 m).

—Gradual descent through forest.

1.9—Junction. Lake O'Hara Fire Road to right. Keep left for Linda Lake.

2.4—Morning Glory Creek bridge.

2.7—Junction. Cataract Brook trail branches right. Trail to Morning Glory Lakes branches left. Keep straight ahead for Linda Lake.

3.7—Linda Lake and junction (2090 m). South shore and Morning Glory Lakes to left. Keep right for north shore trail and Cathedral Basin.

4.5—Junction. Trail to Linda Lake south shore and Morning Glory Lakes branches left. Cathedral Basin to right.

—Gradual uphill.

5.6—Cathedral Lakes.

—Gradual to moderate uphill.

6.1—Junction. Duchesnay Pass alpine route and Last Larch Prospect to left. Keep right for Cathedral Basin.

—Steep uphill via forest and rockslide.

6.6—Uphill ends, trail contours right toward Cathedral Basin.

7.1—Cathedral Platform Prospect (2315 m).

7.4—Cathedral Basin and Monica Lake.

The trail to Linda Lake and the Cathedral Basin is the longest of the spokes radiating from Lake O'Hara — the only hike which usually takes a full day to complete. It is the least crowded of the five major hiking areas, however, and the many pleasant subalpine lakes along the way, coupled with the spectacular overview of the O'Hara environs from the Cathedral Platform Prospect, make it an outstanding trip.

Starting from the north end of the O'Hara Campground, the trail descends through the forest for 1.9 kilometres to a junction with a trail running due west from the O'Hara access road. Keep left at the intersection and follow this trail to Linda Lake in another 1.8 kilometres. Stay right on the shoreline trail and follow it around to the north where there are fine views across the lake to Yukness Mountain and the peaks of the Great Divide beyond Lake O'Hara. For many hikers, a visit to Linda Lake is sufficient exercise for the day, but the real glory of this area lies in the Cathedral Basin, 3.7 kilometres farther along and 225 vertical metres higher up.

To reach the Cathedral Basin, continue around Linda Lake and follow the trail which branches west beyond the far end of the lake. This track climbs gradually through subalpine forest interspersed with meadows. At Kilometre 5.6, the trail crosses a bridge between the first and second Cathedral Lakes (the lower lake is also known as Vera Lake) in a pleasant, meadowy area presided over by the north wall of Odaray Mountain. Just 400 metres beyond, the Last Larch Prospect junction is passed (keep right), and the trail to Cathedral Basin begins its steep ascent.

The last 1.3 kilometres of the journey lies over rough, rocky trail which is frequently more route than track. After 300 metres of steep climbing through a major

rockslide, the trail contours east to the mouth of the Cathedral Basin. Views along this entire stretch are outstanding, but they reach their pinnacle at the lip of the cirque, the Cathedral Platform Prospect. No other viewpoint gives quite so complete an overview of the Lake O'Hara region. High on the side of Cathedral Mountain, you are viewing the area much as the surveyor J. J. McArthur did when he first discovered it from the summit of nearby Mount Stephen in 1887. The upper Cataract Valley is laid out like a map at your feet, stretching southeast to Lake O'Hara and the peaks beyond. The meadows and lakes of the Duchesnay Valley lie immediately below the Prospect, backed by the glowering wall of Odaray Mountain. From the Prospect, it is a short stroll down through alpine meadow to tiny Monica Lake in the heart of the Cathedral Basin cirque.

Alpine Meadows Route. An alternate trail to Linda Lake that is longer, but somewhat more interesting than the direct trail from the campground. This option starts from the trail sign opposite the O'Hara Warden Cabin and follows the trail to the Alpine Meadows. Keep right at the Alpine Club cabins and at the Odaray Plateau junction, and follow the path which skirts a small pond to the north end of the meadow. Beyond the meadow, the trail contours through heavy subalpine forest for 1.8 kilometres and finally descends to cross Morning Glory Creek at the inlet to the second Morning Glory Lake. From the Morning Glory Lakes, the trail becomes very rocky and rooty as it makes a steady, moderately steep ascent through forest and then descends to the south shore of Linda Lake. Total distance from Lake O'Hara to Linda Lake is 4.7 kilometres.

Last Larch Prospect. This old route, originally marked out by Dr. Link, leads to a viewpoint at the head of the Duchesnay Basin. There is little defined trail (watch for faded paint marks and cairns) and much wet and boggy terrain. From the Prospect, experienced rock scramblers can climb around the north side of the upper basin to Duchesnay Pass. Total distance from the junction with the Cathedral Basin trail at Kilometre 6.1 to Last Larch Prospect is approximately two kilometres.

The Alpine Circuit

Lake O'Hara Alpine Circuit—11.8 kilometres (7.3 miles)

Day trip

Allow 4 - 5 hours for circuit

Elevation gain: 495 metres (1,625 feet)

Maximum elevation: 2530 metres (8,300 feet)

Topo maps: Lake Louise 82 N/8

Point of Departure: Travel to Lake O'Hara as described in the *Lake O'Hara* area introduction (see page 234). Walk to the Lake O'Hara Warden Cabin, which is located on the O'Hara Fire Road 0.6 kilometre south of the campground and 0.2 kilometre north of the lodge. To reach the trail head, walk past the warden cabin, pick up the lakeshore trail and follow it north 150 metres to the lake outlet bridge.

0.0—Lake O'Hara outlet (2035 m).

—Follow around north lakeshore.

0.2—Junction. Branch uphill to left from lakeshore on Wiwaxy Gap trail.

—Steady, extremely steep uphill.

2.1—Wiwaxy Gap (2530 m).

—Gradually descending traverse.

4.1—Junction (2275 m). Alpine Circuit crosses *Lake Oesa* trail at Km 3.0.

—Route traverses rock ridge above Lake Oesa, descends to cross outlet stream, then angles up onto Yukness Ledge alpine route.

6.4—Junction. Intersects with *Opabin Plateau* trail at Km 3.6. Turn left and ascend Opabin East Circuit.

6.8—Opabin Lake and junction (2285 m). Keep right to follow Opabin West Circuit.

8.4—Junction. Turn left off Opabin Plateau West Circuit onto All Souls' alpine route.

—Ascends steep scree slopes.

9.3—All Souls' Prospect (2475 m).

—Steep descent via loose rock and ledges.

10.2—Junction. Intersection with Big Larch Route. Keep left for Schaffer Lake.

10.3—Schaffer Lake outlet and junction. Intersection with *Lake McArthur* trail at Km 1.5.

11.8—Lake O'Hara (2035 m).

The Alpine Circuit which skirts the high slopes overlooking Lake O'Hara is not really a trail. While it does utilize segments of three main trails, most of the trip follows paint marks and cairns up across steep scree slopes, through rockslides, and along exposed ledges. The old term "Alpinist's Traverse" is probably a more appropriate name for this trek since bad weather or lingering snow can turn it into a very dangerous exercise. Yet, when the weather is fine and all the snow has disappeared from the rockslides and ledges, the scramble over this inspired route is surprisingly straightforward and logical, and the outing is one of the most glorious in the Rockies. But even under the best conditions, this is a trip reserved for very fit hikers who enjoy exposed heights, and it should be done with the more detailed map of the region published by the Lake O'Hara Trails Club.

Starting the circuit by climbing to Wiwaxy Gap is certainly a more strenuous way to initiate the trip than by heading up to Schäffer Lake and the All Souls' Prospect and moving around the O'Hara basin in the opposite direction. But by labouring up Wiwaxy first you get the toughest climb of the day out of the way early, and if you can scamper up to this lofty col without undue fear and suffering, you'll know that you're tough enough for the trip.

From Lake O'Hara's north shore, just 200 metres beyond its outlet, the steep uphill track to Wiwaxy Gap begins. The distance to the gap is just under two kilometres from the lakeshore junction, but it will seem at least twice that far. In addition to wiggling straight up through forest and across scree, the trail skirts some very exposed ledges—wide enough to walk on comfortably but just inches away from lots of air.

Wiwaxy Gap is a grand viewpoint for the entire O'Hara basin. In addition to looking back down on the lake and out to four or five major hiking areas which radi-

Lake Oesa from the Alpine Circuit

ate from it, the col is a "window" north to Cataract Brook and the mountains near Kicking Horse Pass.

From the gap the route begins a long, descending traverse along the south slope of Mount Huber toward Lake Oesa—a turquoise gem which is frequently visible ahead. Again there are ledges and rockslides to be traversed, but paint marks and cairns are frequent enough that route finding should be no problem.

If you made a reasonably early start and are making decent time, Lake Oesa is a fine place to stop for lunch. The Alpine Circuit crosses the Lake Oesa trail on a rocky knoll just 200 metres west of the lake. Beyond this bluff a new traverse begins (watch for orange paint marks) as the trail drops down to cross the Oesa outlet stream, then climbs to the tumbled cliffs of the Yukness Ledge alpine route— a high contour which takes the hiker around the west slope of Yukness Mountain and into the Opabin Plateau cirque.

After intersecting the Opabin Plateau East Circuit, the climbing and scrambling relents for awhile as you walk the well-graded Opabin Plateau trail to the head of the valley then, at Opabin Lake, turn to descend the opposite side of the plateau on the Opabin West Circuit. The short detour to Opabin Prospect on the northern lip of the plateau is a worthwhile option (another clifftop "thriller" after that "dull" stretch of alpine meadow) since it brings you back onto the Opabin West Circuit just 50 metres above the next major traverse, the All Souls' alpine route.

All Souls' is the last of the three alpine traverses and in some respects the most rugged. It crosses extensive rockslides from Mount Schäffer and climbs steeply to the outstanding All Souls' Prospect — a natural platform on the mountain's north ridge at 2475 metres above sea level. The view across Lake O'Hara, which allows you to retrace the entire Alpine Circuit, is an appropriate finale to the day.

From the Prospect there is one last steep, rocky, thigh-jarring descent to the Big Larch trail near Schäffer Lake. If you are still feeling your oats, return to Lake O'Hara via the rocky but scenic Big Larch trail (see *Lake McArthur* trail, Big Larch Route). Otherwise, continue the last 100 metres to Schäffer Lake and shuffle back down the main Lake McArthur trail.

McArthur Creek

Lake O'Hara to Ottertail River—12.4 kilometres (7.7 miles)

Day trip or backpack

Allow 4 hours one way

Elevation gain: 175 metres (570 feet)
      loss: 730 metres (2,400 feet)

Maximum elevation: 2210 metres (7,250 feet)

Topo maps: Lake Louise 82 N/8

Point of Departure: Travel to Lake O'Hara as described in the *Lake O'Hara* area introduction (see page 234). Walk to the Lake O'Hara Warden Cabin, which is located on the O'Hara access road 0.6 kilometre south of the campground and 0.2 kilometre north of the lodge. The trail begins at the trail sign on the west side of the road, opposite the warden cabin. Northbound travellers can reach the south end of the trail by hiking the *Ottertail River* trail to the junction at Km 14.5.

0.0—Lake O'Hara (2035 m).

—Trail enters Alpine Meadow.

0.6—Elizabeth Parker Hut and junction. Odaray Plateau—Linda Lake to right. Keep left for McArthur Pass.

—Moderate to steep uphill.

1.6—Schaffer Lake and junction. High route to Lake McArthur branches left. Keep right for McArthur Pass.

—Steady climb through forest.

2.1—McArthur Pass (2210 m). Cutoff to Lake McArthur high route branches left. Keep right for McArthur Creek.

2.4—Junction. Lake McArthur low route branches left. Keep right.

—Steep downhill into McArthur Creek valley.

6.4—McArthur Creek bridge.

—Downhill grade moderates, trail passes through avalanche slopes.

12.4—Junction (1480 m). Intersection with *Ottertail River* trail at Km 14.5.

The McArthur Creek trail is a wilderness link connecting the Lake O'Hara region to the Ottertail Valley and points south. After ascending to McArthur Pass from Lake O'Hara, the trail makes a ten kilometre descent of the McArthur Creek valley. Most hikers seem to use the trail as a beginning or an end to the extended backpack stretching from Lake O'Hara to Floe Lake in Kootenay Park; but remember, campground reservations must be confirmed with Parks Canada to include Lake O'Hara in any such itinerary.

If you have a choice, try to hike McArthur Creek from Lake O'Hara rather than the Ottertail, since the climb out of the Ottertail Valley is quite long and gruelling. Starting from the trail head opposite the O'Hara Warden Cabin (see *Lake McArthur* trail description), the hiker climbs to Schäffer Lake via the standard Lake McArthur route. Unless a side-trip to Lake McArthur is planned, most backpackers will want to keep right at the 1.6 kilometre junction and make a direct traverse through McArthur Pass.

From the summit of McArthur Pass, it is all downhill to the Ottertail River. Just beyond the low route cutoff to Lake McArthur, the trail begins a steep descent which lasts for over three kilometres. After crossing McArthur Creek at Kilometre 6.4, the grade becomes less severe as the trail enters the lower section of the valley — an area of dense forest mixed with avalanche slopes and meadows. At the 12.4 kilometre mark, the trail intersects the Ottertail Fire Road at Kilometre 14.5 (see *Ottertail River* trail description). From this junction, turn left and hike up the road 400 metres to reach the McArthur Creek Campground.

The avalanche slopes of McArthur Creek provide some fine views south to Mount Goodsir, but they also create a rich habitat for many large mammals, including grizzly bear. Stay alert while hiking this valley.

Ottertail River

Backpack

Allow 5-7 hours one way

Elevation gain: 360 metres (1,180 feet)

Maximum elevation: 1555 metres (5,100 feet)

Topo maps: Golden 82 N/7
Lake Louise 82 N/8

Point of Departure: Follow the Trans-Canada Highway to the Ottertail River bridge, 8½ kilometres (5½ miles) west of Field. Just 0.2 kilometre east of the bridge, on the south side of the highway, is the parking area and locked access gate for the Ottertail Fire Road.

0.0—Access gate (1195 m).

—Road climbs at gradual rate with some moderately steep pitches.

2.8—Hoodoos viewpoint.

—Gradual uphill above river.

3.5—Giddie Creek

5.2—Moderately steep downhill grade next kilometre.

6.2—Float Creek bridge.

—Road climbs away from river, then continues gradual ascent of valley.

14.5—Junction. McArthur Creek trail to McArthur Pass and Lake O'Hara branches left.

14.6—McArthur Creek bridge.

14.9—McArthur Creek Campground.

15.1—McArthur Creek Warden Cabin.

15.5—Ottertail River bridge.

16.2—Junction. Ottertail Falls to left. Goodsir Pass straight ahead (see *Rockwall Trail* description, Kootenay Park chapter).

17.7—Ottertail Falls (1555 m).

While fire roads usually make rather tedious hiking routes, the one up the Ottertail River is about as pleasant as any in the mountain parks. It climbs gradually along semi-open slopes overlooking the river, passes above a small series of hoodoos, and provides frequent views of the Ottertail Range. The road is mainly used by backpackers as an optional access route for Goodsir Pass and the northern end of Kootenay Park's Rockwall Trail.

From its intersection with the Trans-Canada Highway, the fire road climbs into a mixed forest of lodgepole pine, white spruce and aspen. At the 1.4 kilometre mark, it emerges onto a bench above the Ottertail River, where views open out across the Kicking Horse Valley to the Van Horne Range and up the Ottertail to Mounts Hurd and Ennis. At Kilometre 2.8, the hiker passes above a steep cutbank where a number of hoodoos have been eroded from the calcareous soils and gravels along the river, an area which also serves as a mineral lick for the local mountain goats.

Beyond Float Creek, the road swings away from the river for much of the time and gradually climbs into a subalpine forest of Engelmann spruce and alpine fir. The McArthur Creek trail intersects from the left at Kilometre 14.5 (see *McArthur Creek* trail description), and a well-sheltered campground is passed on the right side of the road 400 metres farther along. The road ends at the McArthur Creek Warden Cabin, 200 metres beyond the campground; the cabin sits on a pleasant, open bench with a spectacular view of the twin summits of Mount Goodsir.

Trail continues beyond the end of the road, running south from the warden cabin and crossing the Ottertail River. A two kilometre-long trail to Ottertail Falls branches left at Kilometre 16.1, while the main trail continues south to Goodsir Pass (see the *Rockwall Trail,* Kootenay Park chapter).

251

Yoho Valley

The Yoho Valley was first explored in 1897 when Jean Habel, an adventuresome alpinist from Berlin, spent seventeen days on an excursion that carried him from Yoho Pass above Emerald Lake to the head of the Yoho Valley and some distance up the Yoho Glacier onto the Wapta Icefield. Habel noted that the area, featuring an impressive array of glaciated peaks, extensive icefields and the stunning 380 metre Takakkaw Falls, was one of exceptional beauty. That reputation has not been diminished over time.

Both the Canadian Pacific Railway and the Alpine Club of Canada took an early interest in the area and are responsible for the construction of its comprehensive trail system. One of the first individuals to make a thorough exploration of the entire region was Edward Whymper, the conqueror of Switzerland's Matterhorn. Though Whymper was 61 years old when the CPR brought him to the Canadian Rockies in 1901, he climbed and hiked extensively throughout the Yoho Valley area, photographing all of the major mountains and valleys. From his long experience in Europe, he saw the recreational potential of the Yoho and recommended the construction of many of the area's trails.

Today the Yoho Valley, together with the adjacent Little Yoho Valley and Emerald Lake basin, constitutes one of the Canadian Rockies' major backcountry recreation areas. While not as compact as many similar regions, such as Lake O'Hara, the Yoho remains very popular, particularly with climbers, backpackers and strong day hikers.

Many of the trails in Yoho Valley region interconnect, creating hiking variations that can be tailored to the strength and available time of almost any hiking party. Thus, starting from Takakkaw Falls, one person may decide to take a short stroll to Duchesnay Lake while another may push on to Twin Falls. A stronger hiker yet may opt to return from Twin Falls via the Highline, while a backpacker will head for the Little Yoho Valley via Twin Falls and the Whaleback. The options are numerous.

As well as the walk-in campground at Takakkaw Falls, there are several small campgrounds scattered throughout the valley (since all of these campgrounds are governed by quotas, you should keep your itinerary flexible). The Twin Falls Chalet stands at the foot of Twin Falls and provides a limited amount of accommodation throughout the summer months (reservations can be made through chalet proprietress Fran Drummond at 403-269-1497). The Alpine Club of Canada's Stanley Mitchell Hut is found at the edge of a meadow near the head of the Little Yoho Valley; this log structure can accommodate approximately 30 and is manned by custodians throughout the summer (information and reservations available from the Alpine Club of Canada, Box 1026, Banff, Alberta T0L 0C0 or by phoning 403-762-4481). As might be expected, the solitude Jean Habel experienced less than a hundred years ago is harder to come by these days, especially during the peak summer season, but the beauty of the area has changed little.

Access: Of the four main points of access to this hiking region, the trail head at the end of the Yoho Valley Road (Takakkaw Falls parking area) is by far the most central and popular. A trail head at the Whiskey Jack Youth Hostel, just 500 metres south of the Takakkaw Falls parking area, provides the most direct access to Yoho Pass. Day

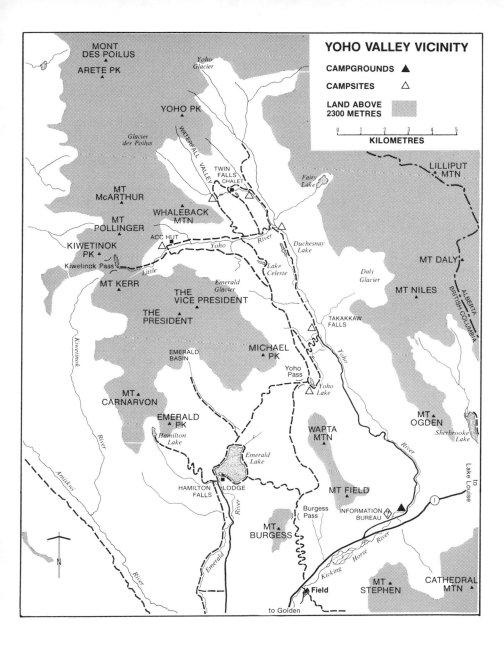

YOHO VALLEY VICINITY

CAMPGROUNDS ▲

CAMPSITES △

LAND ABOVE 2300 METRES

```
0   1   2   3   4   5
```
KILOMETRES

hikers can also reach Yoho and Burgess Passes from Emerald Lake, and backpackers bound for the Highline Trail can initiate their journey at Emerald. The trail leading up from the Trans-Canada Highway to Burgess Pass is popular with backpackers who want to do the full length Highline Trail, and it is a particularly attractive point of access for those utilizing public transport, since the trail head is only a few minutes walk from the VIA Rail station in Field and the Greyhound bus stop at Field Junction. (For detailed access instructions, see individual trail descriptions.)

253

Burgess Pass

Trans-Canada Highway to Burgess Pass—6.6 kilometres (4.1 miles)

Trans-Canada Highway to Emerald Lake Lodge—13.4 kilometres (8.3 miles)

Day trip

Allow 2-3 hours to Burgess Pass

Elevation gain: 930 metres (3,050 feet)
loss: 880 metres (2,880 feet)

Maximum elevation: 2180 metres (7,150 feet)

Topo maps: Lake Louise 82 N/8
Golden 82 N/7

Point of Departure: Follow the Trans Canada Highway to the Field townsite junction. The trail head parking area is located on the north side of the highway just 0.4 kilometre east of the junction and the service station complex.

0.0—Trail sign (1250 m).

—First 300 metres are steep, moderating into well-graded switchbacks.

2.3—First open views.

3.1—Open rockslide.

—Trail continues steady uphill switchbacking.

6.3—Trail crosses steep, grassy slope. Viewpoint.

6.6—Burgess Pass (2180 m).

6.9—Junction. Yoho Pass to right via *Highline Trail.* Keep left for Emerald Lake.

—Steady downhill over open scree slopes.

8.0—Mount Burgess viewpoint.

—Trail switchbacks down through forest.

12.4—Junction. Intersection with *Emerald Lake* nature trail. Keep left.

—Follows lakeshore trail along west and south shoreline.

13.4—Emerald Lake Lodge (1300 m).

The climb up from the Kicking Horse Valley to the summit of Burgess Pass is one of the stiffest in Yoho Park; the trail gains a heart-throbbing 930 vertical metres in just 6.6 kilometres. But the gain is worth the pain, as the summit provides a bird's-eye view of both the Kicking Horse Valley and the Emerald Lake basin. Once Burgess Pass is reached, the way is clear to extend the journey along the Highline Trail or down to Emerald Lake, options which are highly scenic and far less demanding than the gruelling ascent.

The trail strikes off from the Trans-Canada Highway just 400 metres east of Field Junction and immediately begins its relentless, switchbacking climb through the forest. The first views out across the Kicking Horse Valley come at the 2.3 kilometre mark, and when the trail skirts a rockslide at Kilometre 3.1, there is another opportunity for a breather. The trail levels off as it crosses a grassy slope at Kilometre 6.3 — the best viewpoint for the Kicking Horse Valley. Just 300 metres farther along, the hiker crests Burgess Pass and the Emerald Lake basin opens to view. (Be sure to carry a supply of water on the ascent to the pass, as there are few reliable streams.)

Aside from the glaciated peaks of the President Range to the north, the most striking mountain visible from Burgess Pass is the rocky ship's prow of Wapta Peak. It was on the open shale slopes between this mountain and Mount Field in 1909 that the geologist Dr. Charles Doolittle Walcott discovered the most significant bed of soft-bodied Cambrian fossils that has ever been found anywhere in the world. In a quarry that was only 30 metres long and 3 metres wide, the remains of over 150 species were uncovered. Known as the Burgess Shale Beds, this tiny piece of mountainside was declared a World Heritage Site in 1980, and

The President and Wapta Mountain from near Burgess Pass

any disturbance of the area or removal of fossils is strictly prohibited.

Emerald Lake Route. Beyond Burgess Pass, a trail descends along the north slope of Mount Burgess to Emerald Lake. Burgess Pass can be reached just about as easily from this side as from the Kicking Horse Valley side, or transportation can be arranged between the Trans-Canada Highway and Emerald Lake trail heads so that the pass can be traversed as a one way trip. The trail branches left from the Highline Trail 300 metres north of the pass and makes a steady, switchbacking descent, mainly through heavy forest, all the way to Emerald Lake. By staying left on the lakeshore trail, you will reach Emerald Lake Lodge in another kilometre of flat walking. Distance from the pass to the lodge is 6.8 kilometres.

Yoho Pass-Burgess Pass Loop. The trail between Burgess Pass and Emerald Lake Lodge is also used as part of a loop trip which starts and ends at the Emerald Lake parking area. The hike follows the Yoho Pass trail 6.3 kilometres to the summit of that pass, then traverses south along the slopes of Wapta Mountain on the Highline Trail for 6.1 kilometres to the junction 300 metres north of Burgess Pass. Total distance for this very scenic, triangular loop, excluding short side trips to Yoho Lake and Burgess Pass, is 19 kilometres. (See also *Yoho Pass* and *Highline Trail* descriptions.)

The Highline Trail. Burgess Pass can be utilized as part of a 24 kilometre-long highline trip which runs from the Trans-Canada Highway near Field to Twin Falls in the upper Yoho Valley. Once the summit of Burgess Pass is attained at the 6.6 kilometre mark, the remainder of the journey rolls along above the 1800 metre level to provide an unparalleled overview of the Emerald Lake-Yoho Valley region. (See *Highline Trail* description.)

255

Yoho Pass

Yoho Valley Road to Yoho Pass—4.6 kilometres (2.9 miles)
Yoho Valley Road to Emerald Lake Lodge—10.9 kilometres (6.8 miles)

Day trip

Allow 1½-2 hours to Yoho Pass

Elevation gain: 310 metres (1,040 feet)
  loss: 530 metres (1,740 feet)

Maximum elevation: 1830 metres (6,000 feet)

Topo maps: Lake Louise 82 N/8
  Golden 82 N/7

Point of Departure: From its junction with the Trans Canada Highway 3.7 kilometres (2.3 miles) east of Field, follow the Yoho Valley Road north for 12½ kilometres (7½ miles) to the Whiskey Jack Youth Hostel, situated on the edge of a large avalanche path 100 metres to the left of the main road. The trail sign is on the west side of the hostel parking area.

0.0—Trail sign (1520 m).

—Trail climbs at steady uphill grade.

1.1—Junction. Hidden Lakes to left 0.3 km. Keep right.

1.3—Junction. Highline Trail cutoff trail to right. Keep left.

3.7—Yoho Lake (1815 m).

—Trail skirts south end of lake.

4.0—Junction. Intersection with *Highline Trail* at Km 13.0. Keep left for Yoho Pass.

4.6—Yoho Pass and junction (1830 m). Burgess Pass to left via *Highline Trail.* Keep right.

—Steady downhill.

6.6—Falls viewpoint.

7.5—Downhill ends on outwash plain.

9.3—Junction. Emerald Basin trail branches right. Keep left.

9.5—Junction. Intersection with *Emerald Lake* nature trail at Km 1.4. Keep right.

—Trail follows west shore.

10.9—Emerald Lake parking area (1300 m).

Though Yoho Pass can be approached from either the Yoho Valley or Emerald Lake, the trail from the Yoho side is the shortest. The trail is fairly popular because it is one of the shortest day hikes in the Yoho Valley region, and though the pass and Yoho Lake are enclosed by forest, one can achieve some fine overviews of Takakkaw Falls and the Yoho Valley with a little extra effort. The trail is also the quickest way onto the Highline Trail, so it is frequently travelled as a part of longer hikes to and from the upper Yoho Valley.

Starting from the Whiskey Jack Youth Hostel, 500 metres south of Takakkaw Falls, the trail switchbacks up a major avalanche path and into heavy subalpine forest. At Kilometre 1.1, a short side trail branches left to the Hidden Lakes — two tiny, forest-enclosed ponds. Just 200 metres beyond the Hidden Lakes junction, the cutoff to the Highline Trail branches right (you will return down this trail if you make the loop option north from Yoho Lake to the Yoho Valley overlook). The ascent finally ends as the trail levels off at Yoho Lake.

Though this small, green lake is surrounded on three sides by a cool, dense forest of Engelmann spruce and alpine fir, its western shoreline is bordered by a lush meadow where western anemones, globe flowers and yellow violets grow in early summer.

The trail follows around the south shore of Yoho Lake and runs west through the meadow to the summit of Yoho Pass. There is little to indicate one's arrival on the pass other than a trail junction in the midst of the forest. From this point it is possible to turn left and follow the Highline Trail south toward Burgess Pass, or to continue west and descend to Emerald Lake.

Most day hikers will return to the trail head on the Yoho Valley Road once they

Yoho Lake

have visited Yoho Lake and the nearby pass, and the most scenic way of doing this is to follow the Highline Trail north from Yoho Lake. This trail branches from the Yoho Pass trail just beyond the west shore of the lake and, after climbing through forest for the first kilometre, emerges onto open slopes overlooking the Yoho Valley and Takakkaw Falls. At a junction 2.4 kilometres from Yoho Lake, a trail branches down to the right across open meadows and rockslides. By following this cutoff trail downhill for 1.1 kilometres, you will return to the Yoho Pass trail at the Kilometre 1.3 junction. Total distance for the Yoho Lake loop trip is 8.8 kilometres.

Emerald Lake Route. Yoho Pass can also be hiked from the trail head at the Emerald Lake parking area. Though it is nearly two kilometres longer than the Yoho Valley route, this approach is much more open and scenic; the trail skirts the west shore of Emerald Lake for over a kilometre, traverses an open alluvial plain beneath the glaciated summits of the President Range, and passes near a very fine waterfall on the lower slopes of Michael Peak. For those who can arrange transportation between the Yoho Valley and Emerald Lake, it is possible to experience both sides of the pass in one day by traversing Yoho Pass as a one way, 10.9 kilometre hike.

Highline Trail. An interesting entry to (or exit from) the upper Yoho Valley can be made by combining the Yoho Pass hike with the Highline Trail route. One popular itinerary is to hike the Yoho Valley trail to Twin Falls and then return via the Highline and Yoho Pass trails — a very scenic loop trip of 24 kilometres. (See *Highline Trail* description).

257

Twin Falls

Takakkaw Falls to Twin Falls—8.5 kilometres (5.3 miles)

Day trip or backpack

Allow 2½-3 hours to Twin Falls

Elevation gain: 290 metres (950 feet)

Maximum elevation: 1800 metres (5,900 feet)

Topo maps: Lake Louise 82 N/8
　　　　　Hector Lake 82 N/9
　　　　　Blaeberry River 82 N/10

Point of Departure: From its junction with the Trans-Canada Highway 3.7 kilometres (2.3 miles) east of Field, follow the Yoho Valley Road north for 13 kilometres (8 miles) to its termination at the Takakkaw Falls parking area. Keep right and circle around to the far end of the parking area for 0.4 kilometre to a smaller parking lot for the Yoho Valley trail.

0.0—Trail sign (1510 m).

—Trail runs north on old roadbed.

0.8—Takakkaw Falls Campground.

—Trail runs across rocky outwash plain and into scattered forest.

2.6—Junction. Angel's Staircase Viewpoint to right. Point Lace Falls to left 0.2 km. Main trail continues straight ahead.

4.0—Junction. Duchesnay Lake to left 0.2 km. Keep right.

4.2—Yoho River viewpoint to right.

4.7—Laughing Falls. Campground.

4.8—Junction. Little Yoho Valley trail branches left. Keep right.

6.9—Junction. Yoho Glacier trail branches right. Keep left for Twin Falls.

7.1—Twin Falls Campground.

—Steady switchbacking climb.

8.4—Junction. Whaleback trail branches right. Keep left.

8.5—Twin Falls Chalet (1800 m). Connects with *Highline Trail* at Km 24.4.

The 8.5 kilometre trail running up the Yoho Valley from Takakkaw Falls to Twin Falls was originally cut by a CPR trail crew during the summer of 1901. Today it is probably the most frequently hiked route in the Emerald Lake-Yoho Valley region. The trail passes by a number of fine waterfalls as it works its way north along the Yoho River, and it culminates the journey at the spectacular double cataract of Twin Falls. Not only is this a worthwhile trip in and of itself, but it serves as an important access route to three other very scenic trails — the Whaleback, the Highline, and the Little Yoho Valley.

The Yoho Valley trail is relatively flat and straightforward for much of its distance to Twin Falls. The first 2.6 kilometres follow a road-width track which, after skirting the Takakkaw Falls walk-in campground and crossing a rocky alluvial fan, enters a forest of pine and spruce. Three waterfalls are passed on the way upvalley: Angel's Staircase Falls and Point Lace Falls at Kilometre 2.6, and Laughing Falls at Kilometre 4.7. Beyond the Point Lace Falls junction, the trail reverts to a single-file path.

At Kilometre 4.0, a short, 200 metre trail branches left to Lake Duchesnay —a shallow, green lake that slowly dries up to the size of a pond by early autumn. Just beyond the Lake Duchesnay junction is another option, a short trail branching right to the edge of the Yoho River, where the hiker can observe the explosive action of this glacial torrent as it cuts its channel. Across the river views extend to the ice-covered peaks of the Waputik Mountains, dominated by the sharp peak of Trolltinder Mountain (2917 m).

After passing the Little Yoho Valley junction at Kilometre 4.8, the trail crosses Twin Falls Creek and continues its northerly course through heavy forest cover, with occasional breaks in the canopy beyond Kilometre 6.5 that allow quick glimpses of Twin Falls. At the junction with the Yoho Glacier trail, the main trail veers to the left and starts its final, steady ascent to Twin Falls.

The Yoho Valley trail ends at the small Twin Falls Chalet, where one can view the falls as they make a vertical drop of some eighty metres off a massive cliff of Cathedral limestone. The falls are formed by a stream of meltwater from the Glacier des Poilus which splits into two branches just before plunging over the precipice. Before the Twin Falls Chalet was constructed by the CPR in 1923, the left-hand falls sometimes dwindled to a trickle or shut off altogether when an obstruction blocked its channel; CPR employees were dispatched to the lip of the falls to correct this scenic problem —with dynamite! (The appearance of the name "Canadian Pacific Rockies" on early maps of western Canada may not have been all that inappropriate.)

From Twin Falls, hikers have several options for further exploration of the region. The trail over the Whaleback, which strikes off from the junction 100 metres north of Twin Falls Chalet, climbs to an elevation of 2210 metres above sea level and provides some of the finest views available of the upper Yoho Valley region. The Highline Trail begins its southward run at the Twin Falls Chalet and is by far the most scenic route back down-valley to Takakkaw Falls. (See *Whaleback* and *Highline Trail* descriptions.)

Yoho Glacier. From its junction with the Yoho Valley trail at Kilometre 6.9, a 2.3 kilometre trail works its way north through dense forest cover and across relatively level terrain to the edge of a cutbank overlooking the Yoho River and the snout of the Yoho Glacier — a fine observation point for the study of a recently glaciated landscape. (Only those experienced in glacier travel and equipped with rope and ice axe should venture onto the surface of this glacier.)

Twin Falls

259

The Highline Trail

Trans-Canada Highway to Twin Falls—24.4 kilometres (15.2 miles)

Backpack

Allow 1½-2 days to Twin Falls

Elevation gain: 840 metres (2,750 feet)
loss: 290 metres (950 feet)

Maximum elevation: 2090 metres (6,850 feet)

Topo maps: Lake Louise 82 N/8
Blaeberry River 82 N/10

Point of Departure: Follow the Trans Canada Highway to the Field townsite junction. The trail head parking area is located on the north side of the highway just 0.4 kilometre east of the junction and the service station complex. (See also *Burgess Pass* trail description.) Southbound travellers can pickup the north end of the trail by hiking to Twin Falls on the *Twin Falls via Yoho Valley* trail.

0.0—Burgess Pass trail head (1250 m).

6.6—Burgess Pass (2180 m).

6.9—Junction. Trail to Emerald Lake branches left. Keep right.

13.0—Yoho Pass and junction (1830 m). Intersection with *Yoho Pass* trail at Km 4.6. Keep right.

13.6—Yoho Lake, campground and junction. Yoho Valley Road via Yoho Pass trail branches right. Keep left.

16.0—Junction. Cutoff trail to Yoho Pass trail branches right. Keep left.

18.9—Junction (2090 m). Skyline Trail branches left. Keep right.

20.0—Celeste Lake (1995 m).

21.4—Junction. Intersection with *Little Yoho Valley* trail at Km 2.2. Turn right.

21.5—Junction (1905 m). Whaleback trail to left. Keep straight ahead.

22.1—Junction. Yoho Valley trail straight ahead. Turn left for Twin Falls.

23.8—Marpole Lake.

24.3—Twin Falls bridge.

24.4—Twin Falls Chalet (1800 m).

During August of 1901, Edward Whymper, the British mountaineer who first climbed the Matterhorn, journeyed to the Yoho Valley. When he and his party reached Yoho Pass, instead of descending to follow the new trail which had been constructed up along the Yoho River that summer, they stayed high on the west side of the valley and contoured north to the Little Yoho Valley. The following winter, Whymper wrote the CPR and suggested the company build a trail along this high route to provide a more scenic option to the valley bottom trail. Today, Whymper's Highline Trail is considered one of the finest hikes in the Yoho Valley.

While the 11 kilometre-long section of trail running north from Yoho Pass to Twin Falls is officially designated as the Highline Trail, a natural extension of the route continues south to Burgess Pass and down to the Kicking Horse Valley near Field. So, for the purposes of this book, the Highline Trail is the 24.4 kilometre track running north from the Trans-Canada Highway to Twin Falls via Burgess and Yoho Passes and the western slopes of the Yoho Valley.

The first 6.6 kilometres of the Highline follows the Burgess Pass trail (see *Burgess Pass* trail description). Once the 930 vertical metres to this pass are overcome, the remainder of the trip rolls along through the upper subalpine zone, never dropping below the 1800 metre level.

The 6.4 kilometres of trail between Burgess Pass and Yoho Pass give hikers their first taste of the fine scenery this region has to offer. To the north lie the ice-clad peaks of The President and The Vice President (names suggested by Whymper to honour the executives of the Canadian Pacific Railway), while the massive, Cambrian limestone cliffs of Wapta Mountain rise immediately ahead. Open wildflower meadows are scattered along the way, and there are impressive views down to Emerald Lake.

Upper Yoho Valley from the Highline

By the time the trail reaches Yoho Pass, it has re-entered dense subalpine forest. Following the trail east from the summit for 0.6 kilometre, you reach Yoho Lake and the point where the Yoho Pass and Highline trails part ways: the Yoho Pass trail cuts around the lake to the right and descends to the Takakkaw Falls area, while the Highline branches left and continues its northerly journey to the head of the Yoho Valley.

The Highline begins to climb through the forest as it departs the pass environs, and just under two kilometres beyond, it emerges onto open slopes high above the Yoho Valley: below, to the east, is Takakkaw Falls, Canada's highest waterfall, looking like a mere trickle from this elevation; ahead are the peaks of the Waputik Mountains, embraced by the icy blanket of the Wapta Icefield. As the trail progresses north along the slopes beneath the Emerald Glacier, it threads its way across several rocky moraines and outwashes, and encounters some unbridged streams which can be tricky to cross during high water.

Near Kilometre 18.8, after climbing back into subalpine forest, the trail passes along a low, rock ridge, which serves as a fine vantage point for the upper Yoho Valley. Just beyond the viewpoint, the Skyline Trail branches left from the Highline, an important intersection for backpackers bound for the Little Yoho Valley (see *Little Yoho Valley* trail description).

The remainder of the journey is forest-enclosed as the trail gradually descends to the 1800 metre level of Twin Falls. The only real break along this section comes at Lake Celeste, a tiny, turquoise tarn set against the impressive backdrop of The Vice President (3066 m). At Kilometre 21.4, the hiker crosses the Little Yoho River and reaches the intersection with the Little Yoho Valley trail. Keep right at this junction and follow the trail downhill, passing the junction with the south end of the Whaleback trail just 100 metres below. At Kilometre 22.1, the Highline route branches left from the Little Yoho trail and, after skirting the shores of Marpole Lake, reaches Twin Falls. (See also *Yoho Valley* trail description.)

261

Little Yoho Valley

Day trip or backpack

Allow 1½-2 hours to Little Yoho Campground

Elevation gain: 520 metres (1,700 feet)

Maximum elevation: 2135 metres (7,000 feet)

Topo maps: Blaeberry River 82 N/10

Point of Departure: From the Takakkaw Falls Parking Lot, hike the *Twin Falls via Yoho Valley* trail to the 4.8 kilometre junction at Laughing Falls. The Little Yoho Valley trail branches uphill to the left at this junction. The Little Yoho Valley-Skyline Trail circuit is also accessible from the *Highline Trail* at Kms 18.9 and 21.4.

0.0—Yoho Valley Junction (1615 m).

—Steep uphill switchbacks.

1.5—Junction. Intersection with *Highline Trail* route at Km 22.1. Twin Falls Chalet to right. Keep straight ahead.

—Steady uphill at moderate grade.

2.1—Junction (1905 m). Whaleback trail branches right. Keep straight ahead.

2.2—Junction. Intersection with *Highline Trail* at Km 21.4. Yoho Lake via Highline to left. Keep straight ahead for Little Yoho Valley.

5.1—Stanley Mitchell Hut.

5.3—Little Yoho Campground and junction. Kiwetinok Pass trail branches right. Keep left for Skyline Trail.

5.4—Little Yoho River bridge (2075 m). Connects with Skyline Trail running back down-valley to east.

—Trail climbs along rockslides below President Range.

7.0—Skyline Trail Summit (2135 m). Trail contours open slopes.

—Descent into meadows and subalpine forest.

10.4—Junction (2090 m). Intersection with *Highline Trail* at Km 18.9.

The Little Yoho Valley is one of the prime destinations for backpackers in the Yoho Valley region. The campground at the head of the valley and the nearby Stanley Mitchell Hut are ideally situated as base camps for short excursions to such worthy objectives as The Whaleback and Kiwetinok Pass. And the Skyline Trail, which contours high along the foot of the President Range, combines nicely with the Little Yoho Valley trail to make a very scenic loop of this beautiful hanging valley.

Since most hikers to the Little Yoho Valley are backpackers, most are looking for the most direct route to the campground or the Alpine Club hut near the valley's head. That route follows the Yoho Valley trail 4.8 kilometres from Takakkaw Falls to its junction with the Little Yoho Valley trail at Laughing Falls. From this intersection, the trail climbs due west along the north side of the Little Yoho River.

After climbing through the forest via a series of switchbacks, the trail straightens out to make a steady ascent of the valley. At Kilometre 1.5, the trail from Twin Falls intersects from the right (marked as the "Marpole Lake Trail" on the topo sheet). The Whaleback trail branches right at the 2.1 kilometre mark, and just 100 metres farther along, the Highline Trail branches left across the Little Yoho River. The forest becomes progressively more subalpine and open as the trail continues upvalley, until, at Kilometre 5.1, it reaches a large meadow and the Stanley Mitchell Hut (information on accommodation at the hut is available through the Alpine Club of Canada office in Banff); the Little Yoho Campground lies 200 metres farther along. While the head of the valley is enclosed by impressive mountains, the most dramatic and dominating are the heavily glaciated peaks of the President Range, which stand above the meadow to the south.

262

Mount Niles and Daly Glacier from the Skyline

Skyline Trail. Just beyond the campground, the Little Yoho Valley trail bends south to cross the Little Yoho River. This arm of trail descending the south side of the valley is known as the Skyline Trail. From the river crossing, it doubles back along the opposite side of the Stanley Mitchell meadow, and begins its ascent across the shoulder of The Vice President. Once the high point of the trail has been attained beneath the cliffs of The Vice President, the route traverses along the terminal moraines of the Emerald Glacier and descends into an expansive meadowland providing views of much of the Yoho Valley. The Skyline ends by dropping back into the forest and connecting back into the Highline Trail.

Kiwetinok Pass. From a junction across the river from the Little Yoho Campground, there is a short but steep trail which branches west to the 2450 metre summit of Kiwetinok Pass — a rocky and windswept col which boasts its own tiny lake and an outstanding perspective of both the Little Yoho Valley to the east and the Kiwetinok Valley to the west. The spur is only 2.5 kilometres in length, but the last half of the trip is very steep and the track is poorly defined (watch for cairns).

If the Little Yoho Campground is full, it is quite feasible to hike the Little Yoho Valley circuit as a day trip from one of the campgrounds in the Yoho Valley. In fact, strong hikers can trek to the head of the valley from Takakkaw Falls via the Yoho and Little Yoho Valley trails, then return via the Skyline and Highline trails, creating a loop hike of 24 kilometres.

263

Whaleback

Day trip or backpack

Allow 1-1½ hours to Whaleback Summit

Elevation gain: 410 metes (1,350 feet)
loss: 305 metres (1,000 feet)

Maximum elevation: 2210 metres (7,250 feet)

Topo maps: Blaeberry River 82 N/10

Point of Departure: From the Takakkaw Falls Parking Lot, hike the *Twin Falls via Yoho Valley* trail 8.5 kilometres to the junction with the Whaleback trail, just 0.1 kilometre north of the Twin Falls Chalet. The south end of the Whaleback traverse is accessible from the *Highline Trail* at Km 21.5 and the *Little Yoho Valley* trail at Km. 2.1

0.0—Twin Falls Junction (1800 m).

—Trail climbs steeply via long switchbacks.

2.7—Whaleback Campground. Lip of Twin Falls.

2.9—Twin Falls Creek suspension bridge.

—Steady climb up east ridge of Whaleback.

4.5—Whaleback Summit (2210 m).

—Steep downhill switchbacks.

6.6—Junction (1905 m). Intersection with *Little Yoho Valley* trail at Km 2.1 and *Highline Trail* at Km 21.5.

One of the highest and most spectacular trails in the Yoho Valley region runs from the Twin Falls Chalet to the Little Yoho Valley via the rim of the Twin Falls cliff and the eastern flank of the Whaleback. Though the trail can be included in the Yoho Valley-Highline Trail loop from Takakkaw Falls, the 27 kilometre distance is rather strenuous as a day hike. Most hikers will want to visit the Whaleback as a day trip from a campsite in the Yoho or Little Yoho Valleys.

The north end of the Whaleback trail intersects the Yoho Valley trail 100 metres north of Twin Falls Chalet. From this junction, the trail switchbacks up the rock bands that provide the 80 metre precipice for Twin Falls. Gaining the top of the rock bands, the trail descends to Twin Falls Creek and passes the Whaleback Campground. Perched very near the brink of Twin Falls, this is the most spectacular location for any campground in the Canadian Rockies, and not a place for sleepwalkers to spend the night. (Stay clear of Twin Falls Creek near the brink of the falls! This is a dangerous area which has already claimed one life.)

Beyond the campground, the hiker crosses a narrow suspension bridge spanning the turbulent waters of Twin Falls Creek and begins a gradual climb across the flank of the Whaleback. The trail runs close to treeline and offers excellent views back to the north, both to the Yoho Glacier and the upper Waterfall Valley, culminating in the broad expanse of Glacier des Poilus.

The high point of the hike, both in altitude and scenery, comes at the 4.5 kilometre mark, where the trail turns the corner of the Whaleback ridge. Marked by a stone cairn and brass plaque commemorating an avalanche fatality in the area, the viewpoint offers perhaps the most commanding outlook of the Yoho and Little Yoho Valleys of any found on the trails in the region. Many of the

Mount Niles from the Whaleback

nearby peaks visible from the summit —
The President, The Vice President,
Mount Kerr, Mount Pollinger and Isolated Peak, as well as the Whaleback itself
— were named by the British mountaineer Edward Whymper when he visited
the area in 1901.

From the viewpoint, the trail descends
rapidly (300 vertical metres in 2.1 kilometres) to join the Highline Trail. This is the
southern end of the Whaleback traverse,
and here the hiker who wishes to follow
the Highline or Little Yoho Valley trails
will turn west, while the east branch leads
down to the Yoho River or back around
to Twin Falls via Marpole Lake.

265

Hamilton Lake

Day trip

Allow 2-3 hours one way

Elevation gain: 850 metres (2,800 feet)

Maximum elevation: 2150 metres (7,050 feet)

Topo maps: Golden 82 N/7

Point of Departure: From its junction with the Trans Canada Highway 2.6 kilometres (1.6 miles) west of Field, follow the Emerald Lake Road north 8 kilometres (5 miles) to its termination at the Emerald Lake parking area. The trail sign is located at the entrance to the parking area on the west side of the road.

0.0—Trail sign (1300 m).

0.2—Junction. Emerald River trail to left. Keep straight ahead.

—Moderate uphill through forest.

0.8—Hamilton Falls.

—Steady switchbacking ascent.

3.9—Emerald Lake viewpoint.

—Grade moderates.

5.5—Hamilton Lake (2150 m).

A steep trail running up densely forested slopes leads to a small tarn tucked away in a hanging valley between Mount Carnarvon and Emerald Peak. While Hamilton Lake is one of the park's most interesting and enjoyable day trips, most hikers in the Emerald Lake area miss it entirely—a factor which enhances its appeal.

The trail to Hamilton Lake leads west from Emerald Lake and into a mature subalpine forest where Hamilton Falls is encountered within 800 metres. Dropping over a steep limestone cliff in a series of steps, the action of the water has smoothed and dissolved the bedrock to form many pothole depressions. A short distance up the main trail, at a point where it switches back, there is an excellent view of the upper falls as well.

The route is closed-in and arduous beyond the falls, and not until the four kilometre mark does the forest open briefly to disclose a view of Emerald Lake far below. Beyond the overlook the grade moderates somewhat and the trail emerges onto open slopes overlooking the Kicking Horse Valley.

Just as the hiker has relegated himself to another half-hour or so of steep slogging, the trail cuts upward and into the Hamilton Lake cirque. Beautiful as it is unexpected, Hamilton Lake extends to the very lip of its amphitheatre, its water riffled by the occasional down-slope breeze. By stepping across the outlet stream, one can continue along the lake's western shore to a pleasant knoll which provides views back through the cirque's entrance to the Kicking Horse Valley and the mountains beyond. Rising in the distance are the glacier-capped summit of Mount Vaux and the twin towers of Mount Goodsir—the highest mountain in Yoho Park.

Hamilton Lake is named for R. A. Hamilton, an assistant engineer with the CPR who was in charge of trail building in Yoho Park before World War I.

Hamilton Lake and Mount Carnarvon

Emerald Basin

Emerald Lake to Emerald Basin—4.3 kilometres (2.7 miles)

Half-day trip

Allow 1½-2 hours one way

Elevation gain: 300 metres (1,000 feet)

Maximum elevation: 1600 metres (5,250 feet)

Topo maps: Golden 82 N/7

Point of Departure: From its junction with the Trans-Canada Highway 2.6 kilometres (1.6 miles) west of Field, follow the Emerald Lake Road north 8 kilometres (5 miles) to its termination at the Emerald Lake parking area. The trail follows the lakeshore path from the north edge of the parking area.

0.0—Emerald Lake parking area (1300 m).

—Trail follows along west shore of lake.

1.4—Junction. Lakeshore trail branches right. Keep left.

1.6—Junction. Emerald Basin trail branches to left.

—Short, steep climb.

4.3—Emerald Basin (1600 m).

Emerald Basin is a tiny, natural amphitheatre set within the rugged cliffs of the President Range. The route to this rocky pocket is short and pleasant, following the popular Emerald Lake shoreline trail, and then ascending to the basin through a moist, western slope forest on an old climber's access trail. Despite being so near the bustle of Emerald Lake, the basin is seldom visited and makes an excellent place to spend a peaceful afternoon.

From the Emerald Lake parking area, follow the trail north along the west shore of the lake. At a junction near the north end of the lake, where the lakeshore trail turns right, stay left on the Yoho Pass route. At Kilometre 1.6, on the edge of a large, alluvial fan, the trail to the Emerald Basin branches left from the main trail. There is a short, steep climb through a mini-rain forest of Douglas fir, Engelmann spruce and western red cedar as the trail works its way northwest toward the basin, but the grade moderates after this initial pitch.

Though the basin is well below timberline, avalanches have cleared away much of the forest cover from the surrounding slopes (the snow from these winter slides, laced with forest debris, often lingers until mid-summer). Views are open to the surrounding peaks, including the impressive south ridge of The President, a 760 metre wall of limestone looming above the basin to the north.

The Emerald Basin trail also serves as a mountaineer's access route to the President Range — a collection of heavily glaciated peaks which has been a popular climbing area for nearly a century. In fact, the first visit to the Emerald Basin was probably made in the summer of 1901 when the British alpinist Edward Whymper and his Swiss guide Christian Klucker traversed nearby President Pass on their way from the Little Yoho Valley to Emerald Lake.

Emerald River

Day trip

Allow 2-3 hours one way

Elevation loss: 140 metres (450 feet)

Maximum elevation: 1300 metres (4,250 feet)

Topo maps: Golden 82 N/7

Point of Departure: From its junction with the Trans-Canada Highway 2.6 kilometres (1.6 miles) west of Field, follow the Emerald Lake Road north 8 kilometres (5 miles) to its termination at the Emerald Lake parking area. The hike starts out on the Hamilton Lake trail at the entrance to the parking area on the west side of the road.

0.0—Trail sign (1300 m).

0.2—Junction. Hamilton Lake trail continues straight ahead. Turn left for Emerald River.

—Flat to gradual downhill through forest.

2.5—Trail comes abreast of Emerald River.

5.9—Junction. Old trail to Kiwetinok River branches right. Keep straight ahead.

6.0—Junction. Fire road trail branches left and crosses river bridge to Emerald Lake Road (1.0 km).

7.7—Amiskwi Fire Road (1160 m). Trail emerges on access road 200 metres east of Amiskwi River Picnic Area and 1.5 kilometres west of the Natural Bridge junction on the Emerald Lake Road.

For those who can arrange transportation between Emerald Lake and the Amiskwi Picnic Area, the 7.7 kilometre trail which runs along the Emerald River makes a very pleasant, downhill nature walk. Since the trail is enclosed by dense forest throughout its length, views are very limited. But the peacefulness of the scene, the proximity of the river, and the opportunity to study the flora of this unusually lush valley, should more than compensate for the lack of mountain vistas.

Starting the trail from the Emerald Lake end gives a very slight elevation advantage. From the parking lot at Emerald Lake, the hike sets off on the Hamilton Lake trail, but branches left on a well-trod horse trail after only 200 metres. This trail runs due south from Emerald Lake for over two kilometres before it comes abreast of the Emerald River. For the remainder of the journey it is never far from the west bank of the river.

As the trail makes its gradual descent along the river, there may be some wet and boggy areas, particularly where corduroy has not been maintained, but the track is always well defined. At Kilometre 5.9, the old trail to Kiwetinok River branches right, and 100 metres beyond, a broad trail intersects from the east via a bridged crossing of the Emerald River (for those who would make a shorter trip, it is only one kilometre to the Emerald Lake Road via this old fire road). The Emerald River trail continues south, staying on the west side of the river.

The trail finally emerges onto a gravel access road between the Emerald and Amiskwi River bridges, only 200 metres east of the Amiskwi Picnic Area (a good parking area for a vehicle drop-off). From this intersection, it is 1.5 kilometres back to the Emerald Lake Road at the Natural Bridge. (See *Amiskwi River* trail description for detailed access instructions to this end of the trail.)

Amiskwi River

Backpack

Allow 2 days to Amiskwi Pass

Elevation gain: 820 metres (2,700 feet)

Maximum elevation: 1980 metres (6,500 feet)

Topo maps: Golden 82 N/7
Blaeberry River 82 N/10

Point of Departure: From its junction with the Trans-Canada Highway 2.6 kilometres (1.6 miles) west of Field, follow the Emerald Lake Road north 1.5 kilometres (0.9 mile) to the Natural Bridge. Turn left and follow the gravel road that leads west from the edge of the Natural Bridge parking area. Continue on this access road 1.8 kilometres to the Amiskwi River bridge and picnic area.

0.0—Amiskwi Picnic Area (1160 m).

—Road splits. Kicking Horse Fire Road branches left. Keep right on Amiskwi Fire Road.

0.2—Access gate.

—Steady climb to west on broad, well-graded fire road.

15.0—Fire Creek.

17.0—Otto Creek Warden Cabin and campground.

24.0—Amiskwi River bridge. Campground.

29.0—End of fire road.

31.5—Amiskwi Falls.

35.5—Amiskwi Pass (1980 m).

* All distances approximate.

The trail to Amiskwi Pass constitutes one of the longest and most remote wilderness trips in Yoho Park. Despite following along an old access road for some 29 kilometres and passing through large sections of burned-over valley, the trip is peaceful and scenic. Views are open to the surrounding mountains, and the road-sides are thick with the magenta blooms of fireweed in midsummer. And for those who would travel north beyond Yoho Park along the Great Divide, Amiskwi Pass provides the only reasonable route.

The access road strikes off from a picnic area beside the Amiskwi River and climbs steadily for two kilometres before levelling off above the river. This well graded road was created by the last commercial logging operation in the mountain parks (operations ceased in 1968), and old mill sites and log storage areas are still in evidence at several points in the valley.

Beyond Fire Creek, the road makes a steady descent back to the river and crosses a bridge to the east side. Continuing north, it rolls through both burned and unburned sections of forest to end at an old mill site approximately four kilometres beyond the bridge. Now the route becomes an actual trail as it proceeds upvalley. Amiskwi Falls can be seen high up on the shoulder of the valley's eastern wall near Kilometre 31.0. Soon the trail crosses the headwaters of the Amiskwi (a small tributary creek) and enters the unburned forest on Amiskwi Pass. Views from the pass are limited, but an ascent of the long ridge northeast of the summit, reveals the ice-clad Mummery Group in all its splendour.

Backpackers continuing north to the Blaeberry Valley and Howse Pass, should search for trail on the east slope of the valley just beyond the pass (watch for flagging). Once you find it, this track will lead you down to the Blaeberry logging road near the mouth of Collie Creek.

Otterhead River

Day trip or backpack

Allow 5-6 hours to Tocher Ridge Lookout

Elevation gain: 975 metres (3,200 feet)

Maximum elevation: 2135 metres (7,000 feet)

Topo maps: Golden 82 N/7

Point of Departure: From its junction with the Trans-Canada Highway 2.6 kilometres (1.6 miles) west of Field, follow the Emerald Lake Road north 1.5 kilometres (0.9 mile) to the Natural Bridge. Turn left and follow the gravel road that leads west from the edge of the Natural Bridge parking area. Continue on this access road 1.8 kilometres to the Amiskwi River bridge and picnic area.

0.0—Amiskwi Picnic Area (1160 m).

—Road splits. Amiskwi Fire Road branches right. Keep left on Kicking Horse Fire Road.

—Flat travel over old fire road.

4.5—Junction. Kicking Horse Fire Road branches left. Keep right on Otterhead Fire Road.

—Old road runs northwest along Otterhead River.

11.0—Junction. Otterhead Fire Road continues to left. Turn right for Tocher Ridge.

—Steady, switchbacking climb over old, overgrown access road.

16.4—Tocher Ridge Lookout Site (2135 m).

* All distances approximate.

The trail up the Otterhead Valley utilizes an old fire road which served two fire lookouts, one on Mount King and the other on Tocher Ridge. Today, the lookouts are abandoned, and the road is unmaintained and slowly being reclaimed by the lush vegetation of the valley. Yet, the Otterhead remains an interesting area for experienced backpackers who want to get away from it all, and Tocher Ridge provides an outstanding vantage point for the southern half of Yoho Park.

The first section of the route follows the Kicking Horse Fire Road south from the Amiskwi Picnic Area, crossing the sparsely forested, alluvial flats which border the west side of the Kicking Horse River. At the mouth of the Otterhead Valley, the Otterhead Fire Road branches right from the Kicking Horse route and begins its ascent of this narrow, heavily forested valley.

The fire road up the Otterhead is carved from a steep side-slope, so it is prone to washouts, mudslides and brushy overgrowth, obstacles which may cause hikers minor inconvenience. Along the way, the old trail to the Mount King Lookout branches left, but a ford of the Otterhead is required, followed by much scrambling through deadfall on this long-abandoned trail. At the 11.0 kilometre mark, the Tocher Ridge trail branches right from the Otterhead route (the Otterhead Fire Road ends a short distance beyond).

From the Otterhead junction, the route up Tocher Ridge climbs 610 vertical metres over the next 5.4 kilometres, following yet another access road which is overgrown by heavy vegetation for nearly half its distance to the crest of the ridge. From the lookout, portions of every mountain range in Yoho Park are visible, most prominent being the nearby President, Van Horne, and Ottertail Ranges.

271

Mount Hunter Lookout

Trans-Canada Highway to Mount Hunter Lookout—3.5 kilometres (2.2 miles)

Half-day trip

Allow 2 hours one way

Elevation gain: 400 metres (1,310 feet)

Maximum elevation: 1525 metres (5,000 feet)

Topo maps: McMurdo 82 N/2

Point of Departure: Follow the Trans-Canada Highway to the junction with the Wapta Falls access road, which branches south from the highway 5 kilometres (3 miles) east of Yoho Park West Gate or 25 kilometres (15½ miles) west of Field. Park just inside the entrance to the Wapta Falls access road and walk back across the Trans-Canada to the Mount Hunter Lookout trail sign.

0.0—Trail sign (1125 m).

0.3—Cross railroad track.

—Steady uphill through forest.

0.8—Open views next 2 kms.

2.7—Steep climb back into forest.

3.5—Mount Hunter Lookout (1525 m).

Despite its relatively short length and low elevation, the trail to Mount Hunter fire lookout is surprisingly rewarding. There are open views across the Kicking Horse Valley throughout most of the climb, and the dry western slope cover of Douglas fir and juniper found on the open ridgeline makes a pleasant change from the usual Rocky Mountain spruce-fir forest.

After crossing the CPR tracks and climbing for a short distance through a closed forest, the trail breaks out onto the crest of a ridge which leads upwards at a steady grade to the lookout tower. Here the tree cover and vegetation alter dramatically as the predominant spruce forest of the northeast slope is replaced by a much more open environment of Douglas fir and Rocky Mountain juniper on the drier southwest exposure. The ground cover is not as verdant either, as common and creeping varieties of juniper spread across the sunny slope.

The trail stays on this open ridge for nearly two kilometres, the sharp drop on the left providing open views to the Beaverfoot Range and Valley. At Kilometre 2.7 the hiker reenters a more closed forest to make the final steep climb to the lookout tower.

Beneath the fire lookout, the Beaverfoot Valley again dominates the scene. The river serves as the boundary between Yoho Park and provincial forest lands, as evidenced by the steady procession of clearcuts running southward along the slope of the Beaverfoot Range—one of the most poorly managed timber operations in all of British Columbia. More inspiring is the view to the east—the rugged summits of Chancellor Peak (3280 m) and Mount Vaux (3320 m).

Kicking Horse and Beaverfoot Valleys from Mount Hunter Lookout

Ice River

Hoodoos Parking Area to Upper Ice River Cabin—25.2 kilometres (15.7 miles)

Backpack

Allow 2 days to Upper Ice River

Elevation gain: 375 metres (1,200 feet)

Maximum elevation: 1495 metres (4,900 feet)

Topo maps: McMurdo 82 N/2
            Mount Goodsir 82 N/1

Point of Departure: Follow the Trans-Canada Highway to the Hoodoo Creek Campground, located 22½ kilometres (14 miles) west of Field, or 7 kilometres (4½ miles) east of the Yoho Park West Gate. Follow the paved access road 0.6 kilometre to the campground entrance. Branch right just before the entrance and follow the gravel road leading south 0.4 kilometre to the Hoodoos Trail parking area. The Ice River Fire Road begins at the locked access gate to the right of the parking area.

0.0—Access gate (1120 m).

    —Flat fire road through heavy forest and along swampy meadowlands.

6.0—Steep Creek.

10.0—Tallon Creek and warden cabin.

18.8—Lower Ice River Warden Cabin (1280 m). End of fire road.

    —Trail crosses Ice River.

19.0—Junction. Kootenay River trail intersects from right. Keep left for Ice River.

21.2—Mollison Creek.

24.4—Sodalite Creek.

25.2—Upper Ice River Warden Cabin.

27.2—End of trail (1495 m).

Situated on the southern boundary of Yoho Park, the Ice River is yet another low elevation valley that is somewhat short on scenery but long on peace and solitude. For the amateur geologist, the valley offers the bonus of being in the centre of the most significant intrusive igneous complex in the Canadian Rockies.

The first 18.8 kilometres of the journey to the Ice River is over a relatively flat, well-graded fire road which follows along the eastern side of the Beaverfoot River. Views open out to the surrounding mountains wherever the road skirts marshy meadows, but generally travel is through heavy timber, including some very impressive western red cedar and Douglas fir stands.

The road ends at the Lower Ice River Warden Cabin. Just beyond, the trail crosses the Ice River and begins its gradual climb along the east side of the valley. The forest in the lower section of the Ice River valley is composed of Douglas fir, spruce, poplar and alder — a rather luxuriant cover created by the area's high annual precipitation. Beyond Mollison Creek, there are views of Mount Ennis, Hanbury Peak, and the Hanbury Glacier at the head of the valley.

The trail stays on the east (true left) side of the river all the way to the Upper Ice River Warden Cabin at Kilometre 25.2. Beyond the cabin, a faint, overgrown track continues for another two kilometres or so before it fizzles away completely near Zinc Creek. For anyone planning an exploration of the valley, the upper cabin is a good place for a base camp.

The igneous intrusions into the sedimentary strata of the southernmost peaks of the Ottertail Range are unique in the Canadian Rockies. The valley was first explored by the geologist George M. Dawson in 1883, and by the turn of the century miners were working the zinc deposits which occur along the valley's eastern slope.

Short Hikes and Nature Trails

ROSS LAKE — 1.3 kilometres

The short hike to Ross Lake is unexpectedly rewarding for the small amount of time and effort expended in getting there. Set within a beautiful amphitheatre carved from the rugged walls of the Great Divide, this subalpine gem is seldom visited by the hordes frequenting the trails of nearby Lake Louise.

The trail sign is located on the south side of the 1-A Highway 0.9 kilometre (0.6 mile) west of the Great Divide picnic area (Alberta-B.C. boundary), or 2.0 kilometres (1.2 miles) east of the road's junction with the Trans-Canada Highway. The first half of the trail travels over old fire road and through a mature subalpine forest of Engelmann spruce, lodgepole pine and alpine fir. The last 600 metres follows foot trail. The lake lies in a textbook example of a glacially carved cirque. Mount Niblock contains the lake on the east, while the long north ridge of Narao Peak forms its western shore. Vertical cliffs and a steep talus slope serve as its backdrop. *Topo map: Lake Louise 82 N/8.*

ADELINE LINK CIRCUIT (LAKE O'HARA) — 2.8 kilometres

The Adeline Link Circuit is the 2.8 kilometre footpath that circumnavigates the Lake O'Hara shoreline. Dr. George Link and his wife Adeline, along with a few other Lake O'Hara regulars, began work on the trail in 1943. Adeline died of a stroke the following autumn at her home in Chicago, and the trail was dedicated to her memory in 1946. As one might expect, this walk along the shore of one of the Rockies' most beautiful lakes is a very special experience. It is a favourite evening stroll for anyone staying at Lake O'Hara.

After travelling to Lake O'Hara (see *Lake O'Hara* near introduction, page 234), the hiker can walk the lakeshore circuit clockwise from the Cataract Creek bridge (the lake's outlet) at the northwest corner of the lake or counterclockwise from the Lake O'Hara Lodge. Starting from the outlet bridge, follow the trail as it leads east along the north shoreline. The trails to Wiwaxy Gap and Lake Oesa branch away from the lake at the 0.2 and 0.8 kilometre marks respectively. At Kilometre 1.2, the lakeshore path passes beneath the beautiful Seven Sisters Falls. Along the south shore of the lake, the Opabin Plateau East and West Circuits branch away from the lakeshore trail at Kilometres 1.8 and 2.1. Lake O'Hara Lodge is reached at Kilometre 2.4, and from there it is a short, 400 metre walk along the access road back to the northwest corner of the lake. *Topo map: Lake Louise 82 N/8.*

MOUNT STEPHEN FOSSIL BEDS — 2.7 kilometres

This short but very steep trail rises from the village of Field to a shale bed on the west slope of Mount Stephen containing a variety of Cambrian fossils —the remains and imprints of primitive animals which lived under a tepid sea 500 million years ago.

To reach the trail head, follow the Trans-Canada Highway to Field, crossing the Kicking Horse River and railroad tracks to the village proper. Find 1st Street East and follow it uphill to the edge of town. A trail sign near a major stream indicates the beginning of the hike. The trail is a straightforward slog up through a forest of white spruce, Douglas fir, lodgepole pine and a few birch. The fossil beds are reached on an open slope of thinly bedded shale. In addition to the interesting browsing available in the fossil beds, this slope offers fine views back to the Kicking Horse Valley and Mount Burgess. Allow the better part of a day for this trip, since the trail is one of the steepest and most arduous in Yoho Park. And remember, it is illegal to remove geological specimens in a national park; please leave the fossils for others to enjoy. *Topo map: Lake Louise 82 N/8.*

EMERALD LAKE CIRCUIT — 5.0 kilometres

This flat trail running around the shoreline of Emerald Lake requires no more than a couple of hours of easy walking, though dedicated naturalists will probably spend at least a half-day. It is a surprisingly scenic route, with many open views to Mount Burgess and the President Range, and an excellent place to study the vegetation of a very mild and moist western slope forest environment.

From its junction with the Trans Canada Highway 2.6 kilometres (1.6 miles) west of Field, follow the Emerald Lake Road north 8 kilometres (5 miles) to its termination at the Emerald Lake parking area. The lakeshore trail starts from the north end of the parking area, beside the bridge leading to the lodge, and runs along the west shoreline for over a kilometre. A major avalanche slope is crossed at Kilometre 0.5, where there is a classic view across the lake to Mount Burgess and the lodge area. At Kilometre 1.4, the lakeshore trail branches right from the Yoho Pass route and skirts around the north end of the lake. Following back along the west side of the lake, the trail runs through a very heavy forest of Engelmann spruce with a scattering of western red cedar. The Burgess Pass trail junction is passed at Kilometre 3.9, and from this junction it is only 1.1 kilometres along the lake's southern shore to the lodge. (Watch for a cut-off trail 300 metres before the lodge which leads directly to the parking area.) *Topo map: Golden 82 N/7.*

HOODOOS — 3.1 kilometres

A short but steep trail climbs into a narrow mountain valley wherein stand some of the most exceptional hoodoo formations to be found in the mountain parks. These sentinel-like pillars of silt and gravel have been formed by erosion, which has eaten away at a bank of partly consolidated, calcareous glacial debris; cap rocks on top of the pillars help protect the material beneath from these erosive forces.

.Follow the Trans-Canada Highway to the Hoodoo Creek Campground, located 22½ kilometres (14 miles) west of Field, or 7 kilometres (4½ miles) east of the Yoho Park West Gate. Follow the paved access road 0.6 kilometre to the campground entrance. Branch right just before the entrance and follow the gravel road leading south 0.4 kilometre to the Hoodoos Trail parking area. The trail circles around the campground through a lodgepole pine-white spruce forest and eventually arrives at the Hoodoo Creek bridge at Kilometre 1.5. (Campers can reach this point from the rear of the campground.) After this flat forest prelude, the last 1.6 kilometres of trail are steep and rigorous as they ascend the north slope of the Hoodoo Creek valley. At the Hoodoos, the trail splits, with the right-hand path running to the base of these formations and the left branch climbing to a good viewpoint above. Chancellor Peak is the dramatic mountain rising above the valley to the southeast. *Topo map: McMurdo 82 N/2.*

WAPTA FALLS — 2.4 kilometres

The Wapta Falls hike makes a very good afternoon family outing — it is short, the trail is well-marked and, with the exception of a rather steep descent to the lower viewpoint beside the Kicking Horse River, almost level. The objective of the hike is the largest waterfall (for volume of water) in Yoho Park and certainly worth the small amount of effort that goes into the walk.

To reach the trail head, follow the Trans-Canada Highway to the junction with the Wapta Falls access road, which branches south from the highway 5 kilometres (3 miles) east of Yoho Park West Gate, or 25 kilometres (15½ miles) west of Field. The parking area is located at the end of this dirt access road, 1.6 kilometres (1 mile) from the highway. The trail follows an old access road for a bit over 1.1 kilometres before narrowing to a single file path. The forest here is composed of lodgepole pine, white spruce and aspen poplar; a concentration of ferns and Douglas maple makes a dense undergrowth. Forty-five minutes of easy walking brings the hiker to the Wapta Falls upper viewpoint. At this point the trail veers to the right and begins a steep descent to the lower viewpoint, where it is possible to fully appreciate the flow of the Kicking Horse River over this 30 metre ledge. *Topo map: McMurdo 82 N/2.*

Kootenay National Park

Kootenay National Park, bounded on the north by Yoho National Park and on the east by Banff National Park and Mount Assiniboine Provincial Park, is a 1,406 square kilometre tract of rugged mountains and beautiful rivers. The park's east and west boundaries parallel the twists and turns of the Banff-Radium Parkway as it makes its way south and west from the continental divide at Vermilion Pass to Radium, British Columbia, a distance of 94 kilometres.

Of the four contiguous mountain national parks, Kootenay is the least known as a hiking park, but it is a mistake to believe it holds little for the person interested in foot travel. There are over 200 kilometres of trail in Kootenay Park, ranging from a variety of day and half-day trips along the course of the Banff-Radium Highway to the challenging and extremely scenic backpacking trails in the park's northwest corner. For the casual hiker with limited time there are several very short nature walks, some self-guided, such as the Paint Pots and Marble Canyon trails. Slightly longer routes, such as Dog Lake, Cobb Lake, Stanley Glacier and Kindersley Pass, provide scenic half-day and day hikes.

A number of excellent possibilities exist for the backpacker. The Floe Lake, Numa Creek, Tumbling Creek and Helmet Creek trails lead from the highway to the spectacular Rockwall escarpment of the Vermilion Range; these trails can be linked together in a variety of ways to make either short loop trips or extended multi-day excursions along the foot of the Rockwall. The Kaufmann Lake trail takes backpackers to a lofty cirque on the southern slope of the Wenkchemna Peaks — the same mountains which create Banff Park's spectacular Valley of the Ten Peaks. And the trail up the Simpson River and Surprise Creek to Ferro Pass is an increasingly popular way of reaching Mount Assiniboine.

Backpackers are required to obtain a park use permit, designating the party's destination, before beginning an overnight trip. All backcountry campsites have a finite number of tent sites, and the park allows only as many parties on a trail as there are sites. It is possible to pre-book a use permit (up to, but not more than, three weeks in advance) by writing the Superintendent, Kootenay National Park, Box 220, Radium, B.C. V0A 1M0. The permits, as well as information concerning trail conditions and campfire restrictions, are available year around from the Kootenay Crossing Warden Station (51½ kilometres southwest of the continental divide and 42½ kilometres northeast of the park gates at Radium) and, during the summer, from the Marble Canyon Information Centre or Warden Station (7 kilometres west of the divide) and the Information Centre just inside the west gate entrance at Radium. Registration for hazardous activities is a voluntary option, but registrants must report back in by the appointed time to prevent a rescue effort by the Park Warden Service.

Radium serves as a service centre for the park and provides the tourist essentials: restaurants, motels, gas stations and grocery stores. Some stores carry a limited selection of hiking and camping supplies. The park administration building, also in Radium, is located on the road to the Redstreak Campground.

Access: The Banff-Radium Parkway provides the only highway access to the park. On the north and east it intersects with the Trans-Canada Highway at Castle Junction in Banff Park, and to the south and west it connects into Highway 95 at Radium, B.C. The nearest airports serviced by commercial carriers are located in Calgary, Alberta, and at Cranbrook, B.C. (145 kilometres south of Radium). Radium is a stop for Greyhound buses travelling east and west on the southern British Columbia route (access from Calgary and Banff or from Cranbrook and other southern B.C. centres).

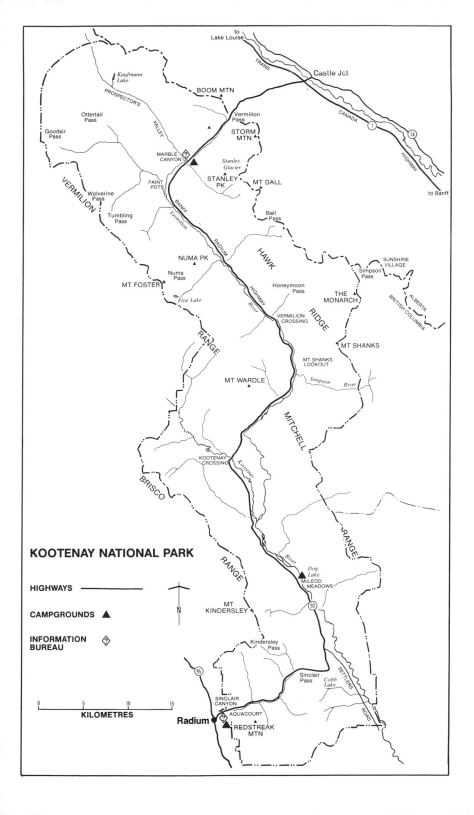

KOOTENAY NATIONAL PARK

HIGHWAYS ————————

CAMPGROUNDS ▲

INFORMATION
BUREAU ◈

0   5   10   15
KILOMETRES

N

Kaufmann
Lake

to
Lake Louise

Castle Jct

BOOM MTN

PROSPECTOR'S

TRANS

Ottertail
Pass

Vermilion
Pass

CANADA

STORM
MTN

1

Goodsir
Pass

VALLEY

MARBLE
CANYON

Stanley
Glacier

1A

HIGHWAY

to Banff

PAINT
POTS

STANLEY
PK

MT DALL

BANFF

Wolverine
Pass

Vermilion

RADIUM

Ball
Pass

VERMILION

Tumbling
Pass

NUMA PK

HAWK

SUNSHINE
VILLAGE

Numa
Pass

Simpson
Pass

MT FOSTER

Floe Lake

HIGHWAY

Honeymoon
Pass

THE
MONARCH

ALBERTA

River

RIDGE

BRITISH COLUMBIA

RANGE

VERMILION
CROSSING

MT SHANKS

MT SHANKS
LOOKOUT

MT WARDLE

Simpson   River

MITCHELL

KOOTENAY
CROSSING

Kootenay

BRISCO

RANGE

River

RANGE

Dog
Lake
McLEOD
MEADOWS

MT
KINDERSLEY

93

Kindersley
Pass

95

Sinclair
Pass

Cobb
Lake

SETTLERS

SINCLAIR
CANYON

Radium ●

AQUACOURT

REDSTREAK
MTN

ROAD

Stanley Glacier

Banff-Radium Highway to Stanley Glacier Basin—4.2 kilometres (2.6 miles)

Day trip

Allow 1½ - 2 hours one way

Elevation gain: 365 metres (1,200 feet)

Maximum elevation: 1950 metres (6,400 feet)

Topo maps: Mount Goodsir 82 N/1

Point of Departure: Follow the Banff—Radium Highway (Hwy 93) to the Stanley Glacier parking area, situated on the southeast side of the highway 3.2 kilometres (2.0 miles) west of the Banff—Kootenay Park boundary at Vermilion Pass. The trail begins at the Vermilion River bridge immediately below the parking area.

0.0—Vermilion River bridge (1585 m).

—Trail switchbacks up through old burn.

2.4—Stanley Creek bridge.

—Steady climb into open basin.

4.2—Stanley Glacier Basin (1950 m).

This 4.2 kilometre trail offers an easy half-day trip which carries the hiker up the southeast slope of the Vermilion River valley and into a beautiful hanging valley, the far end of which supports the slowly retreating ice of the Stanley Glacier. The trail is usually free of snow in early June, and the hike is very pleasant in the spring and early summer when wildflowers blanket the trailside from beginning to end.

After crossing the Vermilion River, the trail rises steadily for over two kilometres through the charred and weathered spars of a forest which was swept by fire in 1968. Lodgepole pine trees have since recolonized and grown to a substantial height, but the slope remains open and sunny enough to support an interesting variety of plants, such as fireweed, yellow columbine, heart-leaved arnica and Labrador tea.

Slightly over two kilometres from the river the trail crosses Stanley Creek. At this crossing the hiker leaves the burn behind and enters the subalpine forest of the Stanley Glacier basin. Off to the right is an imposing face of Cambrian limestone which rises over 450 metres to form the southern wall of the valley and the lower slopes of Stanley Peak. In the early spring dozens of waterfalls cascade down the length of the face, adding much to its carved beauty. Ahead one catches glimpses of the glacier through the thinning forest.

The trail runs gently up the valley for more than a kilometre, following the edge of the creek and a cool, green remnant of Engelmann spruce and alpine fir which was spared by the fire. The last few hundred metres of well-defined trail climb a rocky, sparsely forested slope before ending atop an old moraine in the midst of the basin's boulder fields.

Though the moraine is a fine viewpoint for the valley and makes a pleasant lunch-stop, hikers may continue on for another

Stanley Glacier

kilometre or so, following snippets of trail and cairns, to the larch and fir-topped plateau at the head of the valley (keep to the right-hand side of the valley). Though it is a stiff climb over broken rock (snowfields in early summer), the stream-fed meadow atop the cliff provides an outstanding viewpoint for the toe of the Stanley Glacier. Along the way, watch for the hoary marmots, pikas and ptarmigan which make their home in this rocky amphitheatre.

Look for a pair of small caves at the base of the Stanley Peak cliff about half-way between the end of the trail and the upper plateau (approximately 100 metres beyond the major waterfall which spills over the cliff). These shallow caverns, which can be reached after a short climb up a talus slope, were dissolved from the wall at a time when Stanley Glacier filled this basin. Inside you will find the abundant droppings of the cave inhabitants, little brown bats.

Kaufmann Lake

Banff-Radium Highway to Kaufmann Lake—15.0 kilometres (9.3 miles)

Backpack

Allow 4½ - 6 hours to Kaufmann Lake

Elevation gain: 570 metres (1,870 feet)

Maximum elevation: 2060 metres (6,750 feet)

Topo maps: Mount Goodsir 82 N/1
Lake Louise 82 N/8

Point of Departure: Follow the Banff—Radium Highway (Hwy 93) to the Marble Canyon parking area, situated on the north side of the highway 7 kilometres (4½ miles) west of the Banff—Kootenay Park boundary at Vermilion Pass. The trail starts from the upper parking area above the information bureau.

0.0—Marble Canyon parking lot (1490 m).

—Follows old road track above Marble Canyon.

1.6—Trail narrows to single track.

3.2—Trail emerges onto open flats beside Tokumm Creek.

—Gradual to moderate uphill along creek.

8.5—Tributary stream bridge.

10.3—Tributary stream bridge.

10.4—Junction. Fay Hut to right 2.4 kms. Keep straight ahead.

12.2—Landslide area.

13.2—Tributary stream bridges.

13.5—Trail begins steep switchbacking climb to Kaufmann cirque.

14.7—Grade moderates.

15.0—Kaufmann Lake and campground (2060 m).

Prospector's Valley is one of the more rewarding backpacking areas in Kootenay Park, and most trips up this relatively long wilderness valley usually end at Kaufmann Lake. It is truly a classic Canadian Rockies lake, a beautifully shaped and coloured body of water cradled by the towering, glacier-mantled Wenkchemna Peaks — the same mountains that form the backdrop to Banff's Moraine Lake.

Beyond the Marble Canyon trail head, the route runs northwest in the form of an old access road. In less than two kilometres, the road ends and a single file path begins working its way through a dense coniferous forest of lodgepole pine, Engelmann spruce and alpine fir.

Just beyond the three kilometre mark, the trail opens up onto the valley bottom, and, for some distance, the hiker has good clear meadow walking. For the remainder of the journey up Prospector's Valley, the trail is never far away from the rushing waters of Tokumm Creek, following above its northeastern bank. The valley was named by tourist-explorer Walter Wilcox in 1899, after he discovered an old prospector's camp near its mouth; the name Tokumm apparently comes from the Stoney Indian word for 'red fox.'

The third major tributary encountered breaks into a series of small streams by the time it reaches the trail. While all of these rivulets are bridged, these crossings mark the end of the easy valley bottom hiking, for this is the outlet stream of Kaufmann Lake and there is a steep 1.5 kilometre climb ahead.

At the 15 kilometre mark, the hiker emerges onto the shore of Kaufmann Lake. Deltaform Mountain (3424 m), Mount Tuzo (3249 m) and Mount Allen (3301 m) provide the immediate setting for the lake, and the combination of rock, ice and water make the spot one of the loveliest in Kootenay Park. Occasionally

Kaufmann Lake and the Wenkchemna Peaks

mule deer are seen along the shore, browsing among the yellow columbine, red Indian paintbrush, white fringed grass-of-parnassus and purple asters which colour the meadows into late August.

Fay Hut. Located on the south slope of the Wenkchemna Peaks, above the Prospector's Valley, this one room log cabin was the first climber's hut constructed by the Alpine Club of Canada (1927). Immediately after crossing the second major Tokumm Creek tributary at Kilometre 10.3, the spur trail to the Fay Hut branches up to the right. The trail climbs steeply along the west side of the stream, and then, near the 1830 metre level, it crosses to the east side and angles up and away from the tributary. The trail becomes less defined with altitude, working its way up through cliff bands via steep scree and talus to finally emerge at the well-hidden cabin, some 2.5 kilometres from the Tokumm Creek junction. The cabin is open to the general public (a camping permit is required), and, generally speaking, it is overrun by hikers and packrats.

Helmet Creek—Goodsir Pass

Banff-Radium Highway to Helmet Falls Campground—14.9 kilometres (9.3 miles)
Banff-Radium Highway to Goodsir Pass—18.3 kilometres (11.4 miles)

Backpack

Allow 6 hours to Helmet Falls

Elevation gain: 760 metres (2,500 feet)

Maximum elevation: 2210 metres (7,250 feet)

Topo maps: Mount Goodsir 82 N/1

Point of Departure: Follow the Banff—Radium Highway (Hwy 93) to the Paint Pots parking area, located on the north side of the highway 9½ kilometres (6 miles) west of the Banff—Kootenay Park boundary at Vermilion Pass and 84 kilometres (52 miles) north of the Kootenay Park West Gate at Radium. The trail starts from the sign at the lower edge of the parking lot.

0.0—Paint Pots parking area (1450 m).

—Follows the Paint Pots nature trail across the Vermilion River suspension bridge and through the ochre beds.

1.0—Trail enters forest beyond last ochre spring.

1.3—Junction. Trail from Marble Canyon (3.2 kms) intersects from right.

3.7—Junction. *Tumbling Creek* trail branches left. Keep right.

6.0—Junction. Ottertail Pass trail straight ahead. Turn left for Helmet Creek.

6.3—Ochre Creek crossing and campground.

6.5—Helmet Creek suspension bridge.

—Short series of switchbacks followed by gradual uphill along south side of creek.

12.0—Helmet Creek suspension bridge.

14.3—Junction (1760 m). Connects with *Rockwall Trail* at Km 29.6. Helmet Warden Cabin and campground straight ahead 0.6 km. Keep right for Goodsir Pass.

—Moderate uphill on well-graded trail.

18.3—Goodsir Pass (2210 m).

19.9—Kootenay—Yoho Park boundary.

20.7—Begin steep descent.

26.6—Junction. Intersection with *Ottertail River* trail at Km 16.2 (see Yoho Park).

The Helmet Creek trail is a popular route for two reasons: it yields direct access to the northern end of the spectacular Rockwall; and it leads to the base of the impressive, 365 metre Helmet Falls. The trail can be utilized as a beginning or end to extended trips along The Rockwall or as part of a loop hike over Rockwall Pass to Tumbling Creek, or the campgrounds near the falls can be used simply as a base for day trips to the scenic, larch-fringed meadows of Goodsir and Rockwall Passes.

Although it is possible to start the hike from Marble Canyon, the shortest route begins at the Paint Pots parking area. Initially, the route coincides with the Paint Pots Nature Trail, a short, hard-surfaced path traversing Kootenay's unique ochre beds. At the end of the asphalt, hikers cross a few metres of mineral deposits to find the quiet, forested trail they will follow for the rest of the journey.

Bypassing branches to Marble Canyon at Kilometre 1.3 and Tumbling Creek at Kilometre 3.7, the route follows nearly level terrain along the east side of the Ochre Creek valley. At the 6.0 kilometre mark, the trail branches left from the Ottertail Pass route, crosses to the west side of Ochre Creek and, 200 metres farther along, traverses a suspension bridge over Helmet Creek to begin the ascent of the Helmet Valley proper. The trail quickly gains elevation via a series of switchbacks, then climbs along the south side of the creek at a more reasonable grade. A second suspension bridge takes the hiker to the north side of the creek at Kilometre 12.0, and soon the first glimpses of Helmet Falls are attained. At Kilometre 14.3, the trail to Goodsir Pass joins the Helmet Creek trail from the north, and, from this junction, it is less than a kilometre to the Helmet Warden Cabin and campground.

Goodsir Pass

The highlight of any visit to the Helmet Creek headwaters is undoubtedly Helmet Falls and the sheer escarpment of The Rockwall, which encloses the head of the valley; Limestone Peak (2878 m), Helmet Mountain (3138 m) and Sharp Mountain (3049 m) are the three summits that create the massive amphitheatre, and the Sharp Glacier feeds Helmet Falls. By climbing southward to Limestone Summit on The Rockwall Trail, hikers can attain a loftier perspective of the falls, and from there they can continue to Rockwall Pass, Tumbling Creek and points south (see *The Rockwall Trail* and *Tumbling Creek* descriptions).

Goodsir Pass. Goodsir Pass is a high, long, glorious alpine meadow on the boundary between Kootenay and Yoho Parks. It is hiked either as a day trip from the Helmet Creek campgrounds or traversed by backpackers bound for Yoho Park. The trail begins at the 14.3 kilometre junction on the Helmet Creek trail and climbs 450 vertical metres to the pass in just 4.0 kilometres. Despite the rise, the trail is well-routed and well-maintained, and a steady pace will quickly see hikers

to the thinning larch trees at timberline. Once in the pass meadows, one's attention is drawn to the looming, glaciated spires of Sentry Peak (3267 m) and the twin towers of Mount Goodsir (3561 m), the highest mountain in Yoho Park. The northeast exposure of the Goodsirs, from their summits to the gravel flats of Goodsir Creek, is a stunning 1900 metres, or well over a vertical mile!

From the pass, the trail makes a steady descent, mainly through heavy forest, to Goodsir Creek and the Ottertail River in Yoho Park. The Ottertail bridge and the intersection with the Ottertail River trail lie nine kilometres beyond the pass. (See *Ottertail River* in the Yoho Park chapter.)

Ottertail Pass. From its junction with the Helmet Creek trail at Kilometre 6.0, this trail makes a short, steep climb to the long, unremarkable summit of Ottertail Pass. The trail becomes vague as it crosses the extensive willow meadows on the pass, and it disappears completely as it descends the upper Ottertail River into Yoho Park. This is strictly an explorer's route.

Tumbling Creek

Banff-Radium Highway to Tumbling Glacier—12.6 kilometres (7.8 miles)
Banff-Radium Highway to Wolverine Pass—13.3 kilometres (8.3 miles)

Backpack

Allow 3 - 4 hours one way

Elevation gain: 440 metres (1,450 feet)

Maximum elevation: 1890 metres (6,200 feet)

Topo maps: Mount Goodsir 82 N/1

Point of Departure: Follow the Banff—Radium Highway (Hwy 93) to the Paint Pots parking area, located on the north side of the highway 9½ kilometres (6 miles) west of the Banff—Kootenay Park boundary at Vermilion Pass and 84 kilometres (52 miles) north of the Kootenay Park West Gate at Radium. The trail starts from the sign at the lower edge of the parking lot.

0.0—Paint Pots parking area (1450 m).

—Follows the Paint Pots nature trail across Vermilion River suspension bridge and through the ochre beds.

1.0—Trail enters forest beyond last ochre spring.

1.3—Junction. Trail from Marble Canyon (3.2 kms) intersects from right. Keep left for Tumbling Creek.

3.7—Junction. *Helmet Creek* trail continues straight ahead. Turn left for Tumbling Creek.

4.1—Ochre Creek suspension bridge.

4.2—Campground. Ochre Creek—Tumbling Creek confluence.

—Steady climb along north side of Tumbling Creek.

6.6—Tumbling Creek suspension bridge.

9.4—Tumbling Falls viewpoint.

10.3—Junction and campground (1890 m). Intersection with *Rockwall Trail* at Km 17.1. Tumbling Glacier and Pass straight ahead 2.3 kms. Wolverine Pass to right 3.0 kms.

Yet another access route to The Rockwall area is the Tumbling Creek trail. The trail makes a relatively long approach to the head of the Tumbling Valley, from which point either Tumbling Pass or the Wolverine Plateau may be reached in an hour or less. Both areas offer extensive stands of alpine larch and meadows which are filled with wildflowers in July and August. From their summits, other passes are visible north and south, beckoning hikers to further exploration along this impressive escarpment of the Vermilion Range.

The trail follows the Paint Pots Nature Trail for the first kilometre, then enters heavy forest. After joining the trail from Marble Canyon at Kilometre 1.3, the trail runs northwest for 2.4 kilometres, following above the east side of Ochre Creek. At Kilometre 3.7, the Tumbling Creek trail forks down to the left, away from the Helmet Creek route, and crosses Ochre Creek to begin the long ascent of the Tumbling Valley.

Throughout the remainder of the journey, the turbulent waters of Tumbling Creek are a constant companion. A beautiful waterfall is passed at Kilometre 9.4, and, just a kilometre beyond, a trail junction and campground are reached. The junction marks the intersection with The Rockwall Trail highline route, and backpackers will find this camp an excellent base for trips to either Tumbling Pass or the Wolverine Plateau. (Another campground, on the opposite side of the creek, provides additional campsites.)

Tumbling Pass. The final two kilometres to Tumbling Pass are up a series of steep switchbacks, traversing alongside a high terminal moraine deposited by the Tumbling Glacier. As the trail grinds its way upward, views improve on all sides. Tumbling Glacier and the Rockwall rise above the trail to the west, while back to the north, across the Tumbling Valley,

The Rockwall from near Wolverine Pass

are the open meadows leading to the Wolverine Plateau and Rockwall Pass.

From the summit of the pass, the grey, eastern escarpment of The Rockwall snakes away to the south. The high saddle of Numa Pass is visible between the sharp pyramid of Foster Peak on the right and the rounded summit of Numa Mountain to the left. In the foreground, the trail drops away toward the Numa Creek valley, threading its way across a flower-filled meadow. Perhaps, more than any other view in the Canadian Rockies, this vista captures the spirit of trails that "lead ever ever on."

South of the pass, the trail descends to Numa Creek. By continuing along this route, the hiker can return to the Banff-Radium Highway at the Numa Picnic Area or continue south along the Rockwall Trail to Numa Pass and Floe Lake. (See *Numa Creek* and *Rockwall Trail* descriptions.)

Wolverine Plateau. By following The Rockwall Trail north from the Kilometre 10.3 junction, the hiker can reach the open meadows of the Wolverine Plateau after three kilometres of steady climbing. This summit is every bit as scenic as nearby Tumbling Pass, and the meadows are far more extensive.

The term "Rockwall" takes on new meaning here. In fact, it is not until the hiker is directly beneath the gap of Wolverine Pass that he realizes there is a cleft in the 500 metre high wall. A short side trail leads to this gap, where views stretch as far west into British Columbia as the Purcell Range.

Beyond the Wolverine Pass junction, The Rockwall Trail continues through wildflower meadows to the summit of Rockwall Pass and points north. By persevering along this route, it is possible to make a loop trip back to the Paint Pots via Helmet Creek or continue over Goodsir Pass and into Yoho Park. (See *The Rockwall Trail* and *Helmet Creek* descriptions.)

287

Numa Creek

Banff-Radium Highway to Tumbling Glacier—11.2 kilometres (7.0 miles)
Banff-Radium Highway to Numa Pass—13.7 kilometres (8.5 miles)

Day trip or backpack

Allow 2 hours to Rockwall Trail

Elevation gain: 115 metres (380 feet)

Maximum elevation: 1525 metres (5,000 feet)

Topo maps: Mount Goodsir 82 N/1

Point of Departure: Follow the Banff—Radium Highway (Hwy 93) to the Numa Creek Picnic Area, located beside the Vermilion River on the west side of the highway 14 kilometres (8½ miles) south of the Banff—Kootenay Park boundary at Vermilion Pass and 79½ kilometres (49 miles) north of the Kootenay Park West Gate at Radium. From the far end of the picnic area, walk 100 metres to a footbridge across the Vermilion River—the start of the Numa Creek trail.

0.0—Vermilion River bridge (1410 m).

—Trail contours northwest toward Numa Creek valley.

3.0—Numa Creek bridge.

—Trail follows north side of creek at gradual uphill grade.

6.4—Junction (1525 m). Intersection with *Rockwall Trail* at Km 10.0. Tumbling Pass to right 4.8 kms.

While the Numa Creek trail is the shortest route to Tumbling Pass, the elevation gain is greater than the slightly longer Tumbling Creek approach. (The last 4.8 kilometres to the pass climb an excruciating 685 vertical metres.) Views along the trail are limited as well, particularly on the uphill slog, when the hiker is faced with an unending series of switchbacks up an avalanche slope of massive proportions. However, when hiked downhill in conjunction with either the Tumbling Creek or Floe Lake trails, Numa Creek is a quick and interesting alternate route back to the Banff-Radium Parkway.

The trail starts at the Numa Picnic Area, crosses the Vermilion River, and then contours northwest above the river to the mouth of the Numa Creek valley. After entering the gorge, it crosses to the true left bank of Numa Creek and begins its ascent of this narrow, forested valley. The gradual to moderate climb over the next 3.4 kilometres belies the true nature of what awaits the hiker beyond.

The Numa Creek trail intersects The Rockwall Trail at Kilometre 6.4, and regardless of which way you turn (except back the way you came), there is serious work ahead. The left-hand branch leads to Numa Pass in another 7.3 kilometres — a sobering climb of 830 metres, mainly through enclosed subalpine forest; the right-hand option reaches Tumbling Pass in 4.8 kilometres, after the aforementioned grunt up an interminable avalanche slope.

Most hikers who are using this trail as an approach route will be bound for Tumbling Pass. For those misguided souls, the worst ends approximately 1.5 kilometres below the summit, where the uphill grades moderate and the trail emerges from the avalanche slope into pleasant meadows and open stands of Engelmann spruce, alpine fir and larch. (See also *Tumbling Creek, Floe Lake* and *The Rockwall Trail* descriptions.)

Tumbling Pass

Floe Lake

Banff-Radium Highway to Floe Lake—10.5 kilometres (6.5 miles)
Banff-Radium Highway to Numa Pass—13.2 kilometres(8.2 miles)

Day trip or backpack

Allow 3 - 4 hours to Floe Lake

Elevation gain: 715 metres (2,350 feet)

Maximum elevation: 2040 metres (6,700 feet)

Topo maps: Mount Goodsir 82 N/1

Point of Departure: Follow the Banff—Radium Highway (Hwy 93) to the Floe Lake—Hawk Creek parking area, located on the west side of the highway 22½ kilometres (14 miles) south of the Banff—Kootenay Park boundary at Vermilion Pass and 71 kilometres (44 miles) north of the Kootenay Park West Gate at Radium. The trail starts from the sign at the west edge of the parking lot.

0.0—Parking area (1325 m).

—Trail descends to Vermilion River.

0.4—Vermilion River bridge.

—Trail contours northwest to Floe Creek valley.

1.7—Floe Creek suspension bridge.

—Moderate to steep climb along north side of Floe Creek valley.

5.7—Steep switchbacks for 0.3 km.

7.8—Campground.

8.0—Steep switchbacks for next 2 kms.

10.1—Trail levels off.

10.5—Floe Lake and campground (2040 m). Connects with south end of *Rockwall Trail* at Km 0.0. Numa Pass uphill and due north 2.7 kms.

Set beneath a sheer 1000 metre escarpment, a small glacier feeding its pale blue waters, Floe Lake is easily a match for any beauty spot in the Rockies. Above its north shore lies a subalpine forest of alpine larch and fir which grades upward into the tundra of Numa Pass — a summit which looks down upon the Floe Lake environs to provide a sublime view.

The trail to this high cirque begins near the Vermilion River. It crosses the river and, just over a kilometre beyond, joins the Floe Creek drainage, following that narrow valley upwards for the remainder of the journey. Though travel is mainly through a forest of lodgepole pine, spruce and alpine fir, many areas have been swept clean by avalanches along the way.

Occasionally, the hiker catches a glimpse of the imposing Rockwall ahead, and, at Kilometre 7.2, near the top of a short, steep grade, views open back down the Floe Valley to the Ball Range on the eastern horizon. Just 300 metres beyond this viewpoint, the trail enters a mature spruce forest mixed with a few scattered alpine fir. Here the switchbacks begin that carry the hiker up the last two kilometres to the Floe Lake cirque. Water bottles should be filled at this point, for the trail is steep and there is no water until the lake.

Floe Lake is situated near the 2040 metre level, well into the upper subalpine forest zone. Trees along its northern shore are scattered and somewhat stunted, and, in midsummer, many varieties of wildflowers bloom in the surrounding meadows. In the autumn, the golden needles of alpine larch provide a brilliant foreground for the lake, glacier and Rockwall beyond.

The Rockwall is composed of a dark grey Cambrian limestone (Ottertail Formation) and its east-facing cliffs form the backbone of the Vermilion Range for a stretch of nearly 40 kilometres. A small

Floe Lake

glacier clings to the foot of the wall and plunges to the southern edge of the lake; the resulting ice floes give the lake its name. It is interesting to note the lagoon which has been formed by a terminal moraine, the ridge of which actually loops out into the lake, partitioning off a section of its waters.

Numa Pass. For strong day hikers and those backpacking to Floe Lake, the spur trail to Numa Pass is a must. Branching off from the lakeshore trail just before the warden cabin, the trail rises nearly 300 vertical metres in the 2.7 kilometres to the pass. Views from Numa Pass are some of the most expansive offered by any trail in Kootenay Park. Set between Foster Peak (3204 m) on the west and Numa Mountain (2725 m) to the east, it is by far the best viewpoint for Floe Lake and The Rockwall. To the north, set off by sheer walls, limestone pinnacles and hanging glaciers, the long face of The Rockwall runs toward Yoho Park. The sharp snowy mountains to the far north are the

Wenkchemna Peaks, the summits comprising the Valley of the Ten Peaks in Banff National Park.

Floe Lake serves as the southern terminus for The Rockwall Trail — a 30 kilometre highline route which runs northwest along the face of the Vermilion Range escarpment to Helmet Falls. In addition to crossing three high and very scenic passes, the route intersects with three trails running up Numa, Tumbling and Helmet Creeks to provide a variety of hiking itineraries. (See *The Rockwall Trail* description).

Strong day hikers and backpackers can also complete a loop back to the Banff-Radium Parkway by descending the Numa Creek trail north of Numa Pass — an option which emerges at the Numa Picnic Area eight kilometres north of the Floe Lake trail head. Total distance for the Floe Creek-Numa Creek loop is 27 kilometres. (See *Numa Creek* trail description.)

The Rockwall Trail

Floe Lake Parking Area to Lake O'Hara—66.0 kilometres (41.0 miles)

Backpack

Allow 2 days

Maximum elevation: 2355 metres (7,720 feet)

Minimum elevation: 1760 metres (5,780 feet)

Topo maps: Mount Goodsir 82 N/1

Point of Departure: Hike the *Floe Lake* trail to the Floe Lake campground at Km 10.5—the intersection with the south end of the Rockwall Trail. Southbound backpackers can reach the north end of the trail by hiking the *Helmet Creek —Goodsir Pass* trail to the Goodsir Pass junction at Km 14.3.

0.0—Floe Lake (2040 m).

2.7—Numa Pass (2355 m).

3.3—Steep switchbacking descent next 2 kms.

9.5—Campground.

10.0—Junction (1525 m). Intersection with *Numa Creek* trail at Km 6.4. Keep left for Tumbling Pass.

—Steep switchbacking ascent through open avalanche slope.

14.8—Tumbling Pass (2210 m).

—Trail descends along Tumbling Glacier moraine.

17.1—Junction and campground (1890 m). Intersection with *Tumbling Creek* trail at Km 10.3. Turn left across Tumbling Creek bridge for Rockwall Pass.

17.4—Campground.

—Steep switchbacking ascent.

20.5—Junction. Faint branch trail leads left to Wolverine Pass (0.5 km). Wolverine Warden Cabin and campground in meadow to right (0.2 km).

20.9—Rockwall Pass (2240 m).

24.8—Tributary stream bridge (1920 m).

25.8—Limestone Summit (2170 m).

—Steep descent next 3 kms.

29.0—Campground.

29.6—Junction (1760 m). Intersection with *Helmet Creek—Goodsir Pass* trail at Km 14.3.

After outfitter and guide Walter Nixon took him on a trip to the Wolverine Plateau and Tumbling Pass in the early 1920s, H. B. Clow, the president of the Rand McNally map company, proclaimed it the most wonderful alpine trail he had ever ridden. Today, the trail which runs along the eastern escarpment of the Vermilion Range — The Rockwall — is one of the most popular wilderness backpacking trips in the Canadian Rockies.

The 30 kilometre-long trail which runs along the face of The Rockwall from Floe Lake on the south to Helmet Falls on the north is extraordinary for its variety and beauty. It travels beneath massive limestone walls and hanging glaciers, traversing three alpine passes and numerous wildflower-filled meadows. In the spring, waterfalls tumble from the cliffs above, including one of the highest in Canada, Helmet Falls. In autumn, the passes are bathed in the golden foliage of alpine larch.

The only negative feature of this journey, at least for the overburdened backpacker, is that the trail does not contour along the face of the range as many highline routes do, but rather, rises and falls like a roller coaster as it ascends passes and plunges into the intervening valleys. However, each of these valleys has a trail running up it from the Banff-Radium Parkway, allowing the hiker to enter or exit from The Rockwall Trail at a number of points. (See *Floe Lake, Numa Creek, Tumbling Creek* and *Helmet Creek* descriptions.)

Total distance for the complete Rockwall trip, including the Floe Lake and Helmet Creek approaches, is 54 kilometres. Many backpackers extend the trip northward to Lake O'Hara in Yoho Park, however, to make a journey of 66 kilometres. (This extension requires considerable effort in arranging transportation and careful planning to comply with the Lake O'Hara access regulations.)

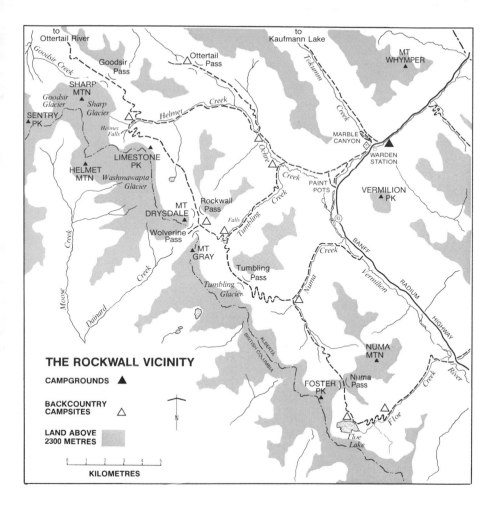

THE ROCKWALL VICINITY

CAMPGROUNDS ▲

**BACKCOUNTRY
CAMPSITES** △

**LAND ABOVE
2300 METRES**

N

0 1 2 3 4 5
KILOMETRES

Hawk Creek

Banff-Radium Highway to Ball Pass—9.7 kilometres (6.0 miles)

Day trip

Allow 3 - 4 hours one way

Elevation gain: 885 metres (2,900 feet)

Maximum elevation: 2210 metres (7,250 feet)

Topo maps: Mount Goodsir 82 N/1

Banff 82 O/4

Point of Departure: Follow the Banff—Radium Highway (Hwy 93) to the Floe Lake—Hawk Creek parking area, situated on the west side of the highway 22½ kilometres (14 miles) south of the Banff—Kootenay Park West Gate at Radium. From the parking area walk back to the main highway and cross to the east side where a well-defined gravel path leads north. Follow this trail beside the highway for 0.4 kilometre to Hawk Creek. Cross the creek using the highway bridge and pick up the trail on the opposite side where it begins the ascent of the Hawk Creek drainage.

0.0—Hawk Creek highway bridge (1325 m).

—Trail runs northeast on old road bed.

0.2—Campground.

0.7—Trail begins to climb along northwest side of canyon.

—Steady ascent at moderate to steep grade.

4.2—Tributary stream bridge.

7.0—Steep switchbacks begin.

8.4—Trail enters subalpine meadow.

—Steep ascent to pass.

9.7—Ball Pass (2210 m). Banff—Kootenay Park boundary. Trail connects with Banff Park's *Shadow Lake—Ball Pass* trail at Km 21.3.

It is amazing how many people day hike to Ball Pass via Hawk Creek. While the pass itself is a scenic defile fringed by alpine larch, the climb up Hawk Creek is relentless, rocky and dry. It is a trail that is better done as a backpack originating from Shadow Lake or Egypt Lake in Banff Park.

The trail starts from the Hawk Creek highway bridge, on the east side of Highway 93 just 400 metres north of the Floe Lake parking area. No sooner does the path leave the highway than it passes a campground, placed in this unlikely spot to serve long distance backpackers hiking through from Banff Park to Floe Lake and the Rockwall. Beyond the campground there is a short stretch of flat walking before the trail begins its ascent of the narrow Hawk Creek valley.

The first few kilometres of trail climb through a pleasant forest and are lined with wild strawberries in late July and early August. But hikers should fill their water bottles at the 4.2 kilometre stream crossing in preparation for the ordeal ahead—a long, steep, waterless traverse across an open, south-facing slope composed of avalanche slopes and massive rockslides. This section is an arid desert on a warm, sunny day, and there is no relief until the stream-fed subalpine meadows just below the pass.

The pass is a narrow notch in the middle of the Ball Range just south of Mount Ball. Rockslides from the slopes above have turned the northern lip of the pass into a rather tumbled and desolate place, but alpine larch and fir interspersed with patches of wildflower meadow command the rest of the summit. Mount Ball with its glacier cap rises above the pass to the north, while the Haiduk Valley stretches away to the northeast.

Banff-bound backpackers will find the first campground of the journey just 2.7 kilometres further along (see Banff Park's *Shadow Lake—Ball Pass* trail description).

Honeymoon Pass

Backpack

Allow 6 - 7 hours to Redearth Pass

Elevation gain: 1145 metres (3,750 feet)
         loss: 320 metres (1,050 feet)

Maximum elevation: 2090 metres (6,850 feet)

Topo maps: Banff 82 O/4†
       †trail not shown

Point of Departure: Follow the Banff—Radium Highway (Hwy 93) to the Vermilion Crossing Lodge, located 30½ kilometres (19 miles) south of the Banff—Kootenay Park boundary at Vermilion Pass and 63 kilometres (39 miles) north of the Kootenay Park West Gate at Radium. Just 200 metres north of the lodge, across the Vermilion River bridge on the east side of the highway, is the parking area for the trail.

0.0—Trail sign (1265 m).

—Trail runs north along highway clearance 50 m then cuts into forest. Steady uphill grade becoming steep switchbacks.

3.7—Uphill grade moderates.

3.9—Open avalanche area.

5.6—Honeymoon Pass (1995 m).

—Steady descent to Verdant Creek.

6.6—Campground.

7.7—Verdant Creek crossing.

—Gradual descent along northeast side of creek. Rough track, boggy.

9.0—Verdant Creek crossing.

11.5—Verdant Creek Warden Cabin and junction (1675 m). Verdant Creek trail continues downvalley. Turn left (northeast) for Redearth Pass and cross Verdant Creek.

—Trail ascends East Verdant Creek drainage. Trail often wet, brushy and indistinct.

18.2—Redearth Pass (2090 m). Banff—Kootenay Park boundary.

18.8—Junction. Intersection with Banff Park's trail to Natalko Lake (see *Egypt Lake* area trips). Natalko Lake to left 1.9 kms. Egypt Lake Shelter and campground straight ahead 2.5 kms.

Except for its role as a direct route from Kootenay Park to the Egypt Lake area of Banff Park, the Honeymoon Pass—Verdant Creek trail has little to recommend it. The grades are steep, the track frequently poor, and there are few open views worthy of mention. It should be reserved for wilderness explorers who enjoy solitude and the challenge of rough track.

The trail to Honeymoon Pass from Vermilion Crossing is a steady, forest-enclosed uphill grind, and views from the pass are limited and certainly not worth the toil of the climb. Beyond the pass the trail makes a quick descent to Verdant Creek and the only designated campground in the valley. Continuing downvalley to the warden cabin, the trail swings across Verdant Creek and back again. The track is wetter and not nearly as well defined as it was in traversing Honeymoon Pass.

From Verdant Creek Warden Cabin, the trail to Redearth Pass branches northeast, immediately crosses Verdant Creek, and begins a rather gruelling ascent of the East Verdant Creek valley. The track is often indistinct, but blazes and markers serve as route-finders in these sections.

Redearth Pass is rather long and undistinguished. At the northern edge of the pass a steep 1.9 kilometre branch trail to Natalko Lake cuts left from a poorly defined junction. Though the lake lies in Kootenay Park, it is usually visited as a day trip from Banff Park's Egypt Lake area, which is only 2.5 kilometres beyond the Redearth Pass junction. There is a campground on Natalko's east shore.

Verdant Creek Option. An old horse trail leads downvalley from the Verdant Creek Warden Cabin, a route which intersects with the Simpson River trail in 10 kilometres. However, the track is not maintained and often disappears for long stretches altogether. It is seldom travelled, even by wardens, and is not recommended.

Simpson River

Banff-Radium Highway to Ferro Pass—22.9 kilometres (14.2 miles)

Backpack

Allow 2 days to Lake Magog

Elevation gain: 1020 metres (3,350 feet)
loss: 105 metres (350 feet)

Maximum elevation: 2270 metres (7,450 feet)

Topo maps: Mount Assiniboine 82 J/13

Point of Departure: Follow the Banff—Radium Highway (Hwy 93) to the Simpson River—Mount Shanks Fire Lookout parking area, located on the east side of the highway beside the Vermilion River 36½ kilometres (22½ miles) south of the Banff—Kootenay Park boundary at Vermilion Pass and 57 kilometres (35½ miles) north of the Kootenay Park West Gate at Radium. Park at the trail sign on the west side of the river, adjacent to a wooden bridge which spans to the east bank.

0.0—Vermilion River bridge (1250 m).

—Follow access road across bridge.

0.2—Junction. Mount Shanks Fire Lookout straight ahead. Keep right for Simpson River.

—Road passes through gravel pit and beside corrals.

0.9—Trail comes abreast of Simpson River.

—Trail follows north side of Simpson Valley at gradual uphill grade.

8.8—Kootenay—Mount Assiniboine Park boundary.

10.9—Junction (1400 m). Simpson River trail continues straight ahead. Turn right and cross suspension bridge for Ferro Pass.

11.0—Surprise Creek Cabin and campground.

—Steep climb next 2½ kms.

18.4—Rock Lake.

19.2—Campground.

—Steady uphill toward pass.

22.9—Ferro Pass (2270 m). Intersection with *Ferro Pass* trail at Km 9.3 (see Assiniboine Park chapter).

32.2—Lake Magog Campground (2165 m).

Other than its value as a pleasant cross-country ski trip in winter, the gentle, forested trail up the Simpson River has little to recommend it. But the trail which branches from the river at Kilometre 10.9 to climb up Surprise Creek and over lofty Ferro Pass is an excellent alternate route to or from the Mount Assiniboine area. The trip over Ferro is long, however, and represents an arduous two day approach to Assiniboine with well over 1000 metres total elevation gain, so the trail might be preferred as an exit rather than approach route.

Beginning at a wooden vehicle bridge across the Vermilion River, the trail works its way south via an old access road to open flats adjacent to the confluence of the Vermilion and Simpson Rivers. From there it swings east to follow along the north side of the Simpson for the next ten kilometres to the mouth of Surprise Creek.

A suspension bridge at Kilometre 10.9 takes the hiker across the Simpson River to the Surprise Creek Cabin (utilized as a hiker's shelter) and campground. From here the trail begins a long and steep climb up the Surprise Creek drainage.

The first portion of the climb, to Rock Lake, is scenically humdrum as the trail confines itself to dense, closed forest of pine, spruce and fir, but above the lake the scenery becomes increasingly impressive, featuring the massive rock wall of Simpson Ridge and Indian Mountain. From Ferro Pass the hiker gains a wonderful view of Mount Assiniboine, The Marshall, Mount Watson and Wedgwood Lake.

Beyond Ferro Pass the trail angles east along the southern slopes of Nestor Peak and drops down to the Mitchell Meadows Campground beside Nestor Creek. But much of the elevation which was lost on the descent from the pass has to be regained as the trail crosses the creek and begins yet another contouring climb to the subalpine meadows of the Sunburst Valley and the Mount Assiniboine environs.

West Kootenay Fire Road

Kootenay Crossing to Park Boundary—9.8 kilometres (6.1 miles)

Day trip or backpack

Allow 4 - 5 hours one way

Elevation gain: 50 metres (165 feet)

Maximum elevation: 1265 metres (4,150 feet)

Topo maps: Spillimacheen 82 K/16

Point of Departure. Follow the Banff—Radium Highway (Hwy 93) to the Kootenay River Crossing Warden Station, situated on the west side of the highway 51 kilometres (31½ miles) south of the Banff—Kootenay Park boundary at Vermilion Pass and 42½ kilometres (26½ miles) north of the Kootenay Park West Gate at Radium. Turn into the warden station and pass through the complex keeping left past the main office and warden's residence. Follow a single lane road 200 metres beyond the station to a locked access gate. Park to the side of the road.

0.0—Access gate (1215 m).

   - Road begins to climb beyond gate.

0.9—Junction. Fire road to *Dolly Varden Creek* branches left. Turn right for West Kootenay Fire Road.

   —Essentially flat travel through lodgepole pine–white spruce forest.

4.5—Downhill grade for 0.5 km.

6.2—Major tributary stream bridge.

6.7—Uphill grade for 0.5 km.

9.7—Junction. Right branch to Kootenay River bridge and east side trail (0.9 km). Keep left for park boundary.

9.8—Kootenay Park boundary (1265 m).

Like many of the fire roads in this section of Kootenay Park, the West Kootenay Road is of more interest to cross-country skiers and bicyclists than it is to hikers. It is an incredibly boring ten kilometre road walk which runs northwest from the Kootenay River Crossing Warden Station to the park boundary. The road is well removed from the Kootenay River throughout its course, so there is little relief from the tedium of pine and spruce forest. A one kilometre branch road at the boundary does lead to a pleasant stretch of the Kootenay River, however, and the possibility of some excellent fly fishing.

From the access gate beyond the warden station, the broad, well-graded fire road climbs onto a benchland above the main river bottom then turns northwest to follow through the forest which fringes the west side of the Kootenay all the way to the park's west boundary. There is little gain or loss of elevation along the way, but near the five kilometre mark the road does descend to the margin of the broad, swampy flats of the Kootenay—a truly unique environment in the mountain parks.

Just 100 metres before reaching the park boundary, a branch road cuts right over a low hill and descends to an old wooden bridge across the Kootenay River. A trail runs back down the east side of the Kootenay River to emerge on the highway just north of the warden station, but it is very brushy and overgrown in this section of the valley.

Dr. James Hector followed this same valley on his way north to the discovery of the Kicking Horse Pass in the summer of 1858. One can imagine the hardships he and his Indian guides endured as they made their way up along the Kootenay to its headwaters. It is likely they would have appreciated this wide fire road far more than do present-day hikers.

Dolly Varden Creek

Kootenay Crossing to Crook's Meadow—11.2 kilometres (7.0 miles)

Day trip or backpack

Allow 2½ - 3 hours one way

Elevation gain: 110 metres (360 feet)
loss: 140 metres (460 feet)

Maximum elevation: 1325 metres (4,350 feet)

Topo maps: Spillmacheen 82 K/16

Point of Departure: Follow the Banff—Radium Highway (Hwy 93) to the Kootenay River Crossing Warden Station, situated on the west side of the highway 51 kilometres (31½ miles) south of the Banff—Kootenay Park boundary at Vermilion Pass and 42½ kilometres (26½ miles) north of the Kootenay Park West Gate at Radium. Turn into the warden station and pass through the complex keeping left past the main office and warden's residence. Follow a single lane road 200 metres beyond the station to a locked access gate. Park to the side of the road.

0.0—Access gate (1215 m).

—Road begins to climb beyond gate.

0.9—Junction. *West Kootenay Fire Road* branches right. Keep left for Dolly Varden Creek.

1.3—Steady uphill grade for 0.5 km.

2.8—Steady downhill for 0.8 km.

3.6—Dolly Varden Creek bridge and campground.

4.1—Junction. Luxor Pass trail branches right from road (4.3 km). Dolly Varden trail continues on road.

6.7—Road crosses series of tributary streams next 0.2 km.

8.2—Old wooden bridge. Road begins descent to valley.

10.6—Access gate. Crooks Meadow group campground.

11.2—Banff—Radium Highway (1185 m). Access gate, Crooks Meadow group campground.

Of all the fire road walks in the Kootenay Valley, the Dolly Varden Creek trail is by far the most pleasant. This dirt road, which starts at the Kootenay Crossing Warden Station and ends at the Crook's Meadow group campground, is a well-graded track that runs through a mixed forest of white spruce, lodgepole pine, aspen and Douglas fir. Along the way it crosses the Dolly Varden Creek meadows and numerous spring-fed streams. Because of its low elevation, this trail makes a very fine early or late season amble.

The north end of the trail starts from the access gate beyond the Kootenay Crossing Warden Station and follows along the same route as the West Kootenay Fire Road for nearly a kilometre. After splitting left from that road, it climbs over a low, forested ridge before plunging down to the willow-covered meadows of Dolly Varden Creek. These meadows provide the only open views on the trail, and there is a pleasant campground near the creek bridge, which makes a fine place for a rest stop.

Beyond Dolly Varden Creek, the road climbs past the Luxor Pass junction, and then rolls along above the valley through an interesting forest of spruce mixed with old Douglas fir and aspen poplar. Many streams are crossed on this stretch of road, so there is no lack of fresh drinking water. The road finally descends to the Banff-Radium Parkway at Crook's Meadow to end the 11.2 kilometre journey. (Mountain bicyclists can make a 20 kilometre loop trip by cycling back to the Kootenay Crossing Warden Station on the Banff-Radium Parkway.)

Luxor Pass. Branching southwest from the Dolly Varden Creek road at Kilometre 4.1, this 4.3 kilometre trail climbs a steep, densely forested slope to a 1905 metre pass in the Brisco Range. The trail offers few open views, is seldom travelled, and has little to recommend it.

East Kootenay Fire Road

Banff-Radium Highway to Park Boundary—29.3 kilometres (18.2 miles)

Day trip or backpack

Allow 4 - 5 hours one way

Maximum elevation: 1220 metres (4,000 feet)

Minimum elevation: 1145 metres (3,750 feet)

Topo maps: Spillmacheen 82 K/16
          Mount Assiniboine 82 J/13
          Tangle Peak 82 J/12

Point of Departure: To reach the northern access point to the central section of fire road, follow the Banff—Radium Highway (Hwy 93) to an unmarked intersection (watch for access gate) on the east side of the highway 5.3 kilometres (3.3 miles) south of the Kootenay River Crossing Warden Station. Park to the side of the access gate.

To reach the southern access point to the fire road, follow the Banff—Radium Highway to an unmarked intersection with a gravel road on the east side of the highway 0.5 kilometre (0.3 mile) north of the Nixon Lake trail head. Follow the gravel road for 300 metres and park to the side of the road at the Kootenay River bridge access gate.

0.0—Access gate (1210 m). Northern access point.

0.2—Kootenay River bridge.

1.4—Junction. North branch of fire road cuts left to Hwy 93 (8.0 kms). Keep right.

1.5—Vermilion River bridge.

1.6—Junction. Fire road branch cuts left up Vermilion River (3.0 kms). Keep right.

5.5—Daer Creek bridge.

6.3—Junction. Daer Fire Lookout trail branches left (1.2 kms). Keep right.

9.7—Junction. Dog Lake north cutoff trail to left (1.2 km). Keep right.

11.9—Junction. Intersection with *Dog Lake* trail at Km 1.2.

15.1—Junction. South branch of fire road continues straight ahead to Pitts Creek (1.6 kms) and park boundary (14.2 kms). Keep right for Hwy 93 southern access point.

15.8—Kootenay River bridge (1145 m). Southern access point.

After a major forest fire swept the Kootenay Valley in 1926, a network of fire roads was constructed to allow park wardens rapid access to all parts of the valley. The East Kootenay Fire Road, stretching from near the Vermilion-Kootenay River confluence on the north to the park's south boundary, was built to service the east side of the valley. Today the road is not considered important for fire control, but it does provide hikers, cyclists and skiers easy access to the east side of Kootenay River. Since the Kootenay Valley is snowfree much of the year, the road can be used for early and late season trips, and the valley provides excellent opportunities for seeing elk, black bear, coyotes, and even wolves.

The northernmost extension of the fire road intersects the Banff-Radium Parkway three kilometres north of the Kootenay Crossing Warden Station, but this section is seldom travelled and not considered a main access route. The usual point of entry from the north is the gravel road branching east from the Banff-Radium Parkway 5.3 kilometres south of the warden station. Southern access to the road is via another gravel cutoff which runs east across the Kootenay River from a junction 500 metres north of the Nixon Creek trail head. A footbridge across the Kootenay at McLeod Meadows provides a third point of entry to the road (see *Dog Lake* description).

The fire road makes a rather unremarkable journey as it rolls gently through valley-bottom forest at some distance from the river. There are several side roads and trails to such humdrum destinations as Hector Gorge and the old Daer Fire Lookout, and trails up Daer and Pitts Creeks are unmaintained. From the junction with the southern access cutoff, the main fire road continues south to a dead end at the park boundary, just a short distance from the Cross River.

Kindersley Pass

Banff-Radium Highway to Kindersley Summit—9.8 kilometres (6.1 miles)
Kindersley Pass-Sinclair Creek Circuit—16.2 kilometres (10.1 miles)

Day trip

Allow 3 - 4 hours one way

Elevation gain: 1055 metres (3,450 feet)

Maximum elevation: 2395 metres (7,850 feet)

Topo maps: Tangle Peak 82 J/12†
†last 1.4 kms of trail not shown

Point of Departure: Follow the Banff—Radium Highway (Hwy 93) to the Kindersley Pass trail head parking area, located on the south side of the highway 9½ kilometres (6 miles) east of the Kootenay Park West Gate at Radium. From the small parking area cross the highway to the trail sign.

0.0—Trail sign (1340 m).

—Moderate uphill through forest.

2.7—Avalanche slope.

—Steady climb along edge of avalanche slope.

6.1—Lookout Point summit ridge.

—Trail enters more open avalanche slopes.

8.4—Kindersley Pass (2210 m). Park boundary.

—Trail cuts up to right. Steep ascent across open slopes to northeast.

9.8—Kindersley Summit (2395 m).

The trail to Kindersley Pass and the high alpine ridges beyond leads hikers onto one of the most scenic day trips in Kootenay Park — and one of the most strenuous.

From the trail head in the upper Sinclair Canyon, the trail climbs steadily up a narrow, densely forested valley which is opened suddenly after Kilometre 2.7 by a number of major avalanche paths. The forest in the initial section is a mixture of Douglas fir, white spruce and lodgepole pine, but as the trail ascends above the first slide area and crosses the small divide just west of Lookout Point, a more typical subalpine cover of Engelmann spruce and alpine fir is encountered.

More avalanche paths are crossed as the trail nears Kindersley Pass, and the huge piles of snow which accumulate in the valley bottom often linger through the entire summer. Along the margins of the retreating snowbanks, glacier lilies and western anemones bloom into late August.

Kindersley Pass is a bit anticlimactic after the rather stiff 8.4 kilometre climb to its summit, yet the small meadow set in a narrow gap just below timberline makes a pleasant rest stop and provides the first good views northward to the long procession of peaks which comprise the Brisco Range.

The true glory of the hike begins at Kindersley Pass. By following the trail which climbs the ridge to the north, the hiker soon ascends through the last stands of alpine larch and emerges onto the treeless alpine tundra. At Kilometre 9.8, the highest point on the hike is reached when the trail crests a 2395 metre ridge situated between two rocky peaks. From this lofty saddle, views open to the headwaters of Sinclair Creek and an endless sea of peaks stretching away to the northeast.

From the trail summit, the hiker can

Kindersley Summit

continue on for another two kilometres as the path contours around the head of the Sinclair Valley, staying just below the ridgeline, and finally descends to the crest of Nixon Creek Summit. This is alpine walking at its best, and though the trail is indistinct at times, there is no problem in discerning its traces where it reappears on the open tundra ahead.

At Nixon Creek Summit, new views open along the crest of the Brisco Range and down to the forested headwaters of Nixon Creek. Experienced rock scramblers can ascend the 2530 metre peak immediately above this col for an even better view.

Sinclair Creek. The Sinclair Creek headwaters provide an excellent alternate route back to the Banff-Radium Parkway. From the Kindersley Summit saddle, descend due east along steep, trackless slopes to the head of the Sinclair Valley. Once the valley floor is reached near a series of small cascades, an obvious trail materializes. The trail follows the west side of the creek for a hundred metres, then crosses to the east, where it remains for the rest of the way down the valley. Once the Banff-Radium Parkway is reached, you have a 1.2 kilometre walk to the parking area at the Kindersley Pass trail head. Total distance for this loop is 17 kilometres. (See *Sinclair Creek* description.)

Sinclair Creek

Banff-Radium Highway to Kindersley Summit—6.4 kilometres (4.0 miles)

Half-day trip

Allow 1 - 2 hours one way

Elevation gain: 545 metres (1,800 feet)

Maximum elevation: 1980 metres (6,500 feet)

Topo maps: Tangle Peak 82 J/12†

†trail not shown

Point of Departure: Follow the Banff—Radium Highway (Hwy 93) to the Sinclair Creek trail parking area, located on the north side of the highway 10½ kilometres (6½ miles) east of the Kootenay Park West Gate at Radium. The parking area is at the upper end of a long guard rail where the highway makes a broad sweeping curve down into the Sinclair Canyon. Walk down to the creek on a section of old road. A few metres after the old roadbed crosses the creek, the trail strikes off to the right up the canyon.

0.0—Trail sign (1435 m).

—Moderate uphill along creek.

1.7—Sinclair Creek bridge.

2.3—Trail begins switchbacking ascent.

4.5—Avalanche slopes.

—Trail climbs along east side of valley.

5.0—End of trail (1980 m). Trail disappears in avalanche slopes at head of valley. Route to Kindersley Summit branches up to left.

The five kilometre-long trail running to the headwaters of Sinclair Creek is a forest - enclosed path which doesn't emerge from the trees until it enters the avalanche slopes near trail's end. Were it not for the fact that it can be linked together with the Kindersley Pass hike, the trail would not likely attract many visitors. But when it is hiked in concert with the Kindersley route, a fine 17 kilometre circuit is created which is the scenic equal of any day hike in the park.

The trail begins its journey along the west bank of Sinclair Creek. After crossing to the east side at Kilometre 1.7, it switchbacks up onto the side of the gorge and then contours northward above the creek. Travel throughout the first four kilometres of the canyon ascent is enclosed by a forest of Douglas fir, spruce and lodgepole pine, and the path becomes rough and rocky as it nears the head of the valley.

Finally, at Kilometre 4.5, the hiker emerges into a series of avalanche slopes where lush vegetation overgrows the trail. (Watch out for devil's club!) While the view is no longer encumbered by forest, the head of the valley is little more than a claustrophobic amphitheatre of brushy slide paths. After crossing back to the west side of the creek, the trail fizzles out near a series of cascades. By angling due west across the open slopes of the valley headwall and climbing a stiff 300 vertical metres over the next kilometre, the hiker will reach the Kindersley Pass trail on the Kindersley Summit col.

While Sinclair Creek provides the shortest route to Kindersley Summit, most hikers prefer the longer but more gradual ascent via the Kindersley Pass trail, using Sinclair Creek for the descent back to the highway. The Kindersley Pass trail head lies 1.2 kilometres below the Sinclair Creek trail head on the Banff-Radium Parkway. (See *Kindersley Pass* description.)

Short Hikes and Nature Trails

JUNIPER TRAIL — 3.2 kilometres

Of the three nature hikes branching from Sinclair Canyon, the Juniper Trail probably offers the most diversity and scenic reward. In just over three kilometres it visits a cool canyon containing a lush growth of western red cedar, switchbacks up an arid south-facing slope where Rocky Mountain juniper and Douglas fir thrive, and climbs along the rim of the canyon to a viewpoint for the Columbia Valley.

Hikers usually take this trail as a loop trip, starting at the trail sign on the north side of the Banff-Radium Parkway just 300 metres inside the Kootenay Park West Gate. The trail descends immediately to the banks of Sinclair Creek, then climbs up open slopes to the canyon rim at Kilometre 1.3. Another 800 metres above the rim, the route reaches its summit, allowing an overview of the Columbia River and the Purcell Mountains beyond. By continuing in an easterly direction, the hiker descends to the Aquacourt area at Kilometre 3.2. From there it is an easy 1.4 kilometre walk back along the highway and through the canyon mouth to the trail head. *Topo map: Radium Hot Springs 82 K/9.*

REDSTREAK CREEK — 2.7 kilometres

This trail makes a short probe up the narrow confines of the Redstreak Creek valley. It is a pleasant forest walk in its initial stages but somewhat disappointing near the end.

The trail can be found along the south side of the Banff-Radium Parkway 4.5 kilometres (2.8 miles) east of the Kootenay Park West Gate. The hike starts at a footbridge across Sinclair Creek, and then climbs through a cool forest of lodgepole pine, white spruce, Douglas fir and aspen for the first 1.3 kilometres. After making a crossing of Redstreak Creek, the track fizzles out in open willow flats, where the hiker is greeted by somewhat limited views of this narrow, heavily forested valley. *Topo map: Tangle Peak 82 J/12.*

KIMPTON CREEK — 4.8 kilometres

Similar to Redstreak Creek, the Kimpton Creek trail runs up a tight, forested valley leading southward from Sinclair Canyon. The drainage is slightly longer, however, so the trail is developed a bit farther from the highway. The well-shaded banks of Kimpton Creek provide a cool respite during the frequent warm spells experienced near Radium.

The trail head is reached by driving the Banff-Radium Parkway to a small roadside parking area on the south side of the highway 7½ kilometres (4½ miles) east of the Kootenay Park West Gate. Walk back down the highway 100 metres from the parking area to the footbridge over Sinclair Creek to start the hike. *Topo map: Tangle Peak 82 J/12.*

COBB LAKE — 2.7 kilometres

A peaceful, forest-encircled lake noted for its mirror-like reflections and fishing. Like most of the trails in the Kootenay Valley vicinity, it is often snowfree from April to November.

The trail starts from a roadside pulloff on the south side of the Banff-Radium Parkway 14½ kilometres (9 miles) from the Kootenay Park West Gate and 0.6 kilometre (0.4 mile) west of the Kootenay Valley Viewpoint. From the barrier rocks at the corner of the paved parking area, the trail switchbacks down for 1.6 kilometres to Swede Creek. The forest is composed of lodgepole pine and white spruce, mixed with a few old Douglas fir giants whose thick, protective bark has been charred by long-forgotten forest fires. After crossing Swede Creek, the trail works uphill at a gradual grade until it reaches the lake. *Topo map: Tangle Peak 82 J/12.*

NIXON LAKE — 1.0 kilometre

This short, forested walk to a small, marshy lake on the west side of the Kootenay Valley makes a good early or late season outing. It is particularly pleasant in late May and early June when calypso orchids and blue clematis are blooming on the forest floor, and shooting stars are springing up among the cattails and equisetum on the soggy flats near the lakeshore.

The trail head is situated on the west side of the Banff-Radium Parkway 23½ kilometres (14½ miles) from the Kootenay Park West Gate and 2.8 kilometres (1.7 miles) south of McLeod Meadows Picnic Area. From the trail sign, which is above the Nixon Creek highway bridge, a good track runs uphill for nearly a kilometre to where a short branch cuts right onto the marshy flats at the south end of the lake (a good area for spring birding). Though the trail beyond the lake cutoff is well defined and looks promising, it ends in a tangle of deadfall after climbing the valley's west slope for another kilometre or so. *Topo map: Tangle Peak 82 J/12.*

DOG LAKE — 2.7 kilometres

The Dog Lake trip is a half-day hike to a shallow, marsh-fringed lake at the foot of the Mitchell Range. The lake's location, on the floor of one of the most temperate valleys in the Canadian Rockies, creates an excellent environment for nature study. It is a popular after-dinner outing for families overnighting at the nearby McLeod Meadows Campground.

To reach the trail, follow the Banff-Radium Parkway to the McLeod Meadows Picnic Area, located 26½ kilometres (16½ miles) from the Kootenay Park West Gate and 0.5 kilometre (0.3 mile) south of the McLeod Meadows Campground. The trail strikes off from the north end of the picnic area and skirts the southeastern side of the McLeod Meadows Campground. (The trail can also be accessed from the rear of the campground.) After crossing the Kootenay River via two sturdy footbridges, the trail swings to the north, crosses the East Kootenay Fire Road, and traverses a low, forested ridge. Through the trees, the hiker has many opportunities to view the expanse of the Kootenay Valley. Directly west of the lake is Mount Harkin (2981 m), a prominent peak of the Mitchell Range which commemorates James B. Harkin, the first commissioner of Canada's National Parks and a leader in the country's conservation movement. *Topo map: Mount Assiniboine 82 J/13.*

MOUNT SHANKS LOOKOUT — 4.2 kilometres

This broad access road leads onto the southwest slopes of Mount Shanks, terminating at a fire tower and cabin. The view from the lookout site is limited to a rather modest panorama of the Vermilion Range, the Hector Gorge section of the Vermilion River valley and the north end of the Mitchell Range. The trail has little to recommend it beyond the lush wild strawberry patches which border the road's first kilometre.

Follow the Banff-Radium Parkway to a point 6 kilometres (3½ miles) south of the Vermilion Crossing Lodge and 14½ kilometres (9 miles) north of the Kootenay Crossing Warden Station. Watch for a wooden bridge that spans the Vermilion River beside the highway. From the trail sign on the highway side of the river, walk across the bridge and follow a gravel road 200 metres to a locked access gate where the road forks. This gate marks the beginning of the lookout road. The road runs flat for the first kilometre, then begins its steady ascent to the lookout site. A major stream is crossed at Kilometre 1.8, the last reliable water on the hike. Like all other remaining lookouts in the mountain parks, this one is unmanned. (Do not climb the tower!) *Topo map: Mount Assiniboine 82 J/13.*

VERENDRYE CREEK — 2.1 kilometres

The Verendrye Creek trail is a forest-enclosed path which extends up this tight side-valley to the base of Mount Verendrye. The trail terminates near the head of the valley in an area swept by avalanches, where there are limited views of the mountain and the sheer eastern escarpment of the Vermilion Range. Unfortunately, this is one view which is better from the highway.

Follow the Banff-Radium Parkway to the Vermilion Crossing Picnic Area, opposite the Vermilion Crossing Lodge, 63 kilometres (39 miles) northeast of the Kootenay Park West Gate and 29½ kilometres (18½ miles) southwest of the park's eastern boundary at Vermilion Pass. From the rear of the picnic area, the trail climbs gradually through a cool, well-shaded forest of lodgepole pine and white spruce. It reaches Verendrye Creek at Kilometre 2.1, where a footbridge once crossed to the creek's north bank (the bridge was washed out many years ago). Most hikers accept the limited view of Mount Verendrye from this crossing and then turn for home, but more dedicated souls can ford the creek and continue upvalley. (This can be a tricky crossing throughout much of the summer, though it is a simple rock-hop in late September and early October.) Beyond the crossing, a rough, unmaintained track with occasional washouts continues along the northwest side of the creek. At Kilometre 3.5, the trail enters an area of avalanche paths and, 800 metres farther along, it finally fizzles out entirely on a large gravel outwash by the side of the creek. *Topo maps: Banff 82 O/4 and Mount Goodsir 82 N/1.*

Waterton Lakes National Park

Waterton Lakes National Park is a 518 square kilometre reserve located in the southwestern corner of Alberta, bounded on the west by the crest of the Great Divide, on the south by the Canada-U.S. border, and on the north and east by the rolling prairies of southern Alberta.

There are over 160 kilometres of trail in Waterton Lakes National Park, making its backcountry the most developed of the mountain parks. The trails, as a whole, are the best constructed in the Canadian Rockies — moderately graded, well-marked, scenically routed and, as might be suspected from such attributes, heavily travelled. Most trails in the park are day hikes, and nearly all lead to small alpine lakes nestled in hanging valleys. Many of the more popular trips branch from the park's main arteries: Rowe Lakes and Carthew Summit are accessible from the Akamina Parkway, while Twin Lakes and Goat Lake are hiked from the end of the Red Rock Canyon Parkway. The Bertha Lake trail, which is the park's most popular day hike, strikes off from the edge of Waterton townsite, and the very special Crypt Lake hike starts from the village marina with a three kilometre boat ride.

While campgrounds are located on many of the shorter trails, serious backpacking opportunities are limited in such a small park. An excellent trip is the Tamarack Trail, which runs along the Great Divide for 36 kilometres from the Akamina Parkway to Red Rock Canyon. Though the 20 kilometre Carthew-Alderson trip from Cameron Lake to Waterton townsite is usually done as a day hike, it can be spread over two days by utilizing the Alderson Lake Campground. In addition, the Lakeshore trail running south from Waterton townsite can be utilized to reach the extensive system of wilderness trails in Glacier National Park, Montana.

All backpackers must obtain a backcountry camping permit before starting their trip. The permits can be obtained from the Information Centre at the townsite entrance, at the administration building near the village centre, or from the park warden office. Advanced bookings are not available and party size must not exceed six. Registration is also required for any mountain climbing trips.

Waterton townsite is the only service centre in the park. Its facilities include grocery stores, restaurants, gas stations, a laundromat, a public swimming pool, and a number of hotels and motels. There is also an outdoor equipment store which stocks a full line of hiking equipment and camping supplies. Waterton is a seasonal village, and most businesses are closed from early October to mid-May.

Access: Two provincial highways offer access to the park. Highway #6 runs south 48 kilometres from the town of Pincher Creek to the park entrance, while Highway #5 intersects at the same point after a journey of 45 kilometres from Cardston to the east. In addition, the Chief Mountain International Highway provides the most direct route from Glacier National Park in the United States, but is open only during the summer months.

The nearest Alberta cities serviced by commercial airlines are Lethbridge (130 kilometres) and Calgary (264 kilometres). Greyhound Lines of Canada runs a bus between the park and Calgary during the summer, while sightseeing buses make daily runs between hotels in Glacier National Park, Montana, and Waterton's Prince of Wales Hotel. Within the park, the outdoor equipment shop in Waterton townsite provides transportation to Cameron Lake and Red Rock Canyon by appointment.

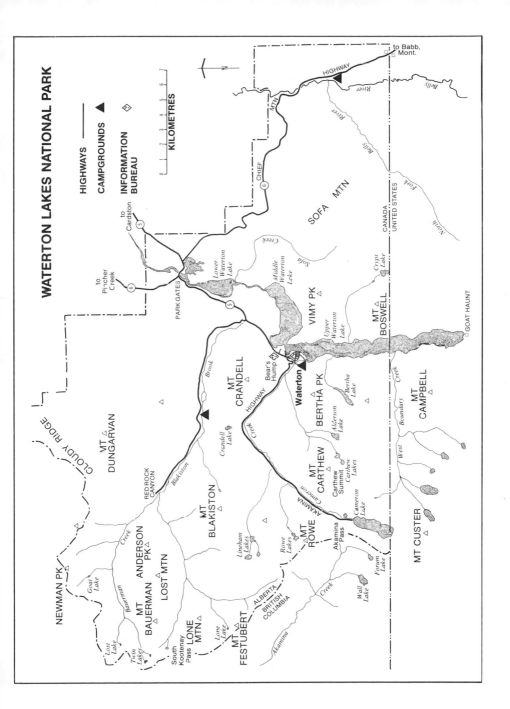

WATERTON LAKES NATIONAL PARK

HIGHWAYS ——————
CAMPGROUNDS ◀
INFORMATION
BUREAU ✧

KILOMETRES

0   1   2   3   4   5   6

N

CLOUDY RIDGE

NEWMAN PK

MT DUNGARVAN

MT ANDERSON PK

MT BAUERMAN

LOST MTN

LONE MTN

MT FESTUBERT

Lost Lake

Twin Lakes

Goat Lake

Bauerman Creek

South Kootenay Pass

Lone Lake

Lineham Lakes

MT BLAKISTON

Blakiston Brook

RED ROCK CANYON

MT CRANDELL

Crandell Lake

Akamina

ALBERTA
BRITISH COLUMBIA

MT ROWE

Rowe Lakes

Akamina Pass

Cameron Lake

Akamina Creek

Wall Lake

Forum Lake

MT CUSTER

MT CARTHEW

Carthew Summit

Carthew Lakes

Alderson Lake

BERTHA PK

Bertha Lake

Waterton

Bear's Hump

HIGHWAY

Cameron Creek

Lower Waterton Lake

Middle Waterton Lake

Upper Waterton Lake

VIMY PK

MT BOSWELL

West Boundary Creek

MT CAMPBELL

GOAT HAUNT

CANADA
UNITED STATES

Crypt Lake

SOFA MTN

Sofa Creek

CHIEF MTN

HIGHWAY

River

Belly River

North Fork

Belly River

to Babb, Mont.

to Cardston

to Pincher Creek

PARK GATES

5

6

307

Crypt Lake

Crypt Landing to Crypt Lake—8.7 kilometres (5.4 miles)

Day trip or backpack

Allow 2½ - 4 hours one way

Elevation gain: 675 metres (2,220 feet)

Maximum elevation: 1955 metres (6,420 feet)

Topo maps: Waterton Lakes National Park

Point of Departure: Book passage on the tour boat that crosses Upper Waterton Lake to the Crypt Landing dock. Crypt Landing can also be reached by hiking the *Vimy Peak—Bosporous* trail—a 13.0 kilometre hike from the Chief Mountain Highway.

0.0—Crypt Landing (1280 m).

—Switchbacks up through forest at moderate grade.

2.4—Last switchback.

3.5—Twin Falls viewpoint.

5.6—Burnt Rock Falls.

—Switchbacks resume.

7.9—Crypt Lake Campground and shelter.

8.1—Tunnel.

8.5—Lip of Crypt Lake cirque. Underground stream and Crypt Falls.

8.7—Crypt Lake (1945 m).

Crypt Lake is unique among all trails in the Canadian Rockies. To reach it the hiker must cross windy Waterton Lake by boat, climb a narrow valley past a series of waterfalls, crawl through a 20 metre long tunnel, and pass by a stream that suddenly materializes from beneath the ground. And if that doesn't satisfy a desire for the bizarre, one may stroll down the lake's emerald waters and visit another country.

To reach the Crypt Lake trail head, passage must be booked on the Canadian-owned motor launch that plies the whitecaps of Waterton Lake. The launch captain drops hikers off across the lake at Crypt Landing on request and arranges for pick-ups there in the evening. There is no other reasonable method of reaching the trail.

From the boat dock the trail begins to climb immediately, gaining elevation via a series of well-graded switchbacks. The way is enclosed by a forest of white spruce, Douglas fir and lodgepole pine. At Kilometre 2.4 the switchbacking ceases temporarily, as the trail heads straight up the Hell Roaring Valley, passing Twin Falls at Kilometre 3.5.

At Burnt Rock Falls, a beautiful 15 metre strand of water that tumbles off a lip of Precambrian strata, the trail takes to the open talus slopes and begins a series of steep switchbacks. After traversing high above a small green lake, it reaches the campsite and kitchen shelter at Kilometre 7.9.

The last 800 metres to Crypt Lake are not well-suited for those suffering from claustrophobia, acrophobia or obesity. A short jaunt across a talus slope brings the hiker to a halt at a sheer wall—an apparent cul de sac but for a ladder leading up into a dark hole in the rock. At the top of the ladder a 20 metre tunnel cuts through the mountain spur—a tight, cramped shaft that nearly requires the hands-and-knees approach. Emerging from the tunnel on

Crypt Lake

the opposite side, the trail is etched along an exposed precipice. A cable has been attached to the rock offering support to the faint-of-heart.

As the path enters a grove of whitebark pine and alpine fir at the mouth of the Crypt cirque, a short spur trail branches to where the outlet stream emerges from beneath a pile of boulders. Not far away the stream plunges over a vertical wall, creating Crypt Falls.

Crypt Lake is certainly no anticlimax to its many-faceted approach. Its waters are of the deepest green and are seldom free from ice, even in the middle of the summer. The brilliant white of floating icebergs serves to accentuate the dark hue of the lake. It is the perfect example of a glacial amphitheatre, with 600 metre high cliffs rising on all but the north side of the lake.

By keeping to the east shore, you can pick a route down to the far end of the lake, which is situated precisely on the International Boundary between Canada and the United States. No customs agent or immigration officer to greet the intruder here, only the odd mountain goat above, patrolling the slopes in search of lichen. Potential smugglers will find, however, that the Wilson Range forms one of the most effective barriers to be found anywhere along the nearly 6500 kilometres of border.

Day hikers should keep an eye on their watches and allow enough time to catch the boat back to Waterton in the late afternoon, and backpackers should be aware that the Crypt Lake campsite is one of the most heavily used overnight stops in the park's backcountry.

Vimy Peak

Chief Mountain Highway to Vimy Basin—11.2 kilometres (7.0 miles)

Day trip or backpack

Allow 4 - 5 hours to Vimy Basin

Elevation gain: 820 metres (2,600 feet)

Maximum elevation: 2105 metres (6,900 feet)

Topo maps: Waterton Lakes National Park

Point of Departure: From the Waterton Park entrance station, follow Highway #5 east 0.9 kilometre to the intersection with the Chief Mountain Highway (Hwy 6). Turn right and follow the Chief Mountain Highway 0.5 kilometre to where the Y Camp access road branches to the right. Park in the pullout on the north side of the highway and start the hike from the locked access gate.

0.0—Access gate (1285 m).

—Follow access road south over flat terrain.

2.6—Y Camp site.

—Road end. Track angles to southeast.

5.5—Sofa Creek crossing.

6.0—Junction (1295 m). Bosporous trail continues straight ahead to Bosporous straits (3.4 kms) and Crypt Landing (7.0 kms). Turn left for Vimy Peak.

—Steep, steady ascent.

11.2—Vimy Basin (2105 m). Trail ends due east of and 280 vertical metres below Vimy Peak.

Rising to a point that is 1100 vertical metres above Upper Waterton Lake, Vimy Peak provides an outstanding viewpoint for much of the Waterton Valley as well as the Crypt cirque to the south. But the trail does have its drawbacks: every one of those vertical metres has to be gained on foot over slopes that can be excruciatingly hot on a sunny summer day; the last 280 metres of vertical to the summit is a steep scramble without the aid of marked trail; and it passes through prime grizzly range where visibility is often limited by dense bush.

The trail follows a good gravel road for the first 2.6 kilometres, but beyond the Y Camp site on the east shore of Lower Waterton Lake it becomes a less defined track which is frequently grassy and overgrown. The grade is essentially flat, however, so it is easy to make good time.

From the Bosporus trail junction, the Vimy Peak trail starts its steep climb to a small basin on the east side of the mountain. All of the trail's 820 vertical metres are gained over this last 5.2 kilometres of trail. From the basin, where the trail ends, rock scramblers can pick the line of least resistance to the summit above.

Bosporus Trail. The Bosporus trail is at the opposite end of the hiking spectrum from the Vimy Peak trail; it is flat and stays in the meadows and mixed deciduous forest near the shores of Middle and Upper Waterton Lakes. It is a pleasant hike for exploring the unique flora of the Waterton Valley, and it can also be used as an optional approach to the Crypt Lake hike (see *Crypt Lake* trail description). From the junction with the Vimy Peak trail at Kilometre 6.0, stay right and continue through aspen groves to arrive at Wishbone Campground on Middle Waterton Lake (Km 9.8), Loon Lake and the short side trail to Bosporus strait (Km 11.0), and Crypt Landing and campground (Km 13.0).

Waterton Lakeshore Trail

Day trip or backpack

Allow 4 - 5 hours one way

Elevation gain: 100 metres (350 feet)
    loss: 115 metres (375 feet)

Maximum elevation: 1395 metres (4,580 feet)

Topo maps: Waterton Lakes National Park

Point of Departure: Follow Evergreen Avenue south along the west side of Waterton townsite to a point 400 metres south of Cameron Falls and directly opposite the townsite campground. Turn right onto a gravel side road that cuts uphill between cottages to a parking area. The trail strikes off to the south from a trail sign at the upper edge of the parking area.

0.0—Trail sign (1295 m).

—Trail climbs south through forest.

1.4—Junction. Trail to viewpoint branches left. Keep right.

1.5—Junction. *Bertha Lake* trail continues to right. Turn left for lakeshore trail.

—Trail descends toward lake.

2.4—Bertha Bay Campground and boat dock.

—Trail rolls along above lakeshore.

5.8—Boundary Bay Campground and boat dock. International Boundary.

6.3—Boundary Creek bridge.

6.4—Junction. *Boundary Creek* trail intersects from right. Keep left.

—Trail rolls along in forest above lakeshore.

11.5—Junction. Boulder Pass trail to right. Keep left.

12.1—Junction. Branch trail right to Rainbow Falls (0.8 km). Keep left.

12.6—Goat Haunt Ranger Station.

—Continue around end of lake for boat dock.

13.0—Goat Haunt boat dock (1280 m).

The 13 kilometre trail running south along the west shore of Upper Waterton Lake from Waterton townsite to the Goat Haunt Ranger Station in the United States offers a number of interesting possibilities: a day hike from the townsite to the international boundary at Boundary Bay and back; a one way trek to the south end of the lake, followed by a return trip to the townsite on the tour boat *International;* or an extended backpack connecting in with one of several fine trails in the northern wilderness of Glacier National Park, Montana.

The lakeshore hike strikes off from the southwest corner of the townsite on the Bertha Lake trail and climbs through a cool, flower-filled forest. The routes split at Kilometre 1.4, the lakeshore trail branching left and descending to Bertha Bay. Beyond Bertha Bay, the trail rolls along the rocky lower slopes of Mount Richards to reach the international boundary and Boundary Bay at Kilometre 5.8. The campground-boat dock in this bay makes a good spot to stop for lunch or a break.

The trail south from the Canada-U.S. border is mainly enclosed in forest. At the south end of the lake, it crosses the Waterton River and angles back to the Goat Haunt Ranger Station on the southern shore. (Hikers must pass an immigration check at this station.) It is just a short walk from the ranger station around to the boat dock on the east shore. (If you plan on riding back to the townsite on the launch, leave plenty of time to catch the last boat at this dock.)

Boundary Creek. This 13.4 kilometre trail branches from the lakeshore route on the south side of the Boundary Creek bridge and runs due west along the creek for some eight kilometres before climbing back into Canada to Summit Lake on the Carthew-Alderson trail. The trail is of marginal scenic interest and frequented by grizzly bears, so travel is not recommended.

311

Bertha Lake

Day trip or backpack

Allow 1½ - 2 hours one way

Elevation gain: 460 metres (1,500 feet)

Maximum elevation: 1755 metres (5,750 feet)

Topo maps: Waterton Lakes National Park

Point of Departure: Follow Evergreen Avenue south along the west side of Waterton townsite to a point 400 metres south of Cameron Falls and directly opposite the townsite campground. Turn right onto a gravel side road that cuts uphill between cottages to a parking area. The trail strikes off to the south from a trail sign at the upper edge of the parking area.

0.0—Trail sign (1295 m).

—Trail climbs south through forest.

1.5—Junction. *Lakeshore* trail branches left. Keep right.

—Trail begins ascent along north side of Bertha Creek.

2.6—Lower Bertha Falls.

—Trail crosses Bertha Creek, begins switchbacking climb along south side of valley.

5.1—Bertha Lake viewpoint. Trail summit.

5.8—Bertha Lake (1755 m). Campground.

—North shoreline trail.

7.4—West end of Bertha Lake.

Lying just 5.8 kilometres from Waterton townsite, Bertha Lake is one of the most popular hikes in Waterton Park. With a campground and kitchen shelter at the lake, the area is frequented by a mixed bag of day hikers, campers, fishermen, and horseback riders. Although the number of people might detract from the attractiveness of the lake, the region has a beauty and tranquility which even the most cynical mountain traveller will find hard to deny.

The trail to the lake is fairly steep but well graded and maintained. From its origin at the extreme southwest corner of the townsite, the trail climbs gradually for the first two kilometres through a forest rich with undergrowth and wildflowers. Near the junction with the lakeshore trail, the trail breaks out of the forest briefly and onto a dry open slope which affords excellent views of Upper Waterton Lake. The rather stunted and bushy looking trees which grow on this sunny exposure are limber pine—a species which thrives in just a few isolated locales throughout the park.

At Kilometre 2.6 the trail crosses the creek beneath the beautiful Lower Bertha Falls and begins its steep climb up to the hanging valley which contains Bertha Lake. Climbing through a forest of alpine fir, Engelmann spruce and lodgepole pine, the trail passes Upper Bertha Falls cascading down across the ochre-red argillite common to the region.

Just 5.1 kilometres from the trail's start the maximum elevation of the hike is reached—a point where the first glimpse of the lake appears. Another 700 metres carries you down to the water's edge and the campground. The trail continues down along the north shore of the lake, eventually encircling the entire body of water.

The high cirque in which Bertha Lake lies was carved thousands of years ago by the action of glacial ice as it slowly accumulated in the valley. The prevailing

Bertha Lake

green hue of the rock and soil surrounding the lake comes from the green argillite of the Appekunny Formation, while the wall at the far end of the lake is composed of the grey dolomite and limestone of the Siyeh Formation and the red argillite of the Grinnell Formation. The thin, dark band stretching across the headwall is an intrusion of igneous rock which was forced between the sedimentary layers in a molten state long before the uplift of the Rockies.

The lake was named for Bertha Ekelund, once a resident of the Waterton area. Bertha is reputed to have tried to pass counterfeit currency. She was sent to jail and never seen in Waterton again, but her name remains.

Carthew-Alderson Trail

Cameron Lake to Carthew Summit—7.9 kilometres (4.9 miles)

Cameron Lake to Waterton Townsite—20.1 kilometres (12.5 miles)

Day trip or backpack

Allow 6 - 7 hours

Elevation gain: 650 metres (2,135 feet)
        loss: 1015 metres (3,330 feet)

Maximum elevation: 2311 metres (7,582 feet)

Topo maps: Waterton Lakes National Park

Point of Departure: From Waterton townsite, drive the Akamina Parkway 16 kilometres (10 miles) to its terminus at Cameron Lake. From the parking lot, walk down to the lakeshore display, turn left and follow the shoreline trail to the Cameron Creek bridge where the Carthew—Alderson Trail begins.

0.0—Cameron Creek bridge (1660 m).

—Gradual but steady climb, switchbacking through dense forest.

3.0—Trail emerges into open, subalpine forest.

4.2—Summit Lake (1935 m).

4.3—Junction. Trail to Boundary Creek branches right. Turn uphill to left for Carthew Summit.

—Trail climbs steeply through dwindling forest.

7.9—Carthew Summit (2311 m).

—Steep descent over open scree slopes.

9.3—Upper Carthew Lake.

9.8—Lower Carthew Lake.

—Trail descends steeply into forest.

13.1—Alderson Lake and campground (1875 m).

—Steady descent along northern slopes of Bertha Peak.

20.1—Waterton townsite (1295 m). Cameron Falls.

The twenty kilometre hike between Cameron Lake and Waterton townsite is one of the few trips in the mountain parks that could be considered "complete" in having all the elements that make alpine travel the pleasurable experience it is: a beautifully constructed trail that carries the hiker through a spectrum of botanical life zones; past lakes and glaciers; over a high and windswept mountain pass; through delicate subalpine meadows featuring a great variety of wildflowers; and at all times through some of the most colourful mountains found in any of Canada's mountain parks.

From Cameron Lake the trail switchbacks up through a lush forest, climbing some 275 vertical metres in just over three kilometres. This early section offers glimpses out from the forest to Cameron Lake below and the surrounding mountains, predominantly Forum Peak (2415 m) to the west and Mount Custer (2708 m), mantled with the Herbst Glacier, to the south. At the three kilometre mark the trail levels off to run to the southeast across a less densely forested plateau to Summit Lake. The shoreline of this small, still lake is a veritable garden in midsummer, replete with the blooms of beargrass, fleabane, valerian, arnica, and many other species of wildflowers, and it is frequently visited by curious mule deer. It is an excellent spot to take a lengthy break.

At Summit Lake the trail to Boundary Creek in the United States forks to the right, while the path to Carthew Summit cuts uphill to the left. Three-and-a-half kilometres and 375 vertical metres from the junction the hiker reaches Carthew Summit after a strenuous switchbacking climb up through steadily diminishing forest cover, across steep scree slopes, and onto the rocky and nearly barren ridgeline of the pass at 2311 metres above sea level. The red scree which the trail runs through is composed of argillites and quartzites of the Kintla Formation and is

Cameron Lake and Mount Custer from Mount Carthew

responsible for the region's striking colour. From Carthew Summit it is a brief fifteen minute scramble to the lower peak of Mount Carthew, an effort which serves to extend the expansive views even further. Here the scenery is dominated by Chapman Peak (2867 m) rising to the south in the United States, with the Hudson Glacier and Lakes Nooney and Wurdeman clearly visible on its northern flank.

From Carthew Summit the trail descends a steep scree slope into the basin containing Upper Carthew Lake. Not far below lies the Lower Carthew Lake, where the hiker again begins to encounter the subalpine forest.

Beyond Lower Carthew Lake the trail descends rapidly (260 metres in just over three kilometres) across two rock formations to Alderson Lake, a diminutive green body of water nestled at the foot of the impressive 700 metre north face of Mount Alderson. The campground at the lake is the only one on the Carthew-Alderson tour, and it is most frequently used by backpackers approaching from Waterton townsite either as a destination or an overnight stop on the long uphill slog to Carthew Summit.

From Alderson Lake the trail runs 6.5 kilometres down the Carthew Creek valley between Buchanan Ridge to the north and Bertha Peak to the immediate south, winding its way through a heavy forest of pine, spruce and Douglas fir. A half-kilometre before reaching Waterton the trail joins Cameron Creek and bypasses the Waterton hydro station to reach the townsite some 50 metres south of Cameron Falls.

Most hikers do the Carthew—Alderson Trail as an arrangement day trip, travelling to Cameron Lake to begin the trek as it is described here (arrange your own transportation or book a ride through the sporting goods shop in the townsite's Tamarack Mall). Other variations include round-trip day hikes to Carthew Summit from Cameron Lake or a base camp at Alderson Lake.

Rowe Lakes

Akamina Parkway to Upper Rowe Lakes—6.4 kilometres (4.0 miles)

Day trip or backpack

Allow 2 hours to Upper Rowe Lakes

Elevation gain: 555 metres (1,820 feet)

Maximum elevation: 2165 metres (7,100 feet)

Topo maps: Waterton Lakes National Park

Point of Departure: From Waterton townsite, follow the Akimina Parkway to the Rowe Lakes trail head parking area, situated on the right side of the highway 10 kilometres (6 miles) from the townsite junction.

0.0—Trail sign (1610 m).

0.3—Rowe Creek cascades.

—Gradual but steady uphill.

2.3—Broad open avalanche slope.

3.9—Junction (1965 m). Lower Rowe Lake 0.2 km to left. Keep right for Upper Rowe Lakes.

5.2—Rowe Basin Campground and junction. *Tamarack Trail* to right. Turn left for Upper Rowe Lakes.

—Steep grade with switchbacks.

6.4—Upper Rowe Lakes (2165 m).

For casual day hikers, the trail to the Rowe Lakes is one of the more pleasant outings in Waterton Park. But for strong hikers who are willing to put in a rather strenuous 15 to 20 kilometre day by extending the trip to the 2560 metre summit of nearby Lineham Ridge, the area offers as much variety and exhilarating scenery as any in the Rockies.

The trail has a very pretty beginning. The first 300 metres follows along the north side of Rowe Creek which, at this point, is a long series of cascades sliding over one of the most colourful stream beds imaginable — a long chute of brilliant red argillite. While you may not have worked up a thirst so early in the hike, you should bottle some of Rowe Creek's sparkling water for the dry three kilometres ahead.

The first part of the climb from the Akamina Parkway is across a semi-open slope scattered with lodgepole pine, but as you ascend the Rowe Creek drainage the pine grades into a mature forest of spruce and alpine fir. The Lower Rowe Lake junction is attained at Kilometre 3.9, and a short spur cuts left from the main trail to reach the shore of the tiny lake in just 200 metres. Despite the lake's diminutive size, the steep walls of the surrounding amphitheatre enhance the setting, and a scattered subalpine forest along the shore helps to create a very pleasant rest stop.

Beyond the junction, the trail to the upper lakes continues its climb, finally emerging in the Rowe Basin meadow at the head of the valley. A bridge at the far edge of the meadow spans a tributary stream and brings the hiker to yet another junction. Here the Tamarack Trail branches right and begins its 500 metre vertical ascent to Lineham Ridge, while the trail to the Upper Rowe Lakes cuts left and contours across a steep slope, climbing into a stand of alpine larch.

The larger of the two Upper Rowe

Upper Rowe Lakes and Mount Rowe from the Tamarack Trail

Lakes is a sparkling body of water backed against the cliffs of the Great Divide and surrounded by a sparse and stunted forest of alpine fir and larch. By hiking down to the smaller of the upper lakes, you can peek over the lip of this hanging valley — a 150 metre cliff — to the waters of Lower Rowe Lake directly below. The slopes above the Upper Rowe Lake are often frequented by flocks of bighorn sheep.

Lineham Ridge. For hikers who get back to the Rowe Basin junction with energy and time to spare, a hike to the summit of Lineham Ridge would be a highlight of the day. Simply follow the Tamarack Trail option from Rowe Basin and reach the crest of the ridge in another 3.4 kilometres of steady climbing. Since this ridge is nearly as high as most of the surrounding mountaintops, the views are magnificent. A sea of mountains stretches out in all directions, and peaks as far away as 50 kilometres can be identified. On the opposite side of the ridge, the beautiful, deep blue Lineham Lakes lie in their verdant basin. (See also *Tamarack Trail* description.)

One note of warning: Lineham Ridge should be avoided during bad weather, since high winds and poor visibility make this a very hazardous area. Hikers should also avoid the ridge early in the season when the trail is obliterated by steep snowfields.

Blakiston Creek

Red Rock Canyon to South Kootenay Pass—11.2 kilometres (7.0 miles)

Day trip or backpack

Allow 3 - 4 hours to South Kootenay Pass

Elevation gain: 700 metres (2,300 feet)

Maximum elevation: 2195 metres (7,200 feet)

Topo maps: Waterton Lakes National Park

Point of Departure: From its junction with Highway #5 just north of Waterton townsite, follow the Red Rock Parkway 15 kilometres (9 miles) to its terminus at the Red Rock Canyon parking area. Walk down to the bottom edge of the parking lot and cross the bridge spanning the lower canyon.

0.0—Red Rock Canyon (1495 m).

—Keep left on Blakiston Falls trail.

1.0—Blakiston Falls.

—Gradual ascent of valley through forest and avalanche paths.

6.5—Blakiston—Lone Creek confluence.

8.8—Grade steepens.

10.1—Junction (1920 m). Intersection with *Tamarack Trail* at Km 21.6. Keep left for South Kootenay Pass.

10.2—Junction. South Kootenay Pass trail branches right from Tamarack Trail.

—Steep ascent.

11.2—South Kootenay Summit (2195 m).

In early September, 1858, Lieutenant Thomas Blakiston, a member of John Palliser's British North American Exploring Expedition, crossed South Kootenay Pass and descended a narrow mountain valley on the eastern slope to the shores of the Waterton Lakes. Today the valley bears his name, and a broad, well defined trail leads up that drainage to the summit of South Kootenay Pass. In addition to its significance as a historical trail, the path up Blakiston Creek serves as an alternate route to the Tamarack Trail. When linked with the Snowshoe Trail-Twin Lakes option, it also becomes part of a 25 kilometre loop trip which starts and ends at Red Rock Canyon.

Starting from Red Rock Canyon, the trail passes Blakiston Falls at Kilometre 1.0 as it begins its steady, if somewhat uneventful, ascent of the valley. Open avalanche paths provide views to two of the highest mountains in Waterton Park, Mount Blakiston (2940 m) to the south and Anderson Peak (2683 m) to the north. At Kilometre 6.5, the trail branches up Lone Creek, the south fork of Blakiston Creek, and climbs to an intersection with the Tamarack Trail. From this junction, you can turn either north or south to complete your journey on the Tamarack Trail or continue west for another kilometre to South Kootenay Pass.

South Kootenay Pass. Less than 100 metres south of the Blakiston Creek-Tamarack Trail junction, the South Kootenay Pass trail branches uphill to the west. The trail is short — only a kilometre in length — and steep, actually climbing to the 2195 metre level on the ridge of Kishinena Peak where it looks down upon the summit of the pass. In addition to a fine view down the length of the Blakiston Valley, there is an excellent panorama to the west of the peaks and valleys which comprise the provincial forest lands of British Columbia.

Blakiston Valley from South Kootenay Pass

Twin Lakes. By following the Tamarack Trail north from its junction with the Blakiston Creek trail, you can reach the Twin Lakes in 2.5 kilometres. From that point, you can return to Red Rock Canyon via the Snowshoe Trail. Total distance for the Blakiston Creek-Twin Lakes-Snowshoe Trail circuit is 25 kilometres. (See *Snowshoe Trail* and *Tamarack Trail* descriptions.)

Snowshoe Trail—Twin Lakes

Red Rock Canyon to Upper Twin Lake—11.4 kilometres (7.1 miles)

Day trip or backpack

Allow 3 - 4 hours to Twin Lakes

Elevation gain: 455 metres (1,500 feet)

Maximum elevation: 1950 metres (6,400 feet)

Topo maps: Waterton Lakes National Park

Point of Departure: From its junction with Highway #5, just north of Waterton townsite, follow the Red Rock Parkway 15 kilometres (9 miles) to its terminus at the Red Rock Canyon parking area. The trail starts at the bridge which spans the canyon just beyond the west edge of the parking lot.

0.0—Red Rock Canyon bridge (1495 m).

—Route follows wide trail through open forest along north side of creek.

4.3—Junction. *Goat Lake* trail branches up to right. Stay straight ahead.

—Gradual climb up Bauerman Valley.

8.2—Snowshoe Warden Cabin, campground and junction (1720 m). Trail to Lost Lake (1.9 kms) and Castle River Divide (3.1 kms) branches right. Intersection with *Tamarack Trail* at Km 27.9. Turn left for Twin Lakes.

—Steady climb through forest and avalanche meadows.

11.4—Upper Twin Lake and campground (1950 m).

12.0—Lower Twin Lake. *Tamarack Trail* continues to south.

The Snowshoe Trail follows an old fire road 8.2 kilometres from Red Rock Canyon to the head of the Bauerman Valley. While this broad, gently rolling track makes for somewhat mundane and tedious hiking, it is the main approach to the north end of the Tamarack Trail and the very scenic Twin Lakes area. The road also serves as access to other worthwhile destinations such as Lost Lake and Goat Lake.

The route from Red Rock Canyon is straightforward as it makes a gradual but steady ascent along Bauerman Creek, traversing to the north of Anderson Peak. The only junction along the way occurs at Kilometre 4.3, where the trail to Goat Lake branches north (see *Goat Lake* description).

The road ends at the Snowshoe Cabin, where trails branch southwest to Twin Lakes and northwest to Lost Lake and Castle River Divide. Tamarack Trail backpackers and most day hikers follow the Twin Lakes option, climbing through heavy timber and across avalanche slopes at the foot of Mount Bauerman to reach Upper Twin Lake in just over two kilometres. Upper Twin Lake is a small, beautifully coloured body of water backed up against the Great Divide, and along with the nearby Lower Twin, it serves as the headwaters for Bauerman Creek. Fishing in both lakes is for brook trout.

Near the north shore of Upper Twin Lake, a steep 1.5 kilometre trail branches west to Sage Pass. This 2165 metre summit on the crest of the Great Divide offers views into British Columbia as well as to the upper Bauerman Valley.

Hikers who are returning to Red Rock Canyon from Twin Lakes can continue south on the Tamarack Trail, then follow the Blakiston Creek trail back to the canyon. This alternate route is only two kilometres longer than the Bauerman Valley approach. Total distance for the Snowshoe Trail-Twin Lakes-Blakiston

Beargrass on the shore of Lost Lake

Creek circuit is 25 kilometres. (See *Tamarack Trail* and *Blakiston Creek* descriptions.)

Lost Lake. Backpackers camped at the Snowshoe Cabin Campground will find the short trail to Lost Lake a pleasant half-day diversion. The trail branches northwest beyond the campground and reaches this tiny but very pretty tarn in just 1.9 kilometres. By continuing past Lost Lake, the hiker can climb to the park boundary on forested Castle River Di-

vide in another 1.2 kilometres. (The trail continues onto the headwaters of the Castle River and eventually connects in with a provincial forest access road.)

The Snowshoe Trail is one of the few trails in Waterton Park open to bicycles. This makes day trips to Twin Lakes and other points along the divide even more feasible, since visitors can cycle to the end of the road, then hike to these destinations.

The Tamarack Trail

Akamina Parkway to Red Rock Canyon—36.1 kilometres (22.4 miles)

Backpack

Allow 2-3 days

Maximum elevation: 2560 metres (8,400 feet)

Minimum elevation: 1495 metres (4,900 feet)

Topo maps: Waterton Lakes National Park

Point of Departure: Northbound hikers can reach the south end of the trail by following the Akamina Parkway 10 kilometres (6 miles) to the *Rowe Lakes* trail head. Southbound hikers can reach the north end of the trail by following the Red Rock Parkway 14 kilometres (8½ miles) to the beginning of the *Snowshoe Trail* at Red Rock Canyon.

0.0—Akamina Parkway (1610 m).

—Follow *Rowe Lakes* trail.

5.2—Rowe Basin Junction (2010 m). Campground. Tamarack Trail branches right from Rowe Lakes trail.

8.5—Lineham Ridge (2560 m).

13.8—Blakiston Creek south fork (1890 m).

15.7—Festubert Saddle (2225 m).

17.7—Lone Lake and campground (2025 m).

21.5—Junction. Trail to South Kootenay Pass branches left (1.0 km).

21.6—Junction. *Blakiston Creek* trail branches right.

22.2—Blue Grouse Basin (1935 m).

24.1—Lower Twin Lake.

24.7—Upper Twin Lake and campground (1950 m).

24.8—Junction. Sage Pass to left (1.5 km).

27.9—Junction (1720 m). Snowshoe Warden Cabin and campground. Intersection with *Snowshoe Trail.*

—Follow *Snowshoe Trail* to Red Rock Canyon.

36.1—Red Rock Canyon (1495 m).

Tracing a major portion of the park's west boundary along the Great Divide, the Tamarack Trail constitutes a rugged and spectacular hike of 36 kilometres. Named for the many stands of "tamarack," or alpine larch, which it passes through, it is one of the finest highline treks in the Canadian Rockies. Because of the length and vertical profile of the hike (nearly 3000 metres of combined ascent and descent), it should be considered only by backpackers who are in fairly good shape.

There is an elevation advantage to starting the trip from its southern end, though you may question the benefit after all the ups and downs. Starting from the Akamina Parkway, the hike follows the Rowe Lakes trail for the first 5.2 kilometres. At Rowe Basin, between the Lower and Upper Rowe Lakes, it branches north and climbs to the highest point on the trip, the 2560 metre summit of Lineham Ridge. The view out over this section of the Rockies is exceptional. (See *Rowe Lakes* description.)

From Lineham Ridge, the trail makes a long, switchbacking descent to the headwaters of Blakiston Creek's south fork. After crossing this tributary, the second tough climb of the trip begins, a 360 metre rise to a saddle on the east ridge of Festubert Mountain. From this lofty viewpoint, the trail drops rapidly to Lone Lake at Kilometre 17.7, the midpoint of the journey.

The trail proceeds north beyond Lone Lake at a relatively level grade, alternately working through beautiful forest and across subalpine meadows. After passing the South Kootenay Pass and Blakiston Creek junctions, it runs through Blue Grouse Basin and across the western ridge of Mount Bauerman to the Twin Lakes. The last leg of the journey follows the Snowshoe Trail-Twin Lakes trail down the Bauerman Valley to Red Rock Canyon. (See *Snowshoe Trail* description.)

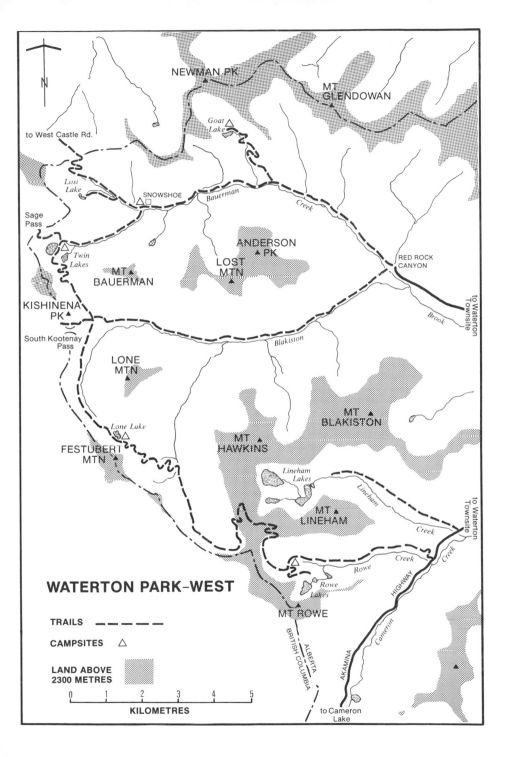

WATERTON PARK-WEST

TRAILS — — — — —

CAMPSITES △

LAND ABOVE
2300 METRES

0 1 2 3 4 5
KILOMETRES

(Map labels)

N

to West Castle Rd.

NEWMAN PK

MT GLENDOWAN

Goat Lake

Lost Lake

SNOWSHOE

Bauerman Creek

Sage Pass

Twin Lakes

MT BAUERMAN

ANDERSON PK

LOST MTN

RED ROCK CANYON

to Waterton Townsite

KISHINENA PK

South Kootenay Pass

Blakiston Brook

LONE MTN

MT BLAKISTON

Lone Lake

MT HAWKINS

FESTUBERT MTN

Lineham Lakes

Lineham Creek

MT LINEHAM

to Waterton Townsite

Rowe Creek

Rowe Lakes

MT ROWE

BRITISH COLUMBIA

ALBERTA

AKAMINA

Cameron

HIGHWAY

to Cameron Lake

Goat Lake

Red Rock Canyon to Goat Lake—6.7 kilometres (4.2 miles)

Day trip or backpack

Allow 2 - 3 hours one way

Elevation gain: 515 metres (1,700 feet)

Maximum elevation: 2010 metres (6,600 feet)

Topo maps: Waterton Lakes National Park

Point of Departure: From its junction with Highway #5 just north of Waterton townsite, follow the Red Rock Parkway 15 kilometres (9 miles) to its terminus at the Red Rock Canyon parking area. The trail starts at the bridge which spans the canyon just beyond the west edge of the parking lot.

0.0—Red Rock Canyon bridge (1495 m).

—Route follows wide trail through open forest along north side of creek.

4.3—Junction. *Snowshoe Trail* continues straight ahead. Branch uphill to right for Goat Lake.

—Steep climb for remainder of trip.

5.4—First of series of switchbacks.

6.2—Grade moderates into Goat Lake cirque.

6.4—Falls. First water since Bauerman Creek.

6.7—Goat Lake (2010 m). Campground.

Goat Lake is a shallow, emerald-coloured tarn surrounded by subalpine forest, lush wildflower meadows, and high ridges of crimson argillite. The small, glacially-carved cirque which contains the lake, perched high above the Bauerman Valley, is a textbook example of a hanging valley. The lake is an excellent objective for day hikers, even though the last 2.4 kilometres climbs 440 vertical metres; the ascent of this south-facing slope will wilt even the most enthusiastic on a warm day.

The first hour or so of hiking follows the Snowshoe Trail along the north side of Bauerman Creek. The track, a restored fire road, offers little inspiration, but the way is flat and there are some fine views of the 700 metre north wall of Anderson Peak — a mountain which displays a narrow, dark band of diorite (intruded igneous rock) across its face.

If you are feeling a little dry by the time you reach Kilometre 4.3 and the branch trail to Goat Lake, you had better fill your water bottle from Bauerman Creek; the way is steep and dry ahead. Climbing from the Snowshoe Trail junction and a dense forest of lodgepole pine, white spruce and Douglas fir, the trail gains elevation rapidly and emerges onto open slopes above the Bauerman Valley in less than 500 metres. Views continue to improve for the remainder of the hike.

As the trail nears the mouth of the Goat Lake cirque, the steep uphill grade moderates. Watch the limestone outcrops along this section of trail carefully, for some of these rocks contain the fossilized remains of algae colonies, visible as a series of rough concentric circles in the rock. These colonies were part of a reef which survived in a shallow Precambrian sea over one billion years ago!

Goat Lake is a quiet body of water reflecting the forest greens that encircle it. The trail continues around the lakeshore to an area of open meadowland to the

Goat Lake

north where, in midsummer, yellow glacier lilies bloom along the edges of snowbanks and many other wildflowers flourish on the abundant meltwater.

A steep scree slope descends to the water's edge on the west shore, etched by the trails of mountain goats. Above the slope stands the long crest of Avion Ridge, capped by the brilliant red argillite that is common throughout Waterton Park. Named for a town in France where Canadians fought in 1917, Avion forms part of the northwest boundary of the park. The summit beyond Avion is Newman Peak (2515 m).

Short Hikes and Nature Trails

BEAR'S HUMP — 1.2 kilometres

The Bear's Hump trail leads up a steep trail to a windswept ledge overlooking the Waterton Valley. It is one of the most popular short hikes in the Waterton Park, and a very pleasant evening outing for anyone staying in the townsite.

The trail strikes off from the Park Information Bureau at the entrance to the townsite. The track switchbacks up the Bear's Hump — the southern ridge of Mount Crandell — travelling through a forest of lodgepole pine, Douglas fir and a few white birch. After gaining 215 vertical metres in just over a kilometre, the trail emerges on a rock ledge overlooking the townsite. From this vantage point, there are excellent views down the length of Upper Waterton Lake into the United States. The trail summit also overlooks the lower Waterton Valley to the prairies beyond. *Topo map: Waterton Lakes National Park.*

CRANDELL LAKE — 0.8 kilometre

Crandell is a pretty, forest-encircled lake sandwiched between Mount Crandell and Ruby Ridge. It can be reached from either the Akamina Parkway to the south or the Red Rock Parkway to the north. With so much accessibility, it is little wonder that it receives very heavy visitation.

The shortest approach to the lake is from the Akamina Parkway, a hike of only 0.8 kilometre. The trail starts at the pulloff on the north side of the highway 7 kilometres (4.5 miles) west of Waterton townsite and follows an old wagon road over a ridge to the lake. Parks Canada has done considerable work around the lakeshore to help absorb the heavy use, and if the shoreline is not too overburdened with bodies, it is a pleasant place to while away an hour or two.

The trail to the lake from the Blakiston Valley is 2.5 kilometres long and gains approximately 120 metres of elevation. It is a route used most often by visitors overnighting at Crandell Campground, 7.5 kilometres (4.5 miles) west on the Red Rock Parkway. Campers can reach the trail by following the main access road through the campground (keeping left at all intersections) until they reach the trail sign. Another trail head, which is located just west of the Crandell Campground on the access road leading into the Canyon Church Camp, provides access for hikers who are not staying at the campground. *Topo map: Waterton Lakes National Park.*

CAMERON LAKE — 1.5 kilometres

This is a pleasant walk that runs through the cool, subalpine forest along the west shore of Cameron Lake. In addition to the lush forest environment, there are a number of fine gravel beaches for lounging and picnicking.

Follow the Akamina Parkway 16 kilometres (10 miles) to its terminus at Cameron Lake. From the parking area, walk down to the lakeshore interpretive display. The lakeshore trail follows the shoreline around to the right. The trail emerges from the trees into a broad section of brushy avalanche paths at the 1.5 kilometre mark. While it is possible to continue on to the Canada-U.S. borderline and the south end of the lake, park authorities recommend turning back here to avoid the possibility of encountering one of the grizzly bears which sometimes frequent these overgrown slopes. *Topo map: Waterton Lakes National Park.*

LINEHAM CREEK — 4.2 kilometres

This trail ascends the Lineham Creek valley to a cascade tumbling from a 100 metre cliff below the Lineham Lakes basin. It is not a popular area with hikers since the real beauties of the valley are well guarded by this cliff, and only experienced climbers who have registered out with the warden service are allowed to traverse the precipice to the hanging valley above. But for those who would like to escape the busyness of Waterton trails, this hike might just be the ticket. And if you have the prerequisite mountaineering skills, the Lineham Basin is a very special place, indeed.

The trail head lies on the north side of the Akamina Parkway 9.5 kilometres (6 miles) from Waterton townsite, just east of the Lineham Creek bridge. The trail is quite straightforward as it ascends the north side of the Lineham Creek valley. After a relatively steep climb along open, south-facing slopes, the ascent moderates in the cool forest of the upper valley. The trail ends near the base of the Lineham Falls cliff — a place where most hikers will turn for home. The route up the cliff is quite exposed, and one corner in particular requires steady nerves and some skill. There are five lakes situated in the basin immediately above the cliff, two ranking as the largest lakes above 2000 metres in the park. The lakes' setting is distinctively subalpine — an open forest of alpine fir and Engelmann spruce with a scattering of alpine larch and whitebark pine. *Topo map: Waterton Lakes National Park.*

BELLY RIVER — 2.4 kilometres

The Belly River, originating in Glacier National Park, Montana, and running northward into Canada, has long been recognized for its excellent fishing. This old wagon road running south from the Belly River Campground to the International Boundary along the east side of the river provides access to this prime trout stream on Canadian territory.

Follow the Chief Mountain Highway (Hwy #6) to the Belly River Campground, 18 kilometres (11 miles) south of its intersection with Highway #5, or 4 kilometres (2.5 miles) north of the Canada-U.S. border crossing. The wagon road runs south from an access gate at the rear of the campground into a forest of lodgepole pine, spruce and aspen. The two-wheeled track is flat all the way to the border and seldom strays far from the river. (Because of U.S. immigration and customs requirements, trips to the upper Belly River in Glacier National Park should utilize the cutoff trail running southwest from the U.S. Customs Station at Chief Mountain.) *Topo map: Waterton Lakes National Park.*

Mount Assiniboine Provincial Park

Mount Assiniboine is a 385 square kilometre park administered by the Province of British Columbia. It is a triangular-shaped park bounded on the east by the continental divide and Banff National Park, on the west by Kootenay National Park, and on the south by B.C. provincial forest lands.

The focal point of the area is the mountain which gives the park its name. At 3618 metres above sea level, Mount Assiniboine is the seventh highest peak in the Canadian Rockies; since its summit is situated on the Alberta-B.C. boundary, it has the distinction of being the highest point in both Mount Assiniboine Provincial Park and Banff National Park. The mountain, which soars spectacularly above its neighbours and is visible for many kilometres in all directions, is distinctive not only for its height but for its pyramid shape, which bears a resemblance to Switzerland's Matterhorn (and thus labelled "the Matterhorn of the Rockies").

Situated beneath Mount Assiniboine's north face at an elevation of 2165 metres above sea level, Lake Magog serves as the core for most of the park's wilderness recreation activity. Many backpackers devote only three days to an Assiniboine trip, usually spending a long day getting to the mountain, another day relaxing along the shores of Lake Magog or strolling to nearby Sunburst Valley, and a final day on the trail back to civilization. But there are many excellent day hikes which can be completed from Lake Magog, trips ranging from half-day jaunts to Nub Peak, Wonder Pass and the Sunburst Valley to full day outings such as Og Lake, Ferro Pass and Og Pass-Windy Ridge. A visit of four days to a week is a prerequisite to uncovering the real glories of the area.

Most backpackers stay at the Lake Magog Campground above the lake's west shore. No firewood is available, so campers should be equipped with white gasoline or cartridge gas stoves. Small spring-fed streams provide the only water for the campground. As of this writing, there is a nightly fee of $5 per tent/party (after you set your camp, park rangers come by to collect this fee). There is no charge at park campgrounds beyond the core area.

The Naiset Cabins are located above Lake Magog's northeast shore. Originally constructed by the Alpine Club of Canada, four of these cabins are currently operated by the parks department as overnight camping shelters, accommodating up to a total of 29 persons. During the summer, these cabins are available on a first-come, first-serve basis, but there is no way of guaranteeing that space will be available. The current nightly charge is $5 per person, collected by the park ranger.

Mount Assiniboine Lodge is also located at the northeast corner of Lake Magog, 500 metres north of the Naiset Cabins. This is the only commercial accommodation in the park, and rates are comparable to other backcountry lodges in the mountain parks. (Information and reservations are available through Mount Assiniboine Lodge, Box 1527, Canmore, Alberta T0L 0M0 or by phoning 403-678-2883.)

B.C. Parks rangers are stationed at the Naiset Cabins (Paintbrush Cabin) and the Sunburst Cabin on Sunburst Lake during the summer. District park headquarters are located at Box 118, Wasa, B.C. V0B 2K0 (phone 604-422-3212).

Access: There are several trails which provide access to the core area of Mount Assiniboine Provincial Park. The most direct and popular run from the Spray Lakes Reservoir area via Bryant Creek and from Sunshine Village via Citadel Pass.

Spray Lakes Reservoir. Traditionally, the trail crossing Assiniboine Pass from Bryant Creek is the most popular route into the park because it is the shortest. Distance from the Spray Lakes Reservoir to the Lake Magog Campground can be as short as 20 kilometres or as long as 27, depending on the point of departure.

328

Mount Assiniboine

The Marvel Lake-Wonder Pass route is a variation on the Bryant Creek approach and far more scenic than the slog over Assiniboine Pass. The trail, which branches from the Bryant Creek route at the Bryant Creek Warden Cabin, adds approximately one kilometre to the journey, but because the climb from Marvel Lake to Wonder Pass is so steep, most hikers prefer to use the trail as an exit route from Assiniboine. (See *Bryant Creek* and *Marvel Lake* descriptions, Banff Park chapter.)

Sunshine Village. The trail running from Sunshine Village in Banff Park to Lake Magog via Citadel Pass and Og Lake is a bit longer than the Spray Lakes Reservoir-Bryant Creek approaches, but it offers many scenic rewards. And since Sunshine Village is higher than Lake Magog, there is a lot less climbing on this route. The major drawback is a long, tedious section through the Valley of the Rocks. Total distance from Sunshine Village to Lake Magog Campground is 29 kilometres. (See *Citadel Pass,* Banff Park chapter, and *Og Lake,* Assiniboine Park chapter.)

Though not nearly so popular as the Spray Lakes and Sunshine Village approaches, the 32 kilometre trail running from the Vermilion River in Kootenay Park via Simpson River, Surprise Creek and Ferro Pass is a frequently travelled route (see *Simpson River,* Kootenay Park chapter, and *Ferro Pass,* Assiniboine Park chapter). It is also possible to reach Lake Magog from the Banff townsite vicinity via Brewster Creek, Allenby Pass and Og Pass — a total distance of 47 kilometres (see *Brewster Creek,* Banff Park chapter, and *Og Pass,* Assiniboine Park chapter). Another trail leading up the Mitchell River from a mining road south of Assiniboine Park is long (30 kilometres), tedious and seldom used.

Other than hiking to Assiniboine Provincial Park, one can also fly there. Commercial helicopter operators based at the heliport in Canmore, Alberta, are permitted to fly campers and lodge guests to the Lake Magog area on Fridays, Sundays and holiday Mondays throughout the summer. As of this writing, one-way fees are running around $40 per person.

Og Lake

Lake Magog Campground to Og Lake Campground—6.7 kilometres (4.2 miles)
Lake Magog Campground to Citadel Pass—19.6 kilometres (12.2 miles)

Backpack

Allow 2 hours to Og Lake

Elevation gain: 195 metres (640 feet)

Maximum elevation: 2360 metres (7,750 feet)

Topo maps: Mount Assiniboine 82 J/13
           Banff 82 O/4†

    † trail not shown

Point of Departure: Travel to Mount Assiniboine Provincial Park as described in *Mount Assiniboine* introduction (see page 328). The trail, as described here, starts from the Lake Magog Campground. (Starting from Assiniboine Lodge subtract 1.4 kilometres and from Naiset Cabins 0.9 kilometre.)

0.0—Lake Magog Campground (2165 m).

—Follow *Assiniboine Pass* trail.

1.6—Junction. Branch trail right to Assiniboine Lodge (0.2 km) and Naiset Cabins (0.7 km).

1.9—Junction. Assiniboine Pass straight ahead. Turn left for Og Lake and Citadel Pass.

2.4—Junction. Horse trail from Sunburst Lake intersects from left.

2.6—Junction. Og Pass and Assiniboine Pass horse trail to right. Keep left.

—Gradual descent across Og Meadows.

6.7—Og Lake and campground (2060 m).

7.5—Trail enters south end Valley of the Rocks.

—Trail winds and rolls through Valley of the Rocks.

12.4—Junction and campground. Trail to Golden Valley and Policeman's Meadows to left. Highline trail to Citadel Pass to right.

15.1—Junction. Trail to Golden Valley and Policeman's Meadows intersects from left.

—Steep climb to Citadel Pass.

19.6—Citadel Pass (2360 m). Assiniboine-Banff boundary. Intersection with *Citadel Pass* trail, Banff Park.

The Og Lake trail rolls through scattered subalpine forest and flower-filled meadows — including the vast Og Meadows — to reach this rockbound lake at the foot of Og Mountain in just over six kilometres. Beyond Og Lake, the trail runs for another 13 kilometres to the park boundary on the 2360 metre summit of Citadel Pass and serves as a main access route to Mount Assiniboine from the north.

The hike to Og Lake is a bit longer than some of the other day trips radiating from Lake Magog, but it is an undemanding walk with little gain or loss of elevation. From the Lake Magog Campground, follow the Assiniboine Pass trail 1.9 kilometres to the Og Lake junction. Here the trail branches due north and makes a gradual descent through a pleasant vale to the Og Meadows. The trail continues north through this extensive meadowland for three kilometres or so. The rocky slopes of Nub Peak rise above the meadows to the west, while the steeply tilted strata of Cave and Og Mountains are constant companions to the east. For hikers approaching the area from Sunshine Village-Citadel Pass, the Og Meadows provide the first good views of Mount Assiniboine.

Og Lake is the creation of a massive rockslide which fills much of the valley from this point north. It is a sink lake, draining down into the boulders and loose rock which form its basin. While views are somewhat limited in this part of the valley, the lake still makes a pleasant lunch-stop and an excellent playground for bouldering and rock scrambling.

The trail continues north from the lake into the Valley of the Rocks, but this extension is of little interest to day trippers from Lake Magog. It is the most tedious part of the journey for backpackers hiking to or from Sunshine Village and Citadel Pass, however, as the

Og Lake

trail rolls and twists through several kilometres of boulder-filled forest. Travellers
should enter the Valley of the Rocks with
full water bottles, since this is a very dry
area.

At the north end of the Valley of the
Rocks, the trail climbs over a low, forested ridge and enters the Golden Valley.
It splits at Kilometre 12.4, allowing hikers
to either descend to the floor of the valley
or stay high on the way to Citadel Pass.
The climb to the pass is long and gruelling, factors which discourage most backpackers from using this route as an exit
from Mount Assiniboine. Once Citadel
Pass is reached, the hiker faces 9.3 kilometres of pleasant meadow-walking to
reach Sunshine Village. (See *Citadel Pass*
description, Banff Park chapter.)

Og Pass — Windy Ridge

Lake Magog Campground to Og Pass—6.8 kilometres (4.2 miles)
Lake Magog Campground to Windy Ridge—8.7 kilometres (5.4 miles)

Backpack

Allow 3-4 hours to Windy Ridge

Elevation gain: 470 metres (1,550 feet)

Maximum elevation: 2635 metres (8,650 feet)

Topo maps: Mount Assiniboine 82 J/13

Point of Departure: Travel to Mount Assiniboine Provincial Park as described in *Mount Assiniboine* introduction (see page 328). The trail, as described here, starts from the Lake Magog Campground. (Starting from Assiniboine Lodge subtract 1.4 kilometres and from Naiset Cabins 0.9 kilometre.)

0.0—Lake Magog Campground (2165 m).

—Follow *Assiniboine Pass* trail.

1.6—Junction. Branch trail right to Assiniboine Lodge (0.2 km) and Naiset Cabins (0.7 km).

1.9—Junction. Assiniboine Pass straight ahead. Turn left for Og Pass-Windy Ridge.

2.4—Junction. Horse trail from Sunburst Lake intersects from left.

2.6—Junction. Og Lake and Citadel Pass to left. Keep right.

—Trail angles due north across Og Meadows.

2.9—Junction. Assiniboine Pass horse trail branches right. Keep left.

4.7—Trail enters forest, begins climb to Og Pass.

6.2—Trail flattens out into rolling terrain of Og Pass.

6.5—Junction. Intersection with *Brewster Creek* trail, Banff Park. Stay right to Og Pass summit (0.3 km), Allenby Pass and Brewster Creek. Keep left for Windy Ridge.

—Moderately steep climb across meadows and open talus slopes.

8.7—Windy Ridge Summit (2635 m).

The trail to Og Pass and Windy Ridge is one of the most rewarding day trips in Assiniboine Park. No other trail provides such an expansive panorama of the Mount Assiniboine environs, and the wildflower meadow on the plateau below Windy Ridge is one of the finest in the Canadian Rockies. And once you reach the trail's 2635 metre summit, overlooking the headwaters of the Brewster Creek valley, you are standing on one of the highest trail-accessible points in the mountain parks.

The route to Og Pass and Windy Ridge begins on the Assiniboine Pass trail, then branches north onto the Og Lake trail. After descending a shallow vale, the hiker passes through a small canyon and emerges onto the broad expanse of the Og Meadows. Here the trail splits right from the Og Lake route and angles due north toward Og Mountain.

The trail over Og Pass was once used by commercial horse parties travelling between Banff and Mount Assiniboine via Brewster Creek. Today it is closed to horses, but the multi-tracks worn into the soft soil over the decades still lead across the Og Meadows and up through timberline forest to the pass. Just beyond the six kilometre mark, the trail emerges from the last dense stands of alpine larch and fir and levels off onto the long, meadowy summit of Og Pass.

At Kilometre 6.5, the trail to Windy Ridge branches north from the eastbound Og Pass trail. The true summit of the pass lies 300 metres from this junction, and a short distance beyond is a very pretty lake backed against the rocky north slope of Cave Mountain. The trail continues eastward into Banff Park and eventually crosses Allenby Pass to Brewster Creek (see *Brewster Creek*, Banff Park chapter).

If the weather is at all reasonable, hikers should continue the journey on the

Brewster Valley from Windy Ridge

Windy Ridge trail. While the trip becomes more strenuous beyond the Og Pass-Windy Ridge junction, the views become more and more rewarding as the trail ascends the west slope of Og Mountain.

Just 1.4 kilometres above the junction, the climb moderates briefly as the trail traverses a grassy ridge. Situated at a lofty 2515 metres above sea level, this small plateau provides a fantastic panorama, stretching from the peaks of the Assiniboine group on the south to Kootenay's Rockwall and Yoho's twin-towered Goodsir Peak on the far northwestern horizon. This ridge also comprises one of the best alpine flower gardens in the park, and in late July and early August, it is replete with blooming wild-flowers, including forget-me-nots, arnica, white paintbrush, contorted lousewort, golden fleabane, alpine speedwell and red-stemmed saxifrage.

After one last uphill grunt along a steep talus slope, the trail crests a high saddle just below Og Mountain's summit. From this point, the hiker has a mountaineer's-eye view of the ranges to the east and the upper Brewster Creek valley (those with sharp vision or binoculars can pick out the Halfway Cabin on the edge of a meadow in that valley). A dizzy precipice drops away from the eastern lip of the Windy Ridge saddle, and hikers can peer warily between their feet 400 vertical metres to a beautiful hanging valley and an exquisite azure lake.

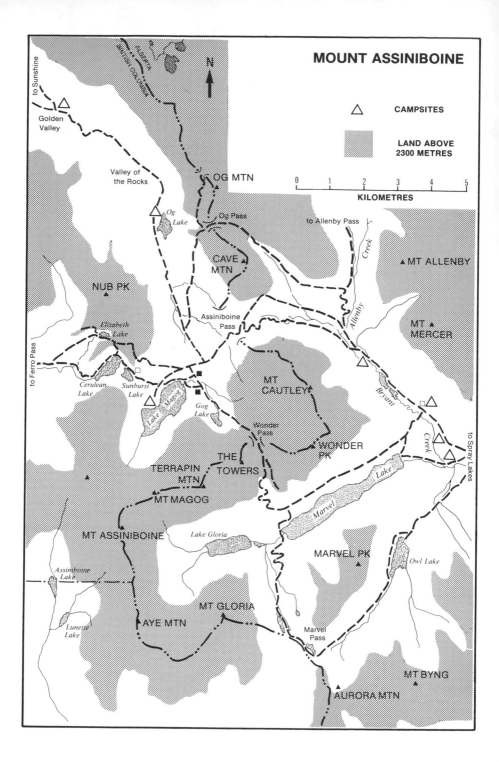

MOUNT ASSINIBOINE

△ CAMPSITES

▨ LAND ABOVE 2300 METRES

0 1 2 3 4 5
KILOMETRES

to Sunshine

ALBERTA
BRITISH COLUMBIA

N

Golden Valley

Valley of the Rocks

Og Lake

OG MTN

Og Pass

to Allenby Pass

▲ MT ALLENBY

CAVE MTN

NUB PK ▲

Elizabeth Lake

Assiniboine Pass

MT ▲ MERCER

Allenby Creek

to Ferro Pass

Cerulean Lake

Sunburst Lake

Lake Magog

Gog Lake

MT CAUTLEY

Bryant

Creek

to Spray Lakes

WONDER PK

Wonder Pass

THE TOWERS

TERRAPIN MTN

Marvel Lake

MT MAGOG

MT ASSINIBOINE

Lake Gloria

Marvel

MARVEL PK ▲

Owl Lake

Assiniboine Lake

Luneue Lake

AYE MTN

MT GLORIA

Marvel Pass

MT BYNG ▲

AURORA MTN ▲

Assiniboine Pass

Lake Magog Campground to Assiniboine Pass—3.7 kilometres (2.3 miles)

Backpack

Allow 1 hour one way

Elevation gain: nil

Maximum elevation: 2165 metres (7,100 feet)

Topo maps: Mount Assiniboine 82 J/13

Point of Departure: Travel to Mount Assiniboine Provincial Park as described in *Mount Assiniboine* introduction (see page 328). The trail, as described here, starts from the Lake Magog Campground. (Starting from Assiniboine Lodge subtract 1.4 kilometres and from Naiset Cabins 0.9 kilometre.)

0.0—Lake Magog Campground (2165 m).

—Follow trail leading north from campground.

0.2—Junction. Sunburst Lake to left (0.4 km). Naiset Cabins to right (1.6 km). Assiniboine Pass straight ahead.

1.5—Junction. Nub Peak trail branches left.

1.6—Junction. Branch trail right to Assiniboine Lodge (0.2 km) and Naiset Cabins (0.7 km).

1.9—Junction. Trail to Og Lake-Citadel Pass and Og Pass branches left.

—Trail rolls through forest and meadow.

3.2—O'Brien Meadows.

3.4—Assiniboine Park trail map.

—Climb through trees to Assiniboine Pass summit.

3.7—Assiniboine Pass (2165 m). Intersection with *Bryant Creek* trail, Banff Park.

The 3.7 kilometre trail running between the Lake Magog Campground and Assiniboine Pass on the park's eastern boundary serves two main purposes: it intersects with Banff Park's Bryant Creek trail to create the shortest and most direct access route to Mount Assiniboine; and, as the central trail bisecting the Lake Magog environs, it serves as the trail head for trips to Nub Peak, Og Lake and Og Pass. The pass can also be hiked from Lake Magog as a half-day outing, but the trip is rather ho-hum compared to other hikes in the area.

Starting from the campground above the west shore of Lake Magog, the trail runs in a northerly direction through willow meadows and scattered stands of fir and spruce. At Kilometre 0.2, a side-trail branches east along the north shore of Lake Magog to provide a direct route to Mount Assiniboine Lodge, the Naiset Cabins and Wonder Pass (see *Wonder Pass* description); a branch running west from this junction reaches Sunburst Lake in 0.4 kilometres. Meanwhile, the Assiniboine Pass trail continues its journey on a northeasterly course, travelling across more open meadowland and passing the Nub Peak junction at Kilometre 1.5.

After passing near Assiniboine Lodge at Kilometre 1.6, the trail rolls through scattered subalpine forest to the summit of Assiniboine Pass. The only major opening along the way comes at Kilometre 3.2, when the trail crosses the O'Brien Meadows — an area which once served as a makeshift airstrip for aircraft flying supplies and guests to Mount Assiniboine Lodge. (A trail map in the middle of the meadows provides orientation for incoming hikers.) After traversing the forested summit of Assiniboine Pass, the trail descends into Banff Park's Bryant Creek valley, which provides access between Mount Assiniboine Park and the Spray Lakes Reservoir (see *Bryant Creek,* Banff Park chapter).

Wonder Pass

Lake Magog Campground to Wonder Pass—4.3 kilometres (2.7 miles)

Backpack

Allow 1½-2 hours one way

Elevation gain: 230 metres (750 feet)

Maximum elevation: 2395 metres (7,850 feet)

Topo maps: Mount Assiniboine 82 J/13

Point of Departure: Travel to Mount Assiniboine Provincial Park as described in *Mount Assiniboine* introduction (see page 328). The trail, as described here, starts from the Lake Magog Campground. (Starting from Assiniboine Lodge subtract 1.2 kilometres and from Naiset Cabins 1.7 kilometres.)

0.0—Lake Magog Campground (2165 m).

—Follow trail leading north from campground.

0.2—Junction. Sunburst Lake to left (0.4 km). Assiniboine Pass straight ahead (3.5 km). Turn right for Wonder Pass.

—Trail skirts above north shore of Lake Magog.

1.6—Junction. Branch trail left to Assiniboine Lodge (0.4 km).

1.7—Naiset Cabins. Paintbrush Ranger Cabin.

—Trail climbs through meadow and scattered forest along Gog Creek.

2.3—Gog Creek bridge.

2.6—Junction. Gog Lake to right 100 metres.

—Steep pitch followed by moderate uphill.

3.0—Trail flattens out into meadow and larch stands.

3.4—Tributary stream bridge.

—Steady climb to Wonder Pass through larch and meadows.

4.3—Wonder Pass (2395 m). Intersection with *Marvel Lake-Wonder Pass* trail, Banff Park.

5.0—Junction. Wonder Pass Viewpoint trail branches left (unmarked junction) from Marvel Lake trail.

5.5—Wonder Pass Viewpoint (2375 m).

For backpackers travelling to Mount Assiniboine and back via Bryant Creek, the Wonder Pass variation to this route is an obvious choice on the return to Spray Lakes Reservoir. For hikers utilizing other access routes, or those who flew to the park by helicopter, Wonder Pass should rank high on a list of priority day hikes from Lake Magog. The approach to the pass from Lake Magog features lush wildflower meadows, pure stands of alpine larch and Gog Lake; the panorama from the summit extends north for over 25 kilometres to the peaks surrounding the Sunshine Meadows; and a short side trip from the main trail to a ridge on the side of Wonder Peak provides breathtaking views down to Marvel Lake.

If you are starting to the pass from the Lake Magog Campground, hike the Assiniboine Pass trail north for 200 metres to the first trail junction. Turn right and follow the trail running east above the north shore of Lake Magog. At a split below Mount Assiniboine Lodge, keep right and climb through a narrow band of trees to the Naiset Cabins. Beyond the cabins, the trail ascends a shallow vale beside Gog Creek, running in a southeasterly direction toward the pass. After swinging across the creek at Kilometre 2.3, the hiker comes abreast of Gog Lake, lying in a marshy meadow beneath the northeast wall of Naiset Point.

Above Gog Lake, the trail climbs in stages through alpine larch stands interspersed with open meadows. This is a particularly beautiful section during the third week of September, when the autumn gold of the larch needles is at its most brilliant. As you crest the summit of Wonder Pass, you pass through the last scattered remnants of these deciduous conifers and receive your first good views back over the core area of Mount Assiniboine Park; the vistas stretch northward along the course of Og Valley to Citadel Pass and beyond. Backpackers departing Mount Assiniboine Park on this route

Wonder Pass

will intersect with Banff Park's Marvel
Lake-Wonder Pass trail on this summit,
beginning the descent that will eventually
bring them back to the Bryant Creek trail
at Bryant Creek Warden Cabin (see *Marvel Lake,* Banff Park chapter.)

Wonder Pass Viewpoint. Day hikers
can continue the journey east of Wonder
Pass as well, descending rocky meadows
between Wonder Peak and The Towers
to an unmarked trail split 700 metres
below the pass. By following the track
which angles left at this junction, you can
contour along the slope of Wonder Peak
for 500 metres or so to the Wonder Pass
Viewpoint — a 2375 metre platform overlooking Marvel Lake and Lake Gloria.
The extensive icefield which stretches
between Aye and Eon Mountains feeds
these two lakes, but since Lake Gloria
filters out most of the silt from this glacier
before it reaches Marvel Lake, its colour
is a milky turquoise as compared to the
darker blue of Marvel. The ice-clad summits of the Assiniboine group create an
impressive amphitheatre above Lake
Gloria, while the forested summit of
Marvel Pass can be seen southwest of
Marvel Lake and Marvel Peak.

Nub Peak

Lake Magog Campground to Nub Ridge—3.8 kilometres (2.4 miles)

Backpack

Allow 1½ hours to Nub Ridge

Elevation gain: 210 metres (700 feet)

Maximum elevation: 2375 metres (7,800 feet)

Topo maps: Mount Assiniboine 82 J/13

Point of Departure: Travel to Mount Assiniboine Provincial Park as described in *Mount Assiniboine* introduction (see page 328). The trail, as described here, starts from the Lake Magog Campground. (Starting from Assiniboine Lodge subtract 1.2 kilometres and from Naiset Cabins 0.7 kilometre.)

0.0—Lake Magog Campground (2165 m).

—Follow *Assiniboine Pass* trail north from campground.

1.5—Junction. Trail to Nub Peak branches left from Assiniboine Pass trail.

—Trail runs northwest across meadow.

1.9—Junction. Horse trail from Assiniboine Pass intersects from right.

2.5—Junction. Horse trail to Sunburst Lake branches left.

—Steady uphill through subalpine forest.

3.6—Trail crests Nub Ridge.

3.8—Nub Ridge Summit (2375 m). Nub Peak to north 2 kms.

—Trail descends west from ridge.

4.8—Junction. Intersection with *Sunburst Valley Circuit*. Elizabeth Lake to right 0.4 km. Cerulean Lake to left 0.5 km.

Nub Peak is a rather unassuming little mountain rising to the north of the Sunburst Valley. While its elevation of 2748 metres above sea level is far short of the Assiniboine Group peaks to the immediate south, its strategic location, in the very centre of the park's core area, makes it an outstanding viewpoint for Mount Assiniboine and all the lakes along the north slope of the Assiniboine Group. A trail climbs from the Magog Meadows to a fine vantage point on Nub Ridge, and any strong hiker with good footwear can scramble another two kilometres to the summit of the peak for the best views of all. And this trail can be tied in quite easily with the Sunburst Valley Circuit to create one of the finest loop day hikes in the Canadian Rockies.

The trail to Nub Ridge branches from the Assiniboine Pass trail just 1.5 kilometres northeast of the Lake Magog Campground. From this junction, it runs northwest across a willow meadow and then climbs into a typical high-level subalpine forest of Engelmann spruce, alpine fir and larch. After just over a kilometre of steady climbing, the hiker emerges onto the crest of Nub Ridge and gets his first good views of Mount Assiniboine and Lake Magog.

The trail continues along the crest of the ridge in a northwesterly direction to a shallow saddle. At this point, it swings due west and begins to descend toward Elizabeth Lake. Less energetic hikers can accept the good views from this section of the ridge, and then either return the way they came or continue on toward Elizabeth Lake and the Sunburst Valley Circuit; more adventurous souls will want to climb the steepening, trackless ridge to the Nublet or Nub Peak.

From any of the main viewpoints along Nub Ridge, the Mount Assiniboine environs are laid out like a map at your feet: the great wall formed by Wedgwood Peak, The Marshall and Mount Watson

Cerulean Lake from Nub Ridge

glowering down upon the heavily forested shores of Wedgwood Lake; Sunburst and Cerulean Lakes wrapped
around the rocky promentory of Sunburst Peak; and the sparkling waters of
the park's largest body of water, Lake
Magog, backed by the incomparable pyramid of Mount Assiniboine.

Sunburst Valley Circuit. By continuing
west on the trail from Nub Ridge, the
hiker can intersect the Sunburst Valley
Circuit at Kilometre 2.1, on a forested
divide just 400 metres east of the Elizabeth Lake outlet. After visiting the lake,
you can either continue around the circuit
in a counterclockwise direction or take
the direct route back over the divide to
Cerulean and Sunburst Lakes (see *Sunburst Valley Circuit* description).

Sunburst Valley

Lake Magog Campground to Elizabeth Lake—2.5 kilometres (1.6 miles)
Sunburst Valley Circuit—8.0 kilometres (5.0 miles)

Backpack

Allow 3 hours round trip

Elevation gain: 135 metres (450 feet)

Maximum elevation: 2300 metres (7,550 feet)

Topo maps: Mount Assiniboine 82 J/13

Point of Departure: Travel to Mount Assiniboine Provincial Park as described in *Mount Assiniboine* introduction (see page 328). The trail, as described here, starts from the Lake Magog Campground. (Starting from Assiniboine Lodge add 1.3 kilometres and from Naiset Cabins 1.5 kilometres.)

0.0—Lake Magog Campground (2165 m).

—Trail runs northwest along north side of campground.

0.4—Junction. Trail from Assiniboine Lodge and Naiset Cabins intersects from right.

0.8—Sunburst Lake.

0.9—Sunburst Cabin (Park Ranger Cabin).

1.4—Cerulean Lake.

1.6—Junction. Ferro Pass and Wedgwood Lake straight ahead. Turn right for Elizabeth Lake.

—Steady uphill through shallow valley.

2.1—Summit and junction (2300 m). Trail from Nub Ridge intersects from right.

—Trail descends to Elizabeth Lake.

2.5—Elizabeth Lake outlet.

—Trail descends through meadow and forest.

3.9—Junction. Intersection with *Ferro Pass* trail. Turn left for Cerulean Lake (1.5 kms) and right for Ferro Pass (5.2 kms).

The Sunburst Valley, lying a short distance west of Lake Magog, is the most popular destination for day hikers in the core of Mount Assiniboine Park. The valley contains Sunburst and Cerulean Lakes, and most visitors include nearby Elizabeth Lake in their itinerary. For hikers willing to commit themselves to a longer outing, Nub Ridge and Chuck's Ridge can be included to make a highly scenic, full day's outing.

The route from Lake Magog Campground to Sunburst Valley follows the trail which climbs along the northern edge of the campground and, after clearing the last campsite, continues in a northwesterly direction along a shallow valley. (From Mount Assiniboine Lodge and Naiset Cabins, simply follow the trail which runs above the north shore of Lake Magog and intersect this route just west of the campground.) The trail reaches Sunburst Lake in less than a kilometre and follows along the northeast shoreline. Along the way, the hiker passes the Sunburst Cabin — an old cabin built by Banff outfitter Pat Brewster in the mid-1930s which now serves as a park ranger residence. Back to the south, Mount Assiniboine is still visible, peeking out from behind the cliffs of Sunburst Peak.

Only a narrow band of trees separates Sunburst from its larger neighbour Cerulean Lake. The trail stays along Cerulean's northeast shore to a junction at the northernmost tip of the lake. While it is possible to continue to the west end of the lake from this intersection (see *Ferro Pass* description), most hikers turn right and climb over the forested divide to the north to tiny Elizabeth Lake. This pretty lake is named for Elizabeth "Lizzie" Rummel, a local mountain woman who operated a tent camp from Sunburst Cabin every summer from 1951 to 1970.

From the outlet bridge at the west end of Elizabeth Lake, hikers can return the

Sunburst and Cerulean Lakes

way they came or continue in a westerly direction through open forest for 1.4 kilometres to a junction with the Ferro Pass trail west of Cerulean Lake. By turning left on the Ferro Pass route, they can return to the junction at the north end of Cerulean to complete a 4.8 kilometre circuit.

Nub Ridge. Without adding a lot of distance to the trip, hikers can have the unique view of Lake Magog and Mount Assiniboine provided by Nub Ridge and the Sunburst Valley lakes, too. Begin the circuit by hiking to Nub Ridge (see *Nub Peak* description), then descend the one-kilometre trail which links the ridge to the junction with the Sunburst Valley circuit just 400 metres east of Elizabeth Lake's outlet bridge. After visiting Elizabeth, finish the trip in either direction, as out-lined in the Sunburst Valley description.

Chuck's Ridge. This 800 metre-long trail branches from the Sunburst Valley circuit just west of the Elizabeth Lake outlet bridge and climbs steeply to a viewpoint on the southwest ridge of Nub Peak. Views from this fine lookout point extend over the Sunburst Valley area and the headwaters of the Mitchell River valley.

Wedgwood Lake. A 3.4 kilometre trail which branches from the Ferro Pass route at the west end of Cerulean Lake (see *Ferro Pass* description). Wedgwood Lake is enclosed by heavy forest, the trail is often muddy, and there is an elevation loss of 900 metres which has to be regained on the return journey, so the trail is seldom hiked except by those in search of solitude.

Ferro Pass

Backpack

Allow 3 hours one way

Elevation gain: 275 metres (900 feet)

Maximum elevation: 2270 metres (7,450 feet)

Topo maps: Mount Assiniboine 82 J/13

Point of Departure: Travel to Mount Assiniboine Provincial Park as described in *Mount Assiniboine* introduction (see page 328). The trail, as described here, starts from the Lake Magog Campground. (Starting from Assiniboine Lodge add 1.3 kilometres and from Naiset Cabins 1.5 kilometres.)

0.0—Lake Magog Campground (2165 m).

—Trail follows *Sunburst Valley* trail northwest.

0.4—Trail from Assiniboine Lodge and Naiset Cabins intersects from right.

0.8—Sunburst Lake.

0.9—Sunburst Cabin (Park Ranger Cabin).

1.4—Cerulean Lake.

1.6—Junction. Elizabeth Lake and Ferro Pass (High Route) to right. Stay left for Ferro Pass (Low Route).

—Trail follows west along Cerulean shoreline.

2.6—Junction. West end of Cerulean Lake. Trail to Wedgwood Lake and Mitchell River branches left. Keep right for Ferro Pass.

—Steady descent, contouring through forest.

4.1—Junction. Ferro Pass (High Route) from Elizabeth Lake intersects from right.

—Trail descends through forest.

5.7—Nestor Creek bridge (1995 m). Mitchell Meadows.

—Steady climb through forest and avalanche paths.

8.4—Series of steep switchbacks.

9.3—Ferro Pass (2270 m). Intersection with *Simpson River* trail at Km 22.9 (see Kootenay Park chapter).

Of all the day trips from Lake Magog, the trail to Ferro Pass is the only one which escapes the busy core area of Mount Assiniboine Park. As a result, it is the hike which provides the most solitude and the greatest sense of wilderness. The pass comprises a small meadow set within a scattered larch forest, and views from the summit stretch out over Wedgwood Lake and the Mitchell Valley to the south and the headwaters of Surprise Creek to the north.

The Ferro Pass follows the Sunburst Valley trail over its initial 1.6 kilometres, skirting along the shorelines of Sunburst and Cerulean Lakes. From the junction at the northern tip of Cerulean Lake, the hiker has the choice of following the low route to Ferro Pass by continuing west along the lakeshore or branching right to Elizabeth Lake on the high route. Despite the gain and subsequent loss of elevation on the high route, many hikers enjoy the inclusion of Elizabeth Lake in their itinerary. (It is actually 200 metres shorter to Ferro Pass via the high option). But, for the purposes of this description, we will stay on the low route (see *Sunburst Valley* trail for high route description).

At the west end of Cerulean Lake, the trail passes the Wedgwood Lake-Mitchell River junction and exits from the west end of Sunburst Valley to begin a long, gradual descent through subalpine forest. The high route rejoins the low trail at Kilometre 4.1 as the steady loss of elevation continues. At Kilometre 5.3, the trail swings north into the Nestor Creek drainage and, 400 metres farther along, reaches its lowest point at the Nestor Creek bridge on the edge of the Mitchell Meadows.

The remainder of the hike is one long, steady ascent. As the trail approaches the pass, it swings across a major avalanche path and makes a series of steep switchbacks to gain the last 135 metres or so of elevation necessary to reach the summit.

Wedgwood Lake from Ferro Pass

(Though the pass would appear to lie at the top of the avalanche path, it is actually the lower, forested notch approximately one kilometre to the west.)

While not spectacular, Ferro Pass is a pleasant summit situated amidst larch trees. Wedgwood Lake, enclosed by dense forest, lies far below the pass to the immediate south, while the massive, glacier-capped wall formed by Wedgwood Peak, The Marshall and Mount Watson serves as a very dramatic backdrop to its sylvan setting. A bit farther west, the lonely Mitchell Valley runs south into the provincial forest lands beyond the park's southern boundary. To the northwest, the long Surprise Creek drainage drops away toward the Simpson Valley; Rock Lake can be seen in the forest just over four kilometres down this

valley, at the far end of the Indian Peak escarpment. (Strong hikers can make a long day of it by hiking down to Rock Lake.) The summit of the pass is also home to a rather large colony of Columbian ground squirrels, and boreal chickadees are frequently seen flitting about in the nearby trees.

The trail running down Surprise Creek and the Simpson River serves as one of the access routes to the core area of Mount Assiniboine Park. The trail ends on the Banff-Radium Highway in Kootenay National Park, near the confluence of the Simpson and Vermilion Rivers. The distance to Lake Magog Campground via Simpson River, Surprise Creek and the Ferro Pass trail is 32 kilometres. (See *Simpson River,* Kootenay Park chapter).

343

Mount Robson Provincial Park

With an area of approximately 2170 square kilometres, British Columbia's Mount Robson is the largest provincial park in the Canadian Rockies. The park's eastern boundary is formed by a 200 kilometre stretch of the continental divide, a border it shares with Jasper National Park in Alberta. On all other sides, the park is bounded by B.C. forest lands.

Despite the park's relatively large size, most visitation is centred around the peak which gives the park its name. At 3954 metres above sea level, Mount Robson is the highest mountain in the Canadian Rockies. It seems likely the mountain was named circa 1820 for the Hudson's Bay Company factor Colin Robertson, and the name was probably corrupted to Robson by the British adventurer W. B. Cheadle when he passed down the Fraser River in 1863. Cheadle did provide the first description of this magnificent peak, however:

"On every side the snowy heads of mighty hills crowded round, whilst, immediately behind us, a giant among giants, and immeasurably supreme, rose Robson's peak . . . We saw its upper portion dimmed by a necklace of light, feathery clouds, beyond which its pointed apex of ice, glittering in the morning sun, shot up far into the blue heaven above."

Mount Robson was one of the last major mountains in the Canadian Rockies to be climbed, and even today it is considered a difficult and dangerous ascent. Attempts to scale its summit were made in 1907, 1908 and 1909, but it wasn't until the Alpine Club of Canada visited the area in 1913 that a party, led by the guide Conrad Kain, reached the top. That same year, the B.C. Legislature created Mount Robson Provincial Park.

The first recreational trail in the park was built along the Robson River to Berg Lake in the spring of 1913, constructed by the Jasper outfitter Donald "Curly" Phillips in preparation for the Alpine Club of Canada camp. That trail remains the most heavily travelled in the park, and the busiest backpacking route in the Canadian Rockies. The park's two other primary recreational trails lead out from Yellowhead Lake just west of Yellowhead Pass: Yellowhead Mountain is the best day trip in the park, and the trail leading to a high basin on the east side of Mount Fitzwilliam makes a good outing for backpackers who are willing to do a bit of exploring and rock scrambling beyond their base camp. Trails leading up the Moose and Fraser Rivers are remote, poorly maintained and, generally, only hiked by a handful of experienced backpackers each season.

Headquarters for Mount Robson Provincial Park are located at Red Pass, just west of Moose Lake on the Yellowhead Highway (Hwy. #16). During the summer months, a visitor centre operates at the Robson Meadows Campground, just south of the Mount Robson Viewpoint on the Yellowhead Highway. Registration or camping permits are not required in the park, but a nightly fee of $5 per tent/party is levied at all campgrounds on the Berg Lake trail (collected by the park ranger after you set your camp). Further information can be obtained through the Park Supervisor, Box 579, Valemount, B.C. (phone 604-566-4325).

The nearest centres providing a full range of services are located outside the park at Jasper, Alberta, and Valemount, B.C. A coffee shop-gas station complex at the Mount Robson Viewpoint offers the only services within the park.

Access: Mount Robson Provincial Park is situated 290 kilometres east of Prince George, B.C., and 390 kilometres west of Edmonton, Alberta, on the Yellowhead Highway (Hwy. #16) — the only highway access through the park. Though VIA Rail passenger trains traverse the park daily on the CNR line, the nearest stations are located beyond park boundaries at Jasper, Alberta, and Valemount, B.C. (a flag stop). Greyhound buses make daily runs east and west on the Yellowhead Highway, and flag stops can be arranged in advance for Yellowhead Pass and Mount Robson Viewpoint.

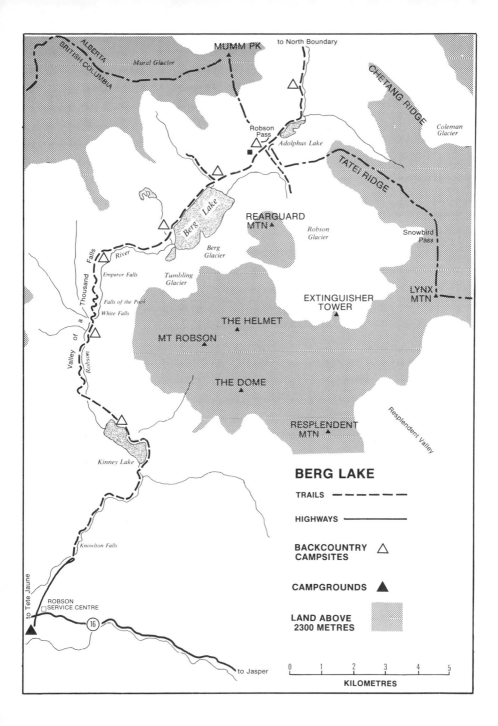

to North Boundary

ALBERTA
BRITISH COLUMBIA

MUMM PK

Mural Glacier

CHETANG RIDGE

Coleman
Glacier

Robson
Pass

Adolphus Lake

TATEI RIDGE

Berg Lake

REARGUARD
MTN ▲

Robson
Glacier

Snowbird
Pass

Falls

River

Berg
Glacier

Emperor Falls

Tumbling
Glacier

EXTINGUISHER
TOWER ▲

LYNX
MTN ▲

a Thousand

Falls of the Pool

White Falls

THE HELMET ▲

Valley

of

Robson

MT ROBSON ▲

THE DOME ▲

Resplendent

RESPLENDENT
MTN ▲

Resplendent Valley

Kinney Lake

BERG LAKE

TRAILS ― ― ― ―

HIGHWAYS ――――――

BACKCOUNTRY
CAMPSITES △

Knowlton Falls

CAMPGROUNDS ▲

to Tete Jaune

ROBSON
SERVICE CENTRE

LAND ABOVE
2300 METRES

(16)

to Jasper

| 0 | 1 | 2 | 3 | 4 | 5 |

KILOMETRES

Berg Lake

Berg Lake Parking Lot to Berg Lake—17.4 kilometres (10.8 miles)

Backpack

Allow 7 - 10 hours to Berg Lake

Elevation gain: 795 metres (2,600 feet)

Maximum elevation: 1652 metres (5,420 feet)

Topo maps: Mount Robson 83 E/3

Point of Departure: Follow the Yellowhead Highway (Hwy #16) west from Jasper townsite 84 kilometres (53 miles) to Mount Robson Viewpoint centre. Take the road that branches north beside the service centre-general store and follow it for 2 kilometres to its terminus at the Berg Lake trail parking area. The trail starts at the Robson River bridge.

0.0—Berg Lake Parking Area (855 m).

4.2—Kinney Lake (outlet bridge).

5.4—Junction. Hiker's trail branches left from horse trail.

6.7—Kinney Lake Campground.

6.9—Junction. Horse trail rejoins hiker's trail from right.

8.0—Robson River bridge.

—Cross outwash flats above Kinney Lake.

10.3—Robson River suspension bridge.

10.5—Whitehorn Campground.

11.3—Robson River suspension bridge.

—Steep switchbacks begin.

11.8—White Falls viewpoint.

12.7—Falls-of-the-Pool viewpoint.

14.3—Emperor Falls viewpoint (0.2 km to right).

15.0—Emperor Falls Campground.

—Steep uphill ends, trail runs flat.

16.9—Major tributary stream bridges.

17.4—Berg Lake (west end).

19.6—Berg Lake Campground.

20.1—Rearguard Campground.

20.9—Warden cabin.

21.6—Robson Pass Campground and shelter.

21.9—Robson Pass (1652 m). Mount Robson—Jasper park boundary. Connects with North Boundary Trail at Km 151.5.

This trail, running along the Robson River to its headwaters in Berg Lake, is the most heavily travelled backpacking route in the mountain parks. And little wonder. This turquoise lake, dotted with icebergs and backdropped by the awesome, ice-bound north wall of the highest peak in the Canadian Rockies, is one of the gems of the mountain world.

From the trail head parking area, a broad, road-width track climbs gradually along the torrent of the Robson River and through a micro-rain forest of Douglas fir, cedar, spruce and hemlock. The lush forest, which is very out-of-place in the Rocky Mountains, is in part created by Mount Robson. Rather than spreading over the broader band of the Rockies, as is usual, precipitation concentrates in this valley when Pacific weather systems run afoul of this huge mountain.

Kinney Lake is the first major point-of-interest on the trail and an excellent example of a glacially fed lake. Its waters are a milky blue, the result of great quantities of finely ground rock material fed into the Robson River by glaciers on Mount Robson and its neighbouring peaks. The lake is named for the Reverend George B. Kinney, a Canadian mountaineer who made the first attempts to scale Mount Robson between 1907 and 1909.

At Kinney Lake, the trail narrows to a normal, well-constructed footpath. After skirting the south end of the lake, it climbs up into the forest briefly, then descends back to the eastern shoreline to continue its northerly journey. After branching left from the horse trail, the hiker's trail passes through the Kinney Lake Campground at Kilometre 6.7, where there are some very fine lakeside views.

The hiker's trail rejoins the horse route at Kilometre 7.2 and emerges from the forest onto the gravel flats at the head of the lake. Here the waters of the Robson

Mount Robson and Berg Lake

River deposit rock and silt over the valley floor to create an extensive outwash plain. At the eight kilometre mark, the trail crosses a bridge to the true right side of the river and swings across the outwash flats to the northwest side of the valley.

After a short, steep climb up from the Kinney Lake outwash plain and two more crossings of the Robson River on suspension bridges, the trail begins its tortuous rise up the spectacular Valley-of-a-Thousand Falls. In the next 3.5 kilometres, the hiker climbs over 450 vertical metres, ascending near the narrow gorge containing the thundering Robson River. Three major waterfalls are viewed on the ascent — White Falls, Falls-of-the-Pool and Emperor Falls.

The trail levels off above the Valley-of-a-Thousand Falls and dips down along the river to provide the first glimpse of the majestic, snow and ice-crusted north wall of Mount Robson. Views of the wall and its glaciers become increasingly spectacular as the trail nears Berg Lake.

The view across the powder-blue waters of Berg Lake to Mount Robson is exceptional to say the least. Two rivers of ice, Mist Glacier and Berg Glacier, cascade down from the uppermost reaches of the mountain, the latter terminating in the lake. The groan and rumble of these two overburdened bodies is constant, with chunks of ice calving from Berg Glacier and drifting into the lake.

The summit of Mount Robson lies more than two vertical kilometres above the lake, at an elevation of 3954 metres above sea level. First climbed in 1913 by a party led by Conrad Kain, it has been the object of many subsequent expeditions and is still considered one of the most difficult ascents in Canada. The mountain also contains the greatest section of Cambrian rock known in Canada —some 4000 metres thick.

Robson Pass lies just over two kilometres beyond the northeast end of Berg Lake and serves as the gateway to the remote northwest corner of Jasper National Park. The trail runs through the pass to Adolphus Lake and the headwaters of the Smoky River. The most popular campgrounds on the Berg Lake trail are all located between the northeast end of Berg Lake and Robson Pass. But for those who relish solitude more than constant views of Mount Robson, there is a less frequented national park campground just north of Adolphus Lake. (See *North Boundary Trail, Jasper Park* chapter.)

Backpackers bound for Berg Lake should be forewarned that heavy weather lingers over Mount Robson for much of the summer, and chances of seeing its summit unencumbered by cloud are not particularly good. Take heed of the journal entry of one J. M. Sellar, who travelled down the Fraser River in 1862: ". . . the guide told us that out of twenty-nine times that he had passed it [Mount Robson] he had only seen the top once before. . . ."

Toboggan Falls. The most popular day trip from Berg Lake leads up along a series of cascades to a fine, high-level viewpoint for Berg Lake and Mount Robson. Start the trip from the Berg Lake Campground (Kilometre 19.6) and climb along the northeast (true left) side of Toboggan Creek. When the trail fizzles out after two kilometres or so, continue upwards through open meadows for the best views of the Berg Lake environs.

Robson Glacier. This trail branches southeast from the main trail near the park ranger's cabin, just one kilometre west of Robson Pass summit. The trail reaches a small, meltwater lake at the toe of the Robson Glacier after two kilometres of level travel across gravel outwash flats. Good route-finders can continue the journey to Snowbird Pass by following cairns up along the lateral moraine on the east side of the glacier. After skirting above the Robson Glacier for three kilometres, the route branches due east and follows a tributary stream to the summit of the pass. Total distance to Snowbird Pass from the park ranger's cabin at Robson Pass is approximately nine kilometres.

Mount Fitzwilliam

Yellowhead Highway to Fitzwilliam Basin—13.0 kilometres (8.1 miles)

Backpack

Allow 5-6 hours to Fitzwilliam Basin

Elevation gain: 945 metres (3,100 feet)

Maximum elevation: 2060 metres (6,750 feet)

Topo maps: Rainbow 83 D/15†

Jasper 83 D/16†

† trail not shown

Point of Departure: Follow the Yellowhead Highway (Hwy. #16) to the Yellowhead Lake Boat Launch and Picnic Area, located on the north side of the highway 7 kilometres (4½ miles) west of the Alberta-B.C. boundary at Yellowhead Pass and 3 kilometres (2 miles) east of Lucerne Campground. Walk to the trail sign, located on the south side of the highway opposite the picnic area entrance.

0.0—Trail sign (1115 m).

—Trail runs west on old roadbed, parallel to highway.

0.7—Junction. Trail branches left from roadbed.

—Steady climb with switchbacks through mixed forest.

2.7—Trail crests forested ridge.

3.3—Underground stream. Trail begins to climb again.

6.3—Rockingham Creek bridge (1605). Campground.

—Rocky, rooty trail. Forest and willow meadows.

10.1—Rockslide area. Trail bends due south toward Fitzwilliam Basin.

—Faint trail through forest above marshy meadow and lake.

11.7—Fitzwilliam Basin headwall.

—Steep scree scramble to upper basin.

13.0—Fitzwilliam Basin (2060 m).

The lake-studded alpine basin on the east slope of Mount Fitzwilliam is a very worthwhile objective for hikers in the Yellowhead Pass area. Unfortunately, despite major improvements to the trail, the last seven kilometres are still rough and travel over this section can be tedious and time-consuming. The trip is best suited to backpackers with some route-finding skills who are willing to overnight at Rockingham Creek and then range up Fitzwilliam Creek for a full day of wandering and exploration.

The trip begins from the well-marked trail head across Highway #16 from the Yellowhead Lake Boat Launch-Picnic Area. After paralleling the Yellowhead Highway for 700 metres, the trail breaks away into the forest and begins the long climb to Rockingham Creek. Upgrading of the lower half of the trail was completed in 1985, and the track is broad and well-graded (though it can be slimy and slippery after a frosty night). While there are no open views on this climb, the forest is a pleasant mixture of lodgepole pine, white birch, aspen and old Douglas fir.

The Rockingham Creek Campground is situated at the north end of an extensive meadow set beneath the western wall of Mount Fitzwilliam. On the east side of the creek, the superhighway trail suddenly becomes a rocky, rooty wilderness track which contours above Fitzwilliam Creek through scattered forest and willow meadows (watch for markers on trees when the track becomes faint).

When the valley bends south around the slopes of Fitzwilliam, defined trail all but disappears. Work your way along the west side of a marshy lake to a 140 metre headwall. Scramble up the steep talus slope on the right-hand (west) side. At the top you will find a truly spectacular basin of meadows and lakes set beneath the walls of Mount Fitzwilliam, Bucephalus Peak, Holloway Rock and Kataka Mountain.

Yellowhead Mountain

Yellowhead Lake to Yellowhead Mountain Viewpoint—4.5 kilometres (3.0 miles)*

Half-day trip

Allow 1½-2 hours one way

Elevation gain: 715 metres (2,350 feet)

Maximum elevation: 1830 metres (6,000 feet)

Topo maps: Rainbow 83 D/15†

† trail not shown

Point of Departure: Follow the Yellowhead Highway (Hwy. #16) to the junction with a gravel access road, located on the north side of the highway 1.7 kilometres (1.1 miles) east of Lucerne Campground and 8½ kilometres (5½ miles) west of the Alberta-B.C. boundary at Yellowhead Pass. Follow this gravel road for one kilometre, crossing an isthmus through Yellowhead Lake to the CNR tracks on the north side of the valley. Park below the railway roadbed where the access road splits and walk to the trail sign on the opposite side of the tracks.

0.0—Trail sign (1115 m).

—Moderate to steep uphill through mixed forest.

1.0—Viewpoint.

—Trail contours east along open slope.

1.2—Trail climbs uphill into forest.

—Steady uphill through lodgepole forest (with blowdown) and meadows.

4.5—End of trail (1830 m). Upper meadows.*

* Distance approximate

Yellowhead Pass has served as one of the important routes across the Canadian Rockies for more than 150 years. Fur traders, gold seekers, tourist-adventurers and railway surveyors all struggled over this summit during the nineteenth century. And there is no better viewpoint for this historic pass than the slopes of Yellowhead Mountain.

The short trail leading up onto the south slope of the mountain starts from the Canadian National Railway tracks on the north side of Yellowhead Lake, a trail head which can be reached by following a gravel access road across the narrows near the west end of the lake. The trail climbs through a forest of aspen poplar mixed with lodgepole pine and white birch. The grade is initially steep, but moderates as the trail contours to the right across the mountain.

At the end of the first kilometre, the trail emerges onto an open slope which provides the first good overview of the Yellowhead Pass environs — Yellowhead Lake, Mount Fitzwilliam and the peaks of the Selwyn Range to the west. This is a particularly fine area in the autumn, when the aspen leaves turn to gold and the first snows dust the ramparts of Mount Fitzwilliam.

After contouring across this opening in the forest for nearly 200 metres, the trail cuts uphill to the left and continues its ascent of the mountain. The track immediately enters a thick lodgepole pine stand which was struck by a windstorm in 1985. As of this writing, the trail has been totally obliterated by this blowdown, but if the trail crew has done its work, you can continue up the mountain into an area of alternating meadow and forest. Each opening allows ever-improving views until the path finally fizzles in a large meadow near the 1830 metre level on the slopes of Tête Roche — the easternmost peak of Yellowhead Mountain.

Moose River

Backpack

Allow 3 days to Moose Pass

Elevation gain: 945 metres (3,100 feet)

Maximum elevation: 2025 metres (6,650 feet)

Topo maps: Rainbow 83 D/15

              Resplendent Creek 83 E/2

              Mount Robson 83 E/3

Point of Departure: Follow the Yellowhead Highway (Hwy. #16) to an intersection with a gravel, railway access road, located on the north side of the highway 3 kilometres (2 miles) east of the Moose Lake Boat Launch (east end of Moose Lake) and 29 kilometres (18 miles) west of the Alberta-B.C. boundary at Yellowhead Pass. (Watch for the road branching north just 500 metres west of the Moose River highway bridge.) Follow the gravel road for 300 metres and park below the railway roadbed. Cross the CNR tracks and walk up a broad, gravel access road.

0.0—Railway tracks (1080 m).

—Follow uphill on access road.

0.3—Junction. Moose River trail branches left from access road.

—Trail climbs over forested ridge of Rainbow Range to Moose River.

11.0—Resplendent Creek-Moose River confluence.

17.0—Resplendent Creek ford. (Difficult multi-channel crossing of glacier-fed stream.)

22.0—Colonel Creek.

28.0—Upright Creek.

—Trail swings back and forth across Moose River four times.

36.0—Steppe Creek fords.

46.0—Moose Pass (2025 m). B.C.-Alta. boundary.

50.0—Campground.

55.5—Coleman Glacier outflow stream. (Difficult ford of glacier-fed stream.)

56.0—Smoky River bridge (1615 m). Intersection with North Boundary Trail at Km 146.1 (see Jasper Park chapter).

* All distances approximate.

Though the Moose River trail is a long, rugged track, it is a highly scenic option for experienced backpackers. It can be used as an alternate access route for the west end of Jasper's North Boundary Trail, or the beautiful wildflower meadows below Moose Pass can be visited as an extension of the Berg Lake trip. However, two major glacier-fed streams must be crossed on this trek, so travel is not recommended during periods of high runoff.

From the Fraser Valley, the trail makes a stiff climb over the end of the Rainbow Range to reach the Moose River. The trail continues northwest alongside the river to its confluence with Resplendent Creek (unseen from the trail). After following up the west side of Resplendent Creek for six kilometres, it crosses the creek (a difficult, multi-channelled ford) and runs east over a forested ridge to rejoin the Moose River.

Between Colonel Creek and Upright Creek, the trail is overgrown and poorly marked (stay near the river's edge). Above Upright Creek, the track is more defined, but there are four unbridged crossings of the Moose and three more in rapid succession on Steppe Creek. After skirting three small lakes near the river's headwaters, the trail crests the 2025 metre summit of Moose Pass. The meadows on the western slope of the pass comprise one of the finest wildflower gardens in the mountain parks, and the glacier-draped summit of Calumet Peak adds to the scene.

The trail descends from the meadows along the south side of Calumet Creek, then bends south around the end of a forested ridge to cross the Coleman Glacier outflow stream (this wide, silty torrent is best forded downstream where it is braided). A log bridge across the Smoky River a short distance upstream from this hazardous crossing, brings you to the junction with the North Boundary Trail (see Jasper Park chapter).

The Great Divide Trail

by Jim Thorsell

There are several feasible long distance routes through the Rockies from south to north which primarily follow existing trails. The best known of these is the Great Divide Trail route first proposed in 1967. The Great Divide Trail has been the focus of many studies since its feasibility was established, and though official policy approval of the trail was announced by Parks Canada in 1971, formal route designation or construction of the missing segments has yet to be undertaken.

Since 1971, two main developments have occurred that should be noted: Parks Canada, fearing that the Great Divide Trail passes through ecologically sensitive areas and through areas where backcountry visitation is already high, has suggested re-routing the trail away from the high ridges close to the Divide to lower, valley-bottom locations. Secondly, a southern extension of the Great Divide Trail from Banff to Waterton in lands outside the national parks has been proposed and, in part, built.*

As this revised edition of *The Canadian Rockies Trail Guide* goes to press, the situation regarding the actual development of the Great Divide Trail is unresolved. The differing views on its possible routes and, indeed, on its very legitimacy make it difficult to offer the prospective traveller a guide on exactly where best to go. All that can be definitely stated is that the route given in the first edition of this book is still essentially valid and passable. Call it what you will, the remainder of this chapter will present an updated account of the park section of the Great Divide Trail route as it originally was publicised in 1969. Remember that only the concept has received government approval and no work has been done on the rougher and missing sections. Remember too that there are other possibilities and that this is merely the one that provides the highest quality route as judged by this author.

Cautions

Remember, the Great Divide Trail has yet to be developed. There are no signs which refer to any segment of the route as 'The Great Divide Trail' and, indeed, directional signs of any kind are scarce. Trail conditions in some sections are poor. Rivers will present special problems for hikers where there are no footbridges. Although there are many primitive campsites along the route, only one shelter is now open for public use. It is important to have good lightweight equipment and be prepared for all weather conditions.

National Park regulations listed elsewhere in this book apply to all travel along this route, i.e. permits are required for any backcountry camping. Permits as well as current trail conditions may be obtained at the trail desks in park information bureaus.

Finally, most elevations in the following route description are approximate as are distances not recorded in tenths-of-kilometres. Further information on most trail segments may be obtained by reading individual descriptions elsewhere in this book (cross reference place names through the index).

---

* For information on the segment outside the parks see *The Great Divide Trail: Banff to Waterton* prepared by the Great Divide Trail Association, Box 5322, Postal Station A, Calgary, 1977.

'MEADOW' SECTION

Palliser Pass to Banff–Radium Highway—86 kilometres

Palliser Pass is at the very southerly tip of Banff Park. It is here that the national park section of the Great Divide Trail begins. Closely following the Divide for 86 kilometres, the Great Divide Trail utilises trails of the upper Spray River through the Mount Assiniboine area to the Sunshine–Egypt Lake complex and out to the Banff–Radium Highway in Kootenay Park.

The nickname 'Meadow' is given to this section because of the above-timberline location of much of the route. The entire section has good existing trails that are marked and well maintained except for a long-abandoned ten kilometre stretch along Currie Creek to Marvel Pass. As recent avalanche debris has made bush-whacking here difficult, the traveller is advised to enter the Assiniboine area via the Bryant Creek trail.

Mount Assiniboine itself is the dominant peak of the section and can be seen from Currie Pass all the way to Healy Pass. Prepare to be distracted by many side trips in Mount Assiniboine Park and around Egypt Lake, both prime hiking areas where there is usually good trout fishing. Profuse alpine flowers in early July and golden larch trees in mid-September make these the most colorful periods for travel.

Access to the southern end of the 'Meadow' Section can be gained from several directions. Palliser Pass can be reached via the North Kananaskis Pass trail running from the Kananaskis Provincial Park at Upper Kananaskis Lake. The upper Spray Valley can also be reached from the Burstall Pass trail which leaves from the Smith–Dorion Creek Road or from the west Spray Reservoir Road at the Bryant Creek trail head.

Similarly, the central part of the section in the Assiniboine–Sunshine segment can be reached by feeder trails from the east and west via Fatigue Creek, Brewster Creek, Mitchell River or Simpson River. The north end of the section emerges on the Banff–Radium Highway at Hawk Creek, although egress can also be made via Redearth Creek or Gibbon Pass to Storm Mountain Lodge.

Distances and Elevations

	kms
Palliser Pass (2090 m) to Currie Creek Jct.	8
Currie Creek Jct. to Currie Pass (2395 m)	8
Currie Pass to Marvel Pass (2150 m)	3
Marvel Pass to Wonder Pass (2375 m)	3
Wonder Pass to Lake Magog (2165 m)	2.9
Lake Magog to Citadel Pass (2360 m)	19.8
Citadel Pass to Sunshine Village (2195 m)	9.3
Sunshine Village to Simpson Pass (2120 m)	5.3
Simpson Pass to Healy Pass (2330 m)	4.0
Healy Pass to Egypt Lake Campsite (1995 m)	3.2
Egypt Lake Camp to Whistling Valley (2300 m)	3.5
Whistling Valley to Ball Pass Jct. (1920 m)	5.2
Ball Pass Jct. to Ball Pass (2210 m)	3
Ball Pass to Banff–Radium Highway (1325 m)	8

Topo maps: Kananaskis Lakes, 82 J/11; Spray Lakes Reservoir, 82 J/14; Mount Assiniboine, 82 J/13; Banff, 82 0/4; and Mount Goodsir, 82 N/1.

'LARCH' SECTION
Floe Creek to Field—88 kilometres

The 72 kilometres of trail from Floe Creek to Lake O'Hara via the Numa, Tumbling, Wolverine, Goodsir and McArthur Passes is one of the finest backcountry trips in the Rockies. With great differences in elevation it is also one of the most rigorous. Highlights of the trip include Floe Lake, the Tumbling Glacier, the Rockwall, the 365 metre Helmet Falls, the Goodsir Towers, and the extensive views from the Goodsir and Numa Passes. Common wildlife include goat, elk and wolverine. Larches reach their northern limit and their most impressive fall colour along this section of the Great Divide Trail. Few other places have wildflowers to match those in the Wolverine Pass meadows.

The trip should present no problem for those in reasonable physical condition. It is well marked and maintained with footbridges throughout. However, for most of the stretch between Lake O'Hara and Field there is no recognized trail; only experienced hikers should attempt the Duchesnay–Dennis Pass route as both sides of the pass are very steep and rocky, and there is heavy bushwhacking to reach the fossil bed trail on Mount Stephen.

The 'Larch' Section extends between the Banff–Radium Highway and the Trans-Canada Highway. Five days are usually required to hike the route from Floe Creek to Lake O'Hara. It is possible to exit via the Ottertail River Fire Road in Yoho, and Parks Canada has designated this as an alternative route for backpackers who would avoid the more heavily travelled Lake O'Hara region. Most hikers will choose to skip the Duchesnay Pass segment and conclude (or begin) the 'Larch' Section at Lake O'Hara.

Distances and Elevations

	kms
Banff–Radium Hwy. to Floe Lake (2040 m)	10.1
Floe Lake to Numa Pass (2353 m)	2.7
Numa Pass to Tumbling Pass (2225 m)	12.1
Tumbling Pass to Wolverine Pass (2207 m)	6
Wolverine Pass to Helmet Warden Cabin (1770 m)	13
Helmet Warden Cabin to Goodsir Pass (2210 m)	5
Goodsir Pass to Ottertail Jct. (1480 m)	11
Ottertail Jct. to McArthur Pass (2210 m)	10
McArthur Pass to Lake O'Hara (2097 m)	2.1
Lake O'Hara to Duchesnay Pass (2666 m)	8
Duchesnay Pass to Dennis Pass (2261 m)	3
Dennis Pass via Fossil Beds to Field (1242 m)	5

Topo maps: Mount Goodsir, 82 N/1 and Lake Louise, 82 N/8.

'GLACIER' SECTION
Field to Saskatchewan River Crossing—92 kilometres

This section extends north from Field, B.C. to Saskatchewan River Crossing, Alberta, a distance of some 92 kilometres. Despite a fifteen kilometre section missing in the middle and a lack of footbridges, the trail presents some exciting travel with a profusion of waterfalls, glaciers and wild rivers. No trail exists from Kiwetinok Pass to the Amiskwi River Fire Road, though by contouring over the northwest ridge of Kiwetinok Valley it is possible to eventually reach the abandoned logging roads leading down to Amiskwi. Likewise, from Amiskwi Pass to the Blaeberry River a thick bushwhack to the Collie Creek logging road can be shortened by keeping above timberline until the last possible moment. The upper Blaeberry trail has been improved in recent years and is now in fair condition (over Howse Pass the trail is faint until the Banff Park boundary marker is reached).

Until the centre portion of the 'Glacier' Section is built, most trail use will be concentrated at either end of this section. The Kiwetinok–Amiskwi portion may be avoided entirely by driving up the Blaeberry forestry road to the trail head 13 kilometres below Howse Pass. For the section in Yoho Park, you may gain access from the Emerald Lake or Yoho Valley Roads. Parks Canada has also designated the Amiskwi Fire Road as an alternate route to the high use Yoho Valley region.

Distances and Elevations

	kms
Field to Burgess Pass (2185 m)	6.6
Burgess Pass to Yoho Pass (1840 m)	6.1
Yoho Pass via Highline to Kiwetinok Pass (2450 m)	13
Kiwetinok Pass to Amiskwi Pass (1995 m)	13
Amiskwi Pass to Howse Pass (1530 m)	27
Howse Pass to Forbes Creek Jct. (1525 m)	2.9
Forbes Creek Jct. to Saskatchewan Crossing (1435 m)	23.0

Topo maps: Lake Louise, 82 N/8; Blaeberry River, 82 N/10; and Mistaya Lake, 82 N/15.

'CARIBOU' SECTION
Norman Creek to Maligne Lake Road—164 kilometres

From the Icefields Parkway at Norman Creek to Maligne Lake runs the longest unbroken stretch of the Great Divide Trail—120 kilometres. A minimum of ten days is required to hike this entire section. Wildlife is relatively plentiful here including caribou which are often seen in the alplands near Amber Mountain and in Jonas Pass. The six passes in this section are all high with extensive alpine meadow and encompassing views. The trails, except for a few kilometres through Cataract Pass, are in good condition and easy to follow.

The 'Caribou' Section of the Great Divide Trail is reached by car at both ends of the trail and also from the Maligne Lake Road at Maligne Lake. Feeder trails from the Icefields Parkway lead in along Nigel and Poboktan Creeks and conveniently divide this section into four roughly equal portions.

From Nigel Pass south to Sunset Pass are found some of the steepest grades on the entire Great Divide Trail. There is no trail over Cataract Pass summit to Nigel Pass, but the country is open and the route should present no problems for hikers. Horses are not allowed on the section of the route that lies within the provincial White Goat Wilderness—a bypass alternate via Coral Creek and Job Pass is suggested for those travelling on horseback.

Distances and Elevations

kms

Icefields Parkway (1525 m) to Sunset Pass (2055 m) 8.2
Sunset Pass to Cataract Creek Jct. (1705 m) 8
Cataract Creek Jct. to Cataract Pass (2515 m) 16
Cataract Pass to Nigel Pass Jct. (2202 m) 6
Nigel Pass Jct. to Jonas Cutoff (1890 m) 6.8
Jonas Cutoff to Jonas Pass (2235 m) 9.8
Jonas Pass to Poboktan Creek Jct. (2105 m) 10.0
Poboktan Creek Jct. to Maligne Pass Jct. (1740 m) 14.1
Maligne Pass Jct. to Maligne Pass (2237 m) 7.3
Maligne Pass to Maligne Lake (1450 m) 34.2
Maligne Lake to Shovel Pass (2285 m) 17.5
Shovel Pass to Signal Mtn. Fire Road (1950 m) 18.1
Signal Mtn. Fire Road to Maligne Lake Rd. (1160 m) 8.5

Topo maps: Cline River, 83 C/2; Columbia Icefield, 83 C/3; Sunwapta, 83 C/6; Southesk, 83 C/11; Athabasca Falls, 83 C/12; and Medicine Lake, 83 C/13.

'MOUNT ROBSON' SECTION

Yellowhead Pass to Mount Robson—87 kilometres

Once the hiker completes the 'Caribou' Section and finds himself in Jasper town-site with energy to spare and a desire to see Mount Robson, what should he do? If he is intrepid (perhaps masochistic?) he may consider the route recommended in the first edition of the trail guide which follows the upper Miette and Moose Rivers. Foot travel here is not easy and is not encouraged by the Warden Service. Nor is the alternate Elysium–Thornton Pass route. Robson, a fitting northern terminus to the Great Divide Trail, can be reached, however, via the Berg Lake or North Boundary trails as described elsewhere in this book. For those still wishing to consider the preferred route, the distances are given with a warning that this section is for explorers only.

Distances and Elevations

kms

Yellowhead Pass (1131 m) to Centre Pass (1965 m) 26
Centre Pass to Grant Pass (1937 m) 8
Grant Pass to Colonel Pass (1870 m) 5
Colonel Pass to Moose Pass (2003 m) 29
Moose Pass to Robson Pass (1651 m) 18
Robson Pass to Berg Lake (1638 m) 1

Appendix

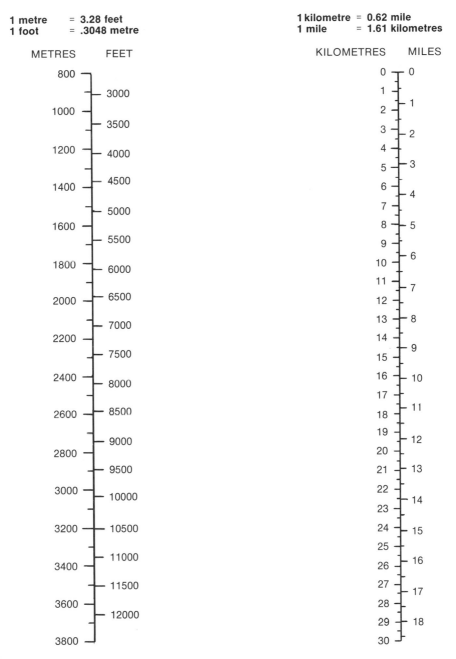

| 1 metre | = 3.28 feet |
| 1 foot | = .3048 metre |

| 1 kilometre | = 0.62 mile |
| 1 mile | = 1.61 kilometres |

METRES	FEET
800	
	3000
1000	
	3500
1200	4000
	4500
1400	
	5000
1600	
	5500
1800	6000
2000	6500
	7000
2200	
	7500
2400	8000
2600	8500
	9000
2800	
	9500
3000	10000
3200	10500
	11000
3400	
	11500
3600	12000
3800	

KILOMETRES	MILES
0	0
1	
2	1
3	2
4	
5	3
6	4
7	
8	5
9	
10	6
11	7
12	
13	8
14	9
15	
16	10
17	
18	11
19	12
20	
21	13
22	14
23	
24	15
25	
26	16
27	17
28	
29	18
30	

Index

Names and pages in bold type refer to the main trail headings as used in this book.

361